P9-ECR-932

THIS IS
MONTANA

A Geography-Geographic History of Montana
Volume I

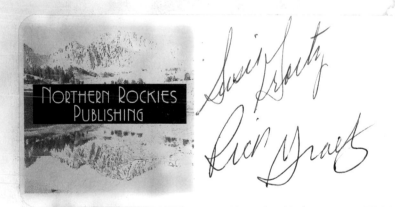

NORTHERN ROCKIES
PUBLISHING

Text and Photos by Rick and Susie Graetz

with contributions by

Dave Alt, Harry Fritz, Jeff Gritzner, A.B. Guthrie, Jr., Joseph Kinsey Howard, Richard Hugo, Wally McRae, Ken Mielke, Tom Palmer, John Pulaski, Lee Rostad, Grant Sasek, Nicholas Vrooman, and Pat Williams

ONE VERY SPECIAL WOMAN MADE THIS BOOK, OUR other titles and newspaper columns far better than they would have been had she not lent her talents. She has the ability to make words declare something beyond the mundane and a capacity to see life and beauty through the eye piece of a camera ... my wife and partner Susie ... I dedicate *This is Montana* to her!

—RICK GRAETZ

Design: GingerBee Creative
    www.gingerbee.com
Maps: Moore Creative Designs
    406-443-2912
Index Minie Smith, Ducksoup Indexing

Printed in the USA
Softcover: ISBN 1-891152-18-1
Hardcover: ISBN 1-891152-19-X

Front cover photo: *One mile east of White Sulphur Springs – Castle Mountains* RICK AND SUSIE GRAETZ
Back cover photo: *A high country lake in the Lee Metcalf Wilderness* RICK AND SUSIE GRAETZ

Published in cooperation with the Foundation For Community Vitality – Jim and Chris Scott and the Montana Geographic Journal. Assistance provided by The University of Montana, Department of Geography and the Montana Geographic Alliance.

CONTENTS

ABOUT THIS BOOK...

T HIS IS MONTANA IS A COLLECTION OF LIVELY ESSAYS TELLING A STORY OF SPACE AND time in one of America's great landscapes. Many of the pieces are edited versions of our syndicated newspaper column, some are new, and others are contributions from well-known writers and journalists.

In some cases, the same information will appear in more than one article. This is by design as each essay must not only stand on its own, but the information is pertinent to several places or events.

Notes about, and quotes from, the Corps of Discovery and their leaders are used liberally; it was Lewis & Clark who pointed the way and began the written knowledge of what would become Montana.

As always, we invite suggestions and criticism. We rely on our Montana friends to help us improve upon our work.

THANK YOU...

A work such as this isn't accomplished in a vacuum. We have received an enormous amount of help by way of suggestions, supplied information and downright encouragement. Our appreciation goes out to all those who have written to us with corrections and new information etc. from reading our newspaper articles and other books. To the many weekly newspaper editors we have contacted for information, thanks for all you shared. And our gratitude to Jeff Gritzner, Chair of the University of Montana Department of Geography, Brian Shovers of the Montana Historical Society, Doug Smith, President of Missouri River Country and an archeologist, Angie Hurley and Tom Lowe of Bannack State Park, Lee Rostad, a writer from Lennep, Lee Willis, a Helena researcher, Jim and Chris Scott of the Foundation for Community Vitality, Linda Peterson of the Office of Public Instruction, Dave and Sandi Ashley and Ken and Linda Carpenter for their assistance.

SOME VERY GOOD MONTANA BOOKS FOR REFERENCE...

Overtime we have utilized numerous Montana books and for reference. The following are just a few of the outstanding titles available... *Roadside History of Montana, Roadside Geology of Montana, Names on the Face of Montana, Floating Montana, Paddling Montana, Wild Montana, The Journals of Lewis and Clark- Volumes 4, 5 and 8* (Moulton-Nebraska), *Moon Handbook of Montana, Montana A History of Two Centuries, Montana High Wide and Handsome, Montana An Uncommon Land, Montana A State of Extremes, Pioneering In Montana* (two volumes), *Montana Margins* and *Montana Legacy*.

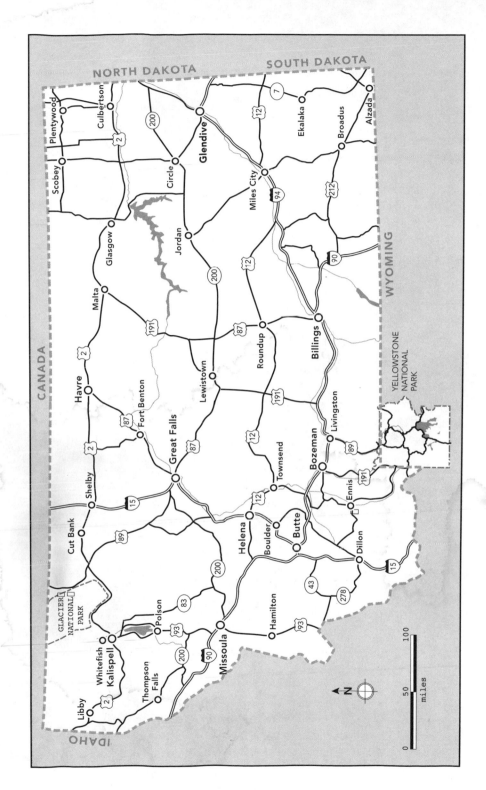

VII

HIGH WIDE AND HANDSOME

"Colorado is high, having more peaks within its borders than any other state. Wyoming is wide, with the breadth of the plains between the Big Horns and the Grand Tetons. California is handsome, with a splendor of success. It takes all three adjectives to describe Montana."

—DONAL CULROSS PEATTIE WRITER FROM THE 1930–1940 ERA

MARGINS

"In Montana ... the elemental and values of life have been too often overlooked — space and freedom, sun and clean air, the cold and majesty of the mountains and the loneliness of the plains, the gaiety of the country dance, the easy friendliness of the people. These are the margins around the sometimes fretful business of earning a living. And these are what Thoreau meant when he said 'I loved a broad margin to my life,' These are the beauties in Montana ..."

—JOSEPH KINSEY HOWARD FROM *MONTANA MARGINS*, 1946

MONTANA ...

"The next passage in my journey is a love affair. I am in love with Montana. For other states I have admiration, respect, recognition, even some affection, but with Montana it is love, and it is difficult to analyze love when you are in it...It seems to me that Montana is a great splash of grandeur. The scale is huge but not overpowering. The land is rich with grass and color, and the mountains are the kind I would create if mountains were ever put on my agenda ... Montana has a spell on me ... of all the states it is my favorite and my loves."

—JOHN STEINBECK FROM *TRAVELS WITH CHARLIE*

DRIVING MONTANA

The day is a woman who loves you. Open.

Deer drink close to the road and magpies spray from your car.
Miles from any town your radio comes in strong, unlikely Mozart
from Belgrade, rock and roll from Butte. Whatever the next
number, you want to hear it. Never has your Buick found this
forward a gear. Even the tuna salad in Reedpoint is good.

Towns arrive ahead of imagined schedule. Absarokee at one. Or
arrive so late — Silesia at nine — you recreate the day. Where
did you stop along the road and have fun? Was there a runaway
horse? Did you park at that house, the one alone in a void of
grain, white with green trim and red fence, where you know you
lived once? You' remember the ringing creek, the soft brown forms
of far off bison. You must have stayed hours, then drove on. In
the motel you know you'd never seen it before.

Tomorrow will open up again, the sky wide as the mouth of a
wild girl, friable clouds you lose yourself to. You are lost in miles
of land without people, without one fear of being found, in the
dash of rabbits, soar of antelope, swirl merge and clatter of
streams.
—RICHARD HUGO

THIS POEM, PENNED BY RICHARD HUGO, WAS FIRST PUBLISHED IN 1972 IN
THE *AMERICAN POETRY REVIEW* AND IS USED WITH THE PERMISSION OF
RIPLEY HUGO. IMMEDIATELY AFTER READING THE WORDS, RIPLEY "FELL IN
LOVE WITH DICK."

THIS IS MONTANA...
AN INTRODUCTION

"The height of Montana summer — early August — a serene Flathead Lake, framed by cedar, ponderosa and spruce confronts me. It is 6 p.m., the sun is still high in its arc, but low enough on the western horizon to fade and blend the low-slung ridges and tops of the Salish Mountains, rising from the lake's western shore, 13 miles or more in the distance."

THE DARK, SEEMINGLY FEATURELESS MASSIFS BECOME PROGRESSIVELY LIGHTER the farther west they extend. A smoke haze from forest fires adds to the silhouetting created by the sun and distance.

Silence has taken over. The water is still. The mechanized watercrafts have been put to bed. Nothing is left to disturb the peace and vision. The human intrusion is vanquished by the expanse of water stretching to the sunset side.

A setting is in place to picture the lake's and northwest Montana's yesterday.

Looking south toward the foot of the lake, my imagination takes me back to March 1812, when explorer and fur trader David Thompson crested a hill to become the first known white man to stand in awe before the sparkling Flathead Lake.

Turning toward the mountains on the west, I envision lonely trappers seeking the elusive beaver and other fur bearing animals along the streams threading the forested uplifts. A bit more conjecture, and it is possible to hear the crack and thud of an ax taking a bite out of a pine tree as logging operations took hold in these same woods at a later date.

A smoke-veiled sky makes it easy to conceive of monster sized steamboats, with antennae-like stacks belching black sooty clouds that hang in the air, and dripping paddle wheels churning a frothy wake as they plied the 27-mile-long lake from about 1885 until 1930.

The thought of all the history and change that has passed through this incredible valley in a relatively short period of its recorded time is exciting and makes me hanker to know more.

But whether it is on Flathead Lake, the banks of the Missouri River or from a Beartooth summit, the surroundings' stories ask to be remembered, beg to be relived, lest all they happened lose importance. It's not difficult to look back on Montana's formulative years; it was such a short time ago. And that is part of what makes this state a grand package of space and time.

Every state boasts of great beauty and a history worth remembering. Montana though, combines geography and an unquiet record of the past

Eastern Montana badlands, Moon Garden out of Jordan. RICK AND SUSIE GRAETZ

into an enviable mix. Our topography is diverse and stunning. The Northern Rockies within Montana's borders equal or surpass mountains found elsewhere, and the prairie lands flowing east of the high country are the most unique and beautiful in the nation. Nowhere on the North American continent do river breaks, island ranges, buttes and badlands come together like they do in Montana's piece of the Great Plains.

Couple this grandeur with great sweeps of landscape unaltered through time and chronicles extending back less than two centuries, and one of the most fascinating and enviable places in America unfolds.

A complete study of a region requires affiliation of place and history. It is especially essential when viewing Montana. Much of what we see here today is intrinsically linked to the past and understanding the past is required to interpret our province of today. A theme based on this premise is carried in the essays throughout this book.

The late K. Ross Toole, an eminent historian and distinguished University of Montana professor, summed up segments of our history and lends us his perspective on its abrupt changes.

"For many years, while immigrants rushed to the West Coast, the facts of geography sealed off the great northern pocket. When at last it was probed, civilization came all at once. It came too fast. There was no ebb to the flow. The plains had sustained millions of buffalo. The sea of grass was endless. To the cattlemen who poured from the south and the west onto this great area in the early 1880s, it was inconceivable that the plains could not sustain their great herds forever. Tough and resourceful as they were, their days on the open range were tragically numbered. In less than a decade their empire had crumbled and the grass was gone.

"Then it was the "honyocker," who like the cattlemen moved onto the land with quick profit as a basic motive. There were a few good years, but then nature struck again. The mass exodus of people left whole communities empty. Eleven thousand farms were abandoned in Eastern Montana in the late teens and early twenties. The boom had been great; so was the bust. The promoters and the ebullient honyockers did not know land. And they left behind them mute towns with tumbleweeds banked high on windward sides of leaning buildings. They also left behind a sorely wounded country.

"In 1880, Nate Leavengood's meadow, where Anaconda now stands, was a lush and quiet place. As far as the eye could see in all directions there was nothing but the valley, the swelling foothills and mountain ramparts.

"Four years later, the meadow was gone, blighted by arsenic fumes from the largest copper smelter in the world. There had been no gradual encroachment of civilization, no creeping in of small farms and little stores. There was no village. First there was nothing, and then all of a sudden there was the world's largest smelter and around it a raw new city."

While Montana's history may be young, it certainly is deep, and much of its evidence is written on the land.

Knowing that an old trail — The Mullan Wagon Road — followed the Clark Fork River, explains cuts along a bench or hillside and the disappearing pieces of logs that supported a bridge. Awareness that Indian tribes traversed the Rock Creek country of northeast Montana explains the circles of stones in succession on a ridgeline — tepee rings.

Recognizing and appreciating Lewis and Clark and the Corps of Discovery's time in Montana is essential. When Lewis penned his journals on the night of April 27, 1805, in essence he was recording the first written history of Montana. Big Sky country was uncharted and cloaked in ambiguity. These explorers mapped the land and noted all they witnessed. Their account was one of not only magnificent topographical and biological wonders, but also of the possibility of wealth. Again K. Ross Toole explains, "Although they left only the ashes of their campfires behind, Montana would never be the same again."

After studying the words of Meriwether Lewis and William Clark, it is essential to learn of the fur trade. The trappers or "mountain men" as they were often referred to, took over where Clark, the topographer, left off. Their wanderings to almost every quarter of Montana provided more detailed mapping — small compensation for what they took in return. Their mark on our terrain was one of exploitation, setting a pattern that continues to this day. In addition, they had a profound and disastrous effect on the Indians.

The ensuing steamboat era, lasting from 1859 through 1888, follows. It began when high waters of the early summer of 1860 allowed the steamboat Chippewa

Lone Mountain, Madison Range, Big Sky, SW Montana. RICK AND SUSIE GRAETZ

passage to Fort Benton, providing accessibility to the soon-to-be Montana Territory. And the chronology of our underpinnings marches on — the mining, the railroad, the so-called Indian Wars and the homestead eras, to name a few. To know these happenings is to better appreciate the terrain of the present.

It's a big chunk of ground, this Montana. Drive from Troy on the Idaho line in the northwestern corner of the state to Alzada in the far southeast and your iron chariot will up its odometer 800 miles. Cruise across the Hi-Line from Troy to the North Dakota border and it's an easy 658 miles.

No doubt, pockets of our state's geography have changed dramatically and lost much of their openness and old Montana flavor. Yet, nearly everywhere in this state, even on the fringe of areas thick with development, it is still possible to find, within a short distance, the simple grandeur of the prairie, a quiet meadow, a rippling stream, or a trail leading to a mountaintop where we can drink in the simple freshness that replenishes our souls and picture the not-so-long-ago Montana.

Here is a vivid portrait; for all who will seek it ... This Is Montana!

RICK GRAETZ
JIM & CHRIS SCOTT'S PLACE
YELLOW BAY, FLATHEAD LAKE, MONTANA
AUGUST 9, 2003

MONTANA EAST
OF THE MOUNTAINS

ONE JUNE EVENING A FEW YEARS BACK FOUND US AT THE SITE OF CHIEF JOSEPH'S surrender, just beyond the northern slopes of the Bear Paw Mountains. A thunderstorm was tailing off in a cloud-laden sky. On the western horizon, a widening gap revealed a setting sun.

The elements and the heavens joined in a prelude to an unfolding performance. As myriad pastel hues of crimson tinted the breaking clouds, the sun slowly disappeared from sight. Then the pinks intensified and began to blend with shades of purple, blue, orange and red; a burning sky in all directions bathed the earth in enchanting light. The tops of the Bear Paw picked up an orange flame, to the east the Little Rockies glowed in gold, and far to the south and north, lightning bolts danced like fireworks. Montana east of the mountains was suspended in an exceptionally brilliant yet dreamlike display as the day came to a close.

Magnificent sunsets and sunrises are common in this uncommon landscape, a region encompassing two-thirds of Montana. The imposing Rocky Mountain Front defines its western flank, the sweep of the open terrain flows east from here. On the north, it stretches 460 miles from Browning and the east slopes of Glacier National Park to the North Dakota. Somewhat less defined, the central boundary begins in the valley of the upper Musselshell River, near Harlowton, and reaches for 300 miles to our state's eastern edge. On the south, it's 250 miles as the golden eagle glides from Red Lodge and the east face of the Beartooth Mountains following the Wyoming border to the South Dakota line.

A distinct region unto itself, and one of America's great pieces of geography, this corner of the Great Plains harbors unique landforms. Grand scenes — badlands, sculptured sandstone, river breaks, canyons, wilderness grasslands, wildlife refuges, lakes and island mountain ranges — intermingle with smaller bits of geologic wonderment. Space, much of it undisturbed, is its greatest commodity. This vast territory of unending sky delivers a feeling of no borders or confinement where a human can stretch and breathe.

At first, the openness, the immensity and the distances may seem overpowering. Gradually, though, you get comfortable with it all; then you notice the beauty and splendor. Not just the imposing geologic structures, but also the abundance of simple grandeur ... cottonwoods along a small creek; a lone tree silhouetted on a hillside; waves of wheat dancing in the summer wind; the first rays of sun illuminating sandstone cliffs; delicate delicate snow patterns drifted against a weathered barn; the northern lights shimmering across the night sky; antelope moving quietly through sagebrush-covered prairie and the soft fusion of earth and sky on horizons that seem endless.

CMR National Wildlife Refuge, across from the UL Bend area. RICK AND SUSIE GRAETZ

Striking features command your attention … the 1,000-foot deep canyons of the Missouri River; the enormity of Fort Peck Lake; stately prairie buttes; isolated mountain ranges including the Little Rockies and Big Snowies; the Makoshika and Terry badlands and the canyons of the Bighorn River.

Montana's mightiest waterways have carved their routes through this territory. Born of mountain snows and springs, the prairie gives them room to grow. They are fabled waters … the Missouri, the Yellowstone, the Marias, the Judith, the Bighorn, the Powder, the Tongue, the Milk and the Musselshell. The wide Missouri and the free-flowing Yellowstone were routes of exploration for Meriwether Lewis, William Clark and other adventurers.

In legend, scenic beauty and recreation, the Missouri stands out. It was the goal of the first fur hunters and of Thomas Jefferson in 1803 as he planned the exploration of the Louisiana Territory.

Serving as a lifeline to Montana, the "Big Muddy," as it is sometimes called, played a major role in creating our state. Among other epics in our history, it witnessed the era of the fur traders, the discovery of gold, Native American trials and tribulations and steamboat travel to Fort Benton … Montana's birthplace.

The Missouri's flow is launched at the meeting of the waters near Three Forks in western Montana. Here the Madison, Jefferson and Gallatin rivers join to power the big river. En route north and east, it picks up more volume from the Dearborn, Teton, Marias, Judith, Musselshell, Milk and other rivers.

This great waterway passes silently through some of the most remote and

8

least inhabited country in the West. Nearly 150 miles of the river, beginning at Fort Benton, have been designated as the Upper Missouri River Breaks National Monument ... protected forever. Its eastern reaches meander through the rugged Missouri Breaks and the huge Charles M. Russell National Wildlife Refuge. At Fort Peck, a dam has turned the river into the fourth-largest reservoir in the world — 125-mile-long Fort Peck Lake, a Montana treasure with a shoreline of 1,600 miles.

As for the Yellowstone River, French trappers, well before Lewis and Clark, entered the lower part naming it "La Roche Jaune" for the tint of the river rocks at low water.

Montana's Yellowstone River drains a 70,000-square mile piece of the west in grand fashion. It gathers some of the finest mountain and prairie topography on the planet ... peaks reaching past 12,000 feet in elevation, the largest high mountain lake on the continent, dense evergreen forests, buttes, colorful badlands, deep canyons, sweet smelling sage and juniper covered hills. Once serving as "a moving highway" into the wilderness, this unique river mirrored the passage of millions of bison, the travels of the Corps of Discovery, creation of the nation's first national park, the foundations of a state and the unfortunate ousting of the regions first occupants — the great Indian population.

Today it provides recreation, irrigation and beauty to eastern Montana. This, the largest undammed river in North America, begins its flow from the north face of Younts Peak in the Teton Wilderness, south of Yellowstone National Park in the Wyoming high country. From there it rushes 670 miles to meet the Missouri in North Dakota, just beyond the Montana line.

It gains strength from waters pouring out of the Absaroka-Beartooth ... the Boulder, Stillwater and Clarks Fork and farther downriver from the Bighorn, Tongue and Powder flows.

With the exception of some stretches of the Yellowstone, most of the rivers of the high plains are mellow — no whitewater excitement, just serenity, solitude, beauty and a sense of the past. The water moves at an easy pace past islands, sandbars and groves of cottonwoods interspersed with a carpet of grasses and other riparian vegetation providing a home to river wildlife. The landscape along the rivers has changed little with time. A modern day floater can imagine sharing the same place with nineteenth-century trappers and explorers.

Not enough can be said about fishing in these parts beyond the mountains, and catching warm water game fish in all the area's lakes and rivers inspires stories. Fort Peck Lake and segments of the Missouri River are the most legendary of all. Walleye, northern pike, lake trout and chinook salmon are just a few of the breeds found in these waters.

Walleye rate their own tournaments, attracting some of the nation's best fishing enthusiasts as entrants. Parts of Fort Peck Lake and the Milk, Missouri and Yellowstone rivers furnish the necessary habitat for the almost prehistoric paddlefish, which average 80 pounds. The largest ever taken was a 142-pound giant caught in the Missouri, upstream from Fort Peck Lake.

Rainbow and brown trout live in the upper reaches of the Marias, Judith, Milk, Teton and Musselshell Rivers. The Bighorn River, fed by the cold waters of Bighorn Lake, is considered one of the best rainbow and brown trout fisheries on earth.

These eastern Montana lands are Big Sky Country. Out here, a formidable canopy of sky provides a constantly changing panorama ... a playing field for clouds and weather. From the moment the sun bursts onto the clear eastern horizon of Montana, beginning its journey toward the closing of day, many surprises may appear depending upon the mood of the heavens.

It is the canvas for artful displays of the morning and evening sun and billowing clouds. With nightfall, an astronomer's dream of brilliant nocturnal displays takes center stage. Diamond dust-like stars cover the Judith Basin on a cold winter night, a full moon illuminates the hills between Scobey and Plentywood and meteors streak off in all directions. It is as big a dome of sky as any on the planet and often brings an early morning and evening light so beautiful that no painter or photographer could ever duplicate it.

Subdued topography allows the sky top billing. Summer thunderstorms build to a towering collection of billowy white and gray clouds that are then swept by the wind up into Canada or out onto the Dakotas or Wyoming plains, leaving brilliant sunshine over the prairie, often only to be replaced by another storm with intense lightning displays. In winter, northern born blizzards roll like turbulent waves across the uncluttered skyline depositing a quiet comforter of snow in their wake.

With the sky comes the wind. Out here the breeze has range and character. As it rakes the land, giving clarity and cleanliness to everything — there's no haze diluting the panorama. The wind brings ferocious blizzards, snow-eating chinooks as well as the pleasant smell of sweet clover. It can sustain a tempered clip one day and hurricane forces the next.

While the wind adds personality to eastern Montana's prairie, the seasons give it color. Each period of the year is distinct, but spring shows off the land at its best. A morning in early May dawns raw and gray ... intermittent snowflakes make an effort to prolong a fading plains winter. But this day the promise of the equinox is about to be fulfilled. The warmth of a rising sun endures. The prairie has turned to face spring.

First, the sagebrush and grasses convert to a vibrant green, then wheat fields come to life and the juniper and scattered pines show signs of new growth. Later in the month, a rainbow of wildflowers joins the celebration. In June, this new beginning moves out of the bottomlands and up the mountainsides and buttes. Spring moisture and the thunderstorms of early summer keep the landscape fresh.

As July heads toward August and rainfall lessens, the vegetation cures and

Historic Matador Ranch east of the Little Rockies. RICK AND SUSIE GRAFTZ

rust, gold and brown prevail. The grasses take on a warm dust color. This is the hot, dry period. In September and early October, the summer yellows become mixed with the flame-orange of cottonwoods in the river bottoms and the reds of low-lying vegetation in the coulees and on the hillsides. The sky can be cloudless for days.

Sometime in November, winds from the north signal the start of winter. By now, fall snowstorms have put a coating of white on the upper reaches of the Big Snowies and most of the other mountains. Lasting snows begin spreading to some areas of the prairie and the Missouri Breaks. Soon cold, strong winds will deposit snowdrifts of every size and shape imaginable. Hillsides will be swept clean and ice will form on the rivers. Winter's harshness also brings a softness — tall golden grass and dark evergreens contrast against a blanket of white, and delicate sunsets and sunrises replace summer's blazing displays. The landscape is at rest. This is the prairie's quiet time.

In the western reaches of the prairie, winter brings a phenomenon known as a chinook ... the snow eater. These mild winds bring temporary respite from the frigid atmosphere that descends on Montana.

A chinook's presence is visible in the form of a "chinook" arch of clouds, at once dark and beautiful. If the sun catches it just right, a stunning sunset paints the arch, embellishing the entire sky with a multitude of colors. Often, these winds vanish as quickly as they arrive, with the push of a ferocious northern blizzard reclaiming its season.

It is said the mountains make western Montana, but east of the Northern

Rock Creek Canyon north of Hinsdale. RICK AND SUSIE GRAETZ

Rockies, they are only a modest share of a diverse province, appearing as islands floating in a big sea. None are lofty, but where they rise from the prairie they make their presence known. The views from their summits are far-reaching and impressive. They are the Little Rockies, the Sweetgrass Hills, the Bear Paw, the Highwoods, the Little Belts, the Moccasins, the Judith, the Big and Little Snowies, the Bull, Pryor, Bighorn, Rosebud, Sheep and Wolf mountains. These highlands serve as watersheds, wildlife sanctuaries and respites from summer heat. They harbor forests of ponderosa pine, Douglas fir, aspen and willows. Ecologically, some are mini-versions of the mountains of the Continental Divide, others are a blend of prairie and alpine zones.

The Big Snowies, in the center of Montana, provide a high stage to view a dozen mountain ranges. From the summit of 8,681-foot Great House Peak, a hiker can take in a 300-mile view, northwest to the Sweetgrass Hills and south to the Beartooth Mountains.

As Lewis and Clark made their way westward, the first major rise of land they viewed was the Little Rocky Mountains. Called Wolf Mountains by the natives, white people came to them for their gold and outlaws used them for hideouts..

One of Montana's most prominent ski areas, Showdown, is centered in the Little Belts, the largest of Montana's outlying ranges.

Ice caves, wild horses and a desert environment below their southern slopes make the Pryors an attraction. With the Bighorn Mountains, they guard the narrowed canyons holding 67-mile-long Bighorn Lake and Bighorn National Recreation Area.

Other elevated features mark the Montana prairies. The Medicine Rocks and Chalk Buttes stand as silent sentinels in southeastern Montana's cowboy country. Black Butte, on the eastern rise of the Judith Mountains, can be seen from more than 50 miles away. Western artist Charlie Russell used the imposing Square Butte near Geraldine and the larger Square Butte, southwest of Great Falls, as backgrounds for his famous paintings.

Badlands — often described as miniature deserts — and river breaks add to the fascination of Montana east of the Rockies. Shaped by wind and water, places such as Makoshika, the Terry Badlands, the Piney Buttes and the Missouri and Yellowstone breaks present vivid colors, a wild landscape and a country void of people.

The short grass prairie is a dominant characteristic beyond the mountains. In some areas flat, in most gently undulating, dissected by coulees and marked in places with sandstone formations, it is part of a serene environment accentuated by space and the sound of the wind.

Before the arrival of white travelers, the land stretching east of Montana's Northern Rockies was a wildlife kingdom and a vast native hunting ground. Millions of bison, great herds of antelope, timber wolves and grizzly bears were common. The wild bison are now gone and the grizzlies have retreated to the mountains, but the prairie is still home to an enormous population of large animals, small critters and winged creatures. Turkeys, burrowing owls, white pelicans, elk, ospreys, deer, blue herons, pronghorn antelope, Canada geese, sandhill cranes, cormorants, ducks, foxes, eagles, bighorn sheep, pheasants, coyotes, Hungarian partridge, grouse, prairie dogs and more than 200 species of birds are some of the wild residents of Great Plains Montana.

Montana's eastern domain presents wildlife entertainment unlike anywhere else — the spectacle of ducks and geese landing to gather on the prairie's waters in the fall before migrating south, the excitement of spring as they convoy home again to refuges, lakes and wetlands scattered from the east slope to the Dakotas. Observing their raucous presence is a spectacular encounter. And the heralding of the summer ahead via the peculiar spring mating dance of the sharptail grouse, performed on favored stages is a special attraction to witness.

Plenty of space, minimal human activity and protected lands ensure thriving wildlife and waterfowl population.

Together, Medicine Lake National Wildlife Refuge, tucked in Montana's northeast corner and Bowdoin National Wildlife Refuge out of Malta make a home for more than 200,000 ducks and geese, as well as lake pelicans. Other havens, such as Half-Breed National Wildlife Refuge at Rapelje, Freezeout Lake near Choteau and War Horse Lake National Wildlife Refuge northwest of Winnett, also attract migratory congregations.

Then there is one of America's special places — the wild, remote and beautiful Charles M. Russell National Wildlife Refuge includes 1,100,000

Off the northern edge of Billings. RICK AND SUSIE GRAETZ

acres in a 200-mile strip encircling Fort Peck Lake. Its deep canyons, rough river breaks and isolation provide a sanctuary for wildlife, big and small. It includes the UL Bend Wilderness, home ground for native elk and transplanted bighorn sheep.

In these parts, history is recent and evident. The old West of legend spanning a short yet wild time was played out here. Only 150 years ago, the great Indian nations hunted enormous bison herds that thundered across Montana territory. They had the plains to themselves, wandering freely in search of food and shelter. Then the 1804–1806 Lewis and Clark Expedition changed the face of the land and the native culture forever. This Corps of Discovery marked the way for the white invaders.

At first, the newcomers—mountain men, trappers, traders and explorers — came in search of beaver pelts and routes west. Soon steamboats began plying the Missouri to Fort Benton. The first one reached Fort McKenzie, just below Fort Benton, in 1859. Gold seekers followed, combing the gulches of the Judith Mountains and Little Rockies. More people entered Indian lands.

Grass was rich, thick and free for the taking. Central and eastern Montana had what seemed an endless supply. By the 1870s, western Montana stockmen ventured into the lush river bottoms and the tall grass to the east, laying claim to the vast open range. They were joined by the legendary drives of longhorns, up 1,800 miles from Texas to winter in Montana.

The era of the big ranches had begun. The Circle C and DHS ranches located in the country between Malta and Lewistown became symbols of Montana.

14

These times bred rustlers, horse thieves, cattle barons and vigilantes. The myths and reality of the American cowboy took root. Outlaws met with frontier justice handed out by "Stuart's Stranglers," named for prominent rancher Granville Stuart. During this time, the Natives took their last stand and lost. The bison were gone and the white man was too powerful. A culture and way of life all but disappeared from eastern Montana.

The cattlemen were soon to have their freedom curtailed as well. The tough winter of 1886–87 caused heavy livestock losses and began the decline of the large operations.

During the 1880s, railroads were pushing their way into Montana from the Dakotas. The Great Northern, Milwaukee Road and Northern Pacific lines brought farmers to plow the virgin sod and fence the land. The cattle empires, weakened by winter, shrunk further as the open grasslands diminished. Sheep moved in on the cattle and by 1900, outnumbered cows on the prairie. For a while, Montana was the number one wool-producing state in the nation.

At the turn of the century, railroad promotions and the building of towns along the steel roads, coupled with generous homestead laws (a grant of 320 acres after 1909) brought a wave of people to eastern Montana. They arrived from points east in the USA and from Europe to cultivate riches from the soil. Some prospered, but many didn't. The time of the homesteader peaked in 1918. The wet years disappeared and drought and low prices set in. Thousands left their places, never to return. Prairie vegetation gradually reclaimed fields that once produced bountiful harvests.

Remnants and vivid reminders of early day eastern Montana are everywhere. Portions of former travel byways such as the Great North Trail, the Nez Perce Trail, the Wood Mountain Trail, the Whoop-Up Trail and the Pony Express Route are still visible, as are the ruins of forts, trading posts and stagecoach stops. Undisturbed areas show signs of travois tracks, wagon wheel ruts and teepee rings.

Evidence of the era of the first sodbusters is plentiful. Old buildings that once housed these settlers and their dreams still stand, only to serve as refuges for small animals, birds and owls.

Although the drought and economic conditions ended their hopes, some hearty pioneer families persisted, stayed on and today are the backbone of the Montana prairie country.

Descendants of the homesteaders and products of cattle outfits that have been in the same family for generations provide the area with a sense of permanency and independence, a strong profile dictated by rural life and past experiences that characterize this corner of the Great Plains.

It might be facetious to say distance between communities is comfortable and elbowroom is plentiful. Here, space dwarfs the human presence whether it is on farms and ranches well apart from neighbors, or in towns with colorful names ... Sunburst, Judith Gap, Roundup, Cut Bank, Plentywood,

Whitewater, Choteau, Big Sandy, Chinook, Lame Deer, Lodge Grass, Ekalaka, Grassrange and Wolf Point as well as Billings, Great Falls, Lewistown and Miles City. The latter four, large towns by Montana standards, are but small outposts on the vast Montana plains.

High school basketball teams often have to travel up to 300 miles one-way for games. The population is dispersed enough to support many one-teacher schools consisting of grades one through eight with an average of 15 students. About 67 of them are still open east of the Rockies.

Towns are the essence of this territory where the natural features capture attention. Social and commercial activities interact within them in a way that is all but disappearing across America. Cafes, hardware and grocery stores are where stockmen, farmers, implement dealers and bankers meet to discuss ag-economics, their families, and the weather. You'll still find drug stores with soda fountains and chances are that you can walk in the door of any business and shake the hand of the owner. A genuine welcoming atmosphere prevails.

To the uninitiated, life in many of these eastern Montana hamlets might seem carefree, but the problems of a lagging agricultural economy, lack of opportunities for the young, and drought are real. The people of these isolated havens that dot the sprawling prairie deal with them and never give up. A "can do" attitude holds sway over town meetings or at the supper table as residents look for answers and new possibilities. Hope always seems to be there.

Livestock operations and dry land farming are the major economic pursuits of Montana east of the mountains, and most of the cultivation involves wheat.

Winter wheat is planted in late summer and gains a foothold before the cold descends. It renews growth with spring's warmth and is harvested in July. Montana's dominant crop, it crowds the horizon of the Golden Triangle … the country north and northwest of Great Falls. Farther east and north, where winter is colder, spring wheat colors the fields. Seeds are sown at winter's end and the crop is cut in late summer. Yields tend to be lower with this strain of wheat.

Strip farming is a trademark. In heavily cultivated areas, successions of wheat, interspersed with fallow earth, stretch as far as the eye can see. This farming practice serves as a deterrent to wind erosion and conserves moisture. Each year the pattern is reversed.

Sugar beet farming doesn't create the same scenic mosaic as the ribbons of wheat fields do, but in the valley of the Yellowstone River, especially between Laurel and Glendive, it adds to the well-being of southeast Montana.

While the big unfenced ranches of the mid — to late 1800s are gone, cattle are still very important on Montana's high plains. Cowboys continue to work the range and substantial ranches exist in Yellowstone and surrounding counties. Miles City in Custer County is known as the "Cattle Capital of Montana."

Powder River country south of Broadus. RICK AND SUSIE GRAETZ

Montana's Indians, to a degree, survived the devastation of their homelands and are a prominent part of this piece of the Big Sky Country. They are the Blackfeet, the Chippewa, the Cree, the Crow, the Northern Cheyenne, the Assiniboine, the Gros Ventre and the Sioux nations. Some still occupy a portion of their ancestral grounds, others do not. Most live on six reservations scattered throughout the Northern Plains. Powwows, rodeos, Milk River Indian Days, North American Indian Days and the Crow Fair are tributes to their proud tribal traditions.

As the first residents of Montana, these natives were good stewards of the land. They respected it and took only what they needed to survive. They passed through and left it as they found it. Their legacy is still present out here in the places that have remained unaltered with the passing of the ages, and their spirit is still carried on the wind. Listen for it and feel it as you explore and marvel at Montana east of the mountains.

—RICK AND SUSIE GRAETZ

WESTERN MONTANA

HEADING WEST ACROSS THE SIMPLE GRANDEUR OF THE VAST MONTANA PRAIRIE, A seemingly white wall shimmers in the distance. You can see it from almost 100 miles away.

In July 1805, Captains Lewis and Clark, the first white travelers coming up the Missouri River, called this vision *"the shining mountains."* Later, immigrants trailing to the Pacific Northwest used the same words. Those voyageurs moving through the Yellowstone Valley were seeing the Beartooth Range; and the Rocky Mountain Front was the vista to the northern prairie explorers.

The panorama on the plains stretches forever to the horizon; now, as the mountains are approached, it reaches up toward the sky. Montana east of the mountains terminates abruptly against these massive uplifts and western Montana's eastern boundary begins. From these frontal rises, its territory reaches west across to the Idaho state line.

The longest stretch of western or "mountainous" Montana is a vertical drop to the south from the Port of Piegan, east of Glacier National Park. Here, an eagle will fly 330 miles before reaching Eighteen Mile Peak in the Beaverhead Range and Idaho's Lemhi River Valley. From the peaks of Glacier in the north, it's about 120 miles along the Canadian line to the western edge of the state. In the central section, the eastern boundary is somewhat less delineated; here it is 220 miles from Two Dot to Lolo Pass. For the southern portion from Red Lodge, just below the Beartooth Range, it's 260 miles through mountains and valleys to Nez Perce Pass in the Bitterroot Range.

Within western Montana's perimeters, the Continental Divide twists and turns from Glacier Park down to the Centennial Range and into Yellowstone National Park. Along the way it touches some of Montana's most fabled wilderness lands, including the Bob Marshall Country, as well as historic mining districts. From this hydrological separation, the big Missouri River is born. Waters flowing east out of springs and snow melt from countless streams feed the Jefferson, Gallatin and Madison rivers at whose confluence the Missouri begins its journey to the Mississippi. Small rivulets of water and creeks draining from the west slope of the Divide power rivers such as the Flathead and the Bitterroot. They fuel the Clark Fork, one of the major tributaries of Washington's Columbia River system, which empties into the Pacific.

One writer described this western Montana country as the "Majestic Land" ... and that it is! Mountain ranges of stunning beauty are interspersed with deep river canyons, broad fertile valleys, conifer forests and clear lakes. The

Flathead Valley and the Swan Mountain Range. RICK AND SUSIE GRAETZ

landscape mix is some of the finest on the North American Continent. The northern half of this terrain is defined with dense forests of pine, fir and tamarack and a multitude of lakes and streams. In the southern part, the timber stands tend to be more open and interspersed with large meadows and broad valleys of sagebrush and grasses. In geographic terms, these openings are called intermountain valleys. Blue ribbon fishing rivers meander through these wider bottomlands.

Thirteen federally designated wilderness areas totaling almost 3,400,000 acres grace this province. One of them, the hallowed Bob Marshall Wilderness complex, embraces the epitome of what the wild American mountainous west once looked like. A territory devoid of roads where wildlife roams free and human travel is by foot or horseback. Views from its interior high points show an untrammeled land.

The mountains of western Montana range from lower lying and timber covered to the alpine heights of the Beartooth where 28 peaks soar above 12,000 feet. Numerous ridges and summits of some of the other other ranges reach beyond 10,000 feet above sea level. Glaciers fill high country cirques on many of the region's upper peaks; in the 1,000,000 acres of Glacier National Park alone, there are currently 50 active glaciers.

The western reaches of Montana cradle an incalculable number of smaller lakes and streams offering some of the nation's finest trout fisheries. Then there are the big rivers ... the Madison, the Big Hole, the Bitterroot, the Gallatin, the three forks of the Flathead, the upper Missouri, the upper

Yellowstone, the Beaverhead and the Smith ... and Flathead Lake, the largest body of freshwater west of the nation's heartland. Starting out as small, high-mountain springs along the Continental Divide, these rivers garner their strength from the contributions of pure alpine creeks and streams along the way. Pertinent to the life of western Montana and a main part of its personality, these waterways are relied on by ranchers, recreationists and communities alike.

Historians agree that the first Indians to settle in northwest Montana were the Kutenai (Kootenai) as well as the Flathead (Salish) and Pend d'Oreille. The Kutenai arrived in the 1500s. The Salish and the Pend d'Oreille soon moved from the northwest to the Three Forks area, then farther east toward the Beartooth. By 1800, the aggressive Blackfeet of the Plains had driven the Salish and Kutenai from the buffalo grounds east of the mountains back into northwest Montana. Various tribes jealously guarded the hunting grounds. The Shoshone were in southwestern Montana before 1600. Eventually, with the advance of the white man into Indian lands, the tribes were forced onto reservations. On July 16, 1885, via the Hellgate Treaty signed near Missoula, the Kootenai, Flathead and Pend d'Oreille were assigned to the Flathead Reservation. This land stretches from the south half of Flathead Lake south to Evaro Hill just north of Missoula.

As their journals and reports described the wonder and possibilities of the land, Lewis and Clark's Corps of Discovery opened the way for whites to come into western Montana. On July 16, 1805, the expedition followed the Missouri River into the mountains near Cascade. On July 19, 1805, Captain Meriwether Lewis entered a narrow and deep canyon of the Missouri. He wrote, "*every object here wears a dark and gloomy aspect. the tow(er)ing and projecting rocks in many places seemed ready to tumble on us ... from the singular appearance of this place, I called it the gates of the rocky mountains.*" The area Lewis wrote about is today's Gates of the Mountains, just to the west of Holter Lake. On July 25, 1805, William Clark reached the three forks of the Missouri River first and named them the Jefferson, the Madison and the Gallatin after President Jefferson and two of his cabinet members.

Fur trappers were the first to follow the Expedition. In the fall of 1807, Finan McDonald entered northwest Montana and built the "Kootenai Post" near present day Libby. In November 1809, David Thompson established "Saleesh House" on the Clark Fork near Thompson Falls, and the rush was on. Thompson explored much of northwest Montana, mapping the Missoula area from the top of today's Mount Jumbo, and probably was the first white man to see Flathead Lake (the Indians called it Salish). His maps of northwest Montana were remarkably accurate.

These traders were not settlers; they just passed through the country. Their kind brought whiskey and disease to the Indians, decimating some of the tribes. The fur trade continued to prosper until about 1840 and then began to slow. The colorful era of mountain men was dying. Catholic priests came

The Big Hole Valley near Jackson. RICK AND SUSIE GRAETZ

on the heels of the trappers, establishing missions at St. Ignatius in the Flathead in 1854 and at St. Mary's in the Bitterroot in 1884.

Gold, however, was the basis for permanent white settlement in western Montana. The first recorded discovery was in the spring of 1858 at Gold Creek, just east of Drummond, by brothers Granville and James Stuart, along with two partners. In July of 1862, a gold rush to Montana was initiated by news of the state's first big strike at Grasshopper Creek. The incoming miners settled nearby, creating Bannack, the first Territorial Capital of Montana.

As word of this strike and other finds reached the eastern United States, gold seekers clambered onto steamboats traveling up the Missouri River to Fort Benton, then ventured overland to the gold camps of western Montana.

One year after Bannack's beginnings, more than 2,000 people had moved into the creek bottom and surrounding hills. The population included some of the most famous characters of the Old West, as well as a collection of all manners of outlaws, crooks and thieves. Among these infamous individuals were Sheriff Henry Plummer and his gang of road agents. Their kind brought on the forming of the Vigilantes, by the citizens of Bannack and nearby Virginia City, to deal out frontier justice. Simply put, no time was wasted; the alleged guilty parties were given a short, if any, trial and the usual sentence — hanging — was carried out on the spot.

Other mineral discoveries followed. In May of 1863, a find in Alder Gulch, 45 miles northeast of Bannack, proved to be the largest of all of Montana's gold strikes and spawned Nevada and Virginia cities. The treasure in Bannack

Gallatin River RICK AND SUSIE GRAETZ

played out and in 1865 Virginia City became the second Territorial Capital, with 10,000 people massed into this rugged area.

In July of 1864, the "Four Georgians" out of Virginia City discovered color in today's Last Chance Gulch ... Helena came into being. As this "gold town" took on some permanence, it replaced Virginia City as the Territorial Capital. In 1889, Montana was granted statehood and Helena became the permanent capital. Gold was still king in the 1880s and Helena had more millionaires per capita than any place in the country — records show that there were 50 of them out of the population. (More than live there today!)

The 1860s through the 1880s was a turbulent, wild time in Montana. But by the 1890s, gold began taking a secondary role to copper. Butte produced the metal and became a major town. Considered one of the most prolific mining districts in the world, Butte earned the title "richest hill on earth." In the late 1880s, it was also a prominent producer of silver, a byproduct of the copper. At one time, it boasted of a population of 90,000 folks.

As the precious metals played out, so did most of the towns surrounding the mines. Only a few of the first camps, including Butte and Helena, prospered and lasted. But overall, Montana grew out of southwest Montana and its placer gold. The miners established the first settlements, and cattlemen soon followed. Communities came to northwest Montana later as a result of the railroad and timber industries taking hold. While some precious metals were found in northwest Montana, most of this activity was confined to the southwestern gulches and valleys.

Western Montana has changed dramatically in the past 30 years. At one time, it was easy to describe the economy of the area as being driven by the timber industry, mining and agriculture. While the forest product sector is still the number one income producer, tourism and government employment have now moved ahead of mining and agriculture in much of the region. Transportation, education and health care are also having an impact.

Mining still plays a role in the Butte-Anaconda area and agriculture is important from Three Forks east through the Yellowstone Valley to Columbus. Ranching continues as the major way of life in the Big Hole, Madison, upper Yellowstone and Centennial valleys, the Big Timber, Livingston and Dillon areas, and the Smith River and Shields River valleys. Missoula, once portrayed as a timber industry community, is probably better known now as a university town (the U of M) and trade center. Bozeman has added the college flavor to its attributes as Montana State University continues to expand. Tourism's growth is evident throughout the region, especially in Bozeman, Whitefish, Kalispell and Red Lodge.

Compared to Montana east of the mountains, western Montana's communities tend to be larger and continue to grow. The human presence on the land is more obvious. From the Bitterroot Valley and Missoula through to the Flathead Valley, this is especially evident.

The eastern two-thirds of the state claim only two large population centers — Great Falls and Billings. In the western one-third, five concentrations of people stand out — Kalispell, Missoula, Butte, Helena and Bozeman. And while Montanans beyond the mountains struggle with shrinking towns and a sagging agricultural economy, their brethren on the opposite side of the state deal with the problems of sprawl and pollution.

Western Montana is attractive, not only for an incredible landscape, but also for all the outdoor recreation it offers. Wilderness experiences that include a chance to see mountain goats, bighorn sheep or even possibly a grizzly bear or wolf, scenic drives, snow sports, fishing, hunting, floating and hiking are just a few of the myriad of activities residents and tourists alike enjoy.

Lower elevation weather is usually drier in the southern half of western Montana than in the northern tier. In the higher reaches, each area receives plenty of snowfall, ranging from 600 to 900 inches a year. Snow measurement courses in the mountains show anywhere from 100 to 150 inches on the ground by winter's end ... up to 200 inches on the western border. The south is somewhat colder than the north and temperatures can drop to 40 and 50 degrees below zero. The national record for cold was set near Helena when the mercury plummeted to minus 70 degrees on January 20, 1954. Summer temperatures are warmer in the southern valleys than in the greener and wetter northwest.

Seasons here are well defined. Winter occupies the longest period ... from five to seven months, depending upon elevation. But this longevity is more than made up for by the beauty created.

Heavy snowfall and moisture filled clouds allow for portraits of snow-laden trees such as the "snow ghosts" found in the Whitefish and Swan ranges of the north. Ice floats the rivers and the forests are silent under a deep blanket of white. Ski tracks take over from foot traffic.

Spring and early summer is the favorite time of year for most western Montanans. Melting snows and frequent rain showers bring a riot of color as wildflowers cover the mountainous landscape. The new green of larch and aspen stand out against the darker pine trees silhouetted against the still snow-covered peaks. Fishing rods come out, kayaks, canoes, and rafts are launched, golf clubs are dusted off and Montana's sport — rodeo — returns to the outdoors. Almost every community, large and small, hosts a fair and a test of men and women against bucking broncs and Brahma bulls. The long light and warm breezes of spring and summer evenings instill a sense of well-being in folks and the land.

Along about mid-September, with daylight fading earlier, a chill hits the air and the nights cool to below freezing. Snow dusts the upper peaks and yellows and oranges bedeck the slopes and bottomlands; first in the cottonwood and aspen trees and later, in the northern area, the tamaracks join in with their brilliant shades of gold. Low lying brush takes on a red and purple hue and the ducks and geese gather to begin their flight south.

The Northern Rockies of western Montana have turned to face fall and the approach, once again, of winter. The air is clear, the sky is blue and wildlife is on the move preparing for the long winter. Hunting takes over from the warm season activities and the Grizzlies and the Bobcats renew their annual pigskin rivalry on the football field.

The diverse weather, the magical scenery and the flavor of the west of yesterday combine to make western Montana a unique place in the Rocky Mountains.

—RICK AND SUSIE GRAETZ

HISTORY AND GEOGRAPHY ...
THE FOUNDATIONS OF A STATE

LEWIS AND CLARK'S
MONTANA TRAIL AND BEYOND

APPOINTED BY PRESIDENT THOMAS JEFFERSON, MERIWETHER LEWIS AND William Clark, with their Corps of Discovery, left Camp Dubois near St. Louis, Missouri on May 14, 1804, to embark on one of history's most storied expeditions the exploration of the northern sector of the recently acquired Louisiana Purchase. Specifically, Jefferson's instructions were: "the object of your mission is to explore the Missouri River & such principle stream of it, as, by its course and communication with the waters of the Pacific Ocean may offer the most direct & practical water communication across this continent for the purposes of commerce."

This journey was one of the most significant events in our nation's history. To quote Roy Appleman in his publication written for the National Park Service: "they carried the destiny as well as the flag of our young Nation westward, from the Mississippi across thousands of miles of mostly unknown land ... up the Missouri, over the Rocky Mountains and on to the Pacific. This epic feat not only sparked national pride, but it also fired the imagination of the American people and made them feel for the first time the full sweep of the continent on which they lived."

Prior to their trip, the West was virgin territory passed through by only a few white explorers; a mysterious place that stirred the imagination. After these two leaders made their journals known, all manners of others followed their pathway, most via the Missouri River.

Lewis and Clark were not only brilliant explorers, but also humanitarians. Appleman noted that hostilities with the Native Americans were limited and "... were undoubtedly far less severe than they might have been were it not for the reservoir of goodwill the expedition had left with nearly all the western tribes ... blending fairness, honesty and strength with patience, respect and understanding, Lewis and Clark recognized the personal dignity of the Indians, honored their religion and culture ... and tried to establish inter-tribal peace. Masters of primitive psychology, they instinctively and unerringly always seemed to make the right decision and rarely offended the natives." Unfortunately, many of those who came later, including the US Government, didn't exhibit this same attitude.

Missouri River, White Cliffs, Lewis & Clark Eagle Creek campsite 5/31/1805. RICK AND SUSIE GRAETZ

It took nearly a year for the party to reach the confluence of the Missouri and Yellowstone rivers, located in present day North Dakota. On April 27, 1805, after having spent a couple of days at the meeting of these great powerhouses, the Corps entered what eventually would become Montana Territory.

Setting foot in country they described as more beautiful than could ever have been imagined, they were particularly impressed with the abundance of wildlife.

The two Captains spent four months following the Missouri through eastern and central Montana, past the future sites of Great Falls and Helena to what is now Three Forks, then routing up the Jefferson River to the Beaverhead and its confluence with Red Rock Creek — today the site of Clark Canyon Reservoir. From there, they traversed west through Horse Creek Prairie to Lemhi Pass, arriving on the Continental Divide and the Montana/Idaho border on Aug. 12, 1805. One of the farthest headwater trickles of the Missouri had been reached.

Their path then proceeded down the west side of the Divide to Idaho's Lemhi River Valley, trailed north to the Salmon River, then back into Montana again somewhere in the area of what would become Lost Trail Pass. Moving up the Bitterroot Valley to a place they called *"Travellers rest"* near present day Lolo, the Corps turned west again, crossing Lolo Pass into Idaho. They eventually found their way to the Pacific Ocean.

On June 29, 1806, on their return journey from the west coast, the

Expedition once more ventured over Lolo Pass to Travelers Rest. From there the leaders split. Lewis headed through present-day Missoula up the Blackfoot River and across today's Lewis and Clark's Pass, west of Lincoln. Attaining the Continental Divide at this point, Lewis and his men trekked to the Sun River and eventually were reunited with the Missouri.

Clark, upon leaving Travelers' Rest, retraced part of their previous route up the Bitterroot River, then entered the Big Hole Valley on his way to a cache they had left near Horse Creek. After navigating the Beaverhead and Jefferson rivers to Three Forks, he turned east through the Gallatin Valley and on to the Yellowstone River, following it to the Missouri. Clark and his men soon rejoined Lewis, and the Expedition continued to St. Louis, reaching the terminus of the adventure on Sept. 23, 1806.

The Montana landscape Lewis and Clark viewed almost 200 years ago, especially along stretches of the Missouri River from the North Dakota line to Fort Benton, has changed little.

Calculations in their journals of latitude and longitude have made it possible to ascertain the approximate location of certain campsites, but others have been altered by the flow of the Missouri. At least 11 of them are now under the waters of Fort Peck Lake. To experience the entire route, one would have to travel on the river or ride horseback.

AFTER THOUGHTS

Counting their odyssey to the Pacific Coast and the return passage to St. Louis, the explorers spent nearly six months in Montana. Their time here was significant, and provided Lewis and Clark with some of their most memorable experiences, as well as periods of extreme hardship.

Previous to their visit, the land that would become Montana was unknown. In describing the topography and mapping the Missouri River, the Captains laid to rest the belief that the big river might offer a navigable water passage to the Pacific. Clark, on his return journey charted a significant portion of the Yellowstone River and Lewis realized from exploring the Marias on his way east that the boundary of the Louisiana Purchase didn't extend beyond the 49th parallel. This ended the hope that America owned a larger portion of the lucrative fur trade territory.

The late historian K. Ross Toole tells us "Lewis and Clark left in their journals not only a story of hardship and courage ... but the story of wealth ... Although they left only the ashes of their campfires behind, Montana would never be the same again." They opened the way for others who came to exploit the land and set a pattern. The colonial economy that began in Montana shortly after the Corps' passage would run strong for more than 100 years and, to a certain extent, still exists.

One could say the Native Americans suffered most as a result of the Expedition. With few exceptions, the Indians Lewis and Clark encountered extended the hand of friendship as well as food, horses and information. Too often though, the white men who followed betrayed this hospitable welcome. Within 80 years of the journey, most tribes were restricted to reservations.

Upon their return to St. Louis on Sept. 23, 1806, the Corps of Discovery was given a well-deserved hero's welcome. It would be difficult to identify another adventure on American soil as great as this one. Reading what these 30 men, one woman, an infant and a Newfoundland dog experienced is nearly unbelievable — the incredible physical toil, often hindered by Mother nature's whims, as well as her creatures, both large and small, seemed to be more than mere humans could handle.

What about afterward? Captain Clark married Julia Hancock, for whom he named Montana's Judith River. He was appointed superintendent of Indian Affairs for the Louisiana Territory, and garnered the rank of Brigadier General of the Militia. He was praised highly for his fairness with the great Indian Nations of the Upper Missouri. He also took on the role of educating Sacajawea's son Jean Baptiste Charbonneau. Clark died Sept. 1, 1838, 31 years after the expedition was completed.

President Jefferson appointed Meriwether Lewis governor of the Louisiana Territory and hoped Lewis would proceed quickly with publishing the journals of the Expedition. Lewis's success as governor was checkered. He drank heavily, paid little attention to his duties, went deep into debt and was unsuccessful in courting, although he did manage to have moments of achievement.

Lewis suffered bouts of depression and other mental issues. In October 1809, he set out for Washington to defend bills he had submitted to the

Missouri River, Gates of the Mountains north of Helena. RICK AND SUSIE GRAETZ

Beaverhead Rock between Dillon and Twin Bridges. RICK AND SUSIE GRAETZ

government, and it is assumed, to have his journals readied for printing. Sometime during the night of Oct. 11, 1809 or the early morning hours of the 12th, at an inn on the Natchez Trace in Tennessee, he committed suicide.

Thomas Jefferson never wavered in his support of his protégé. In 1813, Jefferson defended his reasons for choosing Lewis: "Of courage undaunted, possessing a firmness & perseverance of purpose which nothing but impossibilities could divert from its direction ... with all these qualifications as if selected and implanted by nature in one body, for this express purpose, I could have no hesitation in confiding the enterprise (the exploration of the Louisiana Purchase) to him."

And the late Stephen Ambrose described him as "... a great company commander, the greatest of all American Explorers, and in the top rank of world explorers."

In 1814, Nicholas Biddle arranged with Clark to publish an account of the Expedition based on a paraphrased version of the journals, but left out much of the scientific information. As a result, Lewis and Clark initially didn't get credit for all their discoveries. Ninety years later, Reuben Thwaites did an eight-volume set of the journals. It was with this edition that the explorer's stature began to be elevated.

In the 1980s, Gary Moulton, through the University of Nebraska, published the definitive work filled with outstanding footnotes — some 13 volumes including an Atlas of Clark's maps make up this exceptional effort.

—RICK AND SUSIE GRAETZ

Missouri River near Otis Creek south of Bainville. RICK AND SUSIE GRAETZ

APRIL 27, 1805 —
THE FIRST WRITTEN HISTORY OF MONTANA

Location: Northeast Montana near today's Snowden Bridge just west of the confluence of the Missouri and Yellowstone rivers

During the evening of a day that saw the Corps of Discovery cross into what would become Montana from the Confluence of the Missouri and Yellowstone rivers, Captain Meriwether Lewis describes the day's events in his Journal. These words put to paper commence the first written history of Montana.

Meriwether Lewis April 27, 1805 from the original journals as edited by Gary Moulton...

"This morning I walked through the point formed by the junction of the rivers; the woodland extends about a mile; when the rivers approach each other within less than half a mile; here a beatifull level low plain commences and extends up both rivers for many miles, widening as the rivers recede from each other, and extending back half a mile to a plain about 12 feet higher than itself; the low plain appears to be a few inches higher than high water mark and of course will not be liable to be overflown; tho' where it joins the high plain a part of the Missouri when at it's greatest hight, passes through a channel of 60 or 70 yards wide and falls into the yellowstone river. on the Missouri about 2 ½ miles from the entrance of the yellowstone river, and between this high and low plain, a

small lake is situated about 200 yards wide extending along the edge of the high plain parallel with the Missouri about one mile. on the point of the high plain at the lower extremity of this lake I think would be the most eligible site for an establishment. between this low plain and the Yellowstone river their is an extensive body of timbered land extending up the river for many miles. this site recommended is about 400 yards distant from the Missouri and about double that distance from the river yellowstone; from it the high plain, rising very gradually, extends back about three miles to the hills, and continues with the same width between these hills and the timbered land on the yellowstone river ,up that stream, for seven or eight miles; and is one of the hadsomest plains I ever beheld. on the Missouri side the hills sircumscribe it's width, & at the distance of three miles up that river from this site, it is not more than 400 yards wide. Capt Clark thinks that the lower extremity of the low plane would be most eligible for this establishment; it is true that it is much nearer both rivers, and might answer very well, but I think it reather too low to venture a permanent establishment, particularly if built of brick or other durable materials, at any considerable expence; for so capricious, and versatile are these rivers, that it is difficult to say how long it will be, untill they direct the force of their currents against this narrow part of the low plain, which when they do, must shortly yeald to their influence; in such case a few years only would be necessary, for the annihilation of the plain, and with it the fortification.I continued my walk on shore; at 11 A. M. the wind became very hard from N. W. insomuch that the perogues and canoes were unable either to proceede or pass the river to me; I was under the necessity therefore of shooting a goose and cooking it for my dinner. the wind abated about 4. P. M. and the party proceeded tho' I could not conveniently join them untill night. altho' game is very abundant and gentle, we only kill as much as is necessary for food. I believe that two good hunters could conveniently supply a regiment with provisions. for several days past we have observed a great number of buffaloe lying dead on the shore, some of them entire and others partly devoured by the wolves and bear. those anamals either drownded during the winter in attempting to pass the river on the ice during the winter or by swiming acrss at present to bluff banks which they are unable to ascend, and feeling themselves too weak to return remain and perish for the want of food; in this situation we met with several little parties of them.- beaver are very abundant, the party kill several of them everyday. The Eagles, Magpies, and gees have their nests in trees adjacent to each other; the magpye particularly appears fond of building near the Eagle, as we scarcely see an Eagle's nest unaccompanyed with two or three Magpies nests within a short distance. The bald Eagle are more abundant here than I ever observed them in any part of the country."

This entry then begins a documented history of Montana ... a history at once recent, rich and colorful.

William Clark also penned his journals but it was Lewis who covered more material; Clark was the cartographer. The landscape Lewis described in the above journal account has changed little.

The Missouri and Yellowstone River confluence of Lewis and Clark's time is now about two miles northeast of the where it was when they first reached it. Historic maps made by early scientific expeditions show a stable confluence well after Clark made his chart of the area. A huge ice jam in the 1930s caused widespread flooding in the Yellowstone Valley and along the Missouri sending both rivers out of their banks and caused a shift in their channels. The confluence was forced to the northeast. A recent Landstat image shows clearly a meander scars indicating the former river paths and mixing spot.

The air image also shows Nohly Lake, the body of water Lewis described in his writing. Today Nohly has almost disappeared.

The Captains discussed possible sites for a trading fort near the confluence and Nohly Lake. In 1828 the American Fur Company established. Fort Union, the first fort on the Upper Missouri. Possibly owing to flooding concerns, the place was built two river miles west of the confluence. At that time one could stand on the south side of the fort on the Missouri's banks and look east toward the confluence.

Today, an exact replica of the original structure exists on the former site. However owing to the dynamics of this ever-changing Missouri, the water is about 200 yards south of the post and it is no longer possible to see the confluence now three river miles away.

—RICK AND SUSIE GRAETZ

LEWIS & CLARK'S TRAVELERS' REST

In the nearly 8,000 miles Lewis and Clark traveled during their exploration of the Missouri River and beyond, both heading west and returning, there has been only one confirmed bit of physical evidence to verify the Corps of Discovery's exact presence. On July 25, 1806, Captain William Clark carved his name and the date in the soft sandstone face of Pompey's Pillar, a 200-foot-high outcropping on the south banks of the Yellowstone River east of Billings. After committing this act of historic graffiti, he noted the event in his Journal and named the site after Sacajawea's toddler son Baptiste whom the men of the Corps affectionately called Pomp.

Recently, a new find at the site of "Travellers Rest" may be the second such substantiation. September 9–11, 1805 before heading west over the Bitterroot Mountains and again on their return journey from the Pacific on June 30–July 3, 1806, the explorers camped there.

In 1999, the National Trust for Historic Preservation listed Montana's Travelers' Rest as one of the 11 most endangered historic places in the nation. Now it appears the heart of the area has been preserved!

Travelers' Rest State Park, located west of Hwy 93 a short distance south of the town of Lolo and about ¾ of a mile up Lolo Creek is owned by the State of Montana and managed by a private non-profit group, the Travelers' Rest

Travelers' Rest, Lewis & Clark campsite 9/9-11/1805 and 6/30 to 7/3/1806. RICK AND SUSIE GRAETZ

Preservation and Heritage Association (TRPHA). The Holt family, living adjacent to the 25-acre park, has donated a conservation easement on ten additional acres.

Lewis's journal entry of September 9, 1805 reads, *"Set out at 7 A M. this morning and proceeded down and the Flathead (Bitterroot) river leaving it on our left, the country in the valley of the this river is generally a prairie and from five to 6 miles wide,"* continuing downriver and eventually crossing to the west side *"encamped on a large creek (Lolo Creek) which falls in on the West as our guide informs us that we should leave the river at this place and the weather appearing settled and fair I determined to hault the next day to rest the horses and take some scelestial Observations. we called this Creek 'Travellers rest'."*

In the early 1960s, believing that Lewis and Clark's campsite was located at the confluence of the Bitterroot River and Lolo Creek, the National Park Service declared it a National Historic Landmark. In the mid 1990s, an independent researcher, Bob Bergantino of Montana Tech in Butte, made corrections to the astronomical readings of Lewis and pinpointed the current, farther west location.

Recent findings, oral history, the journal entries and common sense are ample proof in favor of the creek site being their camp.

The Corps had been traveling on horses and would have avoided the brush and rough surface of the river bottoms. Also, they were following a well-used Indian trail (through the Bitterroot Valley) that oral history maintains stayed up on the benches above the river channel. These facts alone indicate they wouldn't have encountered the mix of Lolo Creek and the Bitterroot but rather the east-west orientation of Lolo Creek a ways up from where it meets the Bitterroot and most likely the intersection of the trail across the mountains.

Now, tangible evidence has surfaced. Since this was a military expedition the camps were set up in keeping with a military manual of the time. Using this layout has aided in directing the search for physical evidence of Lewis and Clark's use of the site. It is believed the explorer's central fire used for cooking, the making of ammunition and gunsmithing has been identified. Cracked rocks show an intense fire had burned in this spot at one time; high heat would have been needed to prepare the lead. Indians of that period most likely didn't have the technology to prepare their own ammunition, they traded for it and it is unlikely any trappers or smaller groups who might have preceded the Corps would have built such a large fire. A spent lead ball, circa 200 years old, was found nearby and melted lead was uncovered inside the pit. It is almost certain that the Corps had to manufacture more ammunition, especially in 1806, as they were about to split up.

About 150 yards away from the fire site (in accordance with the military manual), the possible latrine trench was unearthed. Six inches into the trench, archeologists uncovered a length of gray organic matter. Mercury was found at the bottom of this layer and being an inert substance, would have settled to the bottom of the trench. The excavation went down 18 inches and under the organic material ordinary soil was in place. This is the most telling evidence of the expedition's presence. Members of the Expedition had been taking Dr. Rush's pills, an instant purgative containing 60 percent mercury. It is known

7/25/1806, first confirmed proof of L&C campsite, Pompey's Pillar, Yellowstone River. RICK AND SUSIE GRAETZ

from the journals that at least two expedition members were treated with Rush's medication during the 1806 pause at Travelers' Rest, and at this point of the journey it would have been in the systems of the men who had been using the treatment prior to reaching this camp.

Loren Flynn, the Executive Director of TRPHA, contends what has been found here is very compelling evidence that this was an exact Lewis and Clark camp.

Flynn recognizes that while interest in the Lewis and Clark Expedition is starting to build, he is also aware there will be a time when the level of attention will subside. It is his opinion that the park must be sustainable and not overbuilt. The scope of the location should encompass all of the very important events and activities the confluence of Lolo Creek and the Bitterroot River witnessed, not just the Corps of Discovery's time.

What is in position now, and what is planned for the future, will put this historic major trail crossroads into the full light it deserves. A Native American culture was flourishing here well before the Corps discovered the site for white society.

Infrared testing has found numerous tepee rings near the junction of the Lolo and Bitterroot Valley trails. Great Indian Nations ... the Salish, Kootenai, Nez Perce and Shoshone passed through and interacted in this landscape. And to the Salish, the Bitterroot is still a revered homeland. The Native's side of the story, as well as the explorer's experiences, makes for a fascinating and integral part of Montana's past. TRPHA and other partners will employ Native people to tell the Native American history of the area.

About 1850, "Travellers rest Creek" became known as Lolo Creek. Local Indians (most likely the Salish) had trouble with a French Canadian trapper's name. They couldn't pronounce the French uvular r, in Lawrence and shortened it to the easiest part ... Lo-Lo, hence Lolo. And the onerous path the Corps was about to embark on, used for generations by Indians (principally the Nez Perce) on their way to hunt buffalo on the east side of the mountains, and said to be passable only with the knowledge of those who had been shown the way before, was first called the Nee Mee Poo (the Nez Perce's name for themselves) or Nez Perce Trail, then Lolo Trail.

Indeed, Travelers' Rest State Park interprets the times gone by of a region, once considered a hub of western Montana. The natural history of the Bitterroot Country, including plants and animals used for subsistence are part of interactive displays.

—RICK AND SUSIE GRAETZ

MONTANA TERRITORY ...
THE NAMING OF A STATE

E ACH OF THE UNITED STATES OF AMERICA, EXCEPT FOR THE ORIGINAL THIRTEEN, Texas, and California, was first organized as a territory before achieving admittance to the Union as a state. Originating with the Ordinances of 1785 and 1787, the territorial system provided the expanding United States with a method of governing frontier areas until they gained sufficient population and economic maturity to qualify for equality with the states. Territories represented a sort of compromise between colonies and states. They had limited powers of legislative self-government, but their executive and judicial officers were appointed by the federal government. Not surprisingly, residents of frontier territories usually demanded quick admission to statehood so that they could gain full control of their local governments. Until they had such control, federal supervision over their local affairs was the source of constant frustration. Montana's time of frustration lasted for twenty-five years, from the creation of Montana Territory in 1864 until the territory was admitted to statehood in 1889.

The mining boom of the 1860s brought the first sizable influx of whites to Montana and, thus, the first demands for government. Until that time, the large eastern and small western sectors of what would be Montana had simply been attached to huge frontier territories whose centers of population lay hundreds, even thousands, of miles away. The eastern two-thirds of Montana, which occupies the far northwestern corner of the Mississippi-Missouri Basin, had formed the far extremity of Indian Territory until 1805, was part of Louisiana Territory until 1812, Missouri Territory until 1821, a general Great Plains Indian Country until 1854, and Nebraska Territory until 1861, when it became the western sector of newly created Dakota Territory.

The northwest corner of Montana lies on the periphery of a different geographic province, the Columbia River Basin. The United States and Great Britain held this area, known as "Oregon Country," under a joint occupancy agreement until 1846, when they agreed to extend the 49th parallel boundary to the Pacific as the dividing line between the United States and Canada. The western portion of future Montana then became the easternmost portion of Oregon Territory from 1848 until 1853 and of Washington Territory from 1853 until 1863.

Quite by accident, it was the advance of the mining frontier that caused the eastern and western regions of Montana to be joined together in one political unit. In 1861–62, as miners began the rush into the newly opened gold fields of present-day north-central Idaho, settlers demanded a new territory in the Northern Rockies. Congress responded in March of 1863 by creating Idaho Territory. Carved out of Washington, Dakota, and Nebraska territories, Idaho embraced an enormous area, including all of present-day Idaho and Montana and most of Wyoming. Its capital lay on the far western border at Lewiston. Significantly, the creation of Idaho brought eastern and western Montana within a common boundary for the first time.

Idaho Territory was a geographic impossibility. The massive ranges of the Rocky Mountains divided the territory in half, and a thousand miles separated Lewiston in the west from the far eastern extremities. Even in 1863, Idaho's population was shifting rapidly eastward, across the Continental Divide to the mining camps on the upper Missouri. With good reason, the Bannack-Virginia City miners believed that Lewiston — hundreds of miles away over endless, snow-clogged mountain passes — could never govern them properly. The outrages of the Plummer Gang tended to prove their point. Miners began agitating for the creation of a new territory, to be split from Idaho along the crests of the Rockies.

Fortunately for their cause, Judge Sidney Edgerton, the newly appointed chief justice of Idaho, arrived at Bannack in September 1863. Edgerton, a former Ohio congressman, was unable to proceed to Lewiston because of the approach of winter. He soon learned that the governor of Idaho had snubbed him by assigning him to the faraway judicial district lying east of the Divide. Both Edgerton and his nephew, vigilante leader Wilbur Fisk Sanders, took up the settlers' crusade to divide Idaho Territory. Edgerton personally knew the president and many congressmen, so the miners chose to send him to Washington, D.C., to press their case. Carrying two thousand dollars in gold, Edgerton headed east in January 1864. Meanwhile, the Idaho legislature at Lewiston obligingly petitioned Congress to carve a new territory named Jefferson out of Idaho, with the dividing line along the Continental Divide and the 113th meridian, locating Idaho's new eastern boundary just west of the Deer Lodge Valley.

Arriving in Washington, Edgerton consulted with President Lincoln and found him agreeable to the idea of a new territory in the Rockies. More important, Edgerton discovered that his friend and fellow Ohioan, Congressman James M. Ashley, had already begun work on a bill to form the new territory. Ashley, who chaired the House Committee on Territories, had the power to make his wishes felt. His political muscle and reports of the area's wealth of gold, which Edgerton reported as influential "in such a mercenary age as ours," pushed the bill speedily through Congress.

While the bill lay in committee, Edgerton and his allies broke with the Idaho legislature by maneuvering the new territory's northwestern boundary three degrees to the west. This meant that the Idaho-Montana territorial line would generally follow the Bitterroot summits northward to the United States-Canada boundary and that Montana would take a 130-mile-wide bite out of

Downtown Bannack, the state's first city and territorial capital. RICK AND SUSIE GRAETZ

northern Idaho. In this manner, Idaho lost the Flathead, upper Clark Fork, and middle Kootenai valleys to its new neighbor. The arrangement reduced the width of northern Idaho by three-fourths, leaving it an awkward "panhandle," cut off from the southern portion of the territory by the rugged Salmon River Mountains. Idaho petitioned Congress to restore these "stolen" lands, but with no success. The Lewiston area even advocated establishing another territory named Columbia, which would join today's western Montana, northern Idaho, and eastern Washington, but the plan got nowhere. So, by circumstance and scheming, the new territory emerged with its jagged western border.

Congress, preoccupied with the Civil War, devoted little time to the matter of founding another western commonwealth. The one serious threat to passage of the bill arose when the Senate voted to force the new territory to give the vote to African Americans. Even though there were few blacks in the Northern Rockies, this explosive issue caused a deadlock with the House of Representatives. The two houses of Congress finally compromised by restricting the vote to citizens of the United States, thus leaving the newly freed African Americans without a guarantee of the ballot on the distant mining frontier.

The House and Senate also debated the name that Congressman Ashley had placed on his creation. "Montana," from the Latin or Spanish adjective meaning "mountainous," first appeared as a place name in 1858, when Josiah Hinman gave the name to a small mining town near Pike's Peak. Governor

James William Denver of Kansas Territory remembered the name and suggested it to Senator Stephen A. Douglas as a name for a future territory in the Rockies. Ashley picked the name up from Douglas or somewhere else and liked it enormously. After trying unsuccessfully to give the name to what became Idaho in 1863, Ashley determined to apply it to Idaho's new neighbor.

When Ashley's Montana bill reached the floor of the House, the Democrats began harassing the Republican about the name. The Democrats suggested dropping it and substituting the title "Jefferson" to honor the founder of the Democratic party or even "Douglas" to commemorate the prominent Democratic senator from Illinois. Ashley and the Republicans would have none of it. Congressman Jacob Cox of Ohio suggested "Shoshone," but the name was scuttled when the Colorado delegate pointed out that Shoshone meant "Snake," a word that had unfortunate implications during the Civil War, when pro-Confederates from the North were called "Copperheads." The debate reached the point of true absurdity when Representative Elihu B. Washburn of Wisconsin suggested the name "Abyssinia," taunting the Republicans about their fondness for African Americans.

Although Ashley won his battle in the House, two weeks later the Senate again challenged the name "Montana." Again, several members believed the classical name was inappropriate and argued that an Indian word would be better. But no one could suggest a name with any relevance to the place, so they too settled on Ashley's title, but only after this illuminating exchange:

MR. HOWARD: I was equally puzzled when I saw the name in the bill.... I was obliged to turn to my old Latin dictionary.... It is a very classical word, pure Latin. It means a mountainous region, a mountainous country.

MR. WADE: Then the name is well adapted to the Territory.

MR. HOWARD: You will find that it is used by Livy and some of the other Latin historians, which is no small praise.

MR. WADE: I do not care anything about the name. If there was none in Latin or in Indian I suppose we have a right to make a name; certainly just as good a right to make it as anybody else. It is a good enough name.

Montana it became, and Montana it has remained. Following approval by Congress, President Lincoln signed into law the bill creating Montana Territory on May 26, 1864.

FROM MONTANA A HISTORY OF TWO CENTURIES BY MICHAEL P. MALONE, RICHARD R. ROEDER AND WILLIAM L. LANG. PRINTED BY PERMISSION OF THE UNIVERSITY OF WASHINGTON PRESS © 1976

HISTORICAL ERAS:

FUR TRADE

WHILE PELTS HAVE LONG BEEN OBJECTS OF TRADE IN NORTH AMERICA, THE early involvement of Europeans and Asians in the North American fur trade is poorly documented and somewhat controversial. Archeological evidence, inscriptions, the oral traditions of American Indians, and literary references suggest that diverse Old World travelers prior to the voyages of Christopher Columbus visited North America. Vine Deloria, Jr., a Lakota Indian, has noted that almost every tribe has stories of strangers unlike themselves or their neighbors passing through their country or settling nearby. There is reason to believe that furs were among the objectives of travel.

The early history of the fur trade in the upper Missouri and Saskatchewan river basins and Northern Rockies was obscured by secrecy, illiteracy, and the separate histories of those involved. The first English trading post was established at Fort Charles on the Nemiscau River in Canada, and the Hudson's Bay Company was chartered in 1670.

Despite the fact that the quality of the pelts was greatest in northerly low-temperature regions, the more southerly Missouri Basin was the initial gateway to the West. Interest in establishing a fur trade in the Missouri Basin perhaps dates from the travels of Louis Jolliet in 1672–1673. Later, during the course of his 1679–1682 travels on the Mississippi River, René-Robert La Salle learned of "undisciplined" French adventurers who sought furs in the Missouri River Basin, and of Frenchmen who lived among the Indians of the Missouri.

The European presence in the interior of North America during the seventeenth century marked the earliest documented epoch of Métis history. The Métis, a distinct people who emerged from the union of Indian women and European men, are widely regarded as the founders of the organized fur trade. They participated in the trade as couriers de bois ("runners of the woods," or trappers), voyageurs, guides, interpreters, factors, and dock and warehouse workers.

In 1700, Father Merest referred to Spanish commerce on the Missouri River, and to its promise as a source of beaver pelts. According to Father Marc Berger, seventeen Frenchmen ascended the Missouri River and built a fort in 1702. A year later, Pierre Le Moines d'Iberville referred to efforts to encourage settlement along the Missouri, and noted that 20 Canadians had been dispatched into the interior.

Homestead near Circle. RICK AND SUSIE GRAETZ

In 1704, Joseph Céloron Bienville reported that more than 100 Canadians were traveling on the Mississippi and Missouri in small bands of seven or eight individuals, and was given an account of the Indians and Spanish provinces of the Missouri by a Frenchman named Laurain. In 1706, Bienville reported that two Canadians told him that they had spent two years traveling from village to village on the Missouri. In 1706–1707, a party led by François d'Erbanne (Derbanne) ascended the Missouri some 400 leagues (1,200 miles and somewhere in today's North Dakoata), discovering horses and evidence of a Spanish presence — perhaps the Spanish trading colonies among the Mandan Indians described in Hidatsa tribe oral traditions. Similar observations were made by Nicholas La Salle in 1708. Indirect evidence of French trading posts along the Missouri resides in commercial records, such as the effort of Boudon, a Canadian, to provide the outposts with lead.

French involvement in the Missouri fur trade abated in the 1760s owing to the British conquest of Canada in 1759–1760; the 1763 Treaty of Paris that ceded Canada to Great Britain; and the Spanish acquisition of the lands west of the Mississippi under the terms of the treaty ending the Seven Years' War. The British and Spanish became more actively involved in the Missouri fur trade.

Henry Kelsey led a more northerly penetration of the interior in 1690. He was sent into the Assiniboine country "to call, encourage, and invite, the remoter Indians to trade with us." The Hudson's Bay Company sponsored several subsequent expeditions. From 1731 to 1734, Pierre Gaultier de Varennes, Sieur de La Vérendrye, and his sons, François and Louis-Joseph, explored the Saskatchewan River Basin beyond Lake Winnepegosis and the Missouri Basin southwestward to outliers of the Rocky Mountains — the "Shining Mountains." In 1754, Anthony Henday traveled westward from Hudson Bay into the Northern Plains, and on to the Rocky Mountains. The French who had preceded him impressed him: "The French talk several [Indian] languages to perfection; they have the advantage of us in every shape; and if they had Brazile tobacco which they have not would entirely cut off our trade." The journals of La Vérendrye and others frequently refer to unnamed agents or couriers de bois who had preceded them into the wilderness — underscoring the incomplete nature of our data. Commercial exploration in the West increased with the creation of the North-West Trading Company in 1779. The North-West Company drew heavily upon the experience of Métis, as well as the relationships of the Métis with the Indians of the northern forests, and expanded aggressively into the plains and mountains of the interior West. The issue of secrecy increased with the intensification of competition between the North-West Company and the Hudson's Bay Company.

As the fur trade approached the Northern Rockies from the east, a Russian fur trade arose along the Pacific Coast to the west following an expedition in 1741–1742. China, rather than Europe, ultimately became the principal market, as the upper classes sought luxurious pelts for their clothing.

Eventually, the western fur trade moved inland. While the Spanish remained involved in trade within the Columbia River Basin, the basin became an area of intense competition among Hudson's Bay Company, North-West Company, and other British and American companies engaged in the fur trade. While much is known of the Russian and British trade with the Orient, less is known regarding the direct involvement of Oriental trappers and traders in western North American. There is mounting evidence that there was such involvement, and some believe that the Salish oral tradition regarding the Mystery People of Flathead Lake might refer to such a presence.

The Hudson's Bay Company, North-West Company, and independent trappers entered the mountains and plains of what was later to become Montana and adjoining areas of Canada during the 1700s. Hudson's Bay Company's presence in the region was formally heralded by Henday's travels in 1754. Peter Fidler and John Ward spent the winter of 1792–1793 with the Piegan along the Rocky Mountain Front. A continuing Hudson's Bay Company presence was suggested by Fidler's complaint that several Hudson's Bay Company employees who had spent previous winters with the Piegan and had learned their language were unable to accompany them. Among the prominent North-West Company agents were Alexander Mackenzie and David Thompson. In 1793, Mackenzie had completed the first crossing of the North American continent. Four years later, Thompson found an interpreter who knew the Mandan language, organized a trading party of French Canadians, and visited Mandan and Hidatsa villages on the Missouri River (near today's Bismark, North Dakota). In the villages,

Thompson met a Frenchman who had lived among the Mandan for fifteen years, as well as visitors recently arrived from the headwaters of the Missouri River. The river was still within Spanish Louisiana, and the Canadians found themselves competing with Spain's St. Louis-based Company of Explorers of the Upper Missouri that had been established in 1793. The rapid political change that occurred within the region would alter this calculus. In 1800, the Treaty of San Ildefonso ceded Louisiana back to France and, in 1803, an overextended France forced Napoleon to sell Louisiana to the United States.

François-Antoine Larocque, with a party of Canadians and Indians, crossed paths with the Lewis and Clark Expedition in the Mandan villages on the Missouri during the winter of 1804–1805. Larocque, with a party of Canadians and Indians, then explored the commercial promise of the Upper Missouri Basin. Increasingly, however, Americans dominated trade in the Missouri Basin. Fort Remon, popularly known as "Fort Manuel" or "Lisa's Fort," was constructed in 1807 by the Louisiana Spaniard Manuel Lisa and Lewis and Clark Expedition veterans George Drouillard and John Colter at the confluence of the Yellowstone and Big Horn rivers. From Fort Remon, they engaged in a profitable trade with the Crow Indians. In 1809, the St. Louis Missouri Fur Company was established by Lisa, Auguste and Pierre Chouteau, William Clark, Andrew Henry, Reuben Lewis (Meriwether's brother), Pierre Menard, and William Morrison. The St. Louis Missouri Fur Company, or Missouri Fur Company as it was better known, essentially represented a rebirth of the Spanish Company of Explorers of the Upper Missouri under new leadership. In 1810, eager to trade with the powerful Blackfeet, Lisa's men established Three Forks Post (Henry's Fort).

To the west, the British were actively advancing into the Upper Columbia River Basin. The North-West Company, under the leadership of David Thompson and Finan McDonald, opened a trading post in 1808 among the Kutenai Indians near the present site of Libby, Montana. The following year, a North-West Company post, Saleesh House, was established among the Salish-speaking tribes near present-day Thompson Falls. In 1810, Hudson's Bay Company established Howes House, a trading post north of Flathead Lake. In 1811, Thompson surveyed the Columbia in order to establish a trade outlet along the Pacific Coast. Upon reaching the coast, he learned that agents of John Jacob Astor's American Fur Company had arrived before him, but the Americans abandoned the Pacific Northwest owing to disruption in the fur trade caused by the War of 1812. Thompson then surveyed the Upper Clark Fork River, mapped the Missoula area from atop Mount Jumbo, and mapped the Flathead region.

In Canada and the Northwest, the competition between North-West Company and Hudson's Bay Company intensified, and erupted into violence in 1815 with a Nor'Wester attack upon a Hudson's Bay Company colony in the Red River Valley The incident eventually led to the consolidation of the two companies in 1821 under the name of the Hudson's Bay Company. The North-West Company's Montana posts were placed under the authority of the Hudson's Bay Columbia Department headquartered at Fort Vancouver on the Lower Columbia.

The North-West Company's Donald McKenzie had established trapping "brigades" in 1818. They were composed of large groups of trappers, and proved to be highly effective, secure, and profitable. The Hudson's Bay Company under Alexander Ross continued the practice, with the first brigade, made up of 55 men, departing from Saleesh House in early 1824. It returned later in the year with 5,000 beaver pelts. Subsequent brigades led by Skene Ogden traveled as far afield as the Gallatin in the east and the Great Salt Lake, Nevada, and California to the south. In addition to the profitability of the brigade system, it depleted fur-bearing animals within the areas trapped and the Hudson's Bay Company hoped that the Americans would therefore lose interest and abandon their "joint occupation" of the Pacific Northwest. In fact, however, Boston merchants such as Joseph Barrell upon reading the account of Captain Cooks's third voyage had kindled American commercial interest in the Pacific Northwest. They believed that the Northwest's wealth of furs would permit them to more actively enter the China trade. The voyages of the Columbia-Rediviva and the Lady Washington in 1789–1790 and the second voyage of the Columbia in 1790–1793 reinforced this belief. Nevertheless, it was the British who remained most active in the Pacific Northwest fur trade, and in 1833 the Hudson's Bay Company and the highly entrepreneurial American Fur Company agreed to avoid encroachment upon the other's territory. The last of the Hudson's Bay Company posts in Montana, Fort Connah (or Connen), was established in 1846 on Post Creek in the Flathead Valley by Neil McArthur and Angus McDonald.

By 1821, the Missouri Fur Company had expanded westward into the Yellowstone and Big Horn regions. The Rocky Mountain Fur Company was established the following year. Owing to the dangers posed by the Blackfeet and other tribes, the Rocky Mountain Fur Company abandoned fixed posts and relied instead upon far-ranging "free trappers" or "mountain men" who would work on their own and then gather each year at annual trading fairs termed "rendezvous." The rendezvous system was established by William Ashley and Andrew Henry in 1824, and is associated with such colorful individuals as Kit Carson, Hugh Glass, and Jedediah Smith. For the mountain men and participating Indians, the rendezvous was more social than profitable. The gatherings typically involved several days of drinking, debauchery, and re-outfitting for the next trapping season. The St. Louis-based Rocky Mountain partners, on the other hand, purchased the pelts, transported them to St. Louis, and accumulated considerable wealth.

Astor's American Fur Company was established in 1808; came to dominate the Great Lakes-Upper Mississippi region; spread into the Missouri Basin in

1822; and acquired the Columbia Fur Company, a competing company composed of many former Nor'Westers, in 1827. It established Fort Floyd, later known as Fort Union, in 1828. The following year, the American Fur Company dispatched trading caravans to the rendezvous, thus placing it in direct competition with the Rocky Mountain Fur Company — a company owned, at the time, by David Jackson, Jedediah Smith, and William Sublette. The bidding benefited the mountain men, but progressively marginalized the less well-endowed Rocky Mountain Fur Company. In 1831, the American Fur Company's Upper Missouri Outfit erected Fort Piegan near the mouth of the Marias River in order to trade with the Blackfeet. Remarkably, 2,400 beaver pelts were delivered to the fort within the first ten days of business. Fort Piegan was burned in 1832, but was soon replaced by Fort McKenzie, located a short distance from the site of Fort Piegan. In order to dominate trade with the Crow to the south, the American Fur Company constructed Fort Cass near the mouth of the Big Horn River in 1832. Both fort Cass and Fort McKenzie served as outposts of Fort Union. In 1834, the Rocky Mountain Fur Company sold out to the American Fur Company. In the same year, Astor anticipated the end of the fur trade and sold his Western Department to its managers, Pratte, Chouteau and Company. Under the leadership of Chouteau, Alexander Culbertson, and Andrew Dawson, the newly formed Pierre Chouteau, Jr. and Company remained actively involved in the Missouri fur trade until the 1860s when beaver pelts were replaced by bison hides in importance.

The impacts of the fur trade were significant. Divisive competition and the effects of alcohol undermined the integrity of tribal societies. Social relationships, belief systems, and important adaptations were lost. Disease, particularly smallpox, accompanied the fur trade into the interior. The Mandan, who had welcomed European and Métis explorers, trappers, and traders, became extinct. More than half of the Blackfeet succumbed to smallpox, ending their military dominance of the Northern High Plains. In some instances, agriculture was abandoned. As firearms replaced the bow and arrow in hunting, game animals often became scarce or locally extinct. Ecosystem function was altered when the fur trade reduced the numbers of otter, marten, fisher, mink, and black and silver fox. The fashion of top hats made of the felted fur of beaver made beaver the staple of the fur trade. La Salle testified in 1678 that 60 to 80 thousand beaver pelts were being shipped each year from Quebec. A year later, the Hudson's Bay Company received the furs of 10,500 beaver, 1,100 marten, 200 otter, and 700 elk, as well as smaller furs. As beaver populations declined in the waterways of eastern North America, the fur trade was driven into the interior. In the Rocky Mountains and elsewhere, the loss of the beaver and their dams resulted in increased flooding and erosion, reduced ground-water recharge, and significant ecological change.

—JEFF GRITZNER

THE RAILROAD AND THE HOMESTEADERS

Railroads usually connect regions, states, cities, towns. But they also connect time, eras, centuries. In Montana, there is a direct railroad connection between the transportation revolution of the 19th century and the homestead era of the 20th. This is that story.

The coming of the transcontinental railroads to Montana Territory in the 1880s is the single most transformational economic development in the entire history of the state. This careening generalization certainly deserves explication.

Here in the 21st century it is impossible to recall how isolated Montana was in the 19th, how out-of-the-way, how off-the-beaten-trail. Montana's transportation history before 1880s is colorful, exciting, romantic, but ultimately ephemeral. Transportation was seasonal. It was hard to get here in the summer, and even harder to leave in the winter. Most people came on foot. They walked, or picked their way across the plains and over the mountains on horseback. Montana was a long way from nowhere. The Bozeman or Bridger trails from southeastern Wyoming to the gold fields along Alder Gulch were hundreds of dangerous miles long. Sioux Indians resented the intrusion. They forced closure of the trails in 1868. But the next year, the Union Pacific met the Central Pacific at Promontory Point in Utah. Now, the hike straight north to Montana was less than 400 miles.

Along this route — modern I-15 — muleskinners and bullwhackers hauled the mighty Murphy wagons, bringing almost five tons of goods and equipment at a crack to Montana. Stagecoaches also plied this "Corinne Road," maintaining regular schedules to Montana towns. Drivers were called "Jehus," from 2 Kings 9:20: "And the driving is like the driving of Jehu, the son of Nimshi, for he driveth furiously."

Montana also boasted water transportation. For almost six weeks out of the year, booming little Fort Benton on the Missouri River, the "Chicago of the West," became America's most interior port city. When the water was high in the spring, American steam vessels, built to run on a thick dew, could travel 2,600 miles up the river from St. Louis. In terms of costs, figured at price per ton per mile, this was the cheapest way to get supplies, equipment, and people to Montana. Long wagon trains fanned out from Fort Benton to Helena and the Montana mining camps, and even north into Canada. But Montana's rivers run dry in mid-summer, and Fort Benton is drydocked.

These early travel ventures are the stuff of frontier literature, but nobody expected them to last. Railroads represented the coming of age in 19th century America, but until they reached Montana, the territory would remain in its infancy. Long before their arrival, railroads had impacted Montana. In 1853, Isaac Stevens had led a northern-tier transcontinental railroad survey through yet-undefined Montana. No one would build a railroad through unorganized territory however. The first step was to segregate the Indians, so just two years later, the same Isaac Stevens was back in Montana setting up reservations. Stevens's chief lieutenant, John Mullan, later hacked out a mountain road across the Rockies. All this took place before the great gold rushes of 1862–1864.

Miners, merchants, farmers, and cattlemen all arrived in Montana in the 1860s, dreaming of railroads. Early territorial legislatures nearly pledged their patrimony to attract them. Montanans must have experienced rapture when the Northern Pacific Railroad was chartered in 1864. But the N.P., although a land-grant road, suffered from extremely shaky finances, and even went bankrupt during the Panic of 1873. Another line, the north-south Utah Northern, was also curtailed by the Panic.

A reorganized Utah and Northern/Union Pacific finally reached Butte on a sub-freezing day in December 1881. Two years later, the transcontinental Northern Pacific, under the new financial management of, first Frederick Billings, then Henry Villard, drove its last spike at Gold Creek, east of Missoula.

Just four years later a second transcontinental, James J. Hill's Great Northern, cut across the Hi-Line to Havre, then southwest to Helena and Butte.

After all these years, three railroads in the 1880s! Montanans were, literally, transported. The railroads mark a fundamental turning point, the greatest historical watershed in Montana history. The railroads all but ended the captivating river and wagon trades. They linked Montana to vital national markets. They opened the territory (and soon the state) to outside investment and exploitation. They goosed economic growth and development. W. G. Conrad said it all: "The railroad ... changed all the channels of business and many ... were unable to adjust themselves to the new conditions it brought. The coming of the railroads annihilated time and distance ... and annexed the country to the commercial territory of the great eastern merchant princes."

By 1909, a third transcontinental, the Chicago, Milwaukee, St. Paul and Pacific (the "Milwaukee Road") had cut through central Montana just in time to capitalize on the great homesteader boom. Railroads were absolutely essential to homesteading in central and eastern Montana — there's almost a causal connection. Railroads brought farm families into Montana with all their goods, livestock, and equipment. They allowed grain growers and ranchers to ship their products to eastern markets. The Northern Pacific in 1900 was the largest landowner in Montana; it had millions of acres to sell. The Great Northern and the Milwaukee Road depended for their very existence on filling up the plains, recently vacated by Indians and buffalo, with productive, Jeffersonian, agrarian yeomen. Their message to potential farmers all over America and Europe was simple: Come hither, and replenish the earth.

Factors other than railroad promotion and cheap transportation drew settlers to Montana after 1890. Land was free — 160 acres under the Homestead Act of 1862. The acreage doubled in 1909, and the proof period dropped from five to three years. Governments at all levels sought to attract citizens. Rainfall seemed ample; if not, scientific agriculture, or dryland farming, promised good crops anyway. Commodity prices were high.

It all seemed so easy ... free land, railroad competition, instant returns, endless markets, high profits. No wonder people poured into Montana — 103,000 in the 1890s, 133,000 in the 1900's, an incredible 173,000 in the 19-teens. From 1890 to 1920, Montana's population exploded by nearly 300 percent. On a single day in 1910, 250 homesteaders arrived in Havre; in 1913, 700 people filed for land there each month; in March 1916, the number reached 1,200. The plains areas alone accounted for over 70 percent — 220,000 folks — of Montana's population increase in the first two decades of the century.

Everything expanded — prosperity; population; land under cultivation; wheat production (both yield per acre and price per bushel); women, children, and families; the number of towns and counties; railroad trackage. The years 1900 to 1920 were years of frenzied rail construction in Montana. The great transcontinentals sent feeder lines to the farthest hamlet, mine, or forest. Steel rails criss-crossed the state. You could go anywhere, it seemed, on the iron horse.

Every boom, unfortunately, produces a bust. The homestead era began gradually; it collapsed abruptly. When the Great War ended in Europe in 1918, the bottom dropped out of the market. Commodity prices plummeted. A searing drought, for which even scientific agriculture had no remedy, scorched the plains. Crop yields imploded. Fire, wind, hail, plagues of locusts, a flu epidemic, and dust storms of biblical proportions battered Montana's grasslands. Paradise became hell overnight.

The same trains that had carried thousands of settlers into Montana for 30 years, carried thousands away after 1918. Montana was the only state in the nation to record negative population growth in the 1920s. Though no one realized it yet, the railroad era in American history was over. Trains built the country; they made Montana. But when Henry Ford rolled a cheap Model T off the Dearborn assembly lines in 1915, the world changed. Automobiles, trucks, and highway construction constituted the next, and enduring, chapter in Montana's transportation history.

For 15 or 20 years on either side of 1900, it was a great ride. Railroads and homesteaders go together in Montana. Each had its glory days. We still have farmers in Montana, and trains, but the romantic connection is history.

—HARRY FRITZ

WRITINGS OF JOSEPH KINSEY HOWARD — THREE ESSAYS

THE GRASS OF MONTANA'S PRAIRIE

Donald Culross Peattie once wrote:
"Of all the things that live and grow upon this earth, grass is the most important!"

THIS IS THE COUNTRY OF THE "SHORT GRASS" — THE NORTHERN GREAT PLAINS. It is a land of little moisture, searing sun and wind, extreme cold — a land of brief spring greenness, yielding to long, hot summers during which the grasses cure on the ground, turning yellow, then brown.

What was the "short grass" before the white man came, and what is it now?

Now, save in especially favored seasons, it is sick: gray, scrawny, really "short" — a few inches tall at its best, growing sparsely in dun-colored clay fields or powdery sand, struggling to hold its ground against the Russian thistle (tumbleweed), introduced in the Dakotas in some unclean seed, and other less finicky but unpalatable plants. It is still nutritious, rich in protein, mineral salts, carbohydrates; this is because the short maturing season of the high-altitude plains develops protein and carbohydrates (sugar. starch, dextrin) more rapidly than it does crude fiber (roughage). Montana's altitude ranges from 1,800 to 12,850 feet, and its average is 3,400.

Seldom now — only in an exceptionally wet spring — does this grass grow tall enough to "roll in the wind like the sea," as the first white men saw it. It was blue grama, bluestem ("wheat grass") and "buffalo grass" and it stood a foot high — sometimes, especially the buffalo bunch grass, as high as three feet. So closely did it carpet the soil that one early visitor marveled: "You could graze all the cattle of the world upon this plain" and another added: "It [the grass] is the most nutritious that livestock ever fed on."

Maturing rapidly and curing on the ground, the grass provided forage the year 'round; but Nature saw to it that these plains were not overgrazed. Thirty or forty million antelope ranged the Great Plains ... But they were dainty eaters, and restless; and there were no fences. In the foothills and on the higher plateaus where the antelope did not venture, thousands of elk maintained Nature's precarious balance of harvest; and deeper in the forest the deer took over the task.

The "thundering herds" of buffalo dramatically described in western fiction were here, too; but probably not, as too often indicated in novel or movie, all the time. How many? Now it is impossible to tell, but some estimates of their number also go as high as thirty million head. Lewis and Clark in 1805 reported seeing "vast herds" of buffalo in May and early in June on the plains of what is now Montana, at one time recording "a thousand." These explorers may have been watching the spring trek of the great beasts to the north; the first buffalo hunters established their "season" from December 1 to May, pursuing the bison southward through Montana into Wyoming and north again as the herds returned in the spring. The hunters reported large herds unusual before November or later than May, though smaller groups grazed Montana's plains the year around.

Montana's rich grasses were easily accessible to the bison because the almost unceasing wind swept the light snow of the plains from the cushioned sod, and many hundreds of thousands moved annually into this feeding ground from the snowed-under fields of the north and east.

There were scores of varieties of these native grasses. Some have disappeared, others, including the most valuable for forage purposes, have become virtually unobtainable in commercial seed form. Nearly all species, with the exception of those maintained in protected areas such as national forests, have changed drastically in physical character, in ground cover, and in nutritive quality.

The drumming hooves of the stampeding bison invariably provided dramatic opportunity for the pianist in the "silent movie" days, and more recently for the sound-effects technician. But these hooves served an important purpose, and no better instance can be given of Nature's meticulous planning than to cite the value of the bison's trampling.

Sturdy "blue bunch," the great perennial wheat grass of the Montana plains, wiry, drouth-resistant, nutritious, made up a large part of the ground cover of the bison's winter range. It grows only from seed; and the trampling of the bison's hooves (though not in stampede: he was king of the plains unless beset by Indian hunters) planted the seed. It was as simple as that: the grass flourished, matured, and dropped its seed; and as they foraged on the ripened crop, the bison planted it for next season.

But there were no sheep to crop to the roots the tender shoots of new grass when they came up in the spring, there were no cattle penned within fences, insatiably hungry — and above all, there were no desperate or greedy home-steaders to sink the murderous blades of their plows into this matted cushion!

This was Nature's controlled grazing: vast herds of ponderous, hungry bison ranging across millions of unfenced acres, eating their fill — but moving on. The springy sod which had been formed through centuries of growth and death of this grass cushioned pleasantly the great weight on their hooves; and the wind — for always there has been wind — blew the flowering heads of the bluestem against their bellies. The grass was thick, most of the time

Bison once roamed free across the open plains. RICK AND SUSIE GRAETZ

(not always, even then) because the soil was good; the grass was hardy, it needed and it got little moisture. But there were great subsoil reserves of water, and many little springs.

"We found good fields of wild bluestem hay," wrote a buffalo hunter of his experiences in 1878. He and his partner, taking turns with a scythe, cut two hayrack loads in one day a mile or so from their camp, and then continued cutting for a week, "by the end of which time we had six or seven tons stacked in the corral."

Nothing so enrages the Great Plains stockman today as does a picture such as that given above of lush grasses waving in the breeze, the "mythical virgin forest of luscious grass" which he attributes to "theorists with vivid imaginations." (These impatient phrases are from *If and When It Rains*, a stockmen's publication). Some government reports he finds suspect and when they speak of such range conditions he seeks to discredit them on the ground that their authors have a bureaucratic ax to grind.

Nevertheless such a range did exist, though not all of the time. The stockman resents, justifiably, overdrawn descriptions of a paradise of forage, winter and summer, year in and year out; he resents the attendant implication that by overgrazing he brought about destruction of the natural ground cover and dust storms. He protests plaintively that stockmen have long urged and supported controlled grazing. That is not quite true; but neither is it true that he is solely responsible, or even responsible in major part, for the deterioration of the western range.

51

In recent years America has become dust conscious, especially since dust from the northern and central Great Plains has begun blowing clear to the eastern seaboard.

"The little black father," Jesuit Pierre DeSmet, visited Montana in 1841 and 1842. He wrote at that time: "Our beasts of burden were compelled to fast and pine, for scarcely a mouthful of grass could be found." Frontiersman Jim Bridger, about twenty years later, reported "forage unusually scarce, and the animals becoming much emaciated." Emigrants who came into Montana in the '70's reported dust and sand pounding against the weathered tarpaulins of their Conestoga wagons. Weather bureau records in Dodge City Kansas, reveal that there were blinding dust storms there in 1890, 1892, 1893, and 1894.

There have always been drouth and dust on the Great Plains. Averages based upon weather records of thirty-five to fifty years indicate that in most of Montana there are one or two drouth years in every ten, and in the northern portion, two or three.

There were terrible fires which swept suddenly across thousands, perhaps millions, of acres of dry grass, destroying the ground cover for a season. Lightning started some; the Indians — especially after the white man's arrival had made their hunting more difficult — started others to drive game. Early settlers have left records of these fearful, uncontrollable disasters, sheets of roaring flame racing across the prairies thirty or forty miles an hour on a front many miles wide — stopped, sometimes, at the plowed fireguard around the settler's home.

So drouth dried and killed the grass and baked the soil; still the grass stood. And fire took it, leaving mile upon mile of powdery black ash — still its roots twisted and clung in the soil beneath. It would come up again next spring, greener than ever, not quite as rich, needing more rain because the cushioned mulch which held the moisture had burned. . . . But it would come up.

And then there came a man with a plow. Its sharp point crackled as it sliced through the new green grass of spring, the dry mulch of last season, the crisp topsoil. The point went a little harder as it cut deeper, severing the long roots, tough roots, of the native grass. And as the soil curled up beside the plow's gleaming blade the man was happy; for here was good, dark soil, cohesive; soil with moisture in it.

Perhaps the man loved the soil, had grown up on the soil — somewhere else. Perhaps he had been crowded there; and now as he gazed into this vast sky he felt free: here a man could stand up, here a man could do great things, grow incredible wheat crops, become rich. (But that sun was hot. There was nothing between him and the sun. Sure gets hot quick in this country!)

The man bent to his plow. (A man sort of gets a hankerin' to plow. Look at that grass! Wheat'll grow! They say they've got fifty, sixty bushels to the acre. ... God damn, but it's hot!)

But on top of that limestone butte, glistening in the sun a mile away, a horseman is watching the farmer plow; and there is bitterness in his heart. The farmer's fence has cut across his range and his bewildered cattle and horses have blundered into it: the vicious twisted barbs have gashed their legs and he has been treating the wounds with axle grease or mutton fat.

The horseman has greater ground for bitterness than this; for he genuinely loves the grass which the plow is destroying. He knows the farmer will fail. He has told Washington so, but Washington will not listen. It is to the interest of the east, just now, to push its discontented surplus population into the west; and it is to the interest of the railroads to carry the emigrants.

The watcher admits to himself that he, too, has abused this country, that spurred by competition he has overgrazed. But he has been here long enough to learn that cattle cannot be fattened on overgrazed range, that land abuse does not pay. And he has never broken the sod, so on his worst ranges the grass will come back in a year or two. After the farmer has failed, the grass may come back to his plowed fields — in twenty years. Or it may never come back.

The horseman rides off to his herds. The farmer finishes his plowing, waits for rain that doesn't come. It is summer now; the wheat is heading out less than a foot above the ground. The stalk turns yellow, then brown; the heads droop. The farmer takes one in his hand, and it disintegrates into dust. It is not worth harvesting; and all about him the topsoil is cracked and crisped and curled up; gray, now, instead of the rich brown he saw when he plowed this field. He looks across his fence to the field of his distant neighbor, the cattleman. The grass is not so good, but it's better than this wheat. ... And the stockman still has other ranges. (Well, it can't go on like this forever. A few good snows this winter and a wet spring — I'll be laughing at this first dry season. I can clean up!)

One day in the spring of 1883 as a Scandinavian John Christiansen, plowed his fields in Montana's neighbor state of North Dakota, he looked up to find that he was being watched — not by a stockman, as in the imaginary scene described here, but by an old and solemn Sioux Indian. Silently the old Indian watched as the dark soil curled up and the prairie grass was turned under. Christiansen stopped leaned against the plow handle, pushed his black Stetson back on his head, rolled a cigarette. He watched amusedly as the old Indian knelt, thrust his fingers into the plow furrow measured its depth, fingered the sod and the buried grass. Then the old Indian straightened up, looked at the farmer. "Wrong side up," he said, and went away.

For a number of years that was regarded as a very amusing story indeed, betraying the ignorance of the poor Indian. Now there's a marker on Highway No. 10 in North Dakota the spot where the words were spoken — a little reminder to the White man that his red brother was not so dumb.

THE GRASS WAS FREE

Conflict is the first essential of drama. Thus invariably the most dramatic, most glamorous period in the history of any plains state is the era of the "open range."

Yet the searcher after economic and social forces in a regional history at first glance might find this conflict tawdry and the "romantic" industry about and within which the savage battle raged a somewhat ruffianly business. He would find that the initial "capital goods" of the range industry was second hand: broken-down, footsore oxen from the emigrant caravans — and the commodity upon which it built its prosperity, the longhorn steer, an ungainly, unloved freak of the animal world. The range itself, this student would discover, was usually commandeered and frequently stolen outright. The industry's entrepreneurs were often unscrupulous and greedy; their enterprises were brief and bloody struggles against Nature, beast, and man.

But no matter how skeptical might be this scholar's approach, he could hardly conclude his study without having succumbed in some degree to the indubitable romanticism of his subject. And he might end up by buying himself a pair of high-heeled boots and hurrying west. They have been known to do it.

Judged by modern economic practice, everything about the range industry was fantastic. Men hazarded fortunes and often their lives on a meteorological and biological gamble: their herds must increase 20 per cent or more annually because the normal annual loss would be 10 per cent, and in bad winters might be 40 per cent or even 90 per cent. Men born in mansions and graduated from the nation's greatest universities were content to gamble thus, and to live, while the game was played out, in caves dug out of cliffs, or in sod huts, or in dingy log cabins. Other cultured, kindly gentlemen could direct and participate in the mass killing in cold blood of other men — part of the game and essential if one were not to be dealt out.

And a great industry was built up and flourished briefly by undisciplined and heedless exploitation of a resource it did not own and upon which it had virtually no legal or moral claim.

Granville Stuart, a Virginian of Scotch descent, was one of the first in Montana Territory to engage in the beef business; in 1860 he brought in some lame oxen from Fort Hall, Idaho Territory, on the Oregon Trail, fattened them in western Montana, and a year later drove them back to be resold or traded for more "lags." Oxen were merely work cattle; turned out to grass and not worked, they became beef steers. The beef market in the mining camps was excellent and the industry grew rapidly. In 1866 Nelson Story drove in 600 head of longhorns from Texas over the Bozeman Trail — the first Texas drive. Six years later the first Montana Territory brand book was issued by the clerk of the supreme court in Virginia City. It contained 245 brands; in later years there were to be 70,000 brands on Montana grass.

By 1880 overcrowding had already become a problem in the western part of the Territory and in that year Granville Stuart pushed over the divide from the Deer Lodge country to bring the first herd into central Montana. Within five years he was again hunting new range. "It would be impossible," he wrote later, "to make persons not present on the Montana cattle ranges realize the rapid change that took place in two years." He continued in his *Forty Years on the Frontier*: "In 1880 the country [central Montana] was practically uninhabited. One could travel for miles without seeing so much as a trapper's bivouac. Thousands of buffalo darkened the rolling plains. There were deer, antelope, elk, wolves and coyotes on every hill and in every ravine and thicket. In the whole Territory of Montana there were but 250,000 head of cattle, including dairy cattle and work oxen.

In the fall of 1883 there was not one buffalo remaining on the range and the antelope, elk and deer were indeed scarce. In 1880 no one had heard tell of a cowboy ... and Charley Russell had made no pictures of them; but in the fall of 1883 there were 600,000 head of cattle on the range — the cowboy, with leather chaps, wide hat, gay handkerchief, clanking silver spurs and skin-fitting high-heeled boots ... had become an institution."

The cattle business in western Montana, the mountain and valley country, had been conducted largely on the eastern pattern — small herds on farms. But in central Montana the grass was free: it belonged to the people of the United States. The great herds on this last stand of the open range grazed upon millions of acres to which the herds' owners had no right other than the fact that they got there first, a "squatters'" right which was given

Caretakers of the herd. RICK AND SUSIE GRAETZ

recognition of sorts in 1877 in the curious law of "customary range." In many instances, owners of 30,000 or 40,000 head of cattle owned not one square foot of the land those cattle used, — nor even the land upon which their ranch buildings stood.

Along toward the end, one Montana company was shipping more than 9,000 head of cattle annually to market; its herds, more than 30,000 head, had a quarter million acres of range. And at that time this company owned just 450 acres of land.

But no inference should be drawn from this that the vast grass empire was stolen. Many of these companies would have bought land, or leased it (and some did lease, in Canada), had it been possible for them to do so; the basic fault was not theirs — it lay in political maladministration of the public lands, a long and disheartening history of occasionally corrupt, more often stupid bureaucratic bungling.

Much land was stolen: some from the Indians, who got even — as we shall see later in this section; some from the people of the United States, who did not — this by means of illegal fencing of the public domain, fraudulent homestead entry, dishonest manipulation of land grants.

But the central Montana range was merely commandeered, expropriated. If it was to be utilized, this had to happen: for it was not surveyed and could not be bought. Until 1888 everything to the north of the Missouri River was Indian reservation, as was much of the area south of the Yellowstone. Between these two rivers lay a "no-man's-land," subjected to continual Indian raids, blizzard-swept, infested with wolves and outlaws — but a paradise of free grass.

To acquire a portion of this empire, the stockman merely inserted a notice in the nearest weekly newspaper (and it might be hundreds of miles away) listing his brand and establishing by personal decree the extent of his range, bordering it upon creeks or familiar landmarks such as buttes or dry coulees. The same definition of his domain appeared under his brand in the state's brand books.

There then arose the problem of maintaining his dominion, of holding off the "grass pirate" who sought to edge in upon his range. Whereupon into the Montana statutes went the law of the "customary range"; it stands to this day, altered only to the extent of removal of the minimum penalty for violation. Section 1 of this law, adopted in 1877, prohibited branding of another grower's cattle but provided no criminal penalty for this offense, setting out merely that it should constitute grounds for civil action for recovery of damages three times the value of the cattle involved.

This failure to make outright rustling and brand blotting a criminal offense was easily explainable. With herds grazing in common on unfenced range, such an offense was too hard to prove for the Territory to undertake the task with its very limited law enforcement facilities; calves frequently were misbranded by accident and this would provide opportunity for a vindictive cattleman to send a neighbor he disliked to prison. So instead, burden of proof was left upon the stockman directly concerned.

On the other hand, this weakness of the statute undoubtedly contributed to the cattlemen's later impatience with legal procedure and their adoption of the Vigilante system to rid the Missouri badlands of rustlers.

Section 2 of the law, however, sought to make up in part for the impotence of the first paragraph; it was this section which established the principle of "customary range." It read: "Any person who shall drive. or cause to be driven, any cattle, horses, mules, sheep or swine from their customary range without permission of the owner thereof, shall be deemed guilty of a misdemeanor and on conviction thereof before any justice of the peace in the Territory of Montana may be fined in any sum not less than five nor more than one hundred dollars, and may be imprisoned in the county jail not less than ten days nor more than ninety days, or both."

This law, intended to discourage alike the rustler and the "grass pirate" who would shove the first-comer's stock off the range to make room for his own, has been a colossal headache for Montana justices of the peace for more than half a century. It attempted to establish a proprietary right for a private individual upon public property; and though it is still on the books, its constitutional validity is at least questionable. Countless times disputatious neighbors dragged each other before harassed justices and brought charges of violation of the "customary range," a term so broad as practically to defy definition, considering the recklessly migratory habits of range stock driven hither and yon by rain, drouth, lightening, fire, mosquitoes, poisonous weeds, or sometimes just a bad smell. More than one exasperated judge threw a case out of court because the only way to settle it was to get the opinion of the cattle themselves.

But there were other ways to hold one's range; and the most effective of these, at first, was the roundup boycott. Outfits whose "customary range" had been invaded announced publicly that they would not "work" the newcomer's cattle, that he would not be permitted to participate in the common roundup. Thus John H. Conrad of Fort Benton was socially and economically ostracized when he brought a herd onto range claimed by the Niobrara Cattle Company in central Montana in 1885. The local association of cattlemen adopted a resolution: "WHEREAS, The custom of disregarding the prior rights of others on the range is becoming frequent, annoying and damaging in a high degree to range interests. ... RESOLVED, That we discountenance such actions [as Conrad's] as unfair and injurious to the best interests of the country and that we refuse to recognize or work with any parties infringing upon the prior rights of others by turning stock on a range previously occupied, and be it further RESOLVED, That we refuse to work with or in any way handle the cattle of the said J. H. Conrad."

The resolution was widely published, and Conrad, one of the first to be thus publicly stoned, took his herd elsewhere.

This extra-legal appropriation of the public range was greeted somewhat incredulously in Washington, where the General Land Office Commissioner commented: In certain localities in Montana the cattlemen have taken exclusive possession of extensive tracts of grazing lands and hold them by publishing periodically notices that the ranges are full and that no more cattle will be allowed to go on the lands, and by making away with the cattle of other persons found there and driving out all settlers.

Before Washington got around to doing anything about it, however, the roundup boycott had lost its effectiveness. Later interlopers, not as susceptible as Conrad to moral suasion, left their cattle on the disputed range, and far from being dismayed by the boycott, conducted their own roundup — *before* the common roundup began. The established cattlemen could not discipline the newcomer unless he shared membership with them in the general roundup, which divided the unbranded calves among the members according to the section of the range where they were found, or sold them and divided the proceeds. The "sooner," rounding up alone before his neighbors' riders got on the range, could gather up all the mavericks for himself. And he could do worse: in his early roundup he could seriously impair the value of his truculent neighbors' stock. Cattle must not be run more than absolutely necessary, because running cuts down flesh, and flesh is money. And to run them in the early spring when they have not completely shed their heavy winter coats not only seriously reduces their weight but sometimes costs their lives.

Thus the roundup boycott died when it was realized that the "pirates," social outcasts though they might be, were profiting exceedingly, as did the settler upon whose strangely prolific cows Granville Stuart commented: "Near our home ranch we discovered one rancher whose cows invariably had twin calves and frequently triplets, while the range cows in that vicinity were nearly all barren and would persist in hanging around this man's corral, envying his cows their numerous children and bawling and lamenting their own childless state. This state of affairs continued until we were obliged to call around that way and threaten to hang the man if his cows had any more twins."

Not until 1895 did Montana legislators catch up with the "sooners" of the roundup. In that year it became illegal to brand on the open range between December 1 and May 1; but by then it was too late — there was little open range left.

And finally, after the law, moral suasion, threats, and even a few shootings had failed to check this tidal wave which was engulfing their "customary range," the cattlemen built a fence around it.

Federal reaction was as prompt as it had been tardy before. Land office attorneys streamed into federal courts with complaints. By 1887 somewhere near 250,000 acres of public domain in Montana had been illegally inclosed within barbed wire, President Cleveland had ordered every foot of it torn down. United States production of barbed wire tripled between 1880 and 1890, and from the reports of land office registers to the Commissioner in Washington, it appeared that all this increased output had been unrolled in Montana.

The government's war upon illegal fencing continued into the 1900's, and even today an occasional instance crops up, but the practice boomeranged against the cattlemen and it declined in popularity after the disastrous winter of 1886–87. Cattle which prior to that winter had drifted with the storms and had sometimes reached range blown free of snow, piled up instead against the new fences and starved or froze to death.

It was a practice of cattlemen, as soon as they arrived on a new range, to announce portentously that that range was in imminent danger of becoming overcrowded. Perhaps it was this early crying of "Wolf!" which caused the stockmen's later warnings, when they really were justified, to go unheeded.

Throughout the '80's the range industry wrangled over proposals to permit leasing of the public domain for grazing. Such schemes were denounced as class legislation because they would enable the corporate livestock interests to prevent settlement and crowd out the small cattle operator. The Montana Stock Growers' Association changed its position several times, depending upon which faction controlled its convention, and the state's congressional delegation was told one year to seek a leasing system, the next year to defeat it.

But though stockmen might shy away from a lease system which was essentially undemocratic and sure to make trouble, most of them would use almost any other means to acquire range. According to John Clay, pioneer stockgrower and commission man, there was "scarce a ranchman in the west who has not transgressed the land laws of the country." Homestead laws were flagrantly violated, often with the aid of corrupt local officials, especially the Desert Land Act, which required the entryman to construct an irrigation system, and the Timber Culture Act, which required him to plant trees.

A handful of dispirited saplings stuck in the ground where there was no chance for them to grow (and, indeed, sometimes dead before they were planted) often enough constituted "proof" under the latter law. Desert land homesteaders would turn the spring runoff into trenches a few inches deep and obtain affidavits attesting to the fact that the land was being "irrigated," A prominent pioneer citizen of Great Falls had himself dragged in a rowboat by a team of horses through a dry ditch; witnesses testified they had seen a boat traversing the ditch.

It cannot be argued, of course, that the government should knowingly have permitted the expropriation of public property implicit in such illegal land entries and illegal fencing, and the arguments against leasing were valid enough; yet, granted hindsight today, we can see that it might have been better had the government winked at the law violation or overcome its repugnance to class legislation sufficiently to permit leasing.

Because the stockmen in possession of the range, unable to fence, lease, buy, or homestead, had only one way left to hold it: stock it to the limit. And so cattlemen and sheepmen themselves destroyed the industry. Newcomers could not be kept out altogether, and a range stocked to the limit soon became a range hopelessly overgrazed. When this point had been reached, one enemy neither the stockmen nor anyone else could lick — Montana weather — descended upon the range and blotted out the herds almost as if they had never been.

Three rivers — running west to east and throughout much of their course virtually parallel — segment Montana. Each of them has formed a boundary and a pattern for the open range, and each, like the divisions of a sundial, has recorded a period in the industry's brief life.

South of the Yellowstone was Indian country, so the early Texas herds swam that river and were bedded down on the great central Montana range between it and the Missouri. North of that meandering muddy stream was more Indian country, and cutting through it, near the Canadian border, was the Milk River. It was to be the cattleman's last frontier: when the herds crossed it, as they did in the '90's, they went to their doom on the bleak, shelterless prairie of northern Montana and southern Canada, and the story of the range had ended.

Dust hung low over the central Montana badlands of the Missouri River in the summer of 1885 as 100,000 head of cattle streamed onto that range to join the hundreds of thousands already there. President Cleveland had canceled the stockmen's leases on Indian Territory — Oklahoma — and 200,000 head had been forced onto the already overcrowded ranges of other Territories. Texans cursed. "We been votin' Democratic ever since the War between the States," one of them complained to a Montana comrade, "an' the first time we get a Democrat in as President, look what the sonofabitch does to us!"

A few of the cattlemen did more than curse: they hastened to Washington and complained directly to Cleveland. "Gentlemen," he replied imperturbably, "you have been given a certain time to get your cattle out of Indian Territory. Much of that time has now passed. I suggest that you get home and get them moving!"

Then there were the sheep. In the two or three years prior to 1885 the number of sheep in Montana trebled. Sheep first came into the Territory in the '60s, and in 1870 there were 2,000 head. Fourteen years later there were 500,000 and two years after that, almost 1,000,000. By 1893 Montana's sheep numbered 2,225,000 and by 1900 more than 3,500,000.

As this new horde of cattle and sheep moved in on them, stockmen in central Montana clamored for opening of the Indian reservation to the north, but this did not come until 1888. In the meantime, desperate operators moved thousands of head over the Missouri onto the Indian lands anyway, for there lay millions of acres which the Indians did not use, grass untouched since the buffalo had gone; and the cattle faced starvation. This move was easy for a cattleman who happened to have married an Indian woman, and there were many of these, including Granville Stuart. (But when the reservation was opened in 1888, a new law decreed that no white man could hereafter acquire any rights on Indian lands by virtue of marriage into the tribe.)

More cattle streamed across the river and north into Canada, where grouped townships could be leased. A quarter million head crossed the Missouri and the Milk, headed for this new and unfamiliar range. Some of the old-time cattlemen quit rather than cross the Milk River. "I did not like the country and would not move over there," Stuart commented tersely in his memoirs. His partner took over the herd.

So passed the mirage which had charmed and deluded the lords of the grass — the illusion of "customary range."

A Montana cattleman, riding his range one day, found a sheepherder camped up in it, with his flock. He ordered the herder to get off. Returning the next day, he found the lamb-licker still there. Again he demanded that the interloper quit his range.

The herder looked up calmly at the mounted stockman. "You own it, pardner?" he asked.

The cattleman admitted that he didn't, "But it's my range," he retorted, "and I want you off'"

The herder got up slowly, drawing a Winchester rifle from the ground as he did so.

"Listen, friend," he said quietly. "I just got out of prison after shooting one sonofabitch like you, and I'd just as soon go back for shooting another."

The cattleman rode home. "Looking into the barrel of that gun," he told this writer many years later, "you know, I realized for the first time that I didn't own that range. ... And, by God, I didn't even have a gun on me!"

RANCHING, THE WINTER OF 1886-87, THE OPEN RANGE

The best Montana stories deal with the erratic and unpredictable character of Montana weather.

Cowboy "Teddy Blue" and his Texas partners asked an old bullwhacker about Montana's climate. "I'll tell you what kind of a climate it is," he responded. "You want a buffalo overcoat, a linen duster and a slicker with you all the time."

Even today some old-timers will insist speaking of the range era: "It would have been all right, if it hadn't been for the weather."

Always and eternally, the weather: always in Montana the bitter conviction that its vagaries are exceptional and malevolent, though they were so unexceptional and periodic that they ruined, impartially, cattlemen, sheepmen, and wheat raisers.

But most of the veterans will say that the weather could have been contended with successfully had it not been for the settlers cluttering up the range.

That is not the whole truth, either. No industry which functioned as haphazardly as did that of the range could have long endured; nevertheless, the weather came along at the right moment to finish a job begun by other elements, and then so terrible was its onslaught that it was easy to credit grumblings of supernatural malice.

In less than thirty years of cattle drives to Montana from the southwest, more than thirty-five thousand Texans rode into the state. A large share of this number turned right around and rode back, shivering. The inability of the Rio Grande cowboy to withstand Montana's winters was the subject of countless cook wagon jokes, songs, and barroom brawls.

But in the end the Texas cowboy had a free choice: stick it out in Montana until he was acclimated — and at considerably higher wages than he got in Texas — or pack his war bag and go home. The Texas longhorn was not so fortunately situated. Hundreds of thousands of these poor beasts stumbled off the gale-swept plains to die by frozen streams, or staggered on trembling legs into concealed drifts at the heads of coulees, there to be held fast while they slowly starved; or they pushed each other under the ice of the rivers in their frantic stampede to drink at the treacherous air holes.

The wasteful sacrifice of animal life on the open range is hard to credit today. A 10 per cent winter loss was "normal" in Montana; thus a cattleman running 10,000 head could consider his operation reasonably successful if he did not lose more than 1,000 head each winter, though each of these animals had a potential market value of about $50!

The winter toll was heaviest, of course, among the calves, and especially those trailed in that same season from the hot plains of Texas. These losses were increased by the fact that during their first winter on the range the Texas dogies would stand around the ranch house and bawl for their food instead of going out and rustling it for themselves. "This practice is not encouraged" [by feeding], a Miles City newspaper commented callously. "It is hoped they will absorb enough cow sense to go out on the range and eat," Most of them did, when they got hungry enough.

The cattlemen could do little to reduce the 10 per cent loss ratio. Half of it might be attributable to wolves and rustlers, and a constant war was waged against them; but the other half could only be offered on a sacrificial altar to the gods of storm, who would not be placated thereby, either.

Nor was it only winter weather which gnawed at the cattleman's profits. Summer drouth, because it meant a shortage of feed, invariably meant heavier winter kill. There were heavy summer losses, too, through consumption by the stock of poisonous plants which they would not touch when there was sufficient grass. And drouth brought fire.

Nothing in Nature is as terrible as a prairie fire; not even a blizzard. Where such a fire had been, nothing could live. Gophers would come up from their cool chambers and starve to death in the ashes. Game which escaped the holocaust would start a long and hungry trek to find water, grass, and brush, and die before finding them.

Grass fires moved with the speed of the wind. Only the most terrible forest fires, those which are "crowning" — flame leaping from treetop to treetop — can do that; and forest fires, usually in rough country, pause due to shifts or breaks in the wind. The prairie fire did not pause: it swept on at forty or fifty miles an hour, faster than a horse could run, widening its front all the while, a low wall of flame above which rolling masses of black smoke heaved in the wind and then spread to curtain the sky for weeks.

Such a fire would force a range operator to move thousands of head from their customary grazing grounds to a new district strange to him and his stock and perhaps already precariously near overstocking. On his old range no cattle could subsist until the new grass came in the spring; and then, though greener than before, it would lack the nourishment it had had, and because the moisture-retaining mulch would be gone it would not be as hardy.

This move must be made quickly; and so these were the worst drives of all. The cattle would scuffle through mile upon mile of ashes, their hooves bringing up great clouds of sooty, weightless dust until the air was like hot smoke and the world was blotted out. Their hides and the skin of the cursing riders would turn black; flesh would crack and bum with the dryness, despite the scarf flung up to protect the face. Eyes ached from the grayness and the baking heat, and tears which dried before they could be shed gummed eyelids with mud.

Soon the cattle would bawl for water, and there would be none. The rider would curse a little louder, lest the heat and his wretchedness put him to sleep: for now he must be watchful. Many miles away, perhaps in the direction whence they had come, there might be a little stream — too small to water this herd. But a sudden wind might carry the scent of that water to the cattle; if it did, the herd would swing instantly and be gone on a run. It might be impossible, under these conditions, to head them, and they would die — every last cow — of exhaustion, starvation, and thirst.

So the rider tried to straighten his aching back and open his aching eyes and watch the herd for the first sign of madness. He had to watch his horse, too, sometimes; and he caught himself musing over strange fancies which left him even unsure of himself. But above all he must see that the herd, if it were going to stampede, stampeded in the right direction; then the boys were in position to handle it. ... If they were still there; if he were not riding alone in a dead and desolate world, alone with thousands of filthy, half-mad cows. He pulled the bandanna down from his nose and sang out to his partner, riding "point" on the other side of the herd. His voice was cracked; so was the reply, when it came back. But, anyway, it came.

Such were the drives from burned-out range. It is little wonder that cattlemen would spend prodigally, that they and their cowboys would even risk their lives, to forestall such disasters. Owners would not hesitate to have their men slaughter $50 steers and drag their expensive carcasses — over the burning prairie. It was better to take this loss than take a chance on losing the whole herd. The carcass, drawn by ropes from saddlehorns, was dragged between two horses, one on the burned-over side of the flames, the other in the unburned grass, both riders going hell-for-leather in an attempt to smother the fire with their "drag:' It was a sickening ride, but sometimes it worked.

Lightning started most of these fires, but there were other, less innocent agents. Indians resentful of being driven off their buffalo range were responsible for many of the earlier ones; a cattleman coming onto range which had never been used before for domestic stock had to watch constantly for this. Indian hunters occasionally started a fire to stampede a herd of cattle deliberately in order that they might cut out some and get away with them; these hunting parties also set fires to drive game. White rustlers set a few. Some were the result of carelessness — a cigarette (though the cowboy's hand- rolled smoke, which goes out when dropped, is not such a hazard as the tight "tailor-made") or a spark from the chuckwagon stove. Such a spark started the disastrous fire on the X I T ranch in Texas in the fall of 1885, and the cook who started it lit out in a hurry, fearful he would be lynched.

But it was the winters — when icy gales shrilled across the crusted prairies and sliced through the sturdy logs of the ranch houses, when the deadly "white cold" crept slowly down from the Height of Land in Canada's Northwest Territories, when snow fell interminably, burying range, stock, and ranch house — it was the winters which finished the cattlemen.

Even as the first big herds moved onto the plains of central and eastern Montana, the first in a series of bad winters which was to dog the industry was wiping out the herds in the west and on the Sun River-Rockies slope. This was the winter of 1880–81, when blizzards began in December and continued with hardly a break until May: temperatures were seldom less than 20 below and for weeks at a time stayed at -40.

Most of the cattle on the Sun River range had been brought in a few months before the blizzards struck; still unfamiliar with the country, they drifted desperately with the incessant wind and died finally of exhaustion as much as of hunger. Losses on that range were 90 to 98 per cent; thousands of cattle lay dead in the water courses and their ruined owners said, "you can walk from Sheep Creek in the Belts to the Dearborn in the Rockies and never take your foot off a dead cow," Some of the stockmen made frantic efforts to get feed to their animals, but hay was scarce. Ten strawstacks sold for $1,000 at Cascade, though straw was "stuffing," not nutritious feed.

Central and eastern Montana did not suffer so badly that winter because there were as yet few herds on that range, grass was plentiful and the wind kept it freer of snow, and there was still tall brush in the coulees to afford shelter. Nevertheless there were catastrophic instances: an English company which had driven in 5,000 head the previous fall (the cattle thus were thin and weak) had 135 head left in the spring and went bankrupt. Granville Stuart's loss, however, was but 13 per cent and wolves and rustlers accounted for all but 3 per cent of that. He had carefully selected his range, not so much for grass as for shelter, and an early "freak" chinook which apparently blew nowhere else also contributed to his good fortune.

The wolves' toll increased sharply in such winters, as the herds were driven to unfamiliar country. One outfit, which had been running 10,000 head of cattle including 3,000 cows, found at the spring roundup, not one calf. Another counted 700 calves lost to wolves and found its cows bitten in the hams, their tails chewed off, and otherwise bearing the marks of battle with the wolves: the range cow, especially the wild longhorn, would fight fiercely to save her calf from the shrewd gray killers which surrounded her in packs of 15 or 20.

Sometimes it was a race between the wolves and the "grubbers." These latter were skinners who took to the range in the winter and early spring to strip the hides from the dead stock. The first on the field got as much as $5 or $6 a hide, but the market was soon glutted after disastrous blizzards, and it became known as a "grubstake" job — just sufficiently lucrative to keep the skinner alive.

The bad winter of 1880–81 started the overcrowding of the central Montana range and thus led directly to the climactic disaster of 1886; but there were signs and portents in the five intervening years for those who could read. There was, for instance, the Starvation Winter of the Pikuni.

A day or two after Christmas, 1883, a luminous and glittering mist formed over the northern and eastern Rockies slope — where Glacier Park is today. Frantically the Pikuni — Blackfeet — prayed to Aisoyimstan, the Cold Maker, not to persecute their people; pleadingly they sought of their Indian agent a few extra rations. But rations were low: the agent (seeking to make a record for himself) had reported (to Washington) that the Blackfeet were now nearly self-supporting.

The mercury dropped to 40, 50 below zero, and stayed there for sun upon sun. All travel ceased and the hungry Blackfeet huddled in their lodges. Every day was as the day that had gone before; the sun was a faint light in a colorless void, and it set far to the south. There would come slightly warmer days, and it would snow, silently, thinly, hour after hour; tiny, icy crystalline particles which glittered in the gray light.

Now the hunters would go forth to seek game afoot, for their horses had long since died or been killed for food; and when there was no more game, they brought back the inner bark of the fir and pine trees, or tissue scraped from buffalo skulls, or the hooves of cattle, left by the wolves — or even rats hunted out of their homes in the rocks.

They were deserted by their agent, who was being replaced; his successor arrived in the midst of the worst suffering and did his best. Word of their plight reached Montana towns, and rescue expeditions were organized. George Bird Grinnell, famous naturalist and friend of the Blackfeet, stirred the government to action. Cursing freighters fought their way over drifted trails to the reservation with wagonloads of food. They found some of the survivors mad with hunger and grief among the bodies of their kin; they found coyotes and wolves fighting in the lodges of the unburied dead; they found six hundred Indians — one-quarter of the tribe — starved to death.

The next winter was nearly as severe, and the *Mineral Argus* remarked casually in January, 1885: "Many of the Piegan [Pikuni] Indians are reported frozen to death." The *Chicago Times* printed a special dispatch from Montana's cowboy capital, Miles City: "Since December 1st there has been no break in the cold ... until it culminated last night in the dreadful temperature of 52 degrees below zero. The whole valley on all sides of Miles City is filled with cattle, seeking what protection the scant shrubbery affords. Even in the streets of the town great droves of cattle wander back and forth, but there is no food for them."

Losses were mounting annually, but still new herds were being crowded onto the Montana range, as the established cattlemen appealed for opening of the reservation. Market conditions also were worrying them. The average beef price per hundredweight on the Chicago market in 1882 had been $4.75; in 1883 it was $4.70, and in 1884, $4.40. The next year it dropped to $3.90, partially because of the distressed selling of some of the herds President Cleveland had forced out of Indian Territory.

The bonanza days were gone, and some of the old-timers recognized the fact. "There was no way of preventing the overstocking of the ranges," Stuart admitted, "as they were free to all. ... The range business was no longer a reasonably safe business; it was from this time on a gamble, with the trump cards in the hands of the elements."

It soon became apparent that the elements were not going to help the situation any. The summer of 1885 was dry; that of 1886 was parching. Great fires swept the range; those cattlemen who could find new grass began the move through a haze of smoke which hung over Montana for months. "There has hardly been an evening in the last week," said the *Rocky Mountain Husbandman* in August, "that the red glare of the fire demon has not lit up our mountain ridges, while our exchanges bring news of disastrous fires in all parts of the Territory."

The grass began to die in July and all but the largest streams and water holes dried up. Water in the creeks became so alkaline that cattle refused to drink it. Cinders, ashes, and hot alkali dust covered the range and even the furniture in the ranch houses.

That fall wild game moved early from its favored shelters in the Missouri badlands and hurried south and west. Birds which customarily remained all winter fled, too. The horses' winter coats appeared earlier than usual; "even the range cattle," said Stuart, "seemed to take on a heavier, shaggier coat of hair."

Nature had set her stage for the last act.

Kissin-ey-oo-way'-o, the Crees said; "it blows cold." The Crees were the northern people, from the Height of Land; they had many words for cold, degrees of coldness, the effects of cold — but none more literally translating into speech the condition it described: in kissineyooway'o the north wind sang, softly at first, then rising to a wail and a howl. … It blows cold.

It began November 16, though Montana seldom has severe cold or heavy snow until after Christmas. The gale was icy, and it had substance: it was filled with glassy particles of snow, like flakes of mica; it roared and rumbled. After the first day the tonal pitch rose. from a roar it became a moan, then a scream. The snow rode the wind, it thrust forward fiercely and slashed like a knife; no garment or hide could withstand it. The gale piled it into glacial drifts; when cow or horse stumbled into them the flesh on its legs was sheared to the bone.

Now suddenly there appeared white owls of the Arctic. The cattlemen had never seen them before; but the Indians and the metis knew them — and like the beasts and birds, they fled south.

Slowly the temperature moderated. The stockmen prayed for what the Indians called "the black wind" from the arch of black cloud on the western horizon from which it emerged; but it was too early in the season for the chinook. The drifts dwindled but did not disappear; they spread, crusting the range.

In December there were two more blizzards.

January is the Moon of Cold-Exploding-Trees. On the ninth day of that month it snowed without an instant's interruption for sixteen hours — an inch an hour; and the temperature fell to 22 below zero. Intermittent snow continued for another ten days, with temperatures ranging from 22 to 46 below in central Montana; in some other sections it was 40 below day in and day out for more than two weeks.

There was a respite of a little more than a week; then, on January 28, the great blizzard struck. For three days and three nights it was impossible to see fifty feet in any direction and ranch thermometers read 63 below zero. A sudden break in the cold and a wind shift gave promise of a chinook, but the storm set in again and lasted through February 3. A rider who dismounted dropped into snow to his waist on level ground.

"If we can break this fence down, we're on our way to Arizona." RICK AND SUSIE GRAETZ

Cattle which had been pushed over the Missouri in the fall to the better grass on the northern range drifted back, for there was little shelter on the steppes north of the river. Half dead from cold and hunger, their bodies covered with sores and frozen blood, bewildered and blind in a world of impenetrable white, they blundered into the barbed-wire fences, crumpled against them, and perished. They were trapped in drifts above their bellies and stood erect until their bodies froze. They slid into air holes in the rivers.

Cowboys donned two suits of heavy underwear, two pairs of wool socks, wool pants, two woolen shirts, overalls, leather chaps, wool gloves under leather mittens, blanket-lined overcoats, and fur caps. Before putting on the socks they walked in the snow in their bare feet, then rubbed them dry vigorously. After pulling on their riding boots they stood in water, then stood outdoors until an airtight sheath of ice had formed on the boots. Sometimes instead of the riding boots they wore moccasins and overshoes or sheepskin-lined "packs."

Thus prepared, they mounted and fought their way through the snow to extricate cattle stuck in drifts, tried to herd the dying beasts into sheltered ravines and head them off from treacherous rivers. They blacked their faces and eye sockets with lampblack or burnt matches to forestall snow blindness, or they cut holes in their black neckerchiefs and masked their faces, bandit-fashion. They strained and gasped as the icy air stabbed into their lungs and stomachs; they froze hands and feet, and many of them died. Their bodies, frozen stiff, were lashed on the backs of their horses and borne back to the ranch houses, to be thrust into a snowbank until a chinook came because the ground could not be broken for graves.

For all this they got no medals, nor expected any. A cowboy's job was to look after the herd; he was being paid for it — $40 a month. But hundreds of ranchers and riders underwent such hardships in that dreadful winter that they forsook the range forever, crippled in body and spirit.

As the storms and cold continued through February, the tragedy of the range was brought into the towns. Starving cattle staggered through village streets, collapsed and died in dooryards. Five thousand head invaded the outskirts of the newborn city of Great Falls, bawling for food. They snatched up the saplings the proud city had just planted, gorged themselves upon garbage.

Kaufman and Stadler, Helena cattlemen, wrote to their foreman in the Judith Basin to inquire about their herd. When the delayed stage delivered the letter, the foreman tossed it with a derisive grin to one of his riders, a young Missourian who had attained some bunkhouse fame for his pencil and water color sketches.

"Got a postcard?" asked the young artist, whose name was Charley Russell. On it he swiftly sketched in water color a gaunt steer, legs bowed and head down, standing in a drift with a coyote waiting near by. Below he printed a terse legend: "Last of Five Thousand." The card was mailed back to the Helena men without other comment. It was the first Russell work to attain wide circulation; under the title he had originally given it or the later one, "Waiting for a Chinook," it made the artist famous throughout the cow country. It is now owned by the Montana Stockgrowers' Association and hangs in its Helena office. Russell died in Great Falls in 1926; his last painting sold for $30,000.

The chinook did not come until March — a month later than it could have been expected. Before the spring roundups were held to determine the extent of the disaster, the Montana Stockgrowers' Association met in Miles City, scared but hopeful.

"We are not here to bury our industry, but to revive it," said Joseph Scott, association president, whistling bravely in the dark. Then he went on to admit: "Had the winter continued twenty days longer, there would not have been much necessity for this association."

Sadly the stockmen went home for the May roundup. They were in no great hurry to learn the truth; most of them, in short rides near their homes, had seen thousands of rotting carcasses on the plains. There were coulees and sheltered valleys which they could not enter because of the stench of decomposing beef.

The popular estimate of the cattlemen after the roundups had been completed was a 60 per cent loss for the state, or about 362,000 head of cattle. More conservative were official figures, showing a 40 to 50 per cent loss. The drop in cattle on assessment rolls was 200,000, but this did not account for all the loss by any means, since thousands of cattle, including all the fall calf crop, had not been assessed.

Officially, it was reported cattle worth $5,000,000 had perished; actually the cattlemen estimated the loss amounted to $20,000,000. They had to figure in the deterioration in their potential assets, including unborn calves, the cost of restocking, and other more indirect results of the disaster.

Nelson Story of Bozeman, who twenty years before had brought the first trail herd from Texas, lost more than 66 per cent of his stock. On the Yellowstone range losses reached 95 per cent. The Home Land & Cattle Co. had put 6,000 head across the Canadian border; 2,000 survived. James Fergus sold 1,500 hides from his dead stock for $2,000.

The great Swan Cattle Co. of Wyoming, Scotch financed, which had large Montana holdings, went bankrupt. The Niobrara Cattle Co., founded in Texas, collapsed; it had 9,000 head left out of 39,000 and it was $350,000 in debt. Gibb Brothers, typical of the smaller operators, counted 320 head left out of their 2,500. They sold the 320 and quit. Theodore Roosevelt decided the cattle business was not for him and sold his ranch just east of the Montana line in North Dakota. The French Marquis de Mores closed up shop in his ill-fated packing plant at Medora, N. D., and went off to India to hunt tigers.

Ranchers who intended to stick it out but who needed cash found that the forced liquidation of livestock assets had smashed the already tottering Chicago market. Prices slid until the going figure was $3.15 a hundred pounds — less than $38 for a 1,200-pound steer, of which there were few left. Then, on October 8, 1887, came word that a shipment of Montana cattle had been sold in Chicago for $2.50 a hundred — not much more than $25 a head, and with a freight charge of $6 a head to be deducted.

Eastern and foreign investors had lost interest and thrust their companies into bankruptcy; the big herds had nearly vanished. Hundreds of Montanans now became disgusted. "A business that had been fascinating," said Stuart, "suddenly became distasteful. I never wanted to own again an animal that I could not feed and shelter."

The range cattlemen had been fretting for some time under the criticism of eastern humanitarians stirred by highly colored accounts of the "brutal" range industry, gratefully promoted by eastern stock raisers who bought and paid taxes on their pastures and, not unreasonably, saw the free western grass as unfair competition. After the disaster of 1886–87 there was a new burst of condemnatory propaganda and tears were shed in Back Bay drawing rooms.

One of the Montana industry's severest critics was Julian Ralph, who wrote a piece in *Harper's New Monthly* for June, 1891, reporting that the era of large herds on the open range was ended, and continuing: "It is cause for jubilation that this is the case. It seems strange that cruelty should distinguish this branch of food-raising wherever it is seen. ... The reader would not suppose that there was cruelty in the mere feeding of cattle on the plains, but let him go to Montana, and talk with the people there, and he will shudder at what he hears. The cattle owners or cow men are in Wall street or in the south of France, or in Florida, in the winter; but their cattle are on the wintry fields, where every now and then, say once in four years, half of them, or eighty per cent, or one in three (as it happens) starve to death because of their inability to get at the grass under the snow. The poor beasts die by the thousands — totter along until they fall down, the living always trying to reach the body of a dead one to fall upon."

Montana cowmen could be raucously scornful of the eastern writer's picture of a tottering steer hunting for the body of a dead comrade to cushion his expiring fall; but they could not take it so lightly when their own kind turned on them. They were shocked when the *Cheyenne Sun*, cowtown paper, had this to say about them: "A man who turns out a lot of cattle on a barren plain without making provision for feeding them will not only suffer a financial loss but also the loss of the respect of the community in which he lives."

From the Rocky Mountain Husbandman in Montana came another stab in the back: "The range of the past is gone; that of the present is of little worth and cannot be relied on in the future. Range husbandry is over, is ruined, is destroyed — it may have been by the insatiable greed of its followers."

The cattlemen retorted angrily. What could they have done? There was not enough hay in the United States to feed the immense herds on the Great Plains. Their operations had cheapened beef for the eastern consumer. They had improved the dehorning process: it was less painful than formerly. Branding, they insisted, does not hurt the animal much; he will get up and eat immediately, apparently none the worse for his experience.

In September, 1886, before the disaster had struck, the Husbandman had been worried but hopeful:

If we could close our eyes to the fact that there are more stock on the range than ever before and that grass in many localities has been very closely grazed, the outlook would indeed be flattering. But these are stubborn facts that cannot be regarded lightly, although all may yet be well. We shall continue to have faith in a light winter and small losses until forced by polar waves and worlds of snow to change our minds.

The Husbandman's mind was changed in the spring of 1887, and so were those of most of the cattlemen. The overlords of the range-those who were left turned not without relief to a new livestock economy. After all, it had been the stockmen themselves who had heard most keenly the pitiful bawl of famished cows creeping into the creek bed near the home place to die. They began to raise hay: the acreage of this crop increased from 56,000 in 1880 to 300,000 in 1890 and 712,000 in 1900.

Cowboys who had been "line riders" in the first days of the open range, patrolling an unmarked boundary based on creeks or imaginary lines drawn from distant buttes, became fence riders, with wire cutters and pliers replacing the six-shooters in belt scabbards; finally they degenerated into haying hands — or they quit. Most of them, traditionally hostile to any form of labor which could not be performed from a horse's back, quit.

But the snow which had brought ruin in the winter brought rich new grass in the spring and helped the transition to a new type of operation-fewer cattle, more limited but better range, supplemental feeding. Ranchers could restock in 1887 for less than $20 a head; more than 100,000 came in by trail from the south that year. By 1893 Montana had 100,000 more cattle than it had had before the great storm — but individual herds were smaller so that they could be maintained on owned range, fed and sheltered.

Montana old-timers recall that one of the biggest roundups of all time occurred in the middle '90s, along the Canadian border from the Sweet Grass Hills to North Dakota — three hundred miles. It is significant that nearly one thousand riders representing nearly a score of ranches participated; a decade earlier there would have been a few hundred, representing half a dozen companies.

Most of the ranches in this big roundup now owned or leased at least a part of their range. One of these outfits was the famous Circle Diamond of Colorado, which had begun as Thatcher Brothers of Pueblo and became the Bloom Cattle Co. At this writing their foreman, John Survant, is still a prominent citizen of Montana. The Circle Diamond was destined to be the last big outfit on the northern range.

This company's shipments in the '90's had reached an annual total of 9,000 to 12,000 head. In 1902 the firm acquired, by lease, a dozen linked townships along watercourses in Saskatchewan. In the fall of 1906 on this range and in Montana the Circle Diamond had 12,000 head; that winter 9,000 of them perished. The company survived, but within two years it closed out its Montana and Canada cattle operations, and the big herds had disappeared forever from the open range.

In that winter of 1906–07 railroad tracks snapped in the cold and for two months freight shipments were tied up as wreck crews struggled to keep the trains moving. Again starving cattle invaded the towns; one old steer, little more than a scurfy skeleton, stood in the yard of a Chinook newspaper plant until he died. There was nothing to feed him.

Losses would have been as severe as twenty years before were it not for the fact that livestock practice had changed. The story of human heroism in a futile effort to save the stock was repeated: sheepmen and cattlemen rigged up flatboard scrapers to clean the snow off the range in long strips so their animals could get at the grass; again the herders underwent great hardships in efforts to save their charges from accident or starvation.

In April, 1907, the state sadly tabulated the winter's cost: 727,136 head of sheep, 110,628 head of cattle, 6,423 head of horses. It was the worst loss in all America, though it had been a bad winter nearly everywhere. The national average winter kill was 349 per cent for cattle, 6 per cent for sheep; Montana's was 12 and 13 per cent. The last open-range roundup had been held in the fall of 1906; little interest had been shown in it and it had been hard to organize because there were so few outfits left using unfenced grass. In the spring of 1907 it was apparent that there never would be need for another.

John Survant and his riders, snowbound that winter in their Canadian quarters, fought desperately to save the Circle Diamond's stock. They saw the winter as a challenge to the "last big outfit." As long as their hay lasted or more could be bought, they fed the cows-foundation of next year's herd. Finally there was no more hay. Survant sent his men onto the thatched grass roof of an old shed and had them fork the years-old grass and hay down to the cattle. Still there was no chinook and the snow piled deeper.

Now there was no chance of saving the herd; but if he could save something, anything, by his own efforts, Survant felt he would have answered the challenge of the northwest's ancient, inimical gods. The ranch boasted an old milk cow, he explained…

I told the boys I hadn't done much good around there that winter, but by God I was going to save that old milk cow; I was going to save something from that winter. So we kept her in and I carefully fed her the kitchen slops — she would eat anything.

Well, one day the cook boiled up some beans but found they were sour, so he set 'em at the back of the stove until he got around to throwing 'em out. I came along when he wasn't there, and not knowing the beans were bad I swiped 'em and fed 'em to that cow; I figured she needed beans worse than we did.

You should have seen the yard next morning …

And the cow was dead, of course. I felt bad about it, wondering what she thought I'd done to her. But I was licked; guess I was foolish, thinking I could save even one old cow!

—JOSEPH KINSEY HOWARD FROM KISSINEYOOWAY'O

THE PRECEDING THREE PIECES BY JOSEPH KINSEY HOWARD WERE REPRINTED WITH THE PERMISSION OF YALE UNIVERSITY PRESS AND COME FROM MONTANA HIGH WIDE AND HANDSOME COPYRIGHTED 1943 AND 1959

OLD TRAILS

I N EARLY MONTANA, IT WAS THE MIGHTY MISSOURI RIVER AND A SERIES OF OFTEN-crude trails that connected growing population areas to each other and to the rest of the expanding nation.

For prospectors, emigrants and freight headed west, the Missouri River offered an established route for riverboats that reached from St. Louis, Missouri to just east of the Rocky Mountains at Fort Benton, Montana.

By the 1860s, when travelers and goods arrived in Fort Benton, trails were waiting that would lead them through danger, past hardships and with enough grit and a bit of luck, eventually farther west to the Pacific or into the gold fields of the Rocky Mountains.

THE MULLAN ROAD, FROM FORT BENTON
WEST TO WASHINGTON

Among the earliest and most well known of the trails used to travel western Montana was the Mullan Road, a path originally surveyed and used by the U.S. Army to move supplies and troops 640 miles from Fort Benton to Walla Walla, Washington.

Under the direction of John Mullan, a young graduate of the U.S. Military Academy, 100 soldiers and 90 civilians began work on the "road" in the spring of 1859. Ambitious plans called for constructing a 25-foot wide road from Fort Benton, over a low pass across the Continental Divide west of Helena, through the thick forests of western Montana and northern Idaho and into eastern Washington.

The project proved more difficult than at first imagined — especially the portion of the route cutting through the dense woodlands and mountains along the Montana-Idaho border — and at first, sections of Mullan's road turned out to be nothing more than marker poles left behind in the wilderness. Still, by 1862, after an investment of $250,000 by the federal government, Mullan Road connected Fort Benton and the Missouri River with Walla Walla.

Within several years of its completion, Mullan's discovered pass over the Continental Divide (which still bears his name) and route to Washington proved to be of little use to the military, but had grown into a popular route for thousands of pioneers and prospectors. For much of its life, most of the traffic found on Mullan Road was made up of large loads of freight. Today, the section of Interstate 90 that runs from Coeur d' Alene, Idaho to Deer Lodge, Montana follows the same path Mullan surveyed nearly 150 years ago.

—GRANT SASEK

THE BOZEMAN TRAIL, FROM WYOMING INTO MONTANA'S GALLATIN VALLEY.

The Bozeman Trail was nicknamed "The Bloody Bozeman" for a reason.

John Bozeman and partner John Jacobs began in 1863 to mark a route from the Oregon Trail at Fort Laramie, Wyoming into western Montana's gold diggings. It was their brilliant idea to establish a northwestern route for prospectors, pioneers and supplies leading through Wyoming, into Montana's Yellowstone Valley and west to the centrally located and fertile Gallatin Valley. From there the trail would be extended to Virginia City. But the boy's route had what would become a fatal flaw — the Bozeman Trail passed directly through the last remaining decent hunting grounds of the Crow, Sioux and Northern Cheyenne.

As signs of things to come, on Bozeman's first exploratory trip, Indians stole his supplies and the first time he attempted to move a wagon train up his new trail, he was turned back by angry Natives.

Black Elk of the Ogalala Sioux later explained that Indians fought the use of the Bozeman Trail because they believed "It would scare the bison and make them go away, and it would let the other white men come in like a river."

But the US Army saw value in the new trail, and in 1866 three forts were established along the path and a steady stream of wagon trains began to make their way from Wyoming into the Gallatin Valley. But even with the forts and military presence, the Cheyenne and Sioux continued to successfully harass those on the route. In 1868, just five years after John Bozeman marked it, the Army abandoned its recently established posts and turned its back on the Bozeman Trail. Without the military presence, the infamous trail lasted only two more years before falling into disuse.

Interstate 90 parallels portions of the Bozeman Trail in two locations, near the Montana-Wyoming border and between Reed Point and Bozeman.

—GRANT SASEK

THE WHOOP-UP TRAIL, FROM FORT BENTON NORTH INTO CANADA.

Soon after the military's need for a path west had led to the construction of the Mullan Road, different needs prompted the building of another trail from the commercial hub of Fort Benton. In the late-1860s, traders began using the Whoop-Up Trail to haul supplies, mostly whiskey, north into Canada. Originating at Fort Benton, the 240-mile trail passed through some of Montana's richest buffalo lands, crossed the Canadian border near where Sweetgrass now stands and ended at Fort Macleod along Canada's Oldman River in Alberta.

More than 40 "whiskey posts" were set up along the trail where Blackfeet Indians offered buffalo hides for "whoop-up bug juice." The traders remained in business for more than a decade until Indian epidemics of smallpox and alcoholism prompted the Northwest Mounted Police in 1874 to chase the dealers back into Montana.

As the whiskey traders moved off the trail, Fort Benton merchants began using it to supply the Canadian Mounties, and soon "bull trains" of up to 30 wagons, each pulled by eight to ten teams of oxen, relocated up to 100 tons of freight northward at a rate of 15 miles a day. A statue in downtown Helena honors the mule skinners and bull whackers who kept the trains, and supplies, moving. Freight traffic continued on the Whoop-Up Trail until the construction of the Canadian Pacific Rail Line brought rail service to the Canadian area in 1883.

Although no modern road follows the path of the Whoop-Up Trail, a section of Interstate 15 from the Canadian border south to Dutton passes through some of the same areas as Montana's first northward trail.

—GRANT SASEK

THE HELENA-FORT BENTON ROAD, FROM FORT BENTON TO HELENA

The road from Fort Benton to Helena was established about the time gold was discovered at Last Chance Gulch in 1864 and quickly grew into a popular freight route.

Following the already established Mullan Road laid out five years earlier from Fort Benton, the new route split off at the head of the Wolf Creek Canyon and navigated its way to Helena through the narrow gorge. Portions of the Recreation Road still follow the Helena-Fort Benton Road through the canyon and remnants of the original route remain visible.

When the trail left the southern end of the Wolf Creek Canyon, it passed through the Sieben Canyon and arrived in the Helena Valley near the now vanished community of Silver City. Once in the valley, the road split, with the main route taking heavy freight traffic west before heading into the city, while a spur headed south, more directly into central Helena where it converged with other roads leading to Virginia City, Gallatin City, Prickly Pear and Deer Lodge.

The privately owned section of the Helena-Fort Benton Road that passed through Wolf Creek Canyon soon became a toll road and remained a profitable enterprise until 1872 when ownership of many privately owned roads passed to the counties. Traffic gradually diminished during the 1870s, dropped off dramatically in the 1880s after the Northern Pacific Railroad arrived in the Helena Valley and disappeared entirely in the 1890s.

THE CARROLL TRAIL, FROM
THE MISSOURI RIVER TO HELENA

Entrepreneurs in the growing town of Helena eyed the Missouri River and realized Fort Benton wasn't the only place freight could be landed. The Carroll Trail was their attempt to establish another route from the Missouri River into Helena. Faced by similar challenges and doomed to the same fate as many of Montana's other early roads, the Carroll Trail was only used for about a decade.

Established in 1874, the trail was to be part of a route that would move goods from the westernmost reach of the Northern Pacific railroad at Bismarck, North Dakota by boat up the Missouri River to the junction of the Musselshell River and then overland on the Carroll Trail to Helena.

At the time, two alternative routes already existed to bring goods to Helena and nearby gold fields — either from Fort Benton or on a wagon road commencing at Corinne, Utah that ran up past Bannack and Virginia City. But moving goods on the Fort Benton toll road was expensive and the wagon road from Utah stretched more than 450 miles. With both of those entities facing problems of their own, Helena merchants believed a second trail from the Missouri River could be the most profitable solution for supplying their growing town.

The river landing was built about 160 miles downstream of Fort Benton and both it and the trail leading to Helena were named after Matthew Carroll, an official of the Helena freighting company involved in establishing the route. The landing now is under the water of the Fort Peck Reservoir.

From its inauguration, the Carroll Trail was bogged down with problems. Freight shipments from the riverboats were extremely unreliable, the track was often thick with impassible mud and, as with some of Montana's other early trails, travelers, freight and forts, more often than not, found themselves under attack from Sioux war parties. After just a couple of years of operation, use of the Carroll Trail fell off dramatically and with the completion of the Northern Pacific Railroad in 1883, it was abandoned.

US 191 now follows a section of the Carroll Trail between Lewistown and Roy.
—GRANT SASEK

BANNACK-CORRINE FREIGHT ROAD

By the fall of 1862, only a couple of months after the July discovery of gold on southwest Montana's Grasshopper Creek, some 400 people settled about eight miles upstream from the first "showing of colors" giving birth to Bannack. In the spring of 1883, the place had a sizeable population of 3,000 folks.

This populace required not only the necessities of life, but also equipment and other supplies not available in the wilds of what was first part of the Dakota Territory and then the Idaho Territory when it was created in spring of 1863. Everything had to come from St. Louis and needed to be ordered well in advance.

For its first seven years, merchandise arrived in Bannack either by way of Missouri River steamboats providing transport to Fort Benton then via wagons that forged a 300-mile-long road to the town, by pack string from Lewiston, Idaho, or from land freighters pointing west from St. Louis on the long haul to Salt Lake. An estimated 300-mile road was blazed from Bannack to connect with this southern transfer point. It headed out of town through the Horse Prairie Creek Valley (Lewis and Clark's Shoshone Cove) and then up Medicine Lodge Creek on the west side of the Tendoy Mountains. From there it ascended to the Medicine Lodge-Big Sheep Creek divide and then dropped into the Big Sheep Creek-Nicholia Creek Basin before once again climbing, this time, to the Continental Divide passing through the wide, sagebrush-covered 7,679-foot Bannack Pass. The road then lowered to Idaho's Medicine Lodge Creek and eventually came out to the prairie country of southeast Idaho near Dubois and then to the Great Salt Lake.

On May 10, 1869, as tracks of the Union Pacific and Central Pacific railways met at Promontory, Utah and the "golden spike" was driven, the nation's transcontinental railway was completed. Corrine, Utah, 70 miles north of Salt Lake, grew from this event. Its purpose was to serve as a transfer point for train passengers and the freight to be loaded onto wagon trains and stagecoaches headed to the gold camps and towns of Idaho and Montana. The time it now took to get to the Rockies from St. Louis was greatly diminished.

"Traffic" on the Bannack Road increased. By 1873 though, 11 years after its inception, use dwindled as Bannack's gold began playing out. During the height of its life, five stage stations, providing food and shelter for humans and animals, were located along the approximate 60 miles between Bannack and the Montana/Idaho line on Bannack Pass.

On the edge of the remaining buildings of Bannack State Park, the old wagon ruts can be still observed as they pull southward up the hill. Almost the entire route may be seen and followed, most of it is on a well-maintained gravel and dirt county road (wet weather makes parts of it impassable and the upper reaches are snow clogged in winter). At a point in Nicholai Basin, the original trail crossed through the bottoms and signs of years of passage are yet visible. The county road somewhat parallels the old path just to the east and then again meets the onetime freight road before reaching the Continental Divide.

By the way, don't confuse this Bannack Pass with Bannock Pass along Montana Hwy 324 farther to the west. Bannock is the correct spelling for the

Bannack-Corrine Freight Rd., Bannack Pass. RICK AND SUSIE GRAETZ

Indian Tribe that roamed the area. The O was mistakenly changed to an A when a post office was established for the town in November 21, 1862 and the name was submitted to Washington, D.C where the error occurred.

The Southwest Montana Interagency Visitor/Travel Map-West Half, produced by the Forest Service, delineates the way very clearly. Appropriately start from Bannack and then head towards Bannack Pass. You can continue on to Dubois or come back to Big Sheep Creek and take the road to Dell and Interstate Hwy 15.

In exploring this historic road, you'll wander through some of Montana's most remote terrain; a landscape of big, open sage-filled intermountain valleys lined with mountains in every direction. The peaks of the Beaverhead to your west carry the Continental Divide and some of its summits share the 11,000-foot level of elevation, including 11,141-foot Eighteen Mile Peak, the highest summit on Montana's segment of the Divide.

—RICK AND SUSIE GRAETZ

NATIVE LANDS — THE RESERVATIONS

"The history of Montana and the story of the Indian in the state are mixed as sometimes to seem almost the same. A quick look around is enough. The designated battle sites, the towns established because of the presence of Indians or because of trade or fear of attack, real or imagined, testified to that association. Kalispell, Fort Benton and Miles City are three examples. The reservations scattered over the state are added proof. Indians have retained or renewed old customs in the form of celebrations, powwows and re-enactments of historical events. The Indian is no longer ashamed of being Indian, as the young fellows were once made to feel. Thank the Lord ... the Indian has recovered his pride of race. He had no good reason to be ashamed anyhow. His cause was just, though he met defeat. In the course of history, many a just cause becomes a lost cause."

A.B. GUTHRIE, JR. FROM MONTANA A PHOTOGRAPHIC CELEBRATION VOLUME 3

MONTANA'S INDIAN RESERVATIONS

TODAY, THERE ARE SEVEN MONTANA INDIAN RESERVATIONS IN PLACE — THE CROW, Fort Peck (Assiniboine and Sioux), Rocky Boy's (Chippewa and Cree), Fort Belknap (Assiniboine and Gros Ventre), Blackfeet and Northern Cheyenne spread throughout Montana east of the mountains and the Flathead Salish (Flathead) and Kootenai) sited in northwestern Montana. These tribes aren't indigenous to the state. Most were pushed westward by European settlement in the upper Midwest especially along and north of the Great Lakes. The exception is the Salish-Kootenai of the Flathead-Mission Valley country who arrived from the north and the northwest and in the 1500s. The Kootenai are considered to be the first to put down their roots in Montana.

The Crow came from the upper Midwest in about 1620. The Blackfeet were estimated to have come into Montana around the 1730s, followed by the Assiniboine sometime during the 1760s. Next came the Sioux in about 1800 and their allies the Northern Cheyenne ventured into the southeast part of the state in the 1830s. Much later, in 1870, the small bands of the Chippewa and Cree made it to Montana.

At one time, Montana was an immense hunting ground. The great Indian nations who emigrated here lived a nomadic lifestyle in harmony with the landscape, the wildlife and seasons. Tribes east of the Northern Rockies followed immense migratory herds of bison across the vast Montana prairie. Those living west of the Continental Divide often crossed the mountain wilderness and gathered for soirees on the bison hunting grounds.

Before the days of government relegated reservations, the tribes had a more or less self-delineated area they claimed as their territory. However, rivalries and living requirements caused many to encroach on "others' lands."

Early on, the Shoshone were the prevailing power on the plains primarily because they had horses. Once the Blackfeet obtained horses and guns, they used their warrior skills to change the power structure and by the mid-1700s emerged as the dominant Indian force in Montana. This, combined with a large population — an estimated 15,000 strong, helped them become the rulers of the Montana prairies, eventually coercing the Kootenai and Salish off the plains into northwest Montana and the Shoshone into southwest Montana and Idaho.

Although they were forced westward, the displaced tribes still ventured across the mountains for periodic bison hunts. Often these treks resulted in skirmishes with the Blackfeet.

The feared Blackfeet controlled much of northern Montana east of the Rockies and especially around Glacier National Park and south towards today's Augusta and then eastward. The Sioux and Assiniboine roamed northeast Montana. Lands along the Yellowstone River and south were the realm of the Crow.

Together, the Northern Cheyenne and Sioux, who spent most of their time in South Dakota and far eastern Montana and Wyoming, constantly threatened the Crow and hunted on their lands.

Lewis and Clark's 1804–1806 exploration of the upper Missouri River began a dramatic alteration. Trappers followed the Corps of Discovery and brought their whiskey, disease and treachery to the natives. As the fur trade era came to a close, more whites were entering Indian Territory and seeking permanence, claiming the lands of the original owners. Pressure was brought upon the government in Washington by the outside invaders to get rid of the Indians.

At this time, the livelihood of the natives was about to change forever. A passage from *Montana A History of Two Centuries*, best describes what took place. "Except perhaps for Black Slavery, the purposeful destruction of Native American societies is the most sordid chapter of American History ... Whites seized control of vast territories ... Indians were forced to trading for a living." The US Government violated treaty after treaty. The period from 1851 through 1890 is often called an era of "Indian removal." Tribes were pushed off their traditional lands or when allowed to stay were allotted only small portions of the country they once roamed freely.

The Indian people weren't agrarian, but rather nomadic hunters whose lives, for the most part, depended upon the bison; hence, the US Government's planned destruction of these shaggy beasts was meant to devastate the Indians' culture and way of life and "bring them into line."

Overall, the Indians were treated differently than other ethic minorities in the United States. The reservation system came about because unlike other groups, the Indians actually owned land. The first treaties set forth in 1870s granted large tracts of Montana geography to the various tribes. Systematic treaty breaches and outright taking of lands shrunk the acreage severely. At one time, a Federal Indian Policy promoted ending the reservation system and assimilating Indians into the white culture.

Representing only about ten percent of Montana's topography, today's Montana reservations occupy approximately 8,300,000 acres.

A former commissioner of the Bureau of Indian affairs, Philleo Nash, said "The reservation system, with all its faults, is an integral part of Indian continuity, for it is the reservation that gives the tribes territoriality in the modern world."

And despite its problems, these reserves allow the Indian nations to connect with their past; it is their last retreat. Within the boundaries of their land, traditions and customs are protected.

The only reservation, west of the Continental Divide, the Flathead Reservation, home to the Confederated Salish and Kootenai people, occupies the lower portion of the beautiful Flathead Valley and the entire Mission Valley. The name Flathead was a misnomer used by Lewis and Clark in the belief that the Salish flattened their heads. Nowhere has this practice been documented but the name remains.

Approximately 6,950 members are enrolled in the tribe with 4,500 of them living on or near the reservation's 1,242,969 acres. The southern portion of Flathead Lake is on the reservation although non-Indians now own most of the land along the shore.

Tribal offices are located in Pablo (406 675-2700).

The flow of the Montana Prairie ends abruptly against the Rocky Mountain Front. Pointing eastward from its northern reaches and Glacier National Park, four reservations are spaced along Montana's Hi-Line to the North Dakota border. In 1873, this entire span, south to the Missouri River, approximately two-thirds of eastern Montana, was designated as the Blackfeet reserve.

Today's 1,500,000-acre Blackfeet Reservation hugs the western boundary of Glacier National Park. Seven thousand tribal members live on or near it. It is thought that the name Blackfeet came from the color of their moccasin bottoms, so marked either from the soot of fires or from purposeful painting.

From the windswept plains of their land, the Blackfeet, once known as fierce warriors, can gaze toward the setting sun at the spectacular peaks of Montana's Rocky Mountain Front.

Headquarters for the Blackfeet is located in Browning (406 338-7521).

Montana's smallest Indian set-aside, the 121,000-acre Rocky Boy's Reservation, sits south of Havre along the eastern ramparts of the Bear Paws Mountains. The Chippewa-Cree Tribe, about 2,500 strong, call this land home. Named for Rocky Boy, a leader of a band of Chippewa, it is believed that the true translation of the name meant "Stone Child." Established in September 1916, it is the newest of the State's reservations.

Rocky Boy's headquarters is located in Box Elder (406 395-5482).

On the sunrise side of the Bear Paw and stretching into the island range of the Little Rocky Mountains lies the Fort Belknap Indian Reservation. These 737,714 acres are the domain of 5,000 Assiniboine and Gros Ventre Indians.

Many of the tribes are raising bison, but the Assiniboine and Gros Ventre are trying it on the large scale in the Snake Butte area of their reservation.

Central Headquarters for Fort Belknap is located in Harlem (406 353-8471).

Further along US Highway 2, beginning on the east side of Fort Peck Lake extending along the Missouri River towards Culbertson, is the Fort Peck Indian Reservation. This tract encompasses over 2,093,318 acres, making it the second largest Montana reservation. It provides a home for more than 6,800 Assiniboine and Sioux.

The Fort Peck Reservation is the only one in Montana out of sight of mountains. Instead, the wide and scenic valley of the Missouri River dominates it.

Tribe Headquarters for Fort Peck is in Poplar (406 768-5155).

In south central Montana, only about 10 miles from Billings, the 2,235,000-acre Crow Reservation, the largest of Montana's Indian reserves. Home to about 7,500 Absaroka, commonly called Crow, the territory contains large underlying deposits of coal especially along its eastern perimeter.

Many consider the Crow lands to be the most scenic of all of Montana's Indian Reservations. Much of the Pryor Mountains, the Bighorn Canyon and the northern reach of the Bighorn Mountains, as well as the lower-lying Wolf Mountains, are all part of Crow Country. The nationally renowned Bighorn River as well as the historic Little Bighorn flows through central part of the reservation.

Administrative offices are in Crow Agency (406 638-3908).

Contiguous to the Crow's eastern boundary and stretching to the Tongue River, is the 444,679-acre Northern Cheyenne Reservation occupied by 5,000 Northern Cheyenne Natives.

Like Crow Country, the topography of the Northern Cheyenne land is considered especially beautiful. Rather than mountains, the viewscape consists of a labyrinth of river coulees and bottoms and a succession of high buttes and ridges. Coal deposits also underlie the Northern Cheyenne reserve. To date, their religious and environmental beliefs have kept the coal off limits.

Central Headquarters for the Northern Cheyenne is in Lame Deer (406 477-6284).

One tribe doesn't have a designated reservation. Located in Great Falls, the Little Shell, made up of a band of the Chippewa Tribe, have approximately 4,000 enrolled members within the state, with most living in the Great Falls area.

Tribal administration for the Little Shell is located in Great Falls (406 452-2892).

All of the reservations have at least a two-year college and most have a cultural center and museum that proudly display their culture and artifacts. Each reservation is unique in the way the government is structured and the land is managed. Some have a mix of tribal-owned lands and allotted property and others are completely owned by the tribe. Getting to know these reservations and their people is integral part of understanding Montana's heritage.

—RICK AND SUSIE GRAETZ

FLATHEAD RESERVATION...
SALISH AND KOOTENAI

Western Montana's Flathead Indian Reservation is among the most scenic of all of Montana's Indian lands. The picturesque Cabinet Mountains mark the reservation's western boundary; to the east the craggy Mission Mountains define the view and to the southeast lays the Rattlesnake Mountain Wilderness. To the north is Flathead Lake — the largest natural freshwater lake west of the Great Lakes. Cutting through the length of the valley lying between it all is the Flathead River.

It is a place of beauty where American Indians have roamed since antiquity. Artifacts indicate that predecessors of the Kootenai Indians lived in the Lower Flathead River Basin more than 14,000 years ago. Many archeologists believe that the Kootenai who settled south of Flathead Lake, were part of a larger population of Kootenai Indians who ranged from southern Canada into northern Idaho and Montana.

For thousands of years, the Kootenai, leaving only for occasional hunting trips to the plains in the east, apparently had western Montana mostly to themselves. Eventually, after other tribes moved to the area, they would become known as the "fish trap" people for their practice of using traps to catch fish.

When newcomers first began to arrive, probably about 7,000 years ago, they came from the west. It is believed that the members of the Salish tribes who entered northwestern Montana about 5000 BC, came from the Columbia River Plateau. Eventually, these Salish would split into two distinct groups, one that would move, temporarily into the eastern plains and develop a culture around the bison, and another that would remain in western Montana. The former would become known as the Flatheads, the latter would be called the Pend d'Oreille.

The Pend d'Oreille settled primarily in the area near where Paradise, Montana now stands and in other valleys south of Flathead Lake. In the 1700s, the Flatheads, decimated by small pox, crossed back over the Continental Divide and returned to western Montana.

When Lewis and Clark arrived in the Bitterroot Valley in 1805, they found members of the Kootenai and Salish tribes waiting to greet them. An unfortunate, but direct result of the expedition would be a growing pressure for use of the Indian lands.

Four years after the visit by Lewis and Clark, the North West Company established a fort in northern Idaho at Pend d'Oreilles Lake; a short 40 years after the visit, missionaries had already successfully converted many of the area's Indians to Christianity and in 1855, still 34 years before Montana would become a state, the demands had grown great enough that the Kootenai, Flathead and Pend d'Oreille tribes officially settled any lingering fights between themselves and the federal government by ceding much of their traditional lands in western Montana to the United States.

Known as the 1855 Hellgate Treaty, the agreement called for the three tribes to live together on one reservation that included the southern half of Flathead Lake and all land southward through the Jocko Valley. The agreement also called for the creation of another home to the south in the Bitterroot Valley for the Flathead Tribe. But, by 1872, continuing encroachment by white settlers forced many of the Flathead to give up their land in the Bitterroot and to move onto the northern reservation. The pressure never let up; in 1891, under military escort, the last of the Bitterroot Flatheads were moved onto the reservation in the Jocko Valley, which took the name of the Flathead Reservation.

Even though the boundaries of the reservation have remained essentially unchanged since that time, tribal members witnessed the taking of still more of their lands throughout the early 20th Century.

In 1908, surveyors appeared on the reservation and carved the Jocko Valley into small allotments. Under the new plan authorized by Congress, each tribal member was to receive 80 acres of agricultural land or 160 acres of grazing land. The remainder of the reservation lands, and there was much left, was to be sold to white settlers. On April 1, 1910, about 1 million acres of Indian land went up for sale. By the time the Indian Reorganization Act of 1934 finally brought reservation allotments to an end, nearly half of the reservation's land had been sold.

On their remaining land, the tribes reorganized, formed an integrated tribal council and in 1936, officially became the Confederated Salish and Kootenai Tribes of the Flathead Indian Reservation. In 1951, the tribes sued the federal government over unfair payments for land transfers associated with the Hellgate Treaty and for faulty calculations and compensation in the following allotments. The fight was long and it wasn't until 1971 that the tribes won the case and received a $22 million settlement. Indian pride was revived, and a movement began to regain former Indian lands. Between 1986 and 1994, the tribes spent about $16 million to buy back land that had formerly been theirs.

By the turn of the 21st Century, the operations of the Confederated Salish and Kootenai tribes had grown into big business and today they enjoy what is considered by many to be the least depressed economy found on any of Montana's Indian reservations. Along with continuing payments from the US government, much of the reservation's economy is fueled by timber sales, which tribal members proudly claim are managed on a sustainable basis, and regular payments for use of Kerr Dam straddling the Flathead River eight miles south of Polson.

The hydroelectric dam was no small project. Work began in 1929, after an agreement was reached between the tribes and Rocky Mountain Power. Construction that was expected to take three or four years extended to nearly ten because of a lack of available money during the Great Depression. It eventually became the largest electrical producer in Montana Power's series of dams.

With money in the tribal coffers and a swelling pride in their place in history, attention on the Flathead Reservation has turned to education. Public schools emphasize classes in Salish and Kootenai history, a Job Corps training center for Indian people from around the nation can be found near Ronan, and at Pablo, the tribes operate the Two Eagle River School, an alternative high school, and the Salish Kootenai College (SKC), a facility that includes a library with more than 1,200 published items relating to the tribes.

The Flathead Indian Reservation offers world-class scenery and recreation possibilities that reach from Flathead Lake and its myriad of opportunities to the 89,500-acre Mission Mountains Tribal Wilderness, a hiker's paradise with more than 100 lakes, tall mountain peaks and an abundance of wildlife. Because of this beautiful setting, the reservation also enjoys a steady stream of income from tourism — a flow of cash they hope to increase.

In an effort to lure more tourists to the area, the $6.5 million KwaTaqNuk resort and casino has been constructed near Polson and a 6,700-square-foot People's Center in nearby Pablo serves as a tribal museum and a promoter of the tribes' history and customs. Other large-scale tourist destinations also are being considered.

—GRANT SASEK

THE BLACKFEET NATION

At one time, they were feared Plains warriors. Historians believe the Blackfeet, forced out of their ancestral grounds in today's upper Great Lakes region by white advancement, were one of the first Native American tribes to head west. Though there are several stories on how they received their name, the most plausible is that their moccasins were blackened from the long journey across the prairie to reach what would become Montana.

The Blackfeet band now living on the Blackfeet Reservation are descendants of the Piegan branch of the Blackfeet. Two other bands — the Bloods and the North Blackfeet — now reside on Canadian Indian preserves, scattered throughout Alberta.

Blackfeet territory once ranged into southern Canada and south through Montana to Yellowstone National Park. Theirs was a nomadic life. Before acquiring horses, dogs were used to pull the travois as they traveled in search of bison. They were one of the first tribes to use pishkuns — steep cliffs over which herds of bison were driven for harvesting.

Once the Blackfeet obtained horses, they vigorously broadened their territory by pushing other tribes such as the Kootenai, Flathead and Shoshone west of the Continental Divide. Their hunting lands soon covered an enormous landscape. By the early 1800s, they were doing battle with most tribes who ventured into the Northern Great Plains. It is estimated their numbers exceeded 15,000 and this size, coupled with their warrior skills, struck fear in the hearts of all who encountered them.

By the time of the Corps of Discovery, led by Lewis and Clark, moved up the Missouri, the Blackfeet had control of nearly all the Montana terrain the explorers wandered through. Except for one incident, their encounters with the explorers were peaceful. But, they were the scourge of the fur traders who followed the expedition, and it wasn't until the 1830s that they began working with the trappers.

Efforts by the US Government to end inter-tribal warfare began in 1855 with the treaty that gave the Blackfeet and their allies the Gros Ventre, much of Montana east of the Northern Rocky Mountains. But as was the case with all the other tribes in Montana, these lands quickly were whittled down by deception and the misguided efforts of the US Government.

With a gradually shrinking territory, and the disappearance of the bison, the Blackfeet became impoverished. In 1888, left with no other choices, these once proud people were forced to sign the so-called "Sweet Grass Hills Treaty" — an agreement that gave the Blackfeet their present reservation, plus lands in the eastern side of present-day Glacier National Park. Once again though, in 1896, the US Government went back on their word as they forced the tribe to cede the mountain lands that would become part of the national park for $1.5 million.

Today's Blackfeet reserve borders the eastern edge of Glacier and provides a most beautiful backdrop for the undulating hills that stretch eastward towards a north-south perimeter on the western edge of the town of Cut Bank. The Canadian line defines the northern tier of Blackfeet country and its southern point extends just to the west of Dupuyer and the eastern ramparts of the Rocky Mountain Front. Much of the landscape is dissected by creeks and dotted with lakes.

Almost 7,500 tribal members reside on this 1,525,712-acre reservation; a large portion portion of which, in this case nearly 40 percent, is owned by non-Indians.

Another problem is unemployment. Seventy percent of the tribal members with full-time jobs, are employed by either the US Government or the tribe. As more and more people pass through the reservation on their way to the various entrances to Glacier National Park, tourism is becoming more important economically. And the tribe, with its traditions, has much to offer.

The potential is there, for fishing, hunting and sight seeing, tied in with historical preservation. The Museum of the Plains Indians in Browning, one of the great Indian museums in the state, is a leader in attracting visitors.

North American Indian Days, the largest Indian celebration in Montana after Crow Fair, is the highlight of the year in Blackfeet country. It is an authentic, not staged for tourists, event ,that brings out tribal pride and traditions.

Browning is the center of the tribal government, economy and activities. The Blackfeet National Bank, opened here in 1987, has the distinction of being the first tribally owned and controlled, full service bank in the United States. Soon to be renamed the Native American Bank, its healthy capital base will be expanded as other tribes become involved. Blackfeet Community College prepares tribal members in a myriad of fields, including education, to be future leaders and business people.

Overall, an attitude to preserve traditions, including their language and land base, is growing. And the Blackfeet Nation has been instrumental in the fight to keep Montana's Rocky Mountain Front free of development as "The Front" is an integral part of their sacred heritage.
—RICK AND SUSIE GRAETZ

ROCKY BOY'S RESERVATION... CHIPPEWA AND CREE

Officially, it's called Rocky Boy's Reservation, but to many of its residents, it is simply Rocky Boy. The same holds true for the mountains that take up one third of the land within the reservation boundaries. Signs and historians call them the Bears Paw Mountains, others say Bear Paw, while many of the locals, especially those who live within them, label this assemblage of buttes and hills as the Bear Paws. Bear Paw though seems to be the correct term as used by the first folks to head here. There highest point is 6,916-foot Mount Baldy.

Located on the prairie just south of Havre, Rocky Boy is the smallest of all of Montana's reservations. In September 1916, via a Presidential Executive Order, Rocky Boy, with a beginning mass of 55,040 acres, became the last reservation established. Through various methods of land acquisition, today it encompasses 122,000 acres. Many folks, including artist Charlie Russell, William Bole, owner at the time of the Great Falls Tribune, Paris Gibson, founder of Great Falls and author Frank Linderman, helped with the effort to increase the tribe's land.

Initially, the reserve took its title from a Chippewa Chief whose name translated as "Stone Child." However, a white misinterpretation of the name rendered it as Rocky Boy instead. For whatever reason the name stuck.

At one time, the Chippewa, having migrated west from the Great Lakes region, were separate from the Cree, who moved south to Montana from

Canada. Historical notes show the Chippewa probably didn't get to Montana until about 1880. The Cree were here sooner and had aligned themselves with the Assinniboine. Both peoples had guns and horses and were the dominant force on the northern Great Plains until such time as the Blackfeet also came to own rifles and acquired ponies.

The Cree being led by Chief Little Bear and the Chippewa by (Stone Child) Rocky Boy were both essentially landless. Traveling throughout Montana from a period of about 1890 to 1910, the bands maintained their way of life as nomadic people. They harvested berries, roots, and wild plants and hunted, gathered and polished bones and horns for trade. It was a happy life, but it didn't fit in with the white man's desire to get rid of them.

Overall, the story of Montana's Native People is a depressing one. But the Chippewa and Cree received the worst treatment in terms of being able to establish a homeland base. Proposals to carve out reservations were rejected. Many misguided Montanans wanted to send both tribes to Canada. In 1915, a part of Fort Assinniboine, a large military reservation near Havre, was set aside for the two tribes. The residents of Havre approached the Chippewa Cree and proposed creating a park between the town and the reservation. In exchange for the Rocky Boy's support in obtaining the land, the town would aid the reservation in future land acquisition. The result is the 9,000-acre Beaver Creek Park; the second largest city park in the United States.

Chief Rocky Boy passed away in 1916. As a tribute for the major role he played in achieving a home for the Cree and Chipewa, it was given his name.

The establishment of Rocky Boy's hardly solved the tribe's problems. Not only was the land mass was too small to support the members, the terrain was dry and not very productive. The Indians had little or no housing, no schooling and were poorly fed. Overall, a bad attitude existed within the U.S. Government and with others over the plight of the Chippewa and Cree people. Professor Thomas Wessel of Montana State University stated, "The Government has wrongly treated Rocky Boy's as an outdoor asylum for social deviants, who hopefully someday would assimilate into the western world. The Bureau of Indian Affairs, charged with overseeing reservations refused to look at the Rocky Boy's as a community or as an economic entity, and allow the reservation to drift without definition or direction."

It took a great deal of effort by those who came after chiefs Rocky Boy and Little Bear to make the reservation as strong as it is today. Their insistences on pursuing increased land attainment, helped make the reservation more viable.

Rock Boy's now has self-governance status, which allows it to avoid dealing with the BIA and work directly with the Federal Government, a far more beneficial situation.

Up until the last 20 years or so, Rocky Boy's was thought to be void of natural resources save scenery. Recently, the tribe has been successful in finding and negotiating the drilling of natural gas on the reservation. Agriculture though is their dominant source of income. All of the land is tribal owned, but individuals farm or ranch various parcels, and there is some leased land.

Several small businesses operate on the reservation; some owned by the tribe, others by individuals. Competition for any business would come from nearby Havre or Great Falls to the south. Bear Paw Ski Bowl, on Black Mountain, is owned by the tribe and operated by an organization out of Havre. Another large tribal business is the Dry Fork Farm, an irrigated haying operation. Thanks in part to an emphasis on wildlife enhancement, numbers of deer, elk and antelope have increased significantly on the reservation.

Of the more than 6,000 registered Chippewa Cree Tribal members, about 3,400 live on the reservation where the Cree is language still preserved. Stone Child College, with an average enrollment of about 250 mostly tribal folks, is a shining educational light on the reservation.

The Chippewa and Cree people, like all of Montana's natives, take great pride in their history and traditions. For the Rocky Boy's tribes, their annual powwow is the highlight of the year for celebrating who they are.
—RICK AND SUSIE GRAETZ

FORT BELKNAP RESERVATION... GROS VENTRE AND ASSINIBOINE

Montana's Fort Belknap Reservation is made up of two different landscapes and populated by two different tribes — the Gros Ventres and Assiniboine. While the tribes share some history and similar fates, different paths led them to their current, shared homeland in north central Montana.

Like many tribes, the Gros Ventre has a long history of moving from one home to another. Historians believe the tribe, who called themselves the A'a'nin, or White Clay People, lived in North Dakota's Red River Valley from about 1100 A.D. to 1400 A.D. As pressure from the east grew and competition increased among the Plains Indians, the Gros Ventre found themselves forced from their lands, always pushed being farther north or west.

The first known white contact with the Gros Ventres was about 1754 in Canada, between the north and south forks of the Saskatchewan River. It was an unfortunate encounter for the Indians. Left behind for the Gros Ventres was the same smallpox plague that would soon haunt other tribes. As the disease dramatically cut their population and therefore their strength, pressure from the Cree, the largest native population in Canada, and the Assiniboine, who had connections with the larger Sioux nation, compelled the tribe to move again.

The Gros Ventres, along with the Arapaho and Cheyenne tribes, are said to have migrated into what would become Montana about the turn of the 19th Century. While the Arapaho continued south to Wyoming and Colorado, the Gros Ventres and Cheyenne remained in Montana. There, along the

Little Rocky Mountains and the eastern edge of the Fort Belknap Reservation. RICK AND SUSIE GRAETZ

Missouri river in 1826, the tribe met with German explorer Prince Maximilian, who documented their presence in the state. The Gros Ventres were quick to form an alliance with the powerful Blackfeet tribe and by the mid-1800s, the two tribes roamed north central Montana and southern Canada.

By then, the Assiniboine, the tribe that once quarreled with the Gros Ventres in Canada, had also found their way into Montana. Calling themselves the Nakona, or "the Friendly People," they became known by others as the Assiniboine — Chippewa words for "stone boilers" — because of their unique way of cooking with rocks.

According to their oral history, the Assiniboine originally were a branch of the Yanktonai Sioux and a powerful tribe in their own right, making up about 40 distinct bands that reached from the Great Lakes to the Rocky Mountains. For some, the land from where the Milk River flows into the Missouri River all the way to North Dakota was considered to be Assiniboine wintering grounds.

But like the Gros Ventres, the Assiniboine also would suffer from smallpox, see the numbers of their tribe dwindle, and eventually grow vulnerable to the larger tribes. In 1851, the Assiniboine supported the first Fort Laramie Treaty, an agreement that was to end the fighting by designating western lands to each of the tribes.

Four years later in 1855, both the Gros Ventres, who signed as members of the Blackfeet nation, and the Assiniboine, agreed to another treaty that was to bring peace to the area. That treaty set aside land from the Rocky Mountains to the mouth of the Yellowstone River as common Indian hunting grounds, including grounds for both the Gros Ventres and the Assiniboine.

Both tribes remained in central Montana and in 1868, the U.S. Army established Fort Browning along the Milk River to serve as a distribution post for rations and annuities guaranteed to the tribes by the earlier treaties. Unfortunately, the new fort was on Sioux hunting grounds and three years later, it was abandoned. Government officials soon replaced it with Fort Belknap, which was built on the opposite side of the Milk River near where the town of Chinook now stands.

Fort Belknap operated for five years, but in 1876, it too was closed and members of the Assiniboine and Gros Ventres who had been receiving goods there were told to relocate to the agency established to the east at Fort Peck and Wolf Point — land frequented by the Sioux.

Many of the Assiniboine, who shared language and old connections with the Sioux, were willing to move eastward, but members of the Gros Ventres refused to relocate to land they would have to share with old adversaries. Instead, the Gros Ventres, and some lingering Assiniboine, stayed where they were and, for a while, forfeited their annuities.

In 1878, just two years after being closed, Fort Belknap was re-established as a source of supplies for those who had remained in the area. Six years later, in 1884, gold was discovered in the nearby Little Rocky Mountains and the year after that, St. Paul's Mission was established near the foot of the mountains. Finally, in 1888, the tribes of central Montana, under increasing pressure from the continuing influx of whites, ceded 17,500,000 acres to the United States and agreed to live on three new, much smaller reservations.

The Blackfeet Reservation was established along the Canadian border and became home to the Blackfeet Indians; the Sioux nation, including the Assiniboines who had moved to Fort Peck, were located on the Fort Peck Reservation and the Fort Belknap Reservation, officially established on March 2, 1889, became the land of the Gros Ventres and Assiniboine who had remained in the area.

The Fort Belknap Reservation is the smallest of the three, encompassing 1,200 square miles, or about 638,000 acres. It is home to about 3,500 members of the Assiniboine and Gros Ventre tribes. Dry land farming, ranching and tribal government are the main sources of employment.

For the most part, the Gros Ventres settled in the reservation's southern portion in a land marked by rolling grassland, river breaks and the Little Rocky Mountains. About a third of the reservation's population lives in this area and are served by the communities of Hays and Lodge Pole.

Most of the Assiniboine remained in the northern reaches of the reservation, a land of treeless plains and alluvial bottomlands. More than half of the reservation's population lives here, in or near the Fort Belknap Agency or the town of Harlem (which is not located on the reservation).

Each year, reservation residents celebrate their history and traditions with Milk River Indian Days Powwow and Chief Joseph Memorial Days. Other sources of information about the history of those calling the Fort Belknap home can be found at a small museum and visitor center located at the intersection of highways Montana 66 and U.S. 2. The reservation's herd of 300 buffalo and other abundant wildlife often can be seen nearby.

Among the historical sites that can be found on or near the Fort Belknap Reservation are the Chief Joseph Battleground Monument, St. Paul's Mission Church, the Natural Bridge State Monument, the C.M. Russell National Wildlife Refuge and the Missouri River Breaks.

—GRANT SASEK

FORT PECK RESERVATION...
THE ASSINIBOINE AND SIOUX

It stretches across the low hills and sprawling prairie of far northeast Montana. Millions of bison once migrated through the landscape, historic trails crisscrossed it and Lewis and Clark walked the shores of the Missouri River and its southern perimeter...Montana's second largest reservation, home to the Assiniboine and Sioux nations...The Fort Peck Indian Reservation.

In the early 1600s, Europeans displaced the ancestors of the Assiniboine and Sioux from the east coast. By the end of the century, the Sioux had migrated west and south to central Minnesota. Known as a large and powerful nation, they were comprised of seven bands, or council fires, all of whom speak a language of Siouan descent. These seven divisions evolved into what are known today as three different language groups: the Dakotas (Santee Sioux), the Nakotas (Yankton and Yanktonai Sioux) and the Lakotas (Teton Sioux). The Sioux people of the Fort Peck Reservation belong to the Nakota band.

At about the time they arrived in Minnesota, one band of the tribe split into two: the Yankton and the Yanktonai. The Yankton moved west across the northern plains while the Yanktonai went north to Canada.

Historical notes show that the Assiniboine are a branch of the Yanktonai Sioux, having broken away sometime in the 1600s to form the distinct tribe that came to the Fort Peck Reservation in 1871 when it was opened. The name Assiniboine traces back to their Siouan ancestry. The word *ass-ni-pwan* means "stone Sioux," referring to the Assiniboine method of cooking food with hot stones and boiling water. Like the Sioux, sometime during the 17th century, the Assiniboine split into two groups; one staying north in the Canadian woods and the other roaming south to hunt bison on the Great Plains. In the mid 1700s, the southern group divided again with one contingent leaving Canada for the Missouri River Valley region and taking on the name Lower Assiniboine, and the other, trailing west to the Assiniboine and Saskatchewan rivers, being referred to as the Upper Assiniboine.

93

North of Poplar agriculture dominates the Fort Peck Reservation's land. RICK AND SUSIE GRAETZ

Not only had the tribe split several times, thereby decreasing the population, but smallpox decimated the size of the Assiniboines by nearly two-thirds making them vulnerable to other Plains tribes. Unable to defend their hunting grounds, they welcomed the terms of the so called Fort Laramie Treaty in 1851 that "set aside" specific lands for each of the Indian Nations inhabiting what would become Montana and Wyoming.

In 1869, smallpox again reduced the Upper Assiniboine populace. The Lower Assiniboine were not affected, and in order to preserve numbers, stayed away from their Upper brethren and followed Chief Red Stone, to join the Yanktonai Sioux who had migrated to northeastern Montana to hunt bison.

Fort Peck Agency was established in 1871 in part for the Sioux who could not get along with anyone other than their newly found allies, the Lower Assiniboine. Their alliance has remained strong ever since.

Today, nearly 6,000 Sioux and Assiniboine out of about 11,000 enrolled tribal members live on the Fort Peck Reserve. Approximately 110 miles long and 40 miles wide, its western edge is defined by Porcupine Creek near Glasgow and extends east to Muddy Creek, close to the Montana/North Dakota border, and north from the Missouri River to about 50 miles south of Canada.

Wolf Point, once a frontier outpost, and now home to the Wolf Point Wildhorse Stampede, Montana's oldest pro rodeo, is on the Reservation. The town of Poplar is the center for tribal activities and hosts the Assiniboine and Sioux Cultural Center and Museum.

Reservation life is rich with traditions. Powwows are held to renew and strengthen family and friendships as well as to celebrate tribal culture. A myriad of dance styles retrace ancestral customs and celebrate their close connection to the land. These Indian family gatherings not only feature dancing and drumming, but traditional foods and story telling are shared. Visitors are welcome.

Agriculture, in the form of dryland farming and specifically the growing of wheat, cereal grains and barley, is the major economic activity on the reservation.

The Fort Peck Reservation is home to many fascinating artifacts and historical sites including teepee rings, buffalo jumps and sacred sites.

— RICK AND SUSIE GRAETZ

THE CROW TRIBE OF INDIANS

"The Crow Country is good country. The Great Spirit has put it exactly in the right place; when you are in it you fare well; whenever you go out of it, whichever way you travel, you fare worse ... Everything good is to be found there ... There is no country like the Crow Country."

CROW CHIEF EELAPUASH (ARAPOOISH IN SOME OF THE OLDER BOOKS)
IN THE 1830S TO A FUR TRADER

Indeed the lands of the Crow Tribe of Indians are exceptional. They range from the high desert-like Pryor Mountains in the west to the Wolf Mountains and Rosebud Creek on the eastern fringe, and from the Wyoming line north to the edge of Billings and Hardin. These 2.2 million acres take in some of Montana's most noteworthy landscape … the rugged and beautiful Bighorn Canyon, ice caves and wild horses in the Pryors, the 9,000-foot rise of the snowy Bighorn Mountains and the historic Little Bighorn and Bighorn rivers … a place for all seasons.

Apsaalooke (Absarokee), the Crow language, means "children of the large-beaked bird." Other tribes identifying the Crow in sign language would imitate the flapping of a bird in flight. For this reason they came to be called Crow Indians.

Three versions are told of how the Crow came to today's south central Montana. The published, and most accepted, account was researched in depth by tribal elder and historian Joseph Medicine Crow, Ph.D. He tells of the Crow people, part of the Hidatsa Tribe, coming from the Lake Superior region and following a path of migration over a 100 year period. Their odyssey took them first to North Dakota, then to Canada and as far south as Texas and Oklahoma, finally arriving in Montana in the very early 1700s.

Crow Fair dancer. RICK AND SUSIE GRAETZ

Throughout the years of the white man's invasion of Indian Territory, the Crows maintained friendly relations with these outsiders, even serving as military scouts. Through an 1851 treaty with the U.S. government, they were "given" more than 38 million acres in northern Wyoming and southern Montana. In 1868, they were forced to give up much of this territory and were assigned to an eight million-acre reservation that extended from the current eastern boundary west to Livingston and the Paradise Valley. The original Crow Agency was at Mission Creek, five miles east of Livingston. By 1904 however, Crow Country was whittled down by various wrongful acts to its present size.

Today, more than 10,000 tribal members call the Crow lands home. Two-thirds of them live on, or are adjacent to, the present-day reservation. Divided into three subgroups — Mountain Crow, River Crow and Kicked in The Bellies — they live in the reservation's six districts — Lodge Grass (sometimes called Valley of the Chiefs), Wyola (Mighty Few), Reno, Bighorn, Pryor and Black Lodge. A gradual "modern invasion" of the reservation has taken place over many years. Approximately 5,000 whites now live within its confines and have purchased almost 34 percent of the land.

Proud of their history, traditions and language, the Crow are striving to keep them a part of everyday life. One of the best examples is the strong, time honored clan system … a complex matriarchal based extended family. The clan is supportive of each other, shares responsibilities and provides for the needs of their less fortunate members.

In this vein, the best of the old ways are being preserved. Crow leaders are building a strong education base for the future, culminating in the much-admired Little Big Horn College. A guiding principle has been the words of Chief Plenty Coups, last of the tribe's traditional chiefs. He wished young Crows "… to go to school and become well educated … then … to come back home on the reservation and work."

Making a living on the Crow reservation today is difficult and unemployment is high. To combat this, the college has been developing programs to create more jobs through training in areas such as computer science, tourism, guiding, and professional and para-professional positions. Small home-based businesses are also being encouraged.

The Crow have their own constitution and are governed by a general-council consisting of every adult. The council elects four officers for two-year terms. The chair of the tribe has the authority to conduct the general affairs between quarterly council meetings.

Crow Country's physical attractions are luring an increasing number of tourists. Leading the way is recreation on Bighorn Lake and visitation to the Little Bighorn Battlefield National Monument (site of Custer's defeat). Legendary fishing on the Bighorn River is also bringing some economic benefits to the tribe by way of providing jobs for fishing guides.

Then there is Crow Fair, one of the great celebrations in Montana with roots back to 1904. Although it draws many visitors from literally around the world, it is not a staged tourist event, but rather a most colorful and exciting homecoming and gathering for the Crow people. Families reunite, dancers compete and horsemanship at its finest is evident in the contests, races and rodeo that are part of a week-long August affair. With more than more than 1,000–2,000 (depending on the year) tepees raised, it is known as "The Tepee Capitol Of The World."

—RICK AND SUSIE GRAETZ

NORTHERN CHEYENNE COUNTRY

Stretching west through the rambling prairie of southeast Montana, US Hwy 212 crosses the Tongue River near the town of Ashland and enters the eastern periphery of the 447,000-acre Northern Cheyenne Reservation.

For 40 miles from Ashland to Lame Deer and just beyond Busby, Hwy 212 slices the northern tier of the Reservation. Situated on the map below Jim Town and above Birney, with Crow Country contiguous on the western edge in the area of the Wolf Mountains and the Tongue River following much of the eastern boundary, this small reservation occupies some of eastern Montana's most beautiful landscape.

From the muddy waters of the Tongue, the topography rolls along for approximately ten miles, then ascends somewhat abruptly before it gradually slopes downward toward the setting sun. Sculptured sandstone formations rise high on hills surrounded by open forests of junipers and ponderosa pine and large open grassy parks, dropping off into coulees. Some of the highest points on the landscape are in the northern section of the reservation, with Badger Peak lifting to 4,422 feet. An unnamed 4,792-foot knob just north of Bull Creek Lookout (south of the Muddy Creek area) holds the distinction of being king of the hills.

Indeed, the Northern Cheyenne people enjoy what could be described as the epitome of the land of the old western movies. And because so much of the landscape is intact and undisturbed, they boast a large population of whitetail and mule deer as well as antelope, elk, bears and mountain lions.

It is also a place reverberating of legends of not only the Native Americans' heritage but also the formative years of Montana. At one time, 4,316-foot Garfield Peak and other high points across the reservation were employed by the US Military as relay stations to send vital information long distances via the use of mirrors. One of the destinations of this activity was the aptly named Signal Hill near Miles City.

Like many of the Plains Indian tribes, the Cheyenne people came from the country south of Hudson Bay and the Great Lakes region. Burgeoning European settlements in the "New World" began forcing the Natives westward to northern Minnesota sometime in the 1400s. Soon, pressure from this fast-growing white population pushed them even farther west into the Upper Missouri River lands in the Dakotas.

At first the Cheyenne were farmers, but in the mid 1700s, after obtaining horses, they shifted from an agrarian lifestyle to one of hunting. Bison became their main source for meat and skins and in order to keep a full larder, the tribe began following the mighty animal's movements. It is believed that this transition from gatherers to hunters, from stationary to migratory, happened in a period of 25 years.

As the 1800s opened, the Cheyenne found themselves, along with other tribes, living in the Black Hills of South Dakota. They became allies with the Ogala Sioux, both for hunting and for fighting their common enemy the Crow, who resided to the west in what would become Montana.

While in the Black Hills in the 1830s, the tribe split into the Southern and the Northern Cheyenne. Historians feel this was because smaller groups would fare better in a nomadic existence. The Southern Cheyenne, the largest faction, wandered to Colorado, while the Northern Cheyenne remained mostly in the Black Hills, but also moved into territory occupied by the Crow.

The Sioux proved to be great partners to the Cheyenne in their collective battles and activities. Like all Native Americans, the Northern Cheyenne faced the injustice of the US Government through repeated treaty violations that diminished their ancestral lands and witnessed the slaughter of their lifeline, the bison. By the mid 1870s, the US Government demanded that all tribes in

Upper Missouri River area move to reservations. The Northern Cheyenne resisted.

On June 25, 1876, on the banks of the Little Big Horn River (Greasy Grass to the Indians), the Northern Cheyenne with their Sioux friends met the infamous Lt. Colonel George Armstrong Custer in a conflict that came to be known as the Battle of the Little Big Horn. History tells the rest. For a very brief moment some the government's wrongs were revenged, but not for long. Shortly more troops arrived and the Indians lost their free roaming lifestyle forever.

More tragedy was in store for the Northern Cheyenne. Compelled to move south to join their brethren, the Southern Cheyenne in what then was known as Indian Country — Okalahoma — the Northern people were unhappy and didn't want to stay. On Sept. 10, 1878, 300 Northern Cheyenne led by chiefs Dull Knife and Little Wolf, left the Oklahoma reservation for a journey north to the Yellowstone region.

Facing constant danger, the group managed to elude the tracking military until they reached Nebraska where they split up. Many of Chief Dull Knife's followers lost their lives while resisting an attack before he surrendered his band at Fort Robinson. Chief Little Wolf with his troop of 125 made it to Fort Keogh, at today's Mile City, where they were allowed to stay with another gathering of Northern Cheyenne led by Chief Two Moons.

Already, an unofficial reservation was in the making as Northern Cheyenne began to take up residence in the Tongue River and Rosebud Creek areas. Formally established as the Tongue River Reservation in November 1884, the territory was increased in 1900 to include the Tongue River Valley and

Northern Cheyenne Sundance Lodge. RICK AND SUSIE GRAETZ

the name — Northern Cheyenne Reservation was given to the present home ground of the tribe.

For a while, the Federal Government tried unsuccessfully to incorporate the Northern Cheyenne with their traditional enemies and neighbors the Crow, as well as with homesteaders moving into the surrounding areas.

So few folks reside on the reservation that people seem to be unobtrusive here. Total population is 5,400 with 4,200 of those being enrolled tribal members. As other reservations witnessed much of their land sold to whites, the Cheyenne avoided this pitfall and today more than 99 percent is owned by individual tribal members or their government. In the 1960s, a resolution gave the Tribe first option to buy if any members were considering selling their land.

After suffering for many years with an inefficient administration, an extremely effective form of government consisting of a president, vice president and ten council members was adopted. The two leaders serve four-year terms, while the council terms are staggered four-year stints. Elections are held every two years and a mix of up to five new council members join the council while five retire if they are not re-elected. In this way consistency and experience are maintained.

The tribe is proud of the fact that they are trying to develop the economy from within and through input from members of the Reservation's districts rather than only by means of government funding. This is what the Partners for Community Development Action (a grassroots based organization) does. They have had an interest in tourism, but they found through a needs assessment conducted on the Reservation that the majority of the tribal membership favor economic development such as small businesses and cottage industries.

Five communities make up today's reservation: Busby, Lame Deer, Ashland (which includes Rabbit Town), Birney and Muddy. All are participating in determining their economic future.

Logging, once a major part of the economy, is now diminished. The Baby Dean Fire from south of Busby to Buffalo Jump destroyed 64,000 acres of timber in 1994 and the Early Bird Fire that blew up in the summer of 1988, scorching 32,000 acres from Crazy Head Spring to Garfield Peak, are largely to blame. Another hindrance is the closure of the Ashland Sawmill, which put 70 tribal members out of work. An agreement is in the process and hopefully the mill will be running again soon.

The Northern Cheyenne take pride in their scholastic opportunities. The fully accredited Chief Dull Knife College, situated in Lame Deer not only offers quality post-secondary academic and vocational degrees, but also promotes Cheyenne leadership and cultural values. Striving to provide the young people on the Reservation with a connection to their history, Cheyenne language courses are offered at the College, high schools and St. Labre Mission.

A private school for the Northern Cheyenne and the Crow, as well as whites,

St. Labre at Ashland had an interesting beginning. While stationed at Fort Keogh near Miles City in 1884, a Catholic solider informed his Bishop of the sad state of the Cheyenne people along the Tongue River. The Bishop in turn saw to it that land was purchased and four nuns were sent from the Midwest to establish a school and Mission for the Indians. Today, with approximately 750 students, it is a major center for the Cheyenne's ethnic and educational outlook. Funding comes from all forms of philanthropy and the organization provides more than 300 jobs.

In recent years, it was documented that the entire reservation was underlined by a very high grade of coal, forcing the Northern Cheyenne to face the possibility of its development. Due to concerns of impacts to the environment and cultural beliefs including protecting the water, which is of great spiritual importance to the Cheyenne people, the large coal reserves for the most part remain untouched.

Between 1966 and 1971, exploratory lease permits were arranged with several coal corporations. In 1972, a coal company made the tribe an offer that would have put more than 70 percent of their lands under the control of outside energy entities. Much of the tribe was opposed to this and hard-fought attempts were made to have the US Government cancel the earlier leases, which was finally done in 1978.

Much of this position comes from the Northern Cheyenne's enlightened and progressive attitude toward their environment. Simply put, they regard the natural world as a living thing. Major Robinson, construction project manager for the newly developing Youth Services Center and an activist in an organization called Partners for Community Development Action, relates, "It isn't that we are against development but rather we are for our environment … if we give up the environment, we give up everything … we lose ourselves."

A major cultural edifice on the reservation that attracts numerous visitors is the Deer Medicine Rocks. Inscribed by infantrymen, passing tribes and Chief Sitting Bull, these fascinating pictographs give insight into the past.

Presently on private land, the tribe is working to preserve this important landmark of Native American history on the Montana plains. Near here, on June 6, 1876, the great Sioux Chief Sitting Bull held a Sun Dance to entreat the Great Spirit for help defeating the white man. Beneath the shadow of these rocks, in a vision he saw two soon-to-be Indian victories, the battle of the Little Big Horn and the Battle of Rosebud Creek.

Crow scouts traveling with US Cavalry, upon viewing the carved signs of Sitting Bull's vision on the rocks, warned the commanders of the message and wanted to leave; however, the Army leaders could only visualize their own victory and refused to listen.

On June 23, 1876, Custer was on the way to his complete defeat at the Little Big Horn, and camped about 12 miles to the north of the Deer Medicine Rocks on the Rosebud River. Here, horseshoe nails, buttons, spoons and rocks from a fire pit have been excavated. His last camp, before crossing the mountains to the Valley of the Little Bighorn, was just south of the town of Busby.

For a mixture of history with color and excitement, take in the powwows on the Fourth of July at Lame Deer and Labor Day at Ashland. On a more serious note, traditional prayer ceremonies are celebrated during the last weekend in June at the Two Moons Annual World Peace Gathering, along with discussions of current affairs pertinent to Native Americans.
—RICK AND SUSIE GRAETZ

MÉTIS AND LITTLE SHELL

Métis evolved from 'country marriages' between predominantly French and Scot men with mostly Cree and Ojibwa women during the fur trade era. They developed a new culture, blending Indian and European lifeways. After Indians, Métis are next to form true communities of family life within Montana's borders. They were the Voyageurs, Coureurs de Bois, and Bois Brûlé of our history. Wherever we hear French or Scot surnames among tribal peoples, Métis heritage is close at hand.

Métis contributed greatly to Montana's history. In 1801, they created a large spoke wheel attached to a horse travois, inventing the Red River cart. This was the first use of the wheel in the Northwest, allowing the fur trade to continue onto the Plains. There were Cruzatte, Charbonneau, LaBiche, and Revais of the Corps of Discovery. In 1806, Métis Jocko Finley cut a trace across the divide for David Thompson on his trek to the Pacific. The Jocko Valley is named for him.

In 1815, Métis drove the first livestock onto the Plains. By 1840, their cattle covered the Upper Missouri and Milk River country to the Front Range.

From 1841 to 1854 the Hudson's Bay Company recruited Métis to settle Columbia River country to head off American immigration during the fight over Oregon Territory. Many Métis stayed in Montana, bringing fuller presence to the culture group.

During that period, the Métis Grant Clan located in Deer Lodge country. Aware of the decline of the fur trade, they bartered provisions for worn out livestock on the Mormon and Oregon Trail. They pastured the cattle, bred healthy stock, and began the first major cattle enterprise in Montana. The Clan father, Richard, was a Chief Trader for the HBC at Fort Hall, Idaho. The Grants built a ranch modeled on HBC forts all over fur trade territory. The Chief Factor's House exists today as the Grant-Kohrs Ranch, a US National Historic Site.

In 1853, Governor Isaac Stevens began his trip across the Northern Plains to survey a northern Pacific railroad route from St. Paul to Puget Sound. He hired Métis Pierre Bottineau to guide the expedition and reported to Congress that the Métis Red River carts were more adapted to Northern Plains travel than any other vehicle.

At Fort Benton, Stevens met a Métis detachment he had arranged to come from Fort Vancouver. Antoine LaPlante was guide. The meeting of those two exploratory teams defined the northern railroad route. From both ends Métis were leaders.

Another consequence of Stevens' Expedition was that John Mullan, surveyor for the team, met the Grants and learned the carts had traversed the divide for over a decade. In 1859, he hired Métis Gabriel Prudhomme as a guide while constructing his military road over a well-worn animal, aboriginal, and Métis cart road. Prudhomme was the same man who, in 1841, met Father De Smet, bringing him in a Métis cart to Montana on his mission to the "Flathead Indians."

In 1862, the overland trail migration to the Northern Rockies began. That first group leaving St. Paul hired Métis guides and followed the route to Fort Union along the Milk River, to Fort Benton, there connecting with the Mullan Road. Once over the divide, they provisioned at the Grant's place, which by that time had 4,000 head of cattle.

Simultaneously, the government subsidized colonization of the Northwest and allocated monies for expeditions from Fort Abercrombie, N.D. to Fort Walla Walla, W.A. Pierre Bottineau, who led the Stevens Expedition, was chosen for the job and once again, Red River carts were the mode of transport. The success of those trips brought the modern era to the Northern Tier.

By 1866, the Grant's sold out to Conrad Kohrs, one of their beef distributors. It was the time of vigilantes and post-Civil War Confederate refugees. Some of the Grant Clan went to the Bitterroot Valley, intermarried with Salish and Kootenai, and settled in the Flathead region. Others put in along the Front Range, forming communities from Augusta to Heart Butte.

Front Range Métis continued to run cattle. The Forque/LaPierre Clan, who had a contract to supply beef to Fort Benton, became prominent. By 1868, Métis from Dakota and Manitoba moved in with relatives along the Front. All the while, great Métis buffalo hunts continued throughout Montana.

In 1879, famous Métis leader Louis Riel arrived among the Milk River Métis camps. He was responsible, upon the fur trade's demise, for creating the Province of Manitoba, which secured Canadian confederation and nationhood. Riel worked for a circumstance similar to Fort Belknap and Fort Peck Reservations for Métis. That was not to be.

Tribes and Métis grasped to hold their own in a world gone awry. Riel treated with Sitting Bull for a unified front to insure a land base. His words held no sway. The Métis would have to go it alone. By 1880, Métis dispersed north of the Medicine Line, others, including Riel, moved south to the Judith Basin, settling Spring Creek and forming what would become Lewistown.

It was a time of great catharsis. The fur trade was over, the buffalo gone, Indians were placed on reservations, cattle barons claimed turf, and homesteaders fenced what had been unharnessed from time immemorial.

Métis were caught in a squeeze of cultural catastrophism. They weren't homesteaders in the euroamerican sense; they didn't "qualify" for a reservation like Indians; and they were capital poor, having few tangible assets. They traveled in old two-wheeled carts, not wagons and carriages like new immigrants. Folks didn't know where to place Métis in the scheme of things, and often bunched them with river rats, thieves, and scoundrels.

Then in 1884, conditions became critical. As mass immigration came to the Plains, pre-existing claims to land and resources were not taken into account. For Métis the land was one. Their traditional historic homeland bridged the United States and Canada. Métis leader Gabriel Dumont rode from Saskatchewan to St. Peter's Mission, west of Cascade, to entreat Riel to go north and lead a resistance stemming encroachment of their land and communities. Riel, who had become a U.S. citizen, married, had a family, and taught at the mission school, went with Dumont.

In what is called the "Northwest Rebellion," Métis and Cree engaged in a fight with the Canadian government where they were defeated. Dumont, with many other Métis and Cree, escaped to Montana. Riel surrendered, hoping to use the court's forum to justify the case for sovereignty. He was found guilty of treason and hanged in 1885. Canada has since recognized the trial as a political sham, that Riel was unjustly sentenced, and acknowledged executing a United States and Montana citizen.

The ostracism of Métis was intense, many saw them as "illegitimate halfbreeds" and they were forced to hideout in coulees, breaks, and canyons. By the 1890s, it reached such a degree that communities petitioned the government to attend to the "halfbreed problem."

Then in 1896, a deal was struck with Canada. The US Army sent Buffalo Soldiers from Fort Assiniboine, led by Lt. John J. Pershing, on a human cattle drive, herding Métis down the Front Range to Helena, Butte, over to Missoula, and back to Great Falls. Most were put on cattle cars and shipped to Lethbridge, Alberta; some were force marched to the border. A number of descendents of that debacle yet reside in Alberta, though most returned. They came to be called the "Landless Indians," and were comprised of three bands, the Little Bear, Stone Child, and Little Shell. It was then that Hill 57 in Great Falls, Moccasin Flats, Buckskin Flats, and Breedtowns began to form on the outskirts of other communities. Métis scavenged a living on the margins of a newly forming "civilized" Montana society.

Métis slipped into the realm of "concealed history," and it wasn't until just before World War I when the frontier was over, institutions of statehood had taken hold and threats of Indian uprisings were buried at Wounded Knee, that compassion for the Red Man became safe politics.

Public outcry flip-flopped. Calls came to attend to the "Landless Indians." With such luminaries as Charlie Russell, who learned from Métis cowhands in the Judith, public pressure resulted in formation of Rocky Boy's Reservation

Unlike other Montana tribes, the Metis originally were landless. RICK AND SUSIE GRAETZ

in 1915. Poor planning and hard decisions left the Little Shell Band out of the accommodation.

Since then, Little Shell have sought their own sanctuary. Settled Métis enclaves took in their cousins, Breedtowns and Moccasin Flats became entrenched, many married into Tribes, and some forsook their heritage blending into dominant society. Since the 1930s, Montana has formally recognized the Little Shell Tribe. They remain a cohesive people, with their government, social, and cultural structure intact. In 2000, they received provisional federal recognition as a sovereign nation. Final determination still pends in 2003. Although some Little Shell believe they "wait for a day that will never come," no one can deny their central role in Montana's history. Gathering strength from their difficult past, be assured the Métis will flourish in Montana's future.

—NICHOLAS PETERSON VROOMAN

MISSOURI RIVER

"... by every rule of nomenclature, the Missouri being the main stream and the upper Mississippi the tributary, the name of the former should have been given precedence, and the great-river should have been called Missouri from the Rocky Mountains to the Gulf of Mexico."

MANY PEOPLE, ESPECIALLY MONTANANS, AGREE WITH THIS UNKNOWN AUTHOR'S statement. However, the Mississippi was explored first and thus designated the primary stem, leaving the Missouri to receive tributary status. Also included in the argument is whether or not the Yellowstone River, the Missouri's other major partner, should have received top billing ... another question for the ages.

When the Missouri finally contacts the Mississippi, it has covered 2,546 miles, making it longer than the entire Mississippi and more than three times the length of the Yellowstone.

Whatever the Missouri's national standing, for Montana it was a lifeline ... a moving highway that gave birth to the state. On the way to the nation's heartland, it collects the state's memories and history. It is Montana's great river. One nameless writer, speaking of the attributes of other Montana rivers, said it well. "The Missouri is all these and more ... It is the Milk and Mussleshell, the Wind and the Sun, the Big Hole and the Beaverhead and the Marias, streams of mountains and of plains moving toward their compulsive rendezvous with the distant ocean, carving shadows upon rocks, giving perspective to great spaces almost anesthetic in their dizzying emptiness, reflecting blazing suns and mellow moons, bordering their shores with tender trees of willows sweet to the eyes of men in a nearly treeless land."

While the Yellowstone River's original water sources collect very quickly, within a couple of miles, before sending the Yellowstone on its way, major contributors to the Missouri's beginnings initially cover a great deal of ground and establish significant identifications of their own. Consider the Jefferson with its upstream continuations — the Beaverhead and Red Rock rivers. Together, they take in 294 miles. And when the Jefferson, Madison and Gallatin come together to develop the mother river, each arrives swiftly carrying large quantities of water.

From the melding of its tributaries, this celebrated entity will have covered 734 beautiful Montana river miles before picking up the Yellowstone just across the Montana/North Dakota line. It's important to note that 510 of these miles are actual channel miles, while 223 of them are in reservoirs — 134 miles alone in Fort Peck Lake.

The Missouri's Beginnings

August 12, 1805, Meriwether Lewis penned in his journals, *"the road was still plain, I therefore did not dispare of shortly finding a passage over the mountains and of tasting the waters of the great Columbia this evening. At the distance of four miles further the road took us to the most distant fountain of the waters of the mighty Missouri in search of which we have spent so many toilsome days in wristless nights."* Lewis was describing today's Distant Fountain Spring, part of Trail Creek, flowing from the east side of the Continental Divide at Lemhi Pass. Climbing above the trickle, Lewis became the first known white man to have stepped onto and across the Continental Divide.

In accordance with Lewis and Clark's time, we will be telling their story backward ... this trip is downriver and the Expedition went against the current. Hopefully, this won't cause too much confusion.

However, in terms of the most distant waters, he was a bit off. That honor is reserved for a spring and Hellroaring Creek, coming off the Montana side of the Continental Divide just below 9,846-foot Mt. Jefferson at the extreme eastern end of the Centennial Range, west of Yellowstone National Park. Hellroaring has a short life; it is hastily consumed by Red Rock Creek, which begins just off the Divide below Red Rock Mountain at Lillian Lake, 9,000 feet above sea level.

Standing at the headwaters of the Missouri, at Three Forks on July 28, 1805, Lewis noted, *"Both Capt. C. and myself corrisponded in opinion, with rispect, to the impropriety of calling either of these streams the Missouri and accordingly agreed to name them. we called the S.W. Fork, that which we meant*

Lewis & Clark noted the Crimson Bluffs near Townsend. RICK AND SUSIE GRAETZ

to ascend, Jefferson's river in honor of Thomas Jefferson. the Middle fork we called Madison's River in honor of James Madison, and the S.E. Fork Gallitian's river in honor of Albert Gallitian." For whatever reason, Albert's name was corrupted to Gallatin.

At this point, the three tributaries make their presence well known. The Madison and Jefferson, each close to 100 feet wide, join and cover a short distance before meeting the equally broad Gallatin. Of all three tributaries, the Jefferson, counting its suppliers, drains the largest area and the Gallatin the smallest.

Hellroaring and Red Rock creeks are the Jefferson's source. Red Rock River falls out of the mountains and courses through a most beautiful setting, the Centennial Valley and the Red Rock Lakes National Wildlife Refuge. Slowing to fill Upper and Lower Red Rock lakes, it offers haven and nesting ground for species such as the endangered Trumpeter Swan. At the western end of the valley, the river enters 13-mile-long Lima Reservoir. Until this point, the river has been extending westward. Now, beyond the man-made lake, it begins a northwesterly setting until it meets Clark Canyon Reservoir and the waters of Horse Prairie Creek entering from the west. *"The Most Distant Fountain Spring"* as labeled by Lewis, and Trail Creek is at the upper end of Horse Prairie.

In the Corps of Discovery's time, Red Rock River and Horse Prairie Creek coupled in an area the Captains christened Shoshone Cove near their Camp Fortunate (now buried by the waters of Clark Canyon Reservoir). From this point north to the Three Forks, the explorers called the entire stream *"Jefferson's river."* Today, where the creek and river convene somewhere under the reservoir, the Beaverhead River is born and flows forth, switching in and out of narrow canyons and wide valleys before partnering with the Ruby River. A short ways beyond the town of Twin Bridges, it meets the Big Hole River. It is from this point that the present Jefferson River runs to the Three Forks.

The Madison River gains its foothold where the Gibbon and Firehole rivers meet in western Yellowstone National Park. The Firehole begins on the Madison Plateau and Continental Divide just south of Old Faithful near Shoshone Lake. During its journey to meet the Gibbon River at the Park's Madison Junction, it runs north through three geyser basins.

The Grebe Lake area, northwest of the Grand Canyon of the Yellowstone, gives the Gibbon its start. From here it points west taking in two geyser basins, several rapids, and a plunge of 84 feet over Gibbon Falls before finding the Firehole.

From this confluence, the newly made Madison, heading west to northwest, passes herds of bison and elk before crossing out of the Park. It takes a brief rest in Hebgan and Quake lakes (site of a major earthquake in 1959) before rushing full of life into the spacious Madison Valley, where it holds court as one of Montana's premiere fly-fishing destinations. Moving north, between the Madison and Gravelly mountain ranges, it spreads out in Ennis Lake,

A favorite fishing area near Craig. RICK AND SUSIE GRAETZ

then squeezes into Bear Trap Canyon on its way to the Gallatin Valley and its destiny to begin the Missouri.

In the northwest corner of Yellowstone National Park, Three Rivers Peak and Gallatin Lake send off the Gallatin River. It tumbles through a beautiful valley, then eases into Gallatin River Meadows — a favorite for backcountry skiers — before leaving the Park and wedging itself into the constricted and magnificent Gallatin River Canyon, formed by steep rises of the Gallatin Range looking down from the east and the Madison Range across the way. The abrupt demise of the canyon southwest of Bozeman allows the river to spill into the ample and fertile Gallatin Valley and on to the Three Forks.

A hallmark of southwest Montana is its grand valleys ... sage-filled bottomlands surrounded by distant high peaks. The Madison, Gallatin and Jefferson rivers traverse such country.

Leaving The Three Forks

The making of the Missouri at its headwaters' area is a labyrinth of channels, willow bottoms and a general mix of wetlands. From here, it begins an odyssey, heading forth as the river that played an enormous role in the creation of a state. As a route for western expansion, the Missouri River had few equals. Headwaters State Park, at the forks, has excellent interpretive signs and displays documenting the river's illustrious past.

Almost immediately upon departing the Three Forks, the newly formed Missouri is neatly tucked into a mini-gorge. Then, only 16 miles from its inception, the Toston Reservoir and Dam decelerate its flow. After traversing the "Little Gates of the Mountains," so noted on Clark's map of July 25, 1805, as *"2d range of mts — little gate,"* near the small village of Toston, the river will soon ply the last of the big southwest valleys. Officially established when the post office opened in 1882 and named after a local rancher, Tosten bills itself as "the first town on the Missouri."

Wandering north between the Bridger and Belt mountains on its east flank and the Elkhorn Mountains to the west, it finds its way to the Prickly Pear Valley and the Helena area.

Early on the morning of July 24, 1805, Lewis and his men *"passed a remarkable bluff of a crimson coloured earth on Stard. intermixed with Stratas of black and brick red slate."* These are now called the Crimson Bluffs and are located about a mile southwest of Townsend.

Like many Montana communities that were tied to the coming of the rails, Townsend's title comes from a connection to the railroads. In this case it was named for Mrs. Charles Wright, whose husband was president of the Great Northern at one time. Her maiden name was Townsend. At first, the community was called Centerville, but the name changed when the steel road reached the area in 1883. The newspaper in Helena said it would soon become one of the most important towns in Montana and called it the "metropolis of the Missouri Valley." This, the seat of Broadwater County, owed its prosperity to the surrounding ranches and farms. Recreation on the Missouri and Canyon Ferry Lake now adds to the town's well being.

Somewhere along today's lake, in the mid-to-late-1800s, John Oakes ran a ferry to access the gulches, including Confederate, in the Big Belt Mountains. The Missouri's channel he crossed was in a canyon, hence the name Canyon Ferry. A 30-foot-high dam was built in 1889, and construction on the replacement, present-day Canyon Ferry Dam began in May 1948, and was completed in June 1954. The resulting 26-mile-long Canyon Ferry Lake has 76 miles of shoreline.

By this time, the river has covered 42 miles of gentle meanders. Now, it prepares to enter an almost 70-mile-long stretch of the series of Canyon Ferry, Hauser and Holter lakes and dams (all three of which were built to harness the Missouri and create electric power; recreation was secondary). In that section, it will have lost only a little over 500 feet of elevation since the Three Forks.

Hauser Dam was completed in 1911 by Sam Hauser to bring power to the mines in Butte and the smelter in Anaconda. Holter Dam came on line in 1918, and was named for Anton Holter. Both men were Helena area mining tycoons and businessmen. Sam Hauser was a partner with Granville Stuart in the famous DHL Ranch north of Lewistown.

Between Townsend and Helena, the river is covering country that gold settled. On the east side of Canyon Ferry Lake, up in the Big Belt Mountains, was an extraordinarily rich placer gold find. In December of 1864, two Confederate soldiers struck it big here. Naming this site Confederate Gulch after their political leanings, they built four cabins to settle into for the winter. The path in the snow among the cabins formed a perfect diamond, so they christened the camp Diamond City. At one time, 5,000 people crowded in the narrow canyon, and it was said that some of the hillside prospectors garnered more than $1,000 worth of gold from a single pan of gravel. The big boom was over by 1870, and in 1880 only a couple of people remained. Today, not even the town's footings are left; washed away by hydraulic mining once townsfolk realized they had assembled their homes atop the gold.

On the afternoon of July 14, 1864, four men, nursing their bad luck in the gulches and camps of Alder Gulch and Grasshopper Creek to the southwest, and who had been following rumors of gold to the north in the Kootenai country, returned to a gulch they had prospected a bit earlier. This was to be their "last chance." Digging to bedrock in a canyon below today's Mount Ascension and Mount Helena, they hit pay dirt. A camp called Last Chance (later Helena) was mapped out and, as other would-be miners and prospectors migrated to the Prickly Pear Valley, became an overnight boom.

The search for gold continued in the myriad surrounding gulches and canyons including those in the Big Belt Mountains. More ore was found and additional camps, most of which have long since disappeared, were established. Today, as the Missouri passes remnants of those livelier times, she remembers how it was.

The Eldorado Bar, once a gold placer claim, is now worked by current day prospectors looking for sapphires in the gravels just off of the Missouri River.

Downstream from Canyon Ferry Lake, and northwest of Helena, the Missouri's waters edge the western perimeter of the Gates of the Mountains Wilderness. Here, the river's channel narrows to knife its way through steep limestone walls. Lewis's journal notes of July 19, 1805, read in part: *"... this evening we entered much the most remarkable clifts that we have yet seen. these clifts rise from the waters edge on either side perpendicularly to the hight of about 1200 feet ... the towering and projecting rocks in many places seem ready to tumble on us ... for the distance of 5¾ miles ... the river appears to have woarn a passage just the width of it's channel or 150 yds. it is deep from side to side nor is ther in the 1st 3 miles of this distance a spot ... on which a man could rest the soal of his foot ... from the singular appearance of this place I called it the gates of the rocky mountains."*

When the river passes through the Gates, it takes on the Adels, an extension of the Big Belt Mountains. Here, held back by the last of the upriver dams, it fills Holter Lake. After the dam, the Missouri sweeps by the east side of a recreation community, named for Warren Craig who built the first cabin here in 1886. It is now relatively free to run unobstructed for 89 miles until meeting the Sun River at Great Falls.

As the Adels trail off, the Missouri bids farewell to the Northern Rocky Mountains. Near the community of Cascade, a sleepy farm and ranch town with one foot on the prairie and the other in the mountains, the mighty river makes a transition from big valleys and peaks to the open plain where it will hit full stride with space to spread and grow. Cascade was named after waterfalls on the Missouri upriver or as some accounts state, for the great falls of the Missouri 30 miles to the north — this would seem to be a bit of a stretch.

The Missouri Meets The Prairie

When the river puts Cascade behind, it looks out toward the sunset and the distant Rocky Mountain Front, the range of mountains that gave Montana its label, "Land of the Shining Mountains." It also observes to its west an isolated landform, "Charlie Russell Square Butte," used by the famous Montana artist in several of his paintings. Geologically speaking, this is a large laccolith, an intrusion of ingenious rock formed as a large blister of magma between layers of sedimentary rock. Meriwether Lewis's writings of July 15, 1805, noted, "...we *have now passed Fort Mountain on our right it appears to be about ten miles distance."* From his description of it being flat topped and steep on all sides, it is certain he was describing the same formation.

On July 18, Lewis mentioned, *"we passed the entrance a beautifull river 80 yards wide which falls in a Lard. (left side) Which in honour of Mr. Roberts Smith secretary of the navy we called Smiths River. This stream meanders through*

Above the town of Cascade. RICK AND SUSIE GRAET

a most lovely valey to the S.E. for about 25 miles when it enters the Rocky mountains and is concealed from our view." The Smith River, one of Montana's favorites for fly fishing and floating, works its way out of the Little Belt Mountains, then forges west to the Missouri near the hamlet of Ulm. A line of the Great Northern Railway came through in 1887 and what was once part of a ranch established by Bill Ulm became a town. Next door to Ulm sits Ulm Pishkun State Park. Pishkun translates as "deep bloody kettle" in Blackfoot referring to the millions of bison the Natives killed here over two thousand years. An interpretive center tells the story of the many tepee rings found there and how tribes used the bison cliff jump.

The Great Falls of The Missouri

Closing in on the city of Great Falls, a succession of soon to be met dams causes the river to slow and relinquish its freedom to the act of creating power. No longer looking like a big river, it now takes on an appearance of a lake — one of the large inlets is even called Broadwater Bay.

This segment of the river was highly significant in the annals of Lewis and Clark. During their 1804–1805 winter encampment at Fort Mandan, near present-day Bismarck North Dakota, the Corps learned from the Hidatsa Indians that one of the principal landmarks along the water route to the Rocky Mountains was a "great falls."

On the south side of Great Falls, the White Bear Islands, so labeled by Captain Clark owing to the many grizzlies inhabiting them, come up first. They served as the base for the Upper Portage Camp during the very difficult traverse around the falls. When Lewis and Clark came through this country, these giant creatures were yet prairie animals. The islands not only served a feast of washed up buffalo carcasses for the bears, but the sand was soft, enabling them to easily excavate winter dens alongside the cottonwood trees.

The site of the Upper Portage Camp is still visible today, although time has silted in the channel that existed between it and the island they used for storage. The former riverbed is a very obvious depression running through a hay field. A lone cottonwood stands on the edge of what was once the riverbank.

Downriver from the islands on the west edge of Great Falls, the Sun River (another Hidatsa landmark) enters the now lake-like Missouri. Lewis's entry for June 14, 1805 included, *"I determined to procede … convinced that it was the river the Indians call 'medicine' (Sun)."*

Five barriers — Black Eagle, Rainbow, Cochran, Ryan and Morony dams, all within 12 miles of each other, have obliterated the wondrous beauty Lewis described on June 13, 1805. After questioning whether or not the Corps had made the right decision concerning the Marias River not being the Missouri and that they were following the correct waterway, Lewis was desperately searching for the falls the Hidatsa had foretold of, *"… whin my ears were* saluted with the agreeable sound of a fall of water and advancing a little further I saw the spray arrise above the plain like a collumn of smoke ... which soon began to make a roaring too tremendous to be mistaken for any cause short of the great falls of the Missouri." Lewis clambered down a steep cliff in order "to gaze on this is sublimely grand specticle ... the grandest sight I ever beheld."

Struck by a feeling of complete inadequacy to put into words the power and splendor of the sight before him, Lewis wished for the talent of an artist "that I might be enabled to give to the enlightened world some just idea of this truly magnificent and sublimely grand object ... to give the world some faint idea of an object which at this moment fills me with such pleasure and astonishment, and which of it's kind I will venture to ascert is second to but one in the known world." Being so overwhelmed, he set camp on the bank below the falls, since greatly diminished by Ryan Dam.

The next day, Lewis headed off alone to scout the river above the falls. A quick five miles brought him to an unexpected second water cascade he named Crooked Falls. Then being led by "a tremendous roaring above me," Lewis was assaulted by the scene of another "great cataract" that "rivals for glory" the one "which I had discovered yesterday." This once glorious Rainbow Falls has been robbed of much of her splendor by the construction of Rainbow Dam. Almost immediately, Lewis stumbled onto another waterfall (no longer visible); becoming jaded he explained, "in any other neighborhood but this, such a cascade would probably be extolled for it's beauty and magnifficence, but here I passed it by with but little attention ... At a distance of 2½ miles I arrived at another cataract of 26 feet ... below this falls at a little distance a beautiful little Island ... is situated about the middle of the river. In this Island on a Cottonwood tree an Eagle has placed her nest." Another landmark complete with the noble bird's abode, just as the Hidatsa had described it!

The present-day name came more than 70 years later when Thomas P. Roberts, a railway engineer doing survey work, was nearly attacked by a black eagle while viewing the falls. Upon noticing the bird's nest in a cottonwood tree on an island below the thundering curtain of water, he recalled Lewis's mention of the same, and thought it fitting to christen the site Black Eagle Falls.

Somehow, something had been lost in the translation at Fort Mandan that past winter. Initially, from the information given by the Hidatsa, the Captains assumed there would be just one falls and that it would only take a half-day to get around it. With a total of five major falls each separated by rapids, obviously the portage was going to take much longer.

On the 16th of June 1805, Captain Clark, with an extremely ill Sacajawea accompanying him, halted below the confluence of Belt Creek and the Missouri, ("portage creek," to the Expedition), setting up what would become the base camp for their month-long assault around the "great falls." As part of Lewis's effort to cure the young mother, he used the water of a sulphur

June 13, 1805, Captain Lewis reaches the first of five "great falls," at today's Great Falls.
RICK AND SUSIE GRAETZ

spring that is located across the Missouri from the mouth of Belt Creek and called Sacajawea or Sulphur springs. The actual area of the Lower Portage Camp may be glimpsed looking downriver from Sulphur Springs toward a wide flat spot on the opposite shore. Owing to the rock outcrops on either side of the river, it is doubtful the channel has changed much with time. And the rapids Lewis details in his journal are still in place.

To make the portage, the men ascended Belt Creek, crossed the prairie near Malmstrom Air Force Base hauling the boats to the southwest edge of Great Falls, then followed Box Elder Creek (Willow Run in the journals) to the White Bear Islands and the Upper Portage Camp on the Missouri, a distance of about 18 miles.

Less than two miles below Black Eagle Dam, the world's "shortest river," the Roe, extends to the Missouri from its source at Giant Springs. A sign placed by the Lincoln School fifth grade class of 1987–1988 reads, "The Roe River is the world's shortest river, having an average length of 201 feet, as recognized by the Guinness Book of World Records. Lewis and Clark were the first white people to see the river in 1805. The name "Roe" means fish eggs and comes from its proximity to the State Fish Hatchery." The spring is part of the 3,400-acre Giant Springs State Park, which stretches for 14.5 miles along the Missouri at Great Falls.

The springs themselves are a wonderful natural phenomenon. Drs. Dave Alt and Don Hyndman, University of Montana geology professors, and authors of Roadside Geology of Montana, explain, "... enormous volumes of water

115

well up through fractures in the Kootenai sandstone and pour into the river. The great flow of these springs poses an interesting problem because the sandstone does not contain nearly enough open space to produce water in such quantity.

"It seems likely that the water discharging from Giant Springs must be rising from the Madison Limestone, which lies several hundred feet below the surface. Limestones are the usual source of such large springs because they commonly contain caverns capable of conducting an enormous flow. If the Madison Limestone is indeed the source of Giant Springs, then the water probably comes from the Little Belt Mountains about 35 miles south east of Great Falls. That is the closest area where the Madison Limestone comes to the surface."

Paris Gibson of Minnesota read of the wonder of the "great falls" in the journals of Lewis and Clark and in 1880, he traveled to Montana to view them for himself. Rather than admiring the thundering cataracts as the Captains had, Gibson felt that the water simply running over the falls was a waste and saw the possibility of dollars and power being generated instead. Gibson knew he would be able to persuade his friend Jim Hill, architect of the Great Northern Railway, to send a rail line to his city.

Young Paris returned to the falls again in 1882 and filed for ownership of the land that would grow to be Great Falls. In the summer of 1884, he set about building the town site and by 1887, the Montana Central Railway arrived, linking the city with mining camps and other towns in southwest Montana.

As Butte's Anaconda Company grew, new places with cheap power were needed to produce the copper. Gibson's young city by the cascades had all the right ingredients. A new smelter was built on the north side of the river and a dam was constructed to supply the needed electricity. Black Eagle was the first of the magnificent falls to go under. The other dams fell in place over time.

Solid and staid, the grown-up city of Great Falls is the anchor of Montana's best grain growing region — The Golden Triangle. While agriculture rules the economy, the city is filled with art museums and historical venues — just the kind of town to raise a family.

After managing Maroney, the last of the dams, the Missouri will travel 32 miles, for the most part out of sight of roads and people, to Fort Benton. When it finds "Benton," the river will have journeyed 245 miles from its origin and lost 1,386 feet in elevation.

Sixteen miles before Fort Benton, the river passes the Carter Ferry, the first of three commuter "boats" serving backcountry roads and used mainly by ranchers and farmers. Working off of a cable system, the ferries are rudimentary barges with a small engine house on one side. A person needing service presses a buzzer, alerting the operator in his home, then awaits his cruise across the water.

The Virgelle Ferry at Virgelle and Coal Banks Landing is 39 miles below Fort Benton, and the McClelland operation crosses 64 miles downriver from Virgelle. The Carter and Virgelle "boats" are near regularly traveled roads while McClelland isn't close to anywhere. It crosses the Missouri in a very remote segment of the Upper Missouri River Breaks National Monument.

Just before Fort Benton, the Missouri comes into view of the highway at a sweeping, open big bend. An interpretive site, high above the rivers west flank, looks down on cultivated land inside river's curve. From 1845 until 1846, this was the site of Fort Benton's predecessor, Fort Lewis, an American Fur Company trading post.

On the Missouri, Fort Benton has great significance. With the settling in of the first residents during the autumn of 1846, "Benton" began its reign as the oldest continuing town in the state, and hence Montana's birth place. From 1860 until 1888, it was the destination of all steamboat navigation.

A quiet Front Street of today faces the old levee and river. Big cottonwoods and grass have taken the place of the raucous scene of days long gone. At one time, from the moment the ice melted in the spring until the river froze in the fall, the one and one-half-mile-long levee never slept. It was piled with goods going out to the mining camps of southwest Montana or shipments of gold headed east.

Agriculture keeps Fort Benton going now, but the town hasn't forgotten its past. Historic signs and relics of the 1880s line the shady levee. And the venerable Grand Union Hotel, built in 1882, still proudly operates on the banks of the Missouri.

Fort Benton, mile marker 0 for the Upper Missouri River Breaks National Monument. RICK AND SUSIE GRAETZ

From this point on, for the next 300 miles, the big river will maneuver through some of the most storied and magnificent prairie landscape in the West. Save for tiny Loma, guardian of a major tributary, the Marias, the towns are removed from any contact with the river and the importance of the terrain extends much farther from the waterway than it does upstream. Let's call it a giant eco-system.

Upper Missouri River Breaks National Monument

In October 1976, 149 miles of the fabled Missouri River from Fort Benton downstream to the Fred Robinson Bridge and an adjacent 135,350 acres of land gained designation as a National Wild and Scenic River. On January 18, 2001, it was granted National Monument status.

Heading north and east from Fort Benton, mile zero in the Monument, the Big River flows calmly; even the once deadly, steamboat catching rapids such as Deadman and Dauphine hardly make a ripple on the surface. Silently, it passes through fertile river bottoms past some of the west's most remote and least inhabited country. Beautiful rock formations, austere badlands and magnificent river canyon and prairie scenery, coupled with the historical lure of the place, bring floaters back many times over.

The great Indian Nations knew the river first. West of the White Cliffs (about 51 water miles from Fort Benton) was the homeland of the mighty Blackfeet. Below this terrain, the Gros Ventre, Assiniboine and Cree claimed hunting rights.

Lewis and Clark came into what is now the National Monument on May 24, 1805, making camp three miles upstream from today's Fred Robinson Bridge. Pulling the boats upriver, sometimes in water to their armpits, and walking through mud, the men of the Corps of Discovery toiled hard to ascend the "Big Muddy." The explorers exited today's Monument segment of the Missouri on June 13, 1805.

The record of their days spent in this 149-mile length captures some of the most noteworthy moments of the entire Expedition.

On June 2, 1805, the Corps reached the mouth of the Marias River, about 22 river miles from Benton. Camp that evening, beginning a ten-day stay, was at the meeting of the Missouri and Marias rivers. In 1950, a flood diverted the course of the Marias River forcing it to enter the Missouri nearly one mile farther upstream, thereby altering a physical location in history. The former channel is still visible along the cliffs near Loma.

Up until June 2, the information supplied by the Hidatsa Indians during their winter 1804 –1805 encampment proved to be most accurate. On that date however, the Corps encountered something not shown on the crude maps they possessed. The Missouri they had been following for so many months appeared now to split into a north and south fork. The Indians had made no mention of another major waterway coming from the north after the Milk River. They only specified that the explorers would meet a great waterfall, and then soon thereafter the river would enter the mountains.

The two leaders were fairly sure the south fork was the Missouri, but the crew was convinced otherwise. Joseph Whitehouse, a member of the Corps, noted in his journal on June 3, *"our officers and all the men differ in their opinions which river to take."* Characteristic of their excellent leadership, the Captains agreed to explore both branches so all would be assured.

Lewis on June 3, 1805, scripted, *"to this end an investigation of both streams was the first thing to be done ... accordingly we dispatched two light canoes with three men in each up those streams; we also sent out several small parties by land with instructions to penetrate the country as far as they conveniently can permitting themselves time to return this evening and indeavour if possible to discover the distant bearing of those rivers by ascending the rising grounds ... Capt. C. & myself stroled out it to the top of the hights in the fork of these rivers from whence we had an extensive and most inchanting view ... to the south we saw a range of lofty mountains"* (most likely the Highwoods, east of Great Falls).

The *"top of the hights"* the Captains climbed is reached via a dirt road just south of Loma off Hwy 87 and now marked as Decision Point.

After the return of the scouting parties, there was still much uncertainty. It was then decided to explore farther; Clark would follow the south fork (Missouri) and Lewis the north (Marias).

June 4, 1805, the two groups separated. It didn't take Clark long to deduce that the south fork was the correct way to go. Lewis meanwhile, traveled up the north fork a considerable distance (60 to 70 miles) before coming to the same conclusion. On June 6, 1805 he wrote, *"I now became well convinced that this branch of the Missouri had its direction too much to the north for our rout to the Pacific, and therefore determined to return ..."* So assured that the river he was following was not the Missouri, on June 8, Lewis named it Maria's River for his cousin.

On May 31, 1805, the Corps spent the night at one of the Upper Missouri's most scenic campsites, the White Cliffs and Eagle Creek. Lewis penned some of his most poetic words, describing not only the toil of his men, but also the incredible beauty of the scenery.

"... the men are compelled to be in the water even to their armpits, and the water is yet very could ... added to this the banks and bluffs along which they are obliged to pass are so slippery and the mud so tenacious that they are unable to wear their mockersons, and in that situation draging the heavy burthen of a canoe and walking acasionally for several hundred yards over the sharp fragments of rocks ... in short their labour is incredibly painfull and great, yet those faithful fellows bear it without a murmur ... The hills and river Clifts which we passed today exhibit a most romantic appearance. The bluffs of the river rise to the hight of from 2 to 300 feet and in most places nearly perpendicular; they are formed of remarkable white sandstone ... The water in the course of time in decending from

those hills and plains on either side of the river has trickled down the soft sand clifts and woarn it into a thousand grotesque figures, which with the help of a little immagination ... are made to represent eligant ranges of lofty freestone buildings, having their parapets well stocked with statuary; collumns of various sculpture both grooved and plain, are also seen supporting long galleries in front of those buildings; in other places ... we see the remains or ruins of eligant buildings ... the tops of the collumns did not the less remind us of some of those large stone buildings in the U. States ... as we passed on it seemed as if those seens of visionary inchantment would never have an end; for here it is too that nature presents to the view, of the traveler vast ranges of walls of tolerable workmanship, so perfect indeed are those walls that I should have thought that nature had attempted here to rival the human art of masonry had I not, recollected that she had first began her work."

Eagle Creek, in addition to being one of the most picturesque locations along the river and a Lewis and Clark campsite, holds remnants of bison drive lines, Indian processing stations, te'pee rings, rock cairns and flint knapping workshops; all marvelous reminders of the presence of the area's earliest residents. The crew of the government boat Mandan was fond of leaving signs of their passing and their graffiti can still be seen on the river cliffs in several places.

Owing to Indian resistance, whites didn't show up again until 1830, lured, in spite of the dangers, by the fur trade. In the summer of 1831, Fort Piegan Trading Post was established at the confluence of the Marias and Missouri rivers. Only lasting through the winter, it was replaced several miles upriver by Fort McKenzie.

Prince Maximilian, a German scientist, came to the new fort in 1833 to study the Indians and collect animal and plant specimens. Artist Karl Bodmer, who accompanied him, showed the world through his paintings what the Upper Missouri looked like.

Built late in 1832 to trade with the Piegans, Bloods and Blackfeet, the life of Fort McKenzie was cut short in January of 1844, when a party of young Blackfeet warriors returning from the Crow country asked admittance to the fort and were refused by Francois A. Chardon, a hotheaded Frenchman and his lieutenant, Alexander Harvey. The warriors retaliated by stealing and killing some of the fort's livestock. A well-armed party pursued them, but in the fray, Chardon's negro slave was killed and scalped. Vowing revenge, they loaded the fort's cannon with 150 or so lead bullets, aimed it at the approach to the main gate and waited for the next Indian trading party.

In February, a small band of either Piegans or Bloods arrived to trade. Before Harvey could put fire to the cannon, Chardon fired his rifle, killing one chief as the other Indians scattered. Five were hit and two were killed (although some stories say as many as 30 were killed instantly). Further trading at the fort was impossible. Chardon and company moved downriver to the mouth of the Judith about April 5, 1844. Fort McKenzie was then burned either by whites or Indians, and to this day the site is known as Brulé (burned) Bottom.

At first, the river was used extensively for fur trade by keel boats, dug-out canoes and mackinaws. Then on June 17, 1859, a small steamboat called the Chippewa reached Brulé Bottom and became the first to navigate the Upper Missouri. Short on fuel, concerned by a falling river and being yet 12 miles from Fort Benton, Charles P. Chouteau, who was in charge, decided to unload the freight at this point and turn back.

There was no giving up though, and the wild Missouri soon became the lifeline and main "highway" into Montana Territory. On July 2, 1860, the steamers Chippewa and Key West reached Fort Benton just prior to the discovery of gold in the Territory. The rush for the glittering metal started in 1862 at Bannack, followed by Alder Gulch (Virginia City) in 1863 and Last Chance Gulch (Helena) in 1864. Folks came to seek their fortune and steamboats provided the way; an estimated 10,000 in all came on the river vessels. All manners of characters used the river, walked its banks and hid out in its canyons and badlands.

Cow Island, a landmark along the river, is where steamers had to unload freight when the water was too low to make it to Fort Benton. This was also a major ford for Indians and bison.

In the fall of 1877, military supplies had been unloaded. Chief Joseph and his starving band of Nez Perce on their flight to Canada crossed the Missouri here, and after failing to be able to peacefully negotiate for the use of goods with the small military group guarding them, took what they needed and burned the rest.

Woodhawk Creek and Coal Banks Landing were places where steamboats picked up the wood fuel they needed from the woodhawkers who lived lonely and threatened lives on the banks. Familiar sights along the river, such as Steamboat, LaBarge and Pilot rocks, were given their names by the big boat captains.

Settlers followed the would-be prospectors upriver on the sternwheelers, disembarking at points from the Dakota line west.

The steamboat era lasted from 1859 until 1888. Throughout that span, an average of 20 boats a year forged their way up the Missouri through the lands that would eventually become the Upper Missouri River Breaks National Monument and Charles M. Russell Refuge. The years 1860 — 1869 witnessed the highest flow of traffic — 34 boats came through on an average each year. During the 1867 season (spring through early fall), 71 steamboats made it up the river. The last year for the great paddle ships to come up the Missouri was 1888. Previous to that, traffic dwindled some each year. The advent of the railroads into Montana put an end to use of the river as a primary source of transportation Now, migrants to the Territory and later homesteaders traveled on the steel rails to claim land along the Missouri.

After 1910, almost every bottom with enough level ground to make farming worthwhile had been settled. Then, the drought of 1917–1922, combined with extreme weather and isolation, forced most of the "sod busters" off the land. They left as quickly as they had come. Only a few stayed on and are the roots of today's big ranching operations. Eventually the flow and Mother Nature reclaimed much of the land now designated as a National Monument. Faint reminders of these earlier times are still found, but they are lost in the enormity of a mostly unspoiled territory.

The physical geography of this river country is diverse. Rolling hills, table top rims and fertile bottom lands make up the landscape from Fort Benton to Coal Banks, a myriad of coulees and beautiful rock formations stretch from the Eagle Creek and the White Cliffs/Rocks area on through and past Hole-in-the-Wall, then distinctive badlands, steep slopes and wide banks accent the skyline to Fred Robinson Bridge. Here and there, stands of riverside and island cottonwoods add to the river's beauty.

Relief from the water level to the upper rims varies from 400 feet near Fort Benton to more than 1,000 feet in the badlands and breaks areas below Judith Landing. And depths of the river also vary greatly, ranging from a few inches to 15 feet deep.

The White Cliffs/White Rocks country shows some of the most interesting and photogenic scenes on the Upper Missouri. The area's white sandstone crumbles easily while the yellowish-red colored material found here is harder and therefore more erosion resistant. Thus the white pillars with the tinged caps are formed. Toadstools and thin sand stonewalls, common to this area, were created by wind erosion.

Some of the Monument's farthest downstream reaches are actually small desert environments. The badlands, or "les mauvaises terres" as the French trappers called them, are formed when fire or some other disruption destroys the plant cover that normally protects the soil from being eroded. Rainwater hits the denuded surface, compacting it and seeds can't take hold. Runoff then forms gullies and soon, strange looking formations appear.

The namesake of the National Monument, the river breaks, are sculptured by the erosive action of water on the soil and soft rocks underlying the surface. Small gulches and deep canyons are cut out of the higher landscape as streams of rainwater and snowmelt find their paths to the river. The resulting terrain is rough, wild and spectacular.

Weather patterns along this historic waterway vary widely. Summer can bring searing dry heat with temperatures exceeding 100 degrees, violent thunderstorms, heavy rain, and even hail and snow. In winter, north winds whip up ferocious blizzards and the thermometer may lower to 50 degrees below zero, or warm southwest winds can make a January day feel like spring. May and June, although sometimes wet, bring the beauty of wildflowers and green to the landscape and in late September and October, the gold, orange and red of the shoreline and coulees present a magnificent show against a deep blue and cloudless sky.

Vegetation in this environment is diverse and includes groves of cottonwoods, ash, box elder, willows, conifers, grasses, sagebrush, greasewood and low lying riparian growth.

The present lack of cottonwood and willow regeneration is under discussion by the Bureau of Land Management the federal agency charged with management of the river. Silt, carried on the faster, high water brought on by uncontrolled runoff from spring floods, is required to prepare cottonwood seed beds. Because of upstream dams, this no longer happens. Since the dams release less water in the spring than winter, ice jams occur and scour out what seedlings do manage to grow.

Hot weather grazing along the banks also leads to the destruction of newly sprouted cottonwoods. This is an issue the BLM continues to work out with local ranchers. One of the possible solutions is to provide solar powered pumps for water tanks on higher ground. Some operators are voluntarily pulling their stock out of the area during mid-summer.

Wildlife earn a good living along the embankments, coulees and canyons in the sheltered Monument lands. Sixty species of mammals, 230 different kinds of birds and 20 breeds of amphibians and reptiles make this tract of the upper Missouri River and its environs their home. Mule deer, as well as sharp-tailed grouse, are abundant on the slopes and coulees, while the rolling areas above the river bottoms make good habitat for antelope and sage grouse. Golden eagles, prairie falcons and hawks perch and nest in the cliffs above the river.

Badland formations along the upper Missouri. RICK AND SUSIE GRAETZ

Forty-nine varieties of fish have been identified, including gold-eye, sauger, northern pike, sturgeon and walleye. The Upper Missouri River has one of the six remaining paddlefish populations left in the nation.

Even before the lower end of the National Monument is reached, the next great Missouri River prize, the Charles M. Russell National Wildlife Refuge, establishes its upper limit. For ten miles, the Missouri bears the flags of both public treasures to Kipp Landing at the Fred Robinson Bridge.

Incidentally, the bridge was dedicated to Fred Robinson, an elected official of more than 40 years from the Malta area, 60 or so miles to the north. Robinson was the force behind getting the bridge built. Finished in 1959, it allows US Hwy 191 to span the Missouri.

Charles M. Russell National Wildlife Refuge

It's uncommon country ... at once stark, beautiful, imposing and inviting, this Charles M. Russell National Wildlife Refuge. Time has left most of this remarkable landscape with the same appearance as when the indigenous peoples hunted and did battle here. And while some of the wildlife species have disappeared, notably bison and grizzly bears, other animals, including elk and bighorn sheep are coming back strong.

The CMR, as it is commonly referred to, occupies a large swath of Montana's northeast quadrant and is in the center of some of the least inhabited country in the United States. The 1.1 million-acre refuge straddles part of the free flowing Missouri River and takes in the rugged Missouri Breaks, wild prairie grasslands and the 250,000-acre Fort Peck Lake with its 1,600 miles of shoreline. From the western boundary ten miles upstream of the Fred Robinson Bridge near Grand Island, a canoe will cover 150 miles by the time it reaches the spillway of Fort Peck Dam and the eastern perimeter of the refuge. The US Fish and Wildlife Service manages this animal haven.

In many places, the CMR's broken and rough terrain is difficult to negotiate. Nearly 80 percent of the place is made up of steep ridges and a labyrinth of eroded coulees. In wet weather, the underlying shale turns to gumbo, and travel, either by vehicle or on foot, becomes almost impossible.

The mix of landforms of the CMR is impressive. Table-topped uplands give way to rugged ravines, wide and precipitous canyons (some 1,000 feet deep) and spectacular badlands. This much-dissected expanse of ground has been broken by flows of water, such as Seven Blackfeet Creek, Devils Creek, Snow Creek, Hell Creek, the Musselshell River and many smaller, more intermittent creeks. Hence the term "river breaks."

Elevations and relief are low by Montana standards, but when looking up at some of the high points from the bottom of a gulch, the slopes appear as tough to climb as any mountain. When Fort Peck Lake is at full pool, the lowest elevation on the refuge is 2,246 feet. One of the loftiest spots is 3,241 feet on a divide just above the east side of Seven Blackfeet Creek, near the CMR's center.

An open forest of Rocky Mountain juniper, Douglas fir and ponderosa pines covers close to one-third of the refuge. Ponderosa, the dominant tree, is a stunted version of the taller pines that grow west of Montana's Continental Divide. Wildlife use these woodlands for security, and the timber also protects the fragile soils from erosion. Sagebrush and grasslands intersperse the trees and comprise almost 60 percent of the land. Riparian habitats are found along the banks of the Missouri River and many of the smaller creeks.

When flying above the CMR, it is interesting to note that the tree coverage is far more extensive on the south side of the Missouri than to the north. On the south, the forests can extend up to ten miles inland, while in the north they are seldom much more than two or three miles in width. This is especially true east of UL Bend (a U and an L on its back with "feet" sticking up is the shape the river forms here). The slopes ascending from the south banks of the river accumulate more moisture, have better soils and provide a more suitable environment for tree growth than the breaks north of the Missouri.

Fox Hills sandstone and the Hell Creek geologic formations dominate the CMR beyond the southern edge of Fort Peck Lake and the Missouri. The north side of the water was glaciated about 15,000 years ago by continental ice sheets flowing into northeast Montana out of Canada. These glaciers pushed the Missouri River south out of its old channel to its present location (the Milk River now occupies the former Missouri River bed). Scouring glacial ice also removed the quality earth, exposing the fine textured clay-like Bearpaw Shale, which is less conducive to producing vegetation.

Through the centuries, much of the landscape in the southeastern environs of the refuge has been highly eroded by exposure to wind and water. The mudstone and other soils that have been uncovered contain ancient marine life and dinosaur bones. The area continues to yield some of the richest records of prehistoric life in the world.

Enormous expanses of mostly public land (more than two million acres) managed by the Bureau of Land Management surround the Charles M. Russell refuge. Primitive roads cross this BLM land and lead to the CMR.

Unlike most of the refuge, this outlying terrain is predominantly rolling prairie broken by shallow coulees and occasional buttes. Vegetation is predominantly sagebrush, prickly pear cactus and native prairie grass. Rocky Mountain juniper is widely scattered throughout. Drainages that make up the river breaks of the CMR get their start in small draws and deeper gulches of this higher ground beyond the preserve.

The Regions of The CMR

The Missouri River flows freely in the western reaches of the Charles M. Russell National Wildlife Refuge. Its meanders have created wide river bottoms and fertile ground for large stands of cottonwoods, willows and ash trees that provide good white-tailed deer environment. The slopes of the hills in this section are less angular than those farther east, and getting around on foot is easier here than it is downstream.

Large drainages, such as Rock Creek and Sipary Ann Creek, flowing south to the Missouri River from the Little Rocky Mountains and nearby terrain, have dissected the prairie in the northwestern province of the CMR into a north-south pattern of ridges and coulees. South of the Missouri, waterways, including Sand Creek, Two Calf Creek and Crooked Creek flow east to west. Primitive roads follow many of the ridges above these creeks, allowing good access to the protected lands.

In several places on the south side, steep winding roads descend to the river flood plain. As for the north fringe of the river, a road, starting at Hwy 191, parallels the Missouri for about 14 miles. Other byways head north beyond the river toward the Little Rockies and Malta.

In this area, just beyond the Sand Creek Wildlife Station, from a ridge high above the south rim of the Missouri's canyon, on a clear day the horizons extend for up to 100 miles. Many of north central Montana's "island mountain ranges," including the Little Rockies, Big Snowies, Judith, Bear Paw and Moccasins are visible.

Primary access to the western part of the refuge is from above both sides of the Fred Robinson Bridge and Hwy 191.

About 18 miles east of the bridge, the Missouri's progress is slowed as the waters of Fort Peck Lake begin to backup. The flood plain disappears and the river fills the entire channel. When the lake level drops, mud flats appear. Most of the original flood plain of the river is now under the waters of the Fort Peck Lake. At one time, these bottoms provided extensive stands of cottonwoods and riparian land covered by lush vegetation. Lewis and Clark found bison, elk and grizzly bears as they moved along the shore of the river.

From this point east, the river corridor begins to widen. Both sides of the waterway consist of countless coulees and open ponderosa pine forests. As the ebb of water nears the big bend, known as UL Bend, the surface on the north side becomes noticeably flatter and void of trees. Low hills separated by shallow draws blend with level ground; views are distant. As far as the eye can see in any direction, is one of the largest and least disturbed short-grass prairies in the nation. And it supports one of the world's largest networks of prairie dog colonies. The existence of such great numbers of black-tailed prairie dogs on the UL Bend is sustaining the comeback of the black-footed ferret, an endangered and rare mammal. Ferrets need these prairie diggers to survive; they live in their burrows and prey on them. The "Bend" is also a good area to view the colorful mating rituals of sage and sharp-tail grouse.

The horseshoe-shaped landform that makes up the lower portion of the UL Bend region is about seven miles long, one mile across at its narrowest point and 17 miles around. Steamboats plying the Missouri in the mid 1800s

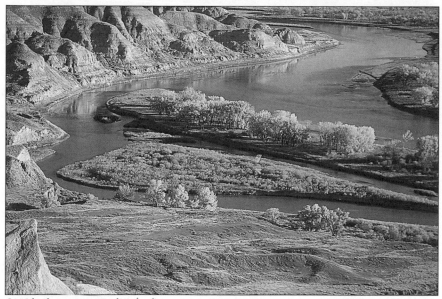

Cow Island – onetime steamboat landing. RICK AND SUSIE GRAETZ

let their passengers off on one side so they could walk across and get their "land legs" back after having spent many days on-board. The boats would continue around and retrieve them on the other side of the peninsula.

The UL Bend National Wildlife Refuge and UL Bend Wilderness are part of this remote area. Both are contiguous to and managed by the CMR through the US Fish and Wildlife Service.

Headwatering in the Castle Mountains of western Montana, the historic Musselshell River winds through its valley from the south, arriving at the Missouri across from the tip of the UL Bend.

East of UL Bend and the Musselshell, the country gets even rougher, the reservoir widens and more bays sculpture the shoreline on both sides of the lake. This is the mid-section of the CMR. Mickey and Brandon buttes, each about 2,900 feet in elevation and home to bighorn sheep, are landmarks on the north side of the water. On the same side of the river, but farther east, Iron Stake Ridge stands out at 3,140 feet and is the southern most reach of the Larb Hills, stands out. South of the river and lake, the sharp divides above Devils Creek, Herman Ridge and Seven Blackfeet reach above some of the most rugged landscape on the CMR. Relief is from 500 to 1,000 feet high.

The mass of the Larb Hills and the untamed geography across the river presents perhaps the most dramatic and beautiful display of upland prairie topography on the continent. Both sides of the river and lake in this span of the refuge create territory for mule deer, elk, bighorn sheep and antelope, as well as smaller critters. Here, nature also displays a fascinating collection of picturesque rock configurations — castles, monuments, towers, arches — all created by differential erosion, such as harder rock sitting atop a softer eroding stone pedestal.

Beyond the mouth of Seven Blackfeet, the inlets become wider and longer; now there is no mistaking the lake for a river. Snow Creek and Hell Creek bays, north of Jordan, both popular recreation areas, stretch south from the main body of water. This side of the lake remains broken and coarse. The north side of the shoreline in this region is extremely irregular. Narrow points of land separate at least ten bays and flat-topped buttes accentuate the ground above them.

As the water spreads out and nears its widest expanse, the landforms on either side become more subdued. The highest hills are 2,500 feet to 2,600 feet above sea level; the relief is not much more than 100 feet. Because of the section's sparse tree cover, elk are scarce. This rolling prairie and open terrain is habitat for the speedy pronghorn antelope.

The eastern edge of the lake takes an abrupt and lengthy turn to the south of the main body of water. Dry Arm, as it is called, (Big Dry Creek before the dam) stretches out for about 40 miles. This finger shaped extension of Fort Peck Lake is greater in length by itself than any other lake in the state. Very few people visit the western fringe of Dry Arm.

Badlands, make up much of the surface geology of the eastern part of this wildlife haven. Views here are austere and beautiful. The Sand Arroyo Badlands are the most distinguished of these dry land creations. Unusual and fascinating rock arrangements that look like toadstools or thin walls are scattered throughout a desert-like environment. Made of sandstone, they were created by wind blowing the finer material away from the rock, leaving the coarser stone standing above the surface.

Although the sunrise side of the CMR is the driest of all the preserve regions, in the Bobcat Creek drainage, pockets of perennial wet areas exist. Just below the surface soils, water moves laterally along impermeable coal seams and seeps out in some of the deeper coulees prompting the growth of green ash trees and other vegetation. In one coulee, aspens have taken hold and in another, black cottonwoods are growing. Usually found in cooler, wetter environs, it is rare for these two species of trees to be so far east of the mountains.

North of Sand Arroyo, the relief increases, dominated by 3,000-foot Deadman's Butte, a promontory just beyond the eastern reaches of the refuge. The summit provides sweeping views of the immense expanse of sky, water and land spread out to the south, west and north. On a clear day, it's possible to see 1,000 square miles of prairie and river.

Roads from Hwy 200 between Winnett and to the east of Jordan lead north into the central and eastern units of the CMR; these dirt roads are not usable in wet conditions. Travel is slow and 60 miles might take more than two hours of drive time. The most popular byways include the Crooked Creek road near Winnett and the route to Hell Creek out of Jordan.

On the eastern margin of the CMR, off of Hwy 24, several routes (dry weather roads) wind to the many recreation areas and boat launches on the Dry Arm. The best access to the northeast part of the Charles M. Russell is out of Fort Peck, just south of Glasgow.

CMR History

The recorded history of the country now designated as the Charles M. Russell National Wildlife Refuge flows with the waters of the Missouri River. The Lewis and Clark Expedition moved west against its current, trappers and natives used it for transportation, steamboats carried life and people to a growing Montana and in the early 1900s, homesteaders settled along the river's rich bottomlands.

Long before these first visitors though, and millions of years prior to the formation of the Missouri, other forms of life existed here. Evidence of their presence is found in the mudstones and other sedimentary formations that blanket the CMR. The Missouri River badlands of the refuge and beyond are producing new discoveries each year. Paleontologists have been provided with one of the world's most fertile fossil sites and an outdoor laboratory to help them understand the evolutionary process.

Tyrannosaurus rex, Triceratops, Albertosaurus, Mosasaurus, aquatic duck-billed dinosaurs and other giant creatures roamed, fought and populated this preserve area. Their remains are now being uncovered. In 1902, one of the first T-rex fossils ever found was discovered near Jordan in the Cretaceous era badlands of Hell Creek. In 1990, the most complete T-rex ever was unearthed here. Each year brings new finds, exciting information and enlightenment about what this land was like more than 70 million years ago.

Indian tribes from the upper Midwest, and farther east, were pushed west into this region by an expanding white population. By the late 1700s, a Plains Indian culture, centered on the movement of bison, had been established.

The original Plains Indians who used these lands, were the Shoshone, Flathead, Pend Oreille and Kutenai. Then the growing Blackfeet nation, especially the most feared Piegan Blackfeet, forced the others to the mountains. While the Blackfeet dominated this region, Assiniboine, Atsina (Gros Ventre), Cree, Absaroka and Sioux also hunted here. The river was supposed to have divided the hunting grounds, but rarely did it stand in the way of trespass, and many major battles were fought over hunting rights.

The first recorded documentation of this Charlie Russell Country began in 1805 with the journals of Lewis and Clark. In May of that year, they spent 16 days traveling through what is now the Charles M. Russell National Wildlife Refuge. Most of their campsites are presently under the waters of Fort Peck Reservoir, but three of the approximate locations are on the western end of the refuge and can be reached by primitive road.

Confluence of the Milk (right) and Missouri rivers. LARRY MAYER

On May 9, 1805, the Corps passed Big Dry Creek and camped near what is now Duck Creek. Lewis wrote, *"today we passed the bed of the most extraordinary river that I ever beheld. it is as wide as the Missouri is at this place or ½ a mile wide and not containing a single drop of runing water."*

May 20, reaching the Musselshell River, they named it the *"Shell River."* Camping here for the night, Lewis penned, *"The hunters returned this evening and informed us that the country continued much the same in appearance as that we saw where we were or broken, and that about five miles ab[ov]e the mouth of shell river a handsome river of about fifty yards in width discharged itself into the shell river on the Stard (north) or upper side; this stream we called Sah-ca-ger we-ah or bird woman's River after our interpreter the Snake woman."*

Two days later, the explorers set up camp just below C K Creek on the north shore of the Missouri. Clark noted in the journals, *"I walked out after dinner and assended a but[te] a few miles [off] to view the countrey, which I found roleing & of a verry rich stickey soil producing but little vegetation of any kind except the prickley pear, but little grass & that verry low"* Clark was probably observing the gumbo soil prevalent on the CMR when it rains.

Fur trappers and traders followed the Corps of Discovery on the Missouri. Activity was minimal until the late 1820s when larger organizations like the American Fur Company moved into the area and established trading posts. Traders labored against the currents of the river with loads of bartered materials, then floated downstream with heaps of furs secured from the Indians and trappers.

After Lewis and Clark and the trappers, and up until the 1880s when the steel rails entered the territory, the Missouri was the main route of travel into Montana. Today's wildlife refuge stretch of the Missouri, and the lands on both sides of the water, were host to everyone who added to the tales and legends of "the Wild West." Rustlers, horse thieves, bank robbers, cattleman, vigilantes, cowboys, Native Americans, trappers, woodhawkers, wolfers, steamboat captains and the U.S. Cavalry passed through or lived here for a short spell. Very few areas experienced as much of the history of the early American west as did this place.

As the fur trade was dwindling in the 1850s, steamboats plying the waters of the Missouri brought legions of new people into Montana and created more access to lonely outposts along the river. The fast current, numerous sandbars and sawyers (submerged trees with lance like tips sticking out of the water) demanded the full attention of river captains. Scores of boats and cargo were destroyed by the river's treachery.

As the water traffic increased, several river front settlements soon sprung up, such as Carroll in the western end of the refuge. At first a trading post, later it became a steamboat landing which enjoyed brief prosperity during the low water years of 1874 and 1875. Freight and passengers were unloaded here to continue the journey west by land over the Carroll Trail to Helena. This good fortune ended when the return of high water allowed the steamboats once again to continue upriver to Fort Benton.

Rocky Point, in the western part of the Russell Wildlife Refuge, was a tough frontier town from the 1860s until the turn of the century. Serving legitimate ranchers and businessmen, as well as the thieves and outlaws, it became the rendezvous and center of trade for wood choppers, trappers, miners, cowboys, whiskey traders and all manner of desperados, including the infamous Kid Curry and his gang. Rocky Point also served as a steamboat landing, with infantry companies occasionally stationed to guard government freight.

Remnants of Rocky Point, like those of Carroll and other riverbank towns, have been washed away, leaving little evidence of their one-time existence.

Perhaps the most fascinating time of the old west and the Missouri River Breaks was in the early 1870s. Western Montana stockmen ventured into the lush river bottoms and tall grass of the north central part of the state. The land was unfenced and un-owned. Pioneer institutions — big outfits such as the DHS Ranch and the Circle C Ranch — ranged their livestock through what is now the CMR. And big cattle drives, up from Texas were brought north into the area to feed on the nutritional grasses.

Outlaws, rustlers and thieves took advantage of the open range and the somewhat easy practice of stealing horses and cattle. They had their favorite haunts and would hole up in the many coulees of the badlands along the Missouri until they could safely dispose of the stolen goods. These outlaws and others on the run from the law hung out in places like Carroll, Rocky

Point and Musselshell. Signs of their camps and corrals that held stolen livestock can be seen in remote areas of the refuge.

In 1867, a northern Pony Express route came through what is now the Wildlife Refuge. Starting at Fort Union on the Missouri and close to today's Montana/North Dakota line, the trail follows Hwy 2, reaching the Missouri River again at Fort Peck (the eastern end of the CMR). Riders stayed on the north side of the Missouri until they reached Fort Hawley, on Hawley Creek west of the UL Bend. Here they crossed the Missouri and headed southwest to the Judith Mountains and Helena. Mail service on this route lasted for just one year.

Where the Musselshell River emptied into the Missouri was a significant intersection in the time of cattle barons and earlier. Here, vast herds of bison crossed the river on their annual migrations, and as a major fording point for the Indians of eastern Montana, battles and skirmishes often occurred there with the white man. A succession of fur trading posts, wood yards, military camps, ranches and homesteads at one time or another occupied the area.

The confluence was also a gathering place for rustlers and other outlaws. Organized horse-stealing rings tormented ranchers in the Missouri Breaks in the late 1800s. Raiding ranches in Montana, Wyoming, the Dakotas and southern Canada, bandits drove the livestock to remote areas of the Breaks, "worked the brands" and drove them to Canada for sale, repeating the process with stolen Canadian livestock on the return trip.

One of the most famous incidents of "vigilante justice" occurred in 1884. Granville Stuart, operator of the DHS ranch, led a group of local stockmen to the Musselshell area to clean out a large horse-thieving ring. Two outlaws were hanged there and two more suffered the same fate at Rocky Point. A few days later, these stockmen, who became known as "Stuart's Stranglers," apprehended more horse thieves at an abandoned wood yard at Bates Point, 15 miles below the mouth of the Musselshell River. Five outlaws were killed in the ensuing gun fight; seven others managed to escape, but five of these were later captured by soldiers in eastern Montana and returned to the vigilantes, who decided their fate would be death by hanging. The vigilante actions received considerable condemnation, but the organized horse rustling business ended in the Missouri Breaks.

The heyday of the wide-ranging cattle industry was about to come to an end. The tough winter of 1886–87 caused heavy livestock losses and began the decline of the big cattle operations. Life in the Missouri Breaks calmed.

Homesteaders, lured to the Montana plains by glowing railroad reports touting prospects of riches to be reaped from the soil and a 1909 liberal homestead law, began making inroads on the eastern Montana prairies. Some settled along the lush bottomlands of the Missouri River. For the most part, the lands that would eventually be set aside for the Charles M. Russell National Wildlife Refuge weren't suited for agriculture and the majority of homestead claims were made along the river.

Small hamlets grew along the Missouri to serve those homesteaders who did settle in the Breaks. At one time, there were 16 post offices located throughout the river country.

At first, these newcomers did well with their crops. In 1917, though, drought set in and worsened during the next three years. This natural calamity, coupled with several severe recessions, destroyed the dreams of many who came to settle in the soon-to-be CMR. Most were forced to leave their places to the wind and let nature reclaim the land. Postal locations such as Round Butte, Big Dry, Wilder, Trenton and Bervie all disappeared.

Those ranchers and farmers who were successful in establishing places along the river and withstood the drought were, in the 1930s, bought out by the US Government as a prelude to the building of Fort Peck Dam.

With the completion of the dam, the river behind it deepened and spread, covering the cottonwoods, floodplain and history alike. The smooth waters have brought a sense of tranquility to the land, drowning the voices of the past. But oftentimes, as the wind rustles across the grass and through the trees, very faintly, those ancient whispers can be heard.

From Fort Peck to The Yellowstone and North Dakota

The Missouri River hasn't seen a town since Loma, 281 miles ago. In 1876, near the site of today's dam, Colonel Campbell Peck and Commander Durfee of the U.S. Army established an Indian Agency and a trading post for the Assiniboine and Sioux people. In the fall of 1933, with the commencement of the dam project, Fort Peck town site, planned and built by the Army Corps of Engineers to house its employees, began its orderly development.

The construction spawned shanty boomtowns that were scattered around the work area. These places disappeared almost as quickly as they grew. Some, including New Deal, are now covered by the lake.

Fort Peck Dam is one of the largest earth-filled river impediments in the world. Its original purpose was not only to control floods, but also to create jobs in a depression saddled economy. At that time, the undertaking was the nation's largest public works project. Completed in 1940, during its peak of activity in 1936, it provided 10,456 jobs. The head gates of the dam were featured on the first cover of Life Magazine.

The Missouri River leaves Fort Peck Lake through the dam's spillway and runs clear again much as it did from its birthplace. Before the dams, and in its natural state, the river was known for its silt and mud. Estimates were that at one time for each one million gallons of water, 120 tons of silt were suspended. Steamboats plying the river had to continually clean mud from their boilers.

Within ten miles of exiting Fort Peck and after regenerating a channel, the Missouri meets the Milk River. The extremely silt-laden waters of the Milk are pushed aside by the stronger flow of the Missouri as it fights to keep the murky color at bay. The intense contrast of the two flows creates a light colored banner along the north bank until finally, the Milk gives up and succumbs to the mightier Missouri.

Meriwether Lewis, May 8, 1805, wrote, *"the water of this river posseses a peculiar whiteness, being about the colour of a cup of tea with the admixture of a tabelspoonfull of milk. from the colour of it's water we called it Milk river. we think it possible that this may be the river called by the Minitares (Hidatsa) 'the river that scolds at all others' ..."* Lewis also noted the Milk River Hills that rise almost 700 feet above the floodplain of the Milk and Missouri. These can be ascended on their south side and reached via MT Hwy 24 across Fort Peck Dam. From these points one can view much of the terrain Lewis and Clark described, both along the Missouri on the north side of the hills and southwest out over Fort Peck Lake.

As the river rolls eastward, the meanders increase, as do the sand bars and islands. While the Missouri is dynamic through its final 185 miles, it doesn't have the strength it had before Fort Peck Dam was completed. And it only drops 220 feet in these last Montana miles. Looking a bit more civilized than the segment between Fort Benton and Fort Peck, it is still, for the most part, void of people.

On May 7, southwest of the small community of Frazer, Lewis gave praise. *"The country we passed today ... is one of the most beautiful plains we have yet seen, it rises gradually from the river bottom ... then becoming level as a bowling green ... as far as the eye can reach."*

Poplar, just off of the Missouri River, serves as headquarters for the Assiniboine and Sioux tribes, and was named for the widespread stands of poplar trees on the riverbanks. Here, the Poplar River comes in from the north and the Redwater River adds a small amount of moisture on the south. The southern boundary of the Fort Peck Indian Reservation is defined by about 130 miles of the Missouri extending from the mouth of the Milk to the Big Muddy River.

The Corps of Discovery overnighted at present day Poplar on May 3, 1805, and the Captains named the *"Porcupine (Poplar) River,"* because of the multitude of needled creatures inhabiting the place. Lewis penned that night, *"the country in this neighborhood of this river, and as far as the eye can reach is level, fertile, open and beatifull beyond description."*

They also christened the present Redwater River, *"2000 mile creek,"* estimating it was 2,000 miles from St. Louis. Many of the place names Lewis and Clark designated lost the original names owing to the delay in the publishing of their journals. Others who followed, not knowing the sites had a label, gave them different monikers.

There are several accounts of how Wolf Point, the next burg on our trip, took its name. The most accepted version was that during a cold late 1860s winter, "wolfers" killed several hundred gray wolves that froze before they could be skinned for their pelts. The hunters stacked the carcasses in high piles at their camp along the Missouri waiting for the spring thaw. Indians took over the landing and camp before the skins could be removed; the putrid piles remained. They became a visible landmark, especially to the steamboats coming upriver in that spring.

Documentation of Wolf Point's exact beginnings is hard to come by. An 1834 map noted an Indian fort at the location. As a settlement, it was probably first established as a trading post for the fur trade. It grew to a cow town when huge cattle herds, up from Texas and elsewhere, came through on their way to the rich and tall grasses of northern Montana. The place was a genuine frontier outpost and featured a dugout hotel along the river.

In 1914, Wolf Point attained a growth spurt brought on by the arrival of farmers when Congress opened up the Fort Peck Reservation to homesteading by non-Indians.

The Big Muddy slowly works its way south from Canada to join the Missouri near the town of Culbertson. The settlement, named for Alexander Culbertson, an early-day fur trapper from the American Fur Company, got its start about 1888, and is considered one of the oldest towns in eastern Montana.

A couple of miles southeast of Culbertson, the Hwy 16 bridge crosses the Missouri. The sweeping river view from here is a favorite of photographers. Beyond the bridge, with 34 miles left before the Missouri prepares to leave Montana and take on the Yellowstone, it rolls through a beautiful mix of bluffs, canyons and badlands. Continually impressed with the pleasant appearance of the landscape, William Clark declared, *"the Countrey on both Sides have a butifull appearance."*

East of Culbertson. RICK AND SUSIE GRAETZ

The Mandans and Hidatsa had warned of the ferocious white bear the Expedition would encounter. Lewis took this admonition lightly, assuming that their superior firepower (the natives didn't posses guns) would more than compensate. On April 29, sometime during midday, before reaching today's Culbertson Bridge, Lewis met his first grizzly. He shot the animal, which then pursued him for almost 80 yards before the second bullet killed it. Lewis, who now gained a new respect for this *"furious and formidable anamal that will frequently pursue the hunter when wounded,"* stated, *"these bear being so hard to die reather intimedates us all; I must confess that I do not like the gentelmen and had rather fight two Indians than one bear."*

Montana's First Written History

A few miles before leaving the state, the Missouri passes Snowden Bridge and the site of the former village of Nohly. Here, Lewis and Clark and their crew on April 27, 1805, spent their first night in what would become Montana. As Lewis began writing in his journals that night, the words he put on paper represent the first written history of Montana. *"This morning I walked through the point formed by the junction of the rivers ... here a beautifull level low plain commences and extends up both rivers for many miles, widening as the rivers recede from each other, and extending back half a mile to a plain about 12 feet higher than itself; ... on the Missouri about 2½ miles from the entrance to the Yellowstone river, and between this high and low plain, a small lake is situated about 200 yards wide extending along the edge of the high plain parallel with the Missouri about one mile."* He is noting Nohly Lake, in close proximity to the town of Fairview.

Once this historic spot is passed, the Missouri appropriates the Yellowstone River, just beyond our border with North Dakota. As the river takes leave, it continues to carry the direction and determination it had when it left Three Forks. It still has a long way to go before catching the Mississippi, but it has left the finest landscapes of its journey behind in Montana.

—RICK AND SUSIE GRAETZ

MOUNTAIN RANGES

T HEY STRETCH FROM A 4,058-FOOT-HIGH POINT IN THE LONG PINES IN THE extreme southeast, to 7,705-foot Northwest Peak of the Purcell Mountains in the opposite corner of the state. Sixty-seven separate ranges make-up these Montana mountains; and when all the sub ranges and connecting hills are added, there are actually 131 of them. Thirteen mountain groups rise to 10,000 feet and higher ... more than 586 of the summits exceed 10,000 feet; 60 surpass 11,000 feet; and 27 eclipse 12,000 feet above sea level.

In a contest for the most height, the Beartooth Mountains west of Red Lodge win since they contain all of the 12,000-footers, including Montana's tallest, 12,799-foot Granite Peak. This lofty mountain range also has 46 peaks reaching 11,000 to 11,999 feet in height and 45 climb from 10,000 to 10,999 feet high. Second place goes to the Madison Range, southwest of Bozeman, which has more than 120 peaks 10,000 feet and higher, with 11,316-foot Hilgard Peak staking claim to the title "Highest Reach Outside Of The Beartooth." The Crazy Mountains in southcentral Montana, crowned by 11,214-foot Crazy Peak, come in third and have 25 pinnacles over 10,000 feet. Contiguous to the Beartooth Country, the Absarokas, led by 11,206-

Lima Peaks near the town of Lima. RICK AND SUSIE GRAETZ

foot Mt. Cowan, is our fourth highest mountain range. No others come close in terms of having tops over 10,000 feet ... more than 166 Absaroka peaks have that distinction. Between Dillon and Butte, the Pioneers shelter 50 summits over 10,000 feet. Mt. Tweedy at 11,154 feet in elevation, makes these lesser-known mountains fifth on the list. The Flint Creek Range between Deer Lodge and Philipsburg and its 10,160-foot Mt. Powell is last on the roster of the 13 ranges with peaks over 10,000 feet above sea level.

Surprisingly, 10,000-foot crests are absent in some of the awesome chains, such as, the Swan, Rocky Mountain Front and Missions. Their highest apexes are only from 8,100 to 9,800 feet, but it is the stunning relief (distance from ground to top) that gives them their stature. Glacier Park mountains (the Lewis and Livingston ranges) have the greatest relief of any range in the state, 10,142-foot Mt. Stinson and 10,052-foot Mt. Jackson ascend from 6,800 to 7,000 feet above their bases.

Blue Mountain, 800 feet higher than the remote plain between Sidney and Glendive, at a whopping 3,084 feet in elevation, is the tallest point in northeastern Montana. Then there are the other less obtrusive ranges, such as the Little and the Big Sheep mountains, a series of hills and eroded badlands between Circle and Glendive, whose highest point at 3,625 feet is no more than 300 feet above the adjacent country. West of Ekalaka, the Chalk Buttes are just over 4,000 feet high and rise only 700 feet above the prairie floor.

The Little Rocky Mountains, south of Malta, can be seen for a long distance. Antone Butte, the highest point at 5,610 feet, is 2,500 feet higher than the surrounding ranchlands. These isolated highlands, as well as others

The Absarokas, West Boulder Valley. RICK AND SUSIE GRAETZ

Peaks of Glacier National Park from the North Fork. RICK AND SUSIE GRAETZ

like them ... the Bear Paw south of Havre, the Judith and Moccasins next to Lewistown, the Bull Mountains at Roundup, and the Highwoods east of Great Falls add perspective to the enormous vistas of Montana east of the main Rockies. Compared to the extensive mountains of western Montana, elevations of mountains in the eastern one-half of the state are low; most of the slopes are less than 5,500 feet, the only exception being the 8,600-foot rise of the Big Snowy Mountains south of Lewistown.

Many names of the Northern Rocky Mountains of Montana are familiar but do you know where the John Longs are? (west of Philipsburg), the Bangtails? (near Bozeman), the Tendoys? (southwest of Dillon), the Coeur d'Alenes? (south of Thompson Falls), the Wolf Mountains? (southeast of Lodge Grass), the Snowcrests? (southeast of Dillon), the Salish? (west of Flathead Lake), or the Lima Peaks? (west of Monida Pass). And a whole mass of mountains between Helena, Deer Lodge and Butte are yet unnamed.

—RICK AND SUSIE GRAETZ

CONTINENTAL DIVIDE

W ITH THE MORNING SUN AT HIS BACK ON AUGUST 12,1805, MERIWETHER Lewis followed a well-worn Indian trail from southwest Montana's Horse Prairie Valley up Trail Creek, gradually topping out on a 7,373-foot pass.

> *"... the road was still plain, I therefore did not dispair of shortly finding a passage over the mountains and tasting the waters of the Great Columbia this evening. At the distance of four miles further the road took us to the most distant fountain of the water of the mighty Missouri in surch of which we have spent so many toilsome days and wristless nights."*

When he walked through today's Lemhi Pass, Lewis became the first known white man to cross the Continental Divide. He was however, mistaken about reaching the most distant waters of the Missouri. That distinction belongs to the earliest trickles of Hellroaring Creek flowing out of the eastern end of the Centennial Mountains and the Divide into the Red Rock River, a good distance to the east.

This Continental Divide, that gives Montana distinct water sheds, is part of a greater hemispheric divide stretching from the Brooks Range of northern Alaska down through the Andes to almost the farthest tip of South America. As a matter of fact, the Continental Divide National Scenic Trail established by Congress allows folks to trek the 3,100 miles from Canada to Mexico following the actual divide as closely as possible.

Bestowing order to every drop of moisture that falls on it, when the spring's sun turns the Divide's blanket of snow into rivulets of water, the Pacific Ocean and the Gulf of Mexico can count on more volume.

Snow melt and rain falling on the west side of Montana's Divide powers the many creeks and rivers leading to the Clark Fork and the fast moving Snake rivers which each meet the Columbia that in turn discharges it's flow into Pacific Ocean.

Sky born liquid landing on the lee or sunrise side of the Continental Divide eventually makes its way to the Missouri River and from there to the Mississippi and on to the Gulf of Mexico.

It's interesting to note in southern Glacier National Park, from the apex of 8,000-foot Triple Divide Peak, water descends to the Pacific Ocean, the Gulf of Mexico and to Canada's Hudson Bay. This is the only summit in the United States that sends its moisture to three seas.

Lemhi Pass, 8/12/1805 Lewis is first known white man to cross the Divide. RICK AND SUSIE GRAFTZ

Pioneers pointing their wagon trains westward to the Oregon Country were unfamiliar with the land and viewed the imposing mountain crests as an immense obstacle. The many Indian Nations inhabiting or migrating through what would become western Montana, knew the easiest crossings well and had used them for centuries as a passageway to the bison hunting grounds of the northern Great Plains.

Montana's Divide respects no geologic structural dictate, but rather snakes at random through the high terrain of the state's Northern Rocky Mountains. With a spectacular start in the remote western reaches of Glacier National Park, at the 49th parallel of latitude where Alberta, British Columbia and Montana join, the northern most point of Montana's Divide begins its run to the south at an elevation of 7,460 feet. It leaves our great state about three miles into Yellowstone National Park at 8,320 feet where Montana, Idaho and Wyoming join in a nondescript, flat, difficult to find timbered landscape.

Elevations along Montana's Divide range from a low of 5,280 feet at Marias Pass near Glacier Park to 11,141 feet at the most southerly situated Eighteenmile Peak.

Once embroiled in politics, the Continental Divide played an important part in Montana's early history. The Idaho Territory, established in 1863, included all of what is now Montana. When Ohio congressman Sidney Edgerton was named Chief Justice of the Idaho Territory and reported to his post, he discovered that his new assignment was to cover only the eastern portion of the new territory.

Initially, Congress determined this mountain crest line was to serve as the border between Montana and Idaho.

A movement was growing in Edgerton's domain to create a new territory (Montana). Initially, the Idaho Territorial Legislature asked Congress to establish the Continental Divide as a boundary. This would mean that half of Glacier Park, Flathead Lake, Missoula and the Bitterroot Valley would today be part of Idaho. Edgerton, with his powerful political connections, as well as being closely acquainted with President Lincoln, asked to have the boundary move west to follow the Bitterroot Divide instead. His request was granted and in July 1864 he became Montana's first Territorial Governor headquartered in the new territorial capital of Bannack.

From the mid 1800s forward, gold, silver and copper played a large role in fueling the population growth of what would become the state of Montana. Today, remnants of the era when hard rock miners worked their claims along the Divide can still be found. Old cabins and mineshafts are testimony to this time in our State's history.

Recognized as Montana's most prominent topographical attraction, the Continental Divide rambles through a myriad of landforms. In many places its course is clear and in others quite obscure, passing through legendary and remote wilderness, glacier scoured terrain and dense forests. It touches on the large mining operations of Butte and skirts just west of Helena. In our southwest corner this contour defines the Montana/Idaho state line. Under its brow, lone miners have worked their claims and ranchers continue to graze cattle, sheep and horses.

Besides influencing the direction of Montana's waters, the Great Divide has an affect on the state's weather, especially in the north. Until they reach this crown of the Continent, wet Pacific air masses heading to Montana are continually moving upward. The Divide causes them to drop a great deal of their moisture on the west side allowing the now much drier air to descend the east slopes resulting in an arid landscape. This process at times creates the very strong and renowned Chinook winds that race across the prairies and along the mountain front rapidly driving temperatures up and often melting several inches of snow overnight.

The northern Divide rises in such a way as to provide gaps for ferocious winds to roar down onto the lowland. Repeatedly, in favored mountain passes, the velocities of winds hitting the plains can exceed 60mph.

Artic air that invades eastern Montana throughout the winter is frequently prevented from touching the western valleys by this high wall.

From Helena north to the Canadian line, the Continental Divide has put its greatest mark on the weather. The national low temperature record was documented just off the Divide on January 20, 1954 at Rogers Pass; the thermometer bottomed out at 70 degrees below zero. Further to the north, state snowfall records have been set on Marias Pass with 44 inches of snow accumulating in a 24-hour period on January 20th, 1972. During the time period of the 17th to the 22nd, the same storm dropped a total of 77.5 inches of white fluffy stuff. Just north of the pass, more than 1,000 inches of snowfall keeps Glacier National Park's many glaciers alive.

In the upper reaches of the Divide, summer is fleeting and autumn arrives early. But the sight of shimmering yellow aspen leaves and later the gold and amber colors of the larch trees interspersed against the rich dark emerald of the evergreens, more than makes up for the chill in the air. Here in the high country, spring can't seem to make up its mind when to show. Even all through the summer months, winter merely hides in the rocks and the summits ready to provide a reminder of its "king of the hill" status on any given July or August day. No season is allowed to escape the wrathful storms Mother Nature can bring along the crest.

Virtually all species of Montana's wildlife spend time along the Divide. In the summer, powerful silvertip grizzlies search for grubs and plants, eagles rise high above on updrafts twisting and turning with the thermals, in the cool evenings the yip of coyotes can be heard and in some places the howls of the wolf. Goats and bighorn sheep cling to precarious ledges and antlered deer quietly slip through the brush to quench their thirst in sparkling mountain streams.

As the Great Continental Divide begins its southward journey from the Canadian border essentially splitting Glacier National Park in half, it becomes a part of North America's most stunning mountain scenery. Bold and beautiful, serene yet dangerous, in places it perilously straddles the knife-sharp edges of sedimentary rocks carved over thousands of years by glaciers from which avalanches continue to clear new paths. Situated below, rugged cirque basins holding turquoise blue lakes tranquilly reflect the Divide's attributes.

Besides trekking along the Continental Divide Trail, many spectacular footpaths permit crossing the Divide in Glacier National Park. In perhaps one of the most remote and rugged parts of the Park, Browns Pass in the north is reached via trails coming up from Waterton Lake on the east and the Kintla Lakes and the North Fork of the Flathead on Glacier's west flank. Further south and overlooking the spectacular terrain of green and red Argillite rocks, Swift Current Pass leading to the popular Granite Park Chalet area intersects it. Continuing on, this separator of waters meets Sperry Glacier and climbs to Gunsight Pass, a magnificent route that opens up a wide range of Glacier's backcountry scenery. For the not so adventurous, the unequivocal Going-to-the-Sun Highway winds its way up and through 6,649-foot Logan Pass revealing with each curve a scene seemingly more breathtaking than the last one. This is the only road that crosses the Divide within the Park.

Rich with ties to Native American history and culture; the Divide here has played a large role both spiritually and physically with the Blackfeet Tribe. Cut Bank Pass, in the southeast corner of the Park, was once used as an east–

west trail by Blackfeet war parties intent on attacking their enemies the Flathead and Kootenai tribes. Two Medicine Pass and the upper and lower Two Medicine lakes were so named when separate gatherings of Blackfeet Indians came together at the lakes to hold religious ceremonies. As they were held at the same time, the area took on the name Two Medicine. This landscape is considered sacred and continues to be used by the Blackfeet Nation today.

Traversing just below Glacier Park's southeast border, Highway 2 crosses one of Montana's most famous mountain passages ...Marias Pass, which at a mile high is the lowest of all the Continental Divide, passes between Canada and Mexico.

In 1880, James Hill, founder of the Great Northern Railway, was planning the layout of tracks for his new venture. He selected John F. Stevens to find the lowest route across the Divide in the northern portion of Montana's mountains. Native Americans knew of a route they described as being a gentle crossing of the peaks, few whites were aware of its existence. In1889, fighting deep snows and bitter cold, Stevens, traveling with an Indian companion, found the way. The first rails where laid across the Pass on September 14, 1891, and in 1893 the initial train chugged up and over. The passageway took its name from the Marias River, a name that, in 1805, Meriwether Lewis had ordained in honor of his cousin Maria Wood.

Leaving Glacier, where it has served as the backbone for some of the nations most extraordinary scenery, the Continental Divide begins a gradual ascent in elevation as it enters the most fabled wilderness in the United States ...the 1.5 million-acre beloved Bob Marshall Country, consisting of the contiguous Great Bear, Bob Marshall and Scapegoat wilderness areas and surrounding wildlands.

Easing through the Badger-Two Medicine, a place hallowed to the Blackfeet Nation, the Divide comes close to the escarpment of the Rocky Mountain Front as it reaches a relatively high cluster of peaks. The bare shear rock summits, most in the 7,000- to 8,000-foot range, resemble the tops of much higher — say, 10,000-foot mountains.

From here the divide swings westward to the internal immense sprawl of the Bob, presiding over valley after valley empty of civilization and populated by dense forest, free running rivers, huge meadows, numerous wild critters and countless canyons and mountains.

Like Glacier, many well known trails allow travel across the barrier. Gateway Pass leading from the headwaters of the Flathead's Middle Fork to the prairie was a major route to the bison herds for the Kutenai and other western tribes. This is one of the few places a hiker can walk on almost level terrain through the Divide. Big River Meadows is on a plain with the pass and then drops sharply down the South Fork of Birch Creek on its sunrise side.

In the heart of the Bob Marshall Wilderness, the Great Divide flows along the rim of one of Montana's celebrated up rises, the 13-mile-long Chinese

Wall rising to 1,000 feet in some places. Part of what is known as the Overthrust Belt, the stunning limestone wall was created when older rocks slid eastward covering up younger sediments. Larch Hill Pass bounds the northern extent of the wall. To view or camp in the wildflower garden beneath the Chinese Wall is the highlight of a lifetime to those who make the trek. Coming up from Benchmark on the east side of the Bob, a popular horse route across the wilderness climbs over White River Pass in the area of the Flathead Alps, descending to the White River and eventually the South Fork of the Flathead.

Second only to the Chinese Wall in Bob Marshall Country notoriety is Scapegoat Mountain, a three-mile-long reef of limestone honeycombed with caves. The Great Divide defines its east edge. South of Scapegoat near Caribou Peak, the Divide leaves the wilderness for an area often called the Lincoln Back Country. Now its journey encounters a more roaded landscape and lowers sufficiently to allow a pass to go through. In 1806, following a trail along the Blackfoot River the Indians called "the river of the road to the buffalo," Captain Meriwether Lewis crossed the Continental Divide back to the prairie here at the now named Lewis and Clark Pass. Today this historic place is protected and only foot or horse travel is permitted

South of Lewis and Clark Pass, the Great Divide meets Rogers Pass and Highway 200, the first road crossing the barrier since Marias Pass 145 miles to the north.

Only a short ways from Roger's Pass, Flesher and Stemple passes provide recreational access to the land of the Divide. In winter, cross-country skiers

The Tobacco Root Mountains near Silver Star. RICK AND SUSIE GRAETZ

from Helena and Great Falls frequent the area. From Stemple Pass, the Divide follows, in some places, a road passing Granite Butte and just east of Nevada Mountain.

Surrounded by logging, the Nevada Mountain Roadless Area, an island of dense stands of lodgepole pine providing high quality elk habitat, straddles the Continental Divide. Serving as sentinels for the area, Nevada Mountain and the somewhat higher Black Mountain are both over 8,000 feet. From their tops some of southwest Montana's big intermountain valleys, including the Helena Valley are visible.

Mid-way into its southward journey and just beyond Nevada Mountain, the Continental Divide traverses above a heavily mined district and the historic town of Marysville one of the state's leading producers of gold. The famous Drumlummon Mine, established here by Thomas Cruse, had an output of almost $50 million of the precious yellow metal. A lasting legacy from Cruse is the beautiful Helena Cathedral built as a tribute and thank you for answered prayers.

Today, hiking, mountain biking and snow sports at the Great Divide Ski Area ... formerly Mount Belmont, have replaced the search for minerals in the Marysville-Bald Butte region.

As the Divide nears Helena, three passes are attained. One, which was prominent in Helena's much younger days, is Mullen Pass named for Lt. John Mullen, who in the early 1860s was in charge of building the military road between Fort Benton and Walla Walla, Washington.

At the 1911 Montana State Fair, a daring stunt pilot named Cromwell Dixon took off from the Helena fairgrounds and made the first flight across the Continental Divide landing in the vicinity of Mullen Pass near the then town of Blossberg. Upon returning to the wild cheers of a large crowd, the 19-year-old aviator collected a $10,000 purse.

Next in line is Priest Pass. This once popular wagon road lost favor when in 1870, when a man named Dundhy built a toll road close by. Due to his extensive use of "log corduroying" over the muddy spots, making travel easier for horse drawn stagecoaches, it soon became the main route to and from Helena. Alexander MacDonald was hired to manage the tollgate and the pass. Today, four-lane Hwy 12 cuts across the top of MacDonald Pass. A well-used public cross-country ski trail system is maintained on the east side of the Pass in the vicinity of Frontier Town.

Long before whites came to Montana, MacDonald, Mullen and Priest passes served as important Indian routes to their prairie hunting grounds in the east.

Between MacDonald Pass and Butte, this hydrological line goes through a mix-match of mining claims, clear-cuts, roadless backcountry and mine remnants. The former mining town of Rimini, complete with shafts and claims, is nestled below the Divide's east side not too distant from Helena.

Though it has been witness to a great deal of Montana's formative years, the range of the peaks between the Capital and Mining cities is yet unnamed.

Geologically, this stretch of topography is known as the Boulder Batholith. Simply put, a large igneous bubble was created when magma rose, spreading up and out across the earth surface before hardening; thus providing for many of the mineral deposits in the vicinity.

The Electric Peak/Blackfoot Meadows Wilderness Study Area, one of the untamed tracts enroute, contains 13 miles of the Continental Divide and is a favorite of hikers and horseback riders.

Still heading south, the Great Divide comes across another major highway when it meets Interstate 15 aiming through Elk Park. An almost level, elevated valley extends to the east of the gap; on the west side, the road dives into Butte where enormous pits were dug to extract copper. The mining of this useful metal fueled the economy of the town and fattened the bank accounts of the famous Copper Kings.

From Elk Park, the Divide quickly gains elevation as it skirts up through granite rocks and past more old mine sites to form an impressive pedestal for the luminescent Our Lady of the Rockies statue overlooking Butte.

Two more thoroughfares are traversed as the Divide meets Homestake and Pipestone passes immediately south of Butte. Interstate 90 goes through Homestake, while MT Hwy 2 winds up and down Pipestone. Both passes are on the fringe of a grouping of mountains called the Highlands. With peaks over 10,000 feet, another striking backdrop for Butte is provided compliments of the Continental Divide.

As the Divide leaves the Highlands behind, it makes a sharp U-turn and charges north back towards Butte. Here, close to Deer Lodge Pass and Interstate 15, the Boulder Batholith exhibits its splendor in the Humbug Spires. Thousands of years of weathering has exposed the central granite core that gives the upwards of 600 feet high towers of rocks such a unique look. Amongst this rugged beauty, the Continental Divide turns and begins a westward course.

After a twisting passage through the Humbug Spires, the Continental Divide eases down in a westerly direction to the wide berth of Deer lodge Pass and Interstate 15 between Butte and Dillon, before beginning its upward climb to the Fleecer Mountain neighborhood. Here it blends with the high ranging country south of Anaconda that also exhibits substantial signs of mining and exploration. A paved back road from Anaconda to the Big Hole River incises across this segment of the Divide.

Backed up on the south edge of the Divide is the Mount Haggin Wildlife Management Area. A short distance to the west of the wildlife quarter, the rugged terrain of the Anaconda-Pintler Wilderness, with many of its peaks soaring to more then 10,000 feet, is next to host the Great Divide.

Not since leaving the Bob Marshall, has the Divide been in such esteemed wilderness. The Anaconda-Pintlers are part of an undeveloped wildland complex totaling 368,000 acres. For 50 miles the Continental watershed now angles in a southwesterly direction through towering glaciated terrain. Like the Bob, this is home to a large population of predator/prey critters.

It is in this wild and distinguished setting that two of Montana's legendary trout streams, Rock Creek and the Big Hole River gather some of their waters.

Plenty of trails crisscross the Divide In this rugged landscape, many leading to high lakes, which characterize the territory. Some of the better known such as Cutaway and Pintler passes are excellent choices for adventure.

Often throughout Montana, the Continental Divide Trail approximates the actual Divide. Not so in the Anaconda Range, here the mountainous topography is far too harsh making it necessary for trekkers to walk well below the Divide. Some trails, such as the Highline path out of Maloney Basin, have a semblance of following the line but not for long.

When the Continental Divide left the Butte area, it wandered in a somewhat east/west direction. Bidding adieu to the A-P wilderness area, it meets the Bitterroot Range Divide, turns on its heel and begins to march true south once again, passing through a region representing both triumph and sadness in the annals of Montana and Idaho history. The Divide now becomes part of the Montana-Idaho border all the way to Yellowstone National Park. Technically, the entire range of mountains forming the Montana-Idaho state line is called the Bitterroot; but there are sub-ranges and it is in this area that the Continental Divide and the Beaverhead Mountains coexist.

Captain William Clark of the Corps of Discovery crossed the mountains in this proximity as he left the Bitterroot in July 1806 on his way back to a cache made the previous summer. And on the Corps' initial journey to the West

The Chinese Wall in the Bob Marshall Wilderness. RICK AND SUSIE GRAETZ

Coast, they also tread the forest between Lost Trail and Chief Joseph passes after following the North Fork of the Salmon as far as they could.

Crossing the Divide, Gibbons Pass leads from the Bitterroot Valley via Prairie and Trail creeks to the Big Hole Valley and Lost Trail Pass, just west of the actual Divide, connects the Big Hole Valley to Idaho's Salmon River country.

Chief Joseph Pass, named for the great Nez Perce chieftain, allows paved road passage across the Divide from the Bitterroot to the Big Hole. Somewhere in this vicinity, Chief Joseph in an effort to bring his people to a safe sanctuary in Canada, led his tribe across the high country to an encampment now called the Big Hole Battlefield. In August 1877, Col. John Gibbon's U.S. forces attacked these peaceful people, killing many women and children. Those who did escape the slaughter eventually surrendered only 20 miles from Canada

Upon meeting the Bitterroot Mountains at Chief Joseph Pass, the Continental Divide abruptly changes its mind directionally and hooking an abrupt left, it saunters south following the Montana/Idaho border. Though still part of the Bitterroot Range, these summits take on the name Beaverhead Mountains and to some folks, the West Big Hole Mountains since they edge the Big Hole Valley. Less rugged than those to the north, the peaks here are loftier, many are over 10,000 feet, and more massive. Monument Peak is one of the highest at 10,343 feet, but the best known and most visible of all the summits is 10,624-foot Homers Young which rises just a bit to the west of the actual Divide.

Part of the proposed West Big Hole Wilderness, footpaths in this untrammeled country follow distinct glacial U shaped canyons and lead to more than 30 alpine jewel-like lakes. Attaining the Divide requires only good conditioning.

Some of the lower peaks south of the Big Hole watershed allow a few roads into the Beaverhead Mountains and to touch the Continental Divide. A dirt track out of the Horse Prairie Valley leads to Lemhi Pass, the route Lewis and Clark used on their journey to the Pacific, and crosses the Divide before taking a sharp drop off to Idaho on the west side. Lemhi's open grassland provides a fine view of the Divide both to the north and the south. The name comes from a character in the book of Mormon named Limhi.

After the Lemhi passage, the mountaintops soar upward again culminating at the impressive 11,141-foot Eighteenmile Peak, the highest Continental Divide pinnacle between Banff National Park in Canada and the Wind River Range of Wyoming.

The Italian Peaks are the next to spurt up. Distinguished by a shear 2,000-foot-high wall on its north side, Italian Peak at 10,998 feet is noted as being the southern most point in Montana. Surrounded on three sides by Idaho, it is much like a peninsula of land. Though roadless, several trails provide access into the proposed Italian Peak Wilderness. These incredible mountains look down on some of the State's least populated space, Big Sheep and Nicholia Basin. Surprisingly, this dry appearing area receives a heavy snow load in the winter.

In the mid 1800s, pioneers and gold seekers crossed the rough mountains leading into this sagebrush terrain on their way to the gold fields further north. Established in 1862, Bannack Pass, a route that still exists today, was the passage for the Bannack Freight Road coming from Corrine Utah.

On the east edge of the Basin, and just beyond Four Eyes Canyon, the Lima Peaks-Garfield Roadless Area-Red Conglomerate Peak Complex completes the Beaverhead Mountains. Most of these Divide summits exceed 10,000 feet and then scale down to 6,870 feet at Monida Pass.

Interstate Hwy 15 whips by the almost ghost town of Monida near the top of the pass. At one time, this was a stage stop for coaches between Salt Lake City and Montana's gold camps.

Barren wind swept foothills east of Monida lead the way up once again to grand heights. The Divide now rides the 9,000 feet and higher Centennial Mountains for much of the final stretch of the Montana/Idaho border.

Below the north face of the Centennials, Red Rocks Lake National Wildlife Refuge, breeding ground of the Trumpeter Swan, is the centerpiece of a lonesome but heartbreakingly beautiful valley that some of Montana's largest and oldest ranches call home.

Just to the west of 10,196-foot Mount Jefferson here in the Centennials, Hell Roaring Creek represents the Missouri Rivers most distant source; and nearby Red Rock Pass terminates the rise of the Centennials portion of the Divide.

From Red Rock Pass, the Divide points north for a short distance then ambles down to Henrys Lake and meets Raynolds Pass and Hwy 87 at the state line. From here, it turns southeast while scrambling into mountains identified as both the Henrys Lake Mountains and the Lionhead Range. This writer, and other geographers, considers them to be the Lionhead Range and a southern extension of the Madison Range. From the town of West Yellowstone, the 10,000-foot peaks of these imposing mountains can be accessed for motorized as well as non-motorized recreation.

Scaling down as Hwy 20 heading from West Yellowstone to Henrys Lake crosses it at Targhee Pass, the mountain range ends abruptly on its southern perimeter. Roughly 30 miles from the pass, still following the Montana/Idaho border, the Divide smacks into Wyoming. Here, just inside Yellowstone National Park, Montana gives up the Continental Divide. After a spectacular debut in Glacier National Park, the indomitable ridge bows out in a rather indistinct and obscure setting lacking any resemblance of the Great Divide that has made its southerly tour through Montana.

—RICK AND SUSIE GRAETZ

ALPINE GLACIERS

WELL BACK IN TIME, PERHAPS ABOUT 10,000 YEARS AGO, WHAT IS TODAY'S Big Sky Country experienced a much colder and snowier climate than we now enjoy. During various ice ages, many of our mountain ranges were almost entirely engulfed in snow and ice. The whole Flathead Valley near Kalispell, as an example, was filled with ice, perhaps as much as 3,000 feet deep. Ice spilled from Glacier Park past Browning and met a continental glacier flowing south from Canada. The Canadian intrusion extended to the present location of the Missouri River in the eastern half of our state.

Miniature remnants of that period still cling to walls and occupy cirques (steep walled, half bowl shaped basins) in some of our higher mountains. There are an estimated 37 active alpine glaciers in Glacier National Park, several in the Mission Mountains, one in the Cabinets, two in the Flathead Range, one in the Swan Range, one in the Crazies and many (they have not been counted) in the Absaroka-Beartooth Mountains.

Most of these ice-age relics are only visible to the backcountry visitor. In Glacier though, some can be glimpsed from the road. Jackson and Blackfoot glaciers are visible from above St. Mary Lake on the Going-To-The-Sun

Mission Mountains. RICK AND SUSIE GRAETZ

Highway, Old Sun on Mt. Merritt is discernible from near Babb and a pullout at the Apikuni Creek Trailhead brings into view Salamander and Gem glaciers in the Many Glacier region.

Several of these icy features are relatively well known. Jackson and Blackfoot glaciers in GNP because of their designated roadway viewpoint and size. Blackfoot at 430 acres is the Park's largest. Grinnell Glacier (217 acres) out of the Many Glacier region and Sperry Glacier (220 acres) are visited by hundreds of trekkers every year via an easy trail. Grasshopper Glacier, so named for the millions of grasshoppers embedded in its ice, abides in the Absaroka-Beartooth Wilderness on the north side of the ridge between Iceberg Peak and Mt. Wilse at the head of the West Rosebud Drainage. It is also a destination for many hikers. Theory has it that these migratory insects were passing over the Beartooth more than 200 years ago, when a storm caught and deposited them on the building glacier.

Late summer, when most of the entire mass is free of new snow, is the best time to see actual glaciers. Blue ice sliced by crevasses and strewn with mud and rock stands out. These writers favorite flows are both on Granite Peak in the Beartooth — the Sky Top Glacier on the south face and Granite Glacier on the north face.

Perennial snowfields in the high country are often mistaken for glaciers. A true glacier moves and needs to be at least 65 feet deep and 25 acres in size. The process of more deposition of snow in the cold season than melt in summer, coupled with continued melting and freezing, turns the body into ice. As it thickens, more weight is added to the lower ice layers. And when the glacier forms on steep slopes, as is the case in Montana, gravity causes the underlying strata to move. Late spring and early summer is when the maximum new snow load is reached and the most movement occurs. Each ice body has its own situation, but on the average in the Northern Rockies, the flow is probably no more than an inch or two a day. In coastal Alaska, a glacier could form in ten years but in the drier Northern Rockies it takes much longer.

Rock glaciers are found in more locales than the solid snow and ice variety. Aside from the ranges listed earlier, they are also active in the Madison, Pioneer, Bitterroot and Pintler ranges. Rockslides cover and insulate the buried ice. Only cold dense air is absorbed within the conglomeration helping to keep the ice intact. Rock glaciers flow very slowly and have steep faces with rippled surfaces.

Glaciers of the past have, especially in Montana's alpine regions, left behind a legacy of good work. They sculptured our mountains into the beautiful forms we have today. Their movement and former presence have left behind cirque filled lakes, deep U-shaped canyons and hanging valleys from which waterfalls plunge. Their abrasive surface action can be seen in long striations carved into the bedrock. And rock flour, a product of the grinding activity,

North facing glaciers on 11,831-foot Mount Wilse in the Beartooths. RICK AND SUSIE GRAETZ

gives a milky color to glacial lake surfaces that turn aqua when sunlight filters through.

Sadly, all of Montana's glaciers are shrinking. Projections, given current weather trends, are that in 30 years they will be completely eradicated from Glacier National Park.

Will the glaciers come back again? Only a trend towards an overall colder and wetter climate would ensure their return. Some folks feel it would be a good thing if they did; urban sprawl would be halted and the ski season would be more predictable and last longer.

—RICK AND SUSIE GRAETZ

BADLANDS

FRENCH TRAPPERS WORKING THE MISSOURI AND YELLOWSTONE RIVERS AND THEIR tributaries well before Lewis and Clark made their epic journey, called the dry land formations they encountered "mauvais terres" (badlands). Painter Karl Bodmer, who accompanied German Prince Maximillian on the Missouri in 1833, was captivated by these unusual landforms and included them in his paintings.

Some stretches of badlands stand out amidst grasslands, while others are mixed with river breaks terrain, especially along the Upper Missouri River Breaks National Monument.

These mini-deserts begin forming once the vegetation cover has been destroyed, usually by wildfire or overgrazing. Water running off of the underlying clay surface and soft bedrock causes erosion. Gullies are formed and seeds of potential new growth of plants and grasses are washed away or unable to take hold in the hardened soil.

Heavy spring and summer downpours accelerate the process. Steeper slopes are etched more quickly, and seemingly smooth surfaced alluvial deposits fan out below them. Soon, the entire disrupted area is void of green growth. Once well into the creation stage, they perpetuate themselves and become permanent. In a few instances, vegetation again takes hold in the disturbed areas and the beginnings of badlands topography is reversed.

While this carved, dry-appearing country receives as much precipitation as adjacent areas, the lack of a protective shield of flora gives it an image of receiving very little moisture.

Exquisite sandstone formations (where sandstone exists) are often intermingled with a badlands environment. Miniature and giant toadstools, castles and cathedrals, fine lined domes, balancing rocks, sentinel-like spires and other beautiful statues of rock add color and personality to these rain-furrowed hills while gremlins and goblins stand watch atop high cliffs. Wind erosion helps fashions them, taking away one grain of sand at a time.

Badlands and sandstone sculpture displays are found throughout Montana east of the main range of the Rockies. Makoshika State Park, on the south edge of Glendive, is perhaps the best-known accumulation of these austere places. Just to the west of Makoshika and across the Yellowstone River from the town of Terry, the Terry Badlands are another good example of this unique type of terrain. East of Jordan, lonesome Highway 200 slices through extensive parcels of "mauvais terres" that range north towards Fort Peck Lake.

The Powder River Country of southeast Montana, the Yellowstone River Breaks south of Sidney, many areas along the entire Hi-Line east of Browning

The Terry Badlands. RICK AND SUSIE GRAETZ

to North Dakota and the land between Scobey and Plentywood also display zones of these fascinating miniature deserts and wind-blasted stones.

The 300-mile stretch of the Missouri River from Fort Benton to Fort Peck is a showcase of sandstone creatures and badlands that illustrate evidence of what passed here 70 million years ago. Sections of McCone, Garfield and Phillips counties north and south of the Missouri were home to Tyrannosaurus Rex, Triceratops, Albertosaurus, Mosasaurus (a marine reptile) and other giant creatures. Due to erosion, some of the richest records of prehistoric life in the world have been, and continue to be, uncovered here. In 1902, one of the first T-Rex fossils ever found was discovered near Jordan in the Hell Creek badlands.

Badlands are intriguing to see anytime of the year and are best photographed as the first light of dawn illuminates them and again when the last rays of the sun turn these masses of earth and rock a rich gold and orange. Newly fallen snow gives them a totally different and beautiful look when framed against the deep blue of a cold winter sky. These natural masterpieces and the surrounding surfaces are fragile, so view and photograph them from the edge, leaving them untracked.

—RICK AND SUSIE GRAETZ

MONTANA'S WEATHER

C LIMATICALLY CHALLENGED IS HOW MONTANA MIGHT BE DESCRIBED...NONE OF that boring year-round 80 degrees and sunshine, our atmospheric circumstances can change abruptly and dramatically. And we get to enjoy extremes...exciting seasonal and unseasonable sky born stuff from all directions of the compass is a part of everyday life.

It gets darn hot and incredibly cold in different parts of this great state. We are visited by occasional tornadoes, plenty of blizzards, noisy thunder and wild lightening storms, drenching rains, our share of drought and the kind of winds that give the land character.

To begin with, our temperature records have an unimaginable 187-degree difference. A chilly January 20, 1954 morning gave us the national record for cold ... 70 below zero on Rogers Pass near Helena, while Glendive and Medicine Lake have heated up to a toasty 117 above. Because of fluctuating arctic fronts and warming Chinooks, our winter temperatures can rapidly drop or rise. We hold two national records in temperature swings. Browning went from a relatively balmy 44 degrees above to a bitter 56 degrees below zero in 24 hours; and in a mere seven minute period, at Great Falls, the mercury soared from 32 degrees below to 15 degrees above zero.

Some interesting precipitation occurrences have been bestowed upon

A ground blizzard along the Rocky Mountain Front. RICK AND SUSIE GRAETZ

us...Montana records for snowfall are: 44 inches in 24 hours at Summit, west of East Glacier; 77.5 inches from a single storm, also Summit; and Cooke City gathered 35 feet over one winter. In the rain department, Billings picked up 1.86 inches in just 30 minutes and Circle accumulated 11.50 inches over a 24-hour span. Summit, the snowy place, logged 55.51 inches of precipitation (water) in one year. And Great Falls recorded an 82 mph wind reading.

It should be emphasized, that all of these records have probably been exceeded, especially in terms of wind and snowfall, in places where there is no official weather observation equipment or facility. The northern Rocky Mountain Front west of Great Falls and the Livingston/Big Timber area have witnessed unbelievable wind speeds. The Beartooth high country, Glacier Park, the northern Swan Range, the Mission Mountains and northwest Yellowstone have all exceeded the snowfall recordings listed above. In some of these places, it snows every day in mid-winter; so much accumulates that it stays on the ground at higher elevations well into August. Estimates are that between 50 to 58 feet can drop in a season.

Rainfall in our mountains can also be heavy and long-lived; just ask anyone who has had to sit in a tent and outwait a storm in the Absaroka Beartooth Wilderness.

In the lofty valleys of southwestern Montana, 50 degrees below zero readings are not uncommon, yet this is not the coldest place in our state. Cooke City holds the distinction of having Montana's chilliest average yearly temperature. Its cool summers, when matched up with reasonably icy winters, help them earn this award. West Yellowstone is a close second and Wisdom is the third coldest spot on an annual average.

Westby, on the North Dakota line in northeastern Montana, has the lowest average winter temperature (5.7 degrees in January) in Big Sky Country. Overall, the prairie lands east of Malta and north of the Missouri River experience the coldest winters. Warming Chinook winds seldom reach this corner of Montana.

Thompson Falls a scant one-tenth of a degree hotter than Big Timber, is our warmest town on a yearly basis. In winter these two communities are also the warmest places in Montana and again are separated by only one-tenth of a degree. Thompson Falls sees very few extreme cold spells and Big Timber is frequented by warming winter winds.

In summer, Glendive in southeast Montana is the warmest town, but Miles City is close on its heels. This eastern prairie territory can witness 40 to 50 days during the warm season with temperatures 90 degrees or higher. Midwest heat, originating in the Gulf of Mexico, often reaches to the eastern one-third of Montana.

Winter's Chinook winds are one of Montana's most talked about weather phenomena. "Snow eaters," as they are often called, occur within 100 to 150 miles east of the Continental Divide and are especially strong off the mountain fronts from Glacier Park to the Livingston area. Further out on the plains, such as in the area around Glasgow, true Chinooks are not felt. What feels like one is just a warm wind blowing across the prairie.

Chinooks come to life in the southwest as warm, water-laden air rises and drops its moisture crossing the Great Divide. The air then heats and dries as it is compressed while rushing down the lee slopes of the mountains. This warm force pushes the cold air over the plains and eastside valleys into oblivion, causing striking temperature rises. Great Falls once went from minus 32 degrees to 15 above in seven minutes.

These temperate winds not only bring respite from the frigid air masses that descend on Montana, but up to three feet of snow can melt overnight. If the air is sufficiently warm and extremely dry, sometimes the snow doesn't have time to melt but instead sublimates, that is it changes directly from a solid to a gas. That is why we often see snow vanish without a trace. And a Chinook can end as quickly as it arrives, with the push of a ferocious northern blizzard reclaiming its season.

—RICK AND SUSIE GRAETZ

WEATHER NOTES

Our big Montana sky is a playing field for wild and unusual weather displays that leave folks shaking their heads in disbelief. Ever wonder why there is such an abrupt temperature change when arctic air enters the state or how hail forms? Well here's a look at various meteorological events and their causes.

Fog can be prevalent in winter, both in mountain valleys and on the prairie. For ground fog to occur, the air just above it must be moist from either a snowmelt or rain. This time of year, fog can occur in two ways. Advection fog, common to the mountain valleys, results from warm, wet air flowing over a cold ground. The cool surface causes the moist air temperature to drop and reach its dew or condensation point forming fog. Radiation fog happens on calm, clear nights when the air near the ground is chilled by radiated heat loss and the low level air is moist enough. Once again the dew point is reached and a cloud literally develops on the ground. As a rising sun warms and dries the air, the mist dissipates. However, a dense fog often takes days to go away.

On the plains, if the snow melts a bit from daytime warming, a layer of moisture occurs at ground level; a falling night temperature then allows fog to form in a widespread area.

The same principles for fog hold with the formation of dew in summer. Have you noticed how wet your legs get walking through tall grass in a high mountain meadow? In this case, the green vegetation protects the air at ground level from moving and drying out. On still, clear nights as the temperature drops, this air reaches its dew point and tiny water droplets form on the ground. The difference between fog and dew is that fog is created in cold weather and involves greater depths of chilled air. Frost is like fog and dew only the moisture freezes because the air is colder.

Those of us living east of the divide, especially from Helena north along the Rocky Mountain Front and all of Great Plains Montana have experienced radical changes in the temperature when an arctic air mass slams into the state. The frigid mass originates far to the north, where constant heat loss during frigid 24 hour nights allows the air to become increasingly colder, heavier and denser. These systems build until a strong, north push of air forces them south. The frigid, moisture laden mass is so weighty that it quickly gathers speed, battering the warmer air up and out of the way. This wall of cold air, when butting up against the warm air in front of it, allows for little transition and the temperature drops rapidly. Browning has seen the temperature fall from 44 degrees above to 56 below zero within 24 hours. Fairfield swung 84 degrees in 12 hours going from 63 above to 21 below.

Often these arctic outbreaks bring heavy snow to places like Helena and the Rocky Mountain Front. As cold air arrives, it pushes warm air up against the east side of the mountains (up sloping) and as this warm air rises and cools, copious amounts of snow can fall at the lower elevations while the amount deposited at higher altitudes is lighter.

Once in place, and especially if it is a high dome, it acts like a mountain and forces moisture-laden warmer air to ride over it (over-running), this air is then cooled to the point of condensation and considerable snowfall is possible.

Blizzards sometimes accompany this cold air from the north, but actually any snowstorm can reach this designation if a fierce, driving accompanying wind creates virtually no visibility. Frigid temperatures have nothing to do with it. Ground blizzards happen when previously fallen snow is whipped up by high winds, reducing sight to near zero in the first few feet above the land.

What about wind chill? Ever wonder what the wind chill would be on your car at 70 mph when the temperature is 30 below? No matter how fast the auto is going, or how hard the wind is blowing against an object, the temperature on that object is that of the still air. Wind chill only affects the human body and warm-blooded animals, and is related to their rate of heat loss — the faster the wind, the quicker the loss. If the temperature is 20 below and the wind is blowing at 25 mph, then your body feels an affect equivalent to 74 below zero, which indicates you would freeze in a hurry.

Wind adds clarity to our Montana sky. In mountainous regions as you climb higher, winds increase. Notice on a hilltop that you experience a breeze you might not feel below. Uneven terrain, with trees and hills, acts as a retardant to airflow, and in valleys, cold dense air is also a deterrent forcing the wind to stay above it. Strong winds though, resulting from an incoming system and caused by a pressure gradient (winds blowing from a high to a low), will affect all altitudes and scour out stagnant air. On the gentler prairie winds are felt at all levels.

Strong winds from the west and southwest can reach incredible speeds in favored areas near Livingston and in gaps in the Rocky Mountain Front. These down slope windstorms accelerate in areas with favorable terrain (they don't occur everywhere) and can be stronger than those just ten miles in either direction. Some places along the Front between Browning and Augusta have experienced winds of between 100 and 125 mph.

Jet stream winds can be very helpful to Montana as they define the storm track. Occurring in the most turbulent section of the atmosphere in the upper troposphere (25,000 to 40,000 feet) they are relatively narrow bands of wind extending from 60 miles to 300 miles across and no more than two miles deep. Wind speeds can be up to 120 mph but have often gone as high as 240 mph. In Montana they're called the "polar jet streams," and they mark the boundary between cold and warm air and are strongest where temperature differences are the greatest.

Wind helps make sailing a popular sport on Montana's lakes. Sea breezes on lakes form during the day as warm air rises from the land causing the cooler air over the water to fill the void, thus creating a lake wind. At night just the opposite can happen when land cools more quickly than water creating a land wind.

Some of Montana's most violent weather comes during the warm months in the form of thunderstorms. When moist air encounters a lifting catalyst such as the warm sun or a mountain, the rapidly rising air creates thunderheads. Fast ascending, moisture-laden air cools as it is elevated and then reaches its condensation point (rain begins to fall). Heat released during condensation adds more warmth to the air causing it to build and lift further. Storms generally build first in western Montana. Heat rises along the slopes of the mountains early in the day helping to trigger thunderstorm updrafts. Later in the day, and into the evening, these same cells can reach eastern Montana. The air in eastern Montana is wetter than the atmosphere in the western part of the state. Sometimes the Montana plains gather air from the Gulf of Mexico as the land slopes downward heading east. Mississippi Valley storms can also extend to eastern Montana, adding more humidity to the sky. For these reasons the storms on the prairie can intensify.

Alpine thunderstorms are often a rude interruption for backpackers and climbers. In the summer, the angle of the sun to a mountain is much higher than in winter (almost perpendicular) so it heats the ground quicker and pockets of warm air grow. When they rise above the mountain, clouds, some of which develop into thunderstorms, form.

Fantastic lightning displays are often part of mountain and prairie thunderstorms. Lightning can only occur in thunderstorms where there is an imbalance between positive and negative charges concentrated inside the storm. The clouds want to return to equilibrium and if the ground has a negative charge and the positive charge in the clouds is big enough, it arcs, causing a flash up from the ground to the cloud, hence the lightning. And it will continue as long as there is turbulence occurring. Lightning takes the path of least resistance so it aims for the highest ground. This is a good reason for not standing in the open during a storm. When in the mountains, hunkering down in a low-lying area away from trees or along a rock wall is your best bet. A car is also a safe place to be.

Thunder echoing like a sonic boom always accompanies lightning. The bolt of light expands the air making noise. Since light travels at 186,000 miles per second and sound creeps along at only 1,100 feet per second, thunder will follow the lightning. When you see lightning, count seconds. If you reach five before the clash, then the lightning is about one mile away.

Hail is no one's friend. It starts out as a snowflake and can only be created by thunderstorms with very strong updrafts of 60–70 miles per hour. As the cooling air reaches higher, the snowflake begins recycling in the turbulence and keeps adding layers (like a rolling snowball) each time it goes around until it's heavy enough to fall out. The strongest updrafts make the biggest hailstones.

Forest fires often create their own clouds and thunderstorms. A major fire can form an enormous cumulous cloud overhead when the rapidly rising heat condenses and grabs on to moisture in the air. Often lightning and rain can come out of these clouds, but there's seldom enough moisture to make a difference on the intense fire below. The cooling of the evening air will make the cloud disappear and spread the smoke out at lower levels.

A storm off on the horizon appears to be dumping rain, but when you arrive there, the ground is dry. In Montana, little moisture resides in the air in summer and therefore the clouds are very high. When precipitation falls, it can evaporate as it travels through the dry air never reaching land. In the humid mid-west where clouds are closer to the ground, drenching and long-lasting rains always reach the surface.

What looks like a long thin cloud following a jetliner across the sky is actually a man-made cloud called a contrail. Water introduced into the cold atmosphere by jet engine exhaust, is quickly cooled to condensation. Since they evaporate, the drier the air the shorter the lifespan of the contrail. If it spreads and lasts, you'll know the air is moist.

Adiabatic cooling is weather speak that describes the rate air cools as you ascend a mountain. In dry air the cooling rate is faster; as you climb, the temperature will drop about 5.5 degrees for every 1,000 feet you go up. If the air is very wet the rate only about 3.3 degrees per 1,000 feet.

Freezing rain creates the black ice that terrorizes drivers. It occurs when rain passes through air colder than 32 degrees but doesn't freeze until it reaches the surface. The subfreezing air above the ground isn't thick enough to freeze the rain. When the liquid hits a cold solid object (roads, tree branches etc.) it freezes on impact.

—RICK AND SUSIE GRAETZ

WINTER WEATHER

In any seemingly "winterless winter," it is important to note this season in Montana is usually allowed to "show its stuff" in the extreme, so don't get accustomed to the "tropical period." Stories abound about conditions changing quickly and in a pronounced way. We hold the national record for cold with a 70 degrees below zero reading near Helena. Research the recorded low for most towns on any given day from early November through March. You will see they range from -20F to -50F or colder. Archives of every Montana newspaper hold facts that give credibility to our reputation as a place where winter isn't whimpy!

Frigid times can come slowly while at other times the transition is abrupt. Take a look back to 1989...January witnessed a disastrous warm spell that tricked some shrubs and trees into believing spring had arrived. Unsuspecting vegetation prepared to show new growth until suddenly, winter reclaimed its place with a vengeance. Much plant life was killed. An Arctic air mass invaded the Northern Rockies bringing record cold temperatures and extreme wind chills. Ahead of the front, on January 30th, down slope winds gusted to 100 mph at Shelby, 102 mph at Browning and 124 mph at Choteau. Twelve empty railroad cars were blown over in Shelby. Elsewhere, roofs were ripped off houses, mobile homes torn apart and trees and power lines downed.

On January 31, temperatures plummeted dramatically. In Helena, it remained colder than -20F for four days including a low of -33F. Wind chills dropped to -75F. The intense cold caused brake failure on a freight train letting it roll, uncontrolled, into Helena where it exploded causing major damage to Carroll College.

Record lows were established in Billings, Bozeman, Missoula and many other towns. At Wisdom the mercury dropped to -52F. As the cold hit Great Falls, the temperature went from 54 degrees above zero to a minus 23 below zero (a 67 degree change) and did not rise to above -20F until February 4th. This included two record low temperatures (-35F and -33F) on the 3rd and 4th of February.

Another abrupt renewal of winter occurred on December 24, 1924; the temperature at Fairfield near Great Falls dropped from a balmy 63F at noon to a bone chilling -21F by midnight. This 84-degree difference still stands as the greatest 12-hour temperature change ever recorded in the United States.

Other stories of long, tough, frigid seasons abound, such as the winter of 1936. January was colder than usual. In February, the mean temperature from 111 reporting stations was 22.4 degrees colder than normal. Temperatures fell on the 13th to -53F at Summit (west of the Continental Divide) and on the 15th, to -57F at Cascade (southwest of Great Falls) and -59F at Frazer and Glasgow. Feed and fuel were scarce, water supplies froze, schools closed and 15 lives were lost. While March saw an overall average temperature, the month ended with well below zero readings. On the 30th, Red Lodge was at -20F,

Chessman Reservoir was at -28F and Summit's low was -29F. Winter's grip held through early April with temperatures bottoming out at -28F at Chessman Reservoir on the 1st. During this winter, many areas of eastern Montana recorded below zero readings for 57 days straight. Ten below was considered to be a warm day and the wind chill often exceeded -100F.

In 1965, a Terry woman reported to the Miles City Star that it had been -20F at her place on November 20th and -20F on March 20th "and darned few days did the temperature rise above 20 below in-between;" a total period of 4 months or 123 days. Pat Gudmundson, writing in a Miles City Star publication, related that the 1977–78 cold season started with heavy November snows and below normal temperatures that continued through each month. A February blizzard isolated many southeastern towns when 15 to 20-foot drifts blocked roads and buried houses up to their rooftops. Snowplow crews struggled to open roads only to be hit by another storm.

To most folks who experienced it, the winter of 1919–20 was considered severe because it lasted from early October until May. But 1886–87 is thought to be the worst because of its impact on the cattle industry. This was the winter Charlie Russell so poignantly titled his sketch "Waiting for a Chinook or The Last of the 5,000 Brand" that started his rise to fame. After an extremely dry summer and fall, grass was scarce. Arctic storms hit in November and December followed by short thaws. By January, a hard icy crust covered what little vegetation there was making it impossible for animals to get at it. Deep snow and a fierce -30F to -40F cold returned and continued unabated until early March. It was the end of an era, 50–95% of the great cattle herds were lost; the days of unmanaged, free-roaming grazing were over.

So don't let an unusually warm and dry winter lull you into believing Montana's winter's have headed north for good…the cold and snow sometimes takes leave but has the option to return with retribution.

—RICK AND SUSIE GRAETZ

70 BELOW AND MAYBE COLDER

Snow had been falling almost continuously for a week and it was very cold; the temperature had only risen to minus 18 degrees. Finally, late in the day, the snow and wind stopped, skies cleared rapidly, and as the sun set the temperature plummeted. Early the next morning on January 20, 1954, Montana's and the continental 48 states' record cold temperature of minus 70 degrees was observed at a mining camp near the Continental Divide a short distance from Rogers Pass near Helena. The reading was observed by one of the National Weather Service's cooperative observers.

The Rogers Pass weather station, located at an elevator 5,470 feet, was established May I, 1953, at the 4 K's Mine located at Highway 200 and three-fourths of a mile west of where the highway crosses Rogers Pass.

Richard A. Dightman, State Climatologist at the Weather Bureau, was not aware of the record it until about February 3 when January's records were received at the Helena office. The January 20 minimum temperature was entered as minus 68 degrees. Dightman noticed that this would be a record, valid, breaking the old national record of minus 66 degrees at West Yellowstone, Montana, on February 9, 1933. So H. M. Kleinschmidt, the observer, was contacted and asked to send in his thermometer to be checked and to provide any other information he could to help evaluate the reading.

He not only sent in the official minimum thermometer, but also included his own alcohol thermometer. He wrote that he was awake most of the severely cold night because of loud and frequent "popping" noises in the cabin. About 2 a.m. he got up and looked at his thermometer located outside an insulated window. It read about minus 68 degrees. He then went outside to the official shelter and found the minimum thermometer indicating a temperature colder than minus 65 which is as low as the scale on it indicates. The minimum index from which the temperature is read had retreated into the bulb and was tilted since the index end had fallen into the bulb.

The two thermometers were sent to the Weather Bureau in Washington, D.C. where they were checked in the lab exactly as the observer described. The index in the official thermometer fell into the bulb and remained at the described angle at a temperature of minus 69.7 degrees. At this temperature, Kleinschmidt's personal thermometer indicated minus 68 degrees.

Conditions had been right for an extreme temperature. The station was located at a high elevation in a saucer shaped depression. During the previous week there were several fresh invasions of very cold arctic air into Montana. Seven days of almost continuous snow increased the snow depth from eight inches to 66 inches at the mine. The night was crystal clear with no wind — ideal conditions for strong cooling.

Perhaps it should be pointed out that the record is an extreme occurring in an extreme location under extreme conditions — in a small, high mountain valley with 5½ feet of snow on the ground, 58 inches of which had fallen recently. The minus 70 degree reading was not representative of the more densely populated areas of the state; that night a low of minus 31 degrees occurred in Butte, minus 43 degrees in Havre, minus 34 degrees in Billings, minus 37 degrees in Great Falls, minus 36 degrees in Helena and minus 14 degrees in Missoula.

The facts that the two thermometers behaved in the lab exactly as described by the observer, that temperatures of minus 57 degrees and minus 59 degrees were recorded in the same general area and that the observer was not aware that he was recording a record temperature were sufficient evidence to adopt the minus 70 degree record.

Most stations are supplied with thermometers similar to Kleinschmidt's that only go to minus 65 degrees. Thus, these thermometers cannot break the record. We know only that on that night it was at least minus 70 degrees; it very well may have gotten colder but the thermometer was unable to record it. The minus 70 degree reading was at 2 a.m. and normally the night's minimum temperature occurs shortly after sunrise.

The record more than likely will have to be broken in a high mountain valley somewhere in Montana or perhaps Wyoming. A few selected weather stations in areas such as this are supplied with colder reading thermometers. And not only must the extreme conditions exist to establish a new record, but someone has to be there to observe!

—RICK AND SUSIE GRAETZ WITH GRAYSON CORDELL

THIS ARTICLE IS A REPRINT OF A VERSION WE WROTE IN THE 1970S WITH THE LATE GRAYSON CORDELL WHO WAS THE METEOROLOGIST-IN-CHARGE AT THE NATIONAL WEATHER SERVICE IN HELENA, MONTANA AND CLIMATOLOGIST FOR THE STATE OF MONTANA. THE PIECE ALSO APPEARED IN LONGER FORM IN A BOOK WE PRODUCED IN 1982 THROUGH OUR MONTANA MAGAZINE TITLED MONTANA WEATHER.

THE FLOODS OF JUNE 1964

Spring 1964 ... Heavy and continuous high country storms create a healthy snow pack. In June, with the first warm weather, the white stuff commences to melt and creeks, tumbling off the mountains throughout western Montana, begin to swell.

In conjunction, an extraordinary meteorological event develops in the Gulf of Mexico and massive amounts of atmospheric moisture head northwest. A storm of the century prepares itself, seeking conditions to be let loose. On June 7th, when it reaches Montana, the catalyst is found. Here, the beast collides head-on with a south moving accumulation of cold Arctic air; condensation of high proportions was about to begin (in other words, we were going to get wet). The gulf humidity was immediately released over Montana; raindrops grew to their maximum size and fell at an incredible rate — in some places, it measured one inch an hour. The southern reaches of Glacier National Park experienced 16 inches of rain in 36 hours.

Misery was not without company. Much of Montana shared in the tempest, but the drainages of Birch Creek, and the Sun, Dearborn, Teton, Marias and Two Medicine rivers east of the Continental Divide and the Flathead system on the west side of the Divide saw the greatest damage. The floods and rampaging water that resulted, were, in the opinion of the National Weather Service in Great Falls, the worst Montana had experienced since record keeping began. President Lyndon Johnson declared Montana a National Disaster Area as 34 people lost their lives and more than $62,000,000 in damages was assessed.

In Glacier National Park, roads, trails, bridges and buildings were destroyed. Nearby, in Bear Creek's valley, barren swaths were created as the torrent took out trees, soil, rock and parts of US Hwy 2. Twisted, sluiced out railroad track could be seen for six miles along the Middle Fork of the Flathead and water filled the Great Northern Tunnel. The Middle Fork itself was a sight to see, as floodwaters were 78 feet above the normal level of the river. At West Glacier, the swell went over a bridge almost 80 feet higher than the water in ordinary flow. In some places, debris was found stranded on the cross arms of power poles 20 feet off the ground. Seventeen continuous miles of highway between Marias Pass and West Glacier was completely washed out.

Sections of the Flathead Valley at Kalispell and Columbia Falls resembled lakes. Elsewhere in western Montana, the water was high as well. The Deer Lodge and Bitterroot valleys experienced extensive flooding. The Great Falls Tribune of June 14, 1964, showed a poignant photograph of a rabbit stranded on a plank floating down the raging Clark Fork River near Plains in the northwest part of the state.

East of the mountains, dams were breached on the Lower Two Medicine River and Birch Creek. When the Swift Dam on Birch Creek gave way, a 20-foot-high wall of water bulldozed its way downstream taking out all that came in its path. In the same area, refrigerators, washing machines, sinks, dead ranch animals, wrecked trucks and all manners of the other rubble were scattered over the prairie. Pavement on a highway in Birch Creek Valley was lifted off the roadbed and deposited in the burrow pit 45 degrees off its original direction. Along the Rocky Mountain Front, Cattle were stranded and homes isolated. Today, nearly 40 years later, some of this widespread damage is still evident.

Choteau, Augusta and Great Falls flooded and at Lewistown, Spring Creek went over its banks. Creeks and rivers changed channels. Portions of bridges were moved to fields while some were completely lost and never located. Many small towns were cut off from food and medical supplies; churches and schools became temporary shelters. Air Force cargo planes landed on highways and in grass fields to deliver supplies where they could. The Blackfeet Reservation in particular was hard hit. Heart Butte, a reservation community, had a number of residents injured. The only early aid available came from a nurse who did what she could while receiving instructions from a physician via the phone.

In an effort to prevent less damage, the gates on Helena's Canyon Ferry Dam were closed to hold back the Missouri River's flow until the surging waters from the Sun River receded and the flooding passed through Great Falls.

Finally, when the storm's energy was spent and the sky's showed clear, Montanans began the arduous task of cleanup and repairs. Some of the toil took months and even longer. The Great Northern Railway fixed their route rapidly with an industrious seven-day-a-week track building effort. On June 29, 1964, trains were again crossing the Continental Divide at Marias Pass.

Many folks blamed the ample snow in the mountains for the flooding — there certainly had been plenty of it. Although this contributed to the problem, it was not the main culprit since the pack was still quite evident after the storm ceased. All analysis showed it was clearly the amount of and intensity of the unleashed precipitation, in such a short time frame, that was the cause of this natural catastrophe.

While all Montana papers carried news and photos of the June, 1964 storm and its aftermath, one newsman in particular covered it in a way that brought acclaim to him, his newspaper and to Montana journalism overall. The late Mel Ruder, owner, publisher and editor of the Hungry Horse News of Columbia Falls, won the coveted grand award of his profession ... the Pulitzer Prize, for his reporting and photography of this episode.

This wasn't just an ordinary case of high water; Ruder knew people needed the story to be recorded. Crisscrossing flooded areas, he detailed the unimaginable power of water on the loose, showing the losses and devastation as well as the human side. Using a large Speed Graphic camera, this newsman captured photos by air, boat and land. And Ruder and wasn't selfish with the information, he supplied reports to the Associated Press and gave live radio updates.

For a week, Mel survived on three hours of sleep a night; he was energized. By Friday, June 12, Ruder and his small staff had all the material they needed and the weekly Hungry Horse News published 6,250 copies — two times its normal run, selling them out immediately. Saturday and Sunday saw additional printings. In all, 12,500 copies, three times the usual press count, were sold.

The story was out. Folks who had been isolated until waters receded, as well as all Montanans, could now see what happened and read why. This epic account was now profiled by one of Montana's best newspaper photographers and it was accomplished in an unequaled way!

Dorothy Johnson, herself a prominent Montana writer, nominated Mel Ruder for the Pulitzer Prize. On May 3, 1965, Mel received word that he was a winner. A man and his newspaper have insured that this incredible 1964 storm, Big Sky Country's mightiest, is forever etched in the archives of Montana's history.

THERMOMETERS

Did you ever notice on a brisk winter morning that we never know how cold to feel until we know the temperature? We may sense that it is brisk, but until we actually check the thermometer or listen to a weather report we don't know how to personally react. Enter the thermometer.

In the grand scheme of things, the thermometer is a relatively new device for measuring temperature. Prior to the first one being developed by Galileo in the early 1600s, actual "degrees" of temperature didn't exist. Rather, weather observers had to use descriptive phrases like cold, chilly, warm, or hot to record or relate to someone how hot or cold their particular "environment" was.

Even Galileo wasn't very scientific about calibrating the "degrees" of warmth or cold that his new device measured. The two most familiar scales used today are the Fahrenheit and Celsius. Gabriel Fahrenheit developed his in about 1724. Using mercury as the fluid in his thermometer, he arbitrarily chose 32 "degrees" as the freezing point of pure water and 212 degrees as its boiling point. In 1742, another scientist, Anders Celsius developed a scale that used the metric system. With his scale, 100 degrees separated the freezing and boiling point of water.

Today, the Celsius scale is used for measuring temperatures by most countries around the world. The United States is one of the last hold-outs to converting to the metric system of measurement.

There are also some very strict criteria used in order for temperatures to be considered "official." The National Climate and Data Center, our national repository for all things weather, recognizes readings from either liquid-in-glass or electronic measuring devices, as authorized and calibrated by the National Weather Service. However, the most critical element is where these instruments are physically located.

"Thermometers must be enclosed in shelters, which act as shields from the sun, rain, snow, and other sources of light, heat, or cold which can cause erroneous readings. Shelters are designed to allow maximum possible free flow of air while providing protection from heat and light. This is accomplished with louvers which slope downward from the inside to the outside of the shelter and with a double top." (as taken from National Weather Service Observing Handbook No.2)

In addition, "the ground over which the shelter is located should be typical of the surrounding area… When possible, the shelter should be no closer than four times the height of any obstruction (tree, fence, building, etc.). It should be at least 100 feet from any paved or concrete surface." (ibid) And, the shelter should be positioned so that the thermometer is located 1.5 meters above the ground surface.

Bottom line, thermometers hanging on the side of a barn, in direct sunlight or the time and temperature billboard located next to a paved bank parking lot do not qualify as official, even though they sometimes give us incredible "record setting" readings.

—JOHN PULASKI

MONTANA BY REGIONS

NORTHWEST MONTANA

M ONTANA'S FAR NORTHWEST CORNER MAY WELL BE THE EPITOME OF WHAT outsiders perceive of Montana … great rivers, vast forests reaching to snow-covered summits, shimmering blue lakes, wilderness, Indian legends and lumberjacks.

Mountain ranges dominate; there isn't much flat terrain. They are the Purcel, Cabinet, Salish, Coeur D'Alene, Bitterroot, Whitefish, Mission, Swan, Rattelsnake, Garnet and the Lewis and Livingston ranges of Glacier National Park, considered by many to be Montana's most beautiful mountains.

The crest of the Bitterroot Range forms the Montana/Idaho border.

On a morning that saw winter doing its best to hang on, we stood high above the eastern flank of Lake Koocanusa (the Kootenai River behind Libby

Dam). It was quiet, with no sign of boats on the lake or cars on road; the silence gave us a chance to reflect. Although much of the country beyond our view had been logged, from our particular vantage point all we saw before us was undisturbed timber and a deep valley. Throughout the sunrise, we imagined the once-wild Kootenai River running below and the Kootenai Indians and the first fur trappers canoeing the rapids or following the tough portage route above the whitewater.

Once a trackless wilderness, the earliest humans coming through the area had to negotiate steep treacherous terrain along the river. In this country, the mountainsides dip sharply to the water; easy shore passage didn't exist then or even now. Legendary fur trader, explorer and cartographer David Thompson, one of the first whites to traverse this geography noted in his journal of a "rude path 300 feet above the river and the least slip would have been sure destruction."

The Kootenai, Salish (Flathead) and Kalispell (Pend d'Oreille), some of the great Indian Nations, arrived in the 1500s, well before the culture of the Plains Indians took root east of the mountains.

In the summer of 1808, Thompson and his crew from the North-West Company, a fur-trading outfit, became the first whites to venture into these woods and mountains. Their mission, as they traveled down the Kootenai River from Canada, was to open up commerce with the Indians. The first "commercial" establishment in western Montana was constructed in October 1808, when Thompson's assistant, Finian McDonald, put up a crude winter camp near the mouth of Pipe Creek on the Kootenai across from today's town of Libby, and opened shop. Three years later, Thompson built the initial "permanent" trading post a few miles upriver. The era of the fur trade was officially in effect in mountainous northwest Montana.

Thompson was also a geographer and explorer. From 1808 to 1809, he mapped much of the northwest, including Missoula. Thompson Falls along the Clark Fork was named in his honor.

Notes on the Kootenai River seem to go back the furthest in time, but there are other prominent waters up here ... the Clark Fork, Yaak, Bull, Vermillion, Thompson and St. Regis rivers, as well as the Flathead system. They too drain a timbered and rough landscape and witnessed their share of early day travelers.

The Clark Fork is western Montana's primary river. Launched between Anaconda and Butte at Warm Springs, after passing through Missoula, it enters a deep canyon just beyond Frenchtown, skirting the Bitterroot Range and the Cabinet Mountains. Until now, Interstate 90 has been following the river; at St. Regis, it makes an abrupt S turn and then US Hwy 200 accompanies it into Idaho on its way to the Columbia River.

In the 1880s, the Great Northern Railroad's track reached the forests of northwest Montana where logging, another activity that spawned lore, had

The home of Charles Conrad, early-day Kalispell businessman. RICK AND SUSIE GRAETZ

taken hold. In its initial years, the timber industry was local and consisted mainly of cutting fence posts and logs for buildings. Later, new and distant markets were opened up for Montana timber. The railroads themselves needed wooden ties, trestles and bridges. In the 1880s and beyond, Butte's expanding copper mines had an enormous appetite for timber to shore up shafts, tunnels and for construction in general.

The wood products industry soon became the hallmark of the area and dominated its social fabric from the last 20 years of the 1800s well through the 1900s.

The first operations were situated deep in the forests. Void of modern mechanization, the logs had to be hauled on horse-driven sleds to the nearest river and floated to the mills. The logging camps were home to the sawyers, a tough breed of characters who lived in the woods all week and raided the nearest town on the weekend to spend their money.

Steam machinery, then diesel trucks eventually took over and the loggers moved into town. Today, the timber industry is a shell of its former presence and the few mills still operating struggle to do so. Communities show evidence of a logging past and present — a checkerboard pattern of clear cuts in various stages of regrowth covers the mountainsides, old rusted tepee burners stand vigilant outside of town and logging trucks barreling out of the woods are part of life.

The industry may never rise again to its former level, but there are those striving to make it more sustainable, albeit smaller.

Here in the northwestern part of our state, in direct contrast to southwestern Montana, the valleys are deep and narrow and the forests consist of many species, such as aspen, larch, lodgepole, ponderosa, cedar, spruce, fir, juniper and white pine. Where they stand is dictated by elevation.

The timbered country is widespread; some counties are 90 percent forested. In the far corner of the northwestern province, trees make a good living — growth is excellent owing to ample moisture. The Kootenai Forest is Pacific-like, with lush hillsides and dense growth; some areas receive up to 50 inches of rain a year. South of Troy and just east of the Idaho boundary, the Ross Creeks Giant Cedars (Red Cedar), a 100-acre grove of trees 12 feet in diameter and up to 175 feet high, thrive in a dark, cool and humid enclave.

The Western larch, or tamarack, is a widespread and dominant tree throughout northwest Montana. In the fall, its needles turn yellow-gold then light orange and the mountainsides take on the look of an impressionistic painting. The needles fall off before winter, carpeting the forest floor. Initially, the new growth in the spring is a delicate light green color; a startling contrast with the darker evergreens and snow covered peaks.

Larger Western larch is more common than the alpine variety and grows at lower elevations. These beautiful trees can live 600 years; stand dead for 100 years and decay for another couple hundred years, giving them a 900- to 1,000-year life cycle. They can take fires and temperature extremes and the wood is dense and durable, making for strong structural support.

Trees and wildflowers are everywhere, but one particular flowering plant is the toast of late spring and early summer in many areas of northwestern Montana. When beargrass blooms, it comes to life on a tall stem (up to five feet) as a bell or egg-shaped delicate creamy flower. In a good year, beargrass often creates stunning seas of white. Supposedly, the plant's flowering cycle is once every seven years. Indians wove the tough and wiry grass part into clothing and baskets. Bears don't eat it, but goats and elk do. Beargrass is the official flower of Glacier National Park.

Fifty percent of the northwest's woodland topography is federally owned in National Forest and Wilderness. Management of these lands by the U.S. government at times can be in direct conflict with the wishes of locals. The fact that the public forests are administered as a national resource gets lost in arguments and expectations.

Much of the landscape of the western half of the region is roaded, with roadless areas existing only in pockets such as the Cabinet Wilderness and the Great Burn. Hunting and fishing are major activities for leisure and food. Wildlife, like the trees are plentiful — Grizzly, deer, elk, cougars, eagles, coyote, moose and their neighbors roam here. Even a few woodland caribou hang out in the vicinity of Northwest Peak Scenic Area in the Yaak region and the Purcell Mountains of the farthest corner of the northwest.

The eastern half of northwest Montana has extensive unroaded wildlands in Glacier Park, and the Great Bear, Bob Marshall, Mission Mountain and Rattelsnake wilderness areas. The legendary Bob Marshall Country is a hallowed piece of western Montana. It is part of a huge ecosystem extending north from Hwy 200 through the Bob Marshall Country into Glacier National Park and Canada. Only two roads cross it in an almost 200 mile stretch.

In the center of the province, the only wide valley, geologically known as the Rocky Mountain trench and carved out by a succession of massive valley glaciers, cuts northwest Montana into two and is itself broken into a northern and southern segment. The northern stretch starts at the foot of the Whitefish Range at the Canadian border and extends south to the Mission Valley. The big Polson glacial moraine interrupts it to hold back Flathead Lake, the largest freshwater lake west of the nation's heartland. Whitefish, Kalispell, Polson and other smaller communities take up a small bit of space within the valley. However, the Flathead Indian Reservation claims a fair chunk of the it and surrounding mountains.

The southern piece picks up just south of Polson. An area called Evaro Hill, beyond Arlee fills it in. Then it becomes distinct again north of Missoula. From there it continues south through the Bitterroot Valley, but that territory belongs to southwest Montana.

On the morning side of the Mission Mountains, the Swan Valley, bordered to the east by the Swan Range, is another long but narrow valley, continuing for 90 miles from Salmon Lake to the Bigfork area.

Of the two major towns in the northwestern part of the state, Missoula came early and Kalispell late. In 1860, two businessmen, Higgins and Worden,

City Beach on Whitefish Lake. RICK AND SUSIE GRAETZ

established a trading post in a tent where the Bitterroot and Clark Fork rivers converge, calling it Hellgate and giving Missoula a jump-start. The traders soon moved from Hellgate to near Rattlesnake Creek; modern Missoula was born and grew on timber, railroads and the University of Montana.

Kalispell didn't assert itself until 1891, when it came on line courtesy of a hot bit of news railroad tycoon Jim Hill gave to Charles Conrad. Insider trading at its best, Hill told Conrad, who had already gained wealth in the freighting business at Fort Benton, to move to the northern Flathead because his steel rails would soon be heading that way. Conrad moved there and got a town going just in time. Railroad, logging and tourism fueled Kalispell's economic well-being, as well as that of Mr. Conrad.

The university town is considered the hub of five rivers and valleys ... Jocko, Upper Clark Fork, Lower Clark Fork, Big Blackfoot and the Bitterroot. Kalispell is viewed as the western gateway to Glacier National Park and the hub of the northern Flathead Valley.

By Montana standards, northwestern Montana's weather is thought of as moderate. Summer temperatures can be warm but not as blistering, as is the case in the southwestern and eastern parts of the state. The reverse is the case in winter. Ample snow falls, but temperatures colder than 25 degrees below zero are rare. As the area is west of the Continental Divide, Pacific born air masses influence its weather, especially in winter. Long periods of cloudy days and nights are common, and temperature inversions are a fact of life in the fall and winter in western Montana. Warm overriding air often traps colder air and fog in the valleys, while the higher terrain is in the sunshine and considerably warmer. It takes winds and system changes to correct the situation.

Oh, and before we forget, another bit of geographic information on Northwest Montana. The state's lowest point — 1,820 feet — is found where the Kootenai River leaves Montana just beyond Troy, which has the lowest elevation of any Montana town — 1,892 feet.

—RICK AND SUSIE GRAETZ

THE BITTERROOT RANGE TO LOLO PASS

At a point in northwest Montana where the Cabinet Gorge allows the Clark Fork River to continue its journey beyond the state, forested slopes rise abruptly, 2,300 feet above the water, to create the northern tip of the Bitterroot Range. Twisting and turning, ascending and lowering, the crest stretches south for 470 miles to form almost the entire Montana-Idaho border. Half-way along, at Lost Trail Pass (named for Lewis and Clark because they lost their way here), the Continental Divide joins in and stays with this high barrier the rest of the way.

Three sub-groups compose the main range. From their beginnings in the north to Lost Trail Pass, the peaks are named the Bitterroot Mountains. South to Monida Pass, they are the Beaverheads. At Monida they become the

The Bitterroot Range begins off of the Clark Fork at Noxon Dam. RICK AND SUSIE GRAETZ

Centennials and turn east to the vicinity of Henrys Lake and Raynolds Pass and the terminus of the Bitterroot Range.

Montana's largest mountain chain drains a wide area, discharging water to both the Pacific Ocean and the Gulf of Mexico. On the north side of Lost Trail Pass, the Bitterroots and Sapphires form a bowl spawning the Bitterroot River and the start of a 245-mile-long north by northwest pointing conduit for runoff from the east face of the range, to meet the Pacific via the Clark Fork of the Columbia.

Lost Trail Pass serves as the separating point for the watershed of the Bitterroots. All flow from south of it connects with major tributaries of the Missouri, such as the Big Hole, Beaverhead and Red Rock rivers and eventually pours into the Gulf of Mexico.

From the Cabinet Gorge southward to Lolo Pass west of Missoula, the peaks (6,000–7,000 feet) are relatively low and tree covered. This is timber country and as a result, quite a few logging roads get close to the divide. Lookout Pass, a major thoroughfare across the mountains, connects Montanans with Idaho and Washington. North of the pass, on some maps, the Bitterroots use a local name at times…the Coeur D' Alene Mountains.

Pockets of wildlands, including the proposed Great Burn wilderness, spot the Bitterroots. The Great Burn takes its name from the forest fires that devastated this part of Montana in 1910.

Unlike their southern extension where wide valleys flank the sunrise side, the east margin of the range here in the northwest descends to a narrow bottomland. Mountains again rise quickly just across the way. Alberton, Superior, Plains, Thompson Falls and Trout Creek, communities born from logging, are well spaced along the Clark Fork River, the Bitterroots eastern guardian.

Under a couple of sub-range banners, the Bitterroot Range continues south following the Montana Idaho border to within 20 miles of Yellowstone National Park. We pick up this journey in the Southwest Montana chapter.
—RICK AND SUSIE GRAETZ

MOUNTAIN NOTES

Coeur D' Alene Mountains

A part of the Bitterroot Range, this sub range extends for almost 75 miles, with peaks ranging from 5,000 to 7,000 feet, between the lower Clark Fork River and the St. Regis River south of Thompson Falls.

The Cabinet Mountains

The Cabinet Mountains, just to the west of Libby, are the dominant range of northwestern Montana. They extend about 80 miles along a northwest-southeast axis and are bordered by the Idaho state line on the west, the Clark Fork River and Hwy 200 on the south, Thompson River on the east, and the Kootenai River and Hwy 2 on the north.

The Cabinet Mountain Wilderness forms the core of the range. This 35-mile-long wild area of nearly 100,000 acres consists of jagged peaks, high lake basins and open country with spectacular alpine views. The summits are relatively low, but the surrounding elevations are among the lowest in Montana, and so the resulting relief creates formidable-looking mountains. The highest point in the range is 8,712-foot Snow Shoe Peak. The Cabinets themselves are the highest mountains between Glacier National Park and the Cascade Range of Washington to the west. As such, they form one of the first major mountain barriers to eastward-flowing Pacific storms that can drop up to 100 inches of precipitation here each year.

The mountains of the southeast portion of the Cabinets are less rugged than the wilderness summits. Several peaks are more than 7,000 feet high, including 7,429-foot Mount Headley.

The Bull River Valley separates the Cabinet Mountain Wilderness Area from the rest of the range to the northwest. The tops of this segment are the lowest in the range, reaching elevations of about 6,500 feet.

Many of the peaks and the surrounding forestlands of the northwest part of the state have been heavily logged; the country around the Cabinets is no exception. Nonetheless, 75,000 acres of this area — the Scotchman Peaks in the West Cabinets — are pristine wildlands. Ross Creek and its giant cedar trees (some are more than 8 feet in diameter and 175 feet tall) are in this

Snow ghosts at the Big Mountain Ski Resort in the Whitefish Range.

locale. Savage Mountain, at 6,900 feet, is the highest pinnacle in the West Cabinet/Scotchman Peaks. From here the range slopes downward and north to 1,802 feet above sea level, the lowest point in the state — where the Kootenai River leaves Montana just west of Troy.

Purcell Mountains

Home of the Yaak River Valley and the Northwest Peak Scenic Area, the Purcells rise in the extreme northwest corner of Montana. They're just north of Libby and the Kootenai River, Idaho is to their west, Canada to the north, and 35-mile-long Lake Kookanuska stretches along the eastern perimeter.

As elsewhere in northwestern Montana, elevations here are relatively low. The highest mountains of the Purcells are found in and around the Northwest Peak Scenic Area. Northwest Peak, at 7,705 feet, is their highest pinnacle.

Much of the region is roaded and logged, but the Northwest Peak Scenic Area has been set-aside to be protected from timbering, and contains several lake basins (including seven high lakes) and superb mountain scenery. The remains of a 1930s lookout tower, offers big vistas of the adjacent Yaak River wildlands as well as far north into Canada.

Across a labyrinth of roads and clear-cut forests, the prominent points of Purcell Peak and 7,243-foot Mount Henry stand out.

Just beyond the Northwest Peaks Area, and a few miles to the west and above the Yaak River, the 25-mile-long roadless Buckhorn Ridge — ascending between 6,000 feet and 6,500 feet — is an important wildlife sanctuary.

The Whitefish Range

A major range, stretching 60 miles north of Columbia Falls to the Canadian line, most of its peaks are in the 7,000-foot neighborhood, but relief of up to 4,000 feet on the west side is impressive. The highest summit in the Montana segment (part of the Whitefish Range extends into Canada) is Nasukoin Mountain at 8,095 feet.

Major portions of the range remain roadless. Ten Lakes Scenic Area was established for hiking, but the North Fork Flathead wildlands, consisting of Tuchuck, Mount Hefty and Thompson Seton — lack lasting federal wilderness protection. Their heavy timber provides excellent grizzly bear habitat.

The range is bordered by the North Fork of the Flathead River and the peaks of Glacier Park to the east, and the Tobacco Valley on their western edge.

The most famous attraction in the Whitefish Range is the Big Mountain Ski Area, a major destination resort.

Salish Mountains

This range of timbered hills and mountains runs for 100 miles from just south of Eureka to the west of Polson and Flathead Lake. The highest summits are short of 7,000 feet. Named for the Salish Indians, they feature many large lakes, including Lake Mary Ronan, Little Bitterroot, McGregor, Hubbert, Thompson, Ashley and Talley, all well-known recreation areas. Blacktail Mountain, at 6,757 feet, just west of Lakeside, is the state's newest ski area. Baldy Mountain, at 7,464 feet, and just west of Hot Springs in the extreme southern end of the range, is the highest peak.

Rattlesnake Mountains

The Rattlesnakes are Missoula's mountains, dominating the northeast horizon of this university town. The Rattlesnake Wilderness Area, as well as the Rattlesnake National Recreational Area and the Tribal Primitive Area to the north, protect the land. Trails meander throughout it. McCloud Peak at 8,620 feet is the highest summit. Stuart Peak, a favorite trek, is 7,960 feet high. More than 50 creeks and 30 lakes grace the upper reaches of the Wilderness section. The northern segment of the area, managed by the Confederated Salish/Kootenai Tribes, is off limits to all but tribal members because it is a sacred site.

Missoula Snowbowl Ski Area sits in the Rattlesnake Mountains.

—RICK AND SUSIE

GREAT BURN

"Winds felled trees as if they were blades of grass; darkness covered the land; firewhirls danced across the blackened skies like an aurora borealis from below; the air was electric with tension, as if the earth itself was ready to explode into flames. And everywhere people heard the roar, like a thousand freight trains crossing a thousand steel trestles."

So reads Stephen Pyne's vivid description of the summer from hell that visited the forests of the northern Bitterroot Divide — Montana/Idaho border in 1910.

From May through August of that year very little rain fell, and the snow had disappeared from southern slopes by April; vegetation was rendered tinder-dry. In July, hundreds of fires, some lightning caused, most by careless people, were burning. For a while they were controlled, but on August 20th, high winds (called "Palouse Winds" because they came from eastern Washington), brought smoldering embers and smaller fires to life, sparking an enormous conflagration and fire tornadoes. It wasn't until September 4th, that the rains finally came and halted the inferno's advance. When it was over, more than three million acres had been consumed and the mining town of Wallace, Idaho destroyed. The landscape was forever changed.

The forests came back and some were burned again; however, ninety years

The Yaak River in the far NW corner of the state. RICK AND SUSIE GRAETZ

later, reminders of that fiery summer can still be found. The event is still very much evident in the magnificent 250,000-acre stretch of wild country, 30 miles west of Missoula, called the Great Burn. Its landscape reaches across the Montana/Idaho line ... 98,000 acres are in Montana. This, the largest unprotected roadless area left in the lower 48 states, stretches from Granite Pass on the south to Hoodoo Pass in the north. In a straight line on the Montana side it covers about 32 miles.

Thousands of standing dead snags and large open spaces define the place. Had it remained free of fire since 1910, dense tree cover would have probably dominated the area. However, subsequent fires burned the regrowth lodgepole before they could sprout seeds. Hence, grasses took over, creating vast stretches of meadows and parklands filled with wild flowers. Bill Cunningham, author of Wild Montana, calls them the "lowest elevation true tundra in Montana." These fire induced tundra lands resemble those found in the Beartooth at elevations from 4,000 — 6,000 feet higher.

The Great Burn doesn't have towering jagged summits and ridges like those of the Bitterroots south of Lolo Pass, but it is still rugged and mountainous. Elevations range from 3,200 to 7,700 feet creating some impressive relief. Slopes are steep and in many places dense with tag alder. Hiking off-trail is tough. Stair-step waterfalls cascade clear cold water from the higher terrain into creek bottoms lush with ferns. In some places, these narrow valleys shelter 600-year-old red cedars that escaped the 1910 holocaust. More than 30, deep blue lakes spot the length of the divide and provide habitat for cutthroat, rainbow and golden trout. Some 1,000 elk call this pristine country home.

As these mountains are well west of the Continental Divide, they are often visited by clouds and ample moisture. Afternoon summer thunderstorms are common and snow lies deep in winter.

A 140-mile trail system on the Montana side covers the area well. The most interesting of all of them is the 40-mile State Line Trail that follows the northern Bitterroot Divide, skirting the western edge of the Montana segment. Past Goose Lake and north, this route stays with the divide, south of here it deviates somewhat from the crest.

The best entry to the Great Burn Roadless Area is from the Clearwater Crossing trailhead, about 17 miles west of Interstate 90, north of Alberton and accessed via the Fish Creek Road. Hoodoo Pass is reached from the Trout Creek Road (on the north end, near Superior, Montana) and Granite Pass off a trail leading northward from Lolo Pass. In the winter, plowed roads (check with the Lolo National Forest) open up good cross-country skiing opportunities.

Although the area is not in the Federal Wilderness system, the Great Burn is as wild as any other designated place (to date the Forest Service has protected it) and deserves the lasting safety, that Wilderness status would give it. Foolish politics have prevented its inclusion so far.

The best overall map is the Lolo National Forest Visitor Map. It shows the USGS topographic maps that you would need, depending upon the area you plan to enter. Bill Cunningham's book, *Wild Montana*, published by Falcon Press has more information on hiking and use here.

—RICK AND SUSIE GRAETZ

CLARK FORK RIVER

While the Missouri and Yellowstone rivers drain an enormous part of eastern Montana, the Clark Fork is western Montana's waterway. Two creeks — Silver Bow and Warm Springs — provide the necessary ingredients to give it a launch.

In 1864, prospectors found placer gold on Silver Bow Creek and Butte, one of Montana's largest mining camps, had its start. The mining progressed to silver and eventually to the mineral that sent the town soaring ... copper.

Originating above Butte's north side in Yankee Doodle Gulch, the creek drops off of Butte Hill and proceeds westward.

Warm Springs Creek falls out of a small lake just below Twin Peaks in the Flint Creek Range northwest of Anaconda. When it meets Silver Bow, the Clark Fork is off and running 331 miles through south and then northwestern Montana to Idaho. And from its start at 4,800 feet, it will have lost about 2,600 feet in elevation by the time it leaves the state.

The Clark Fork's first passage is through the extensive Deer Lodge Valley where, about 38 miles into the trip, near Garrison Junction, it takes on the Little Blackfoot River. The Clark Fork started out bearing to the north, but

The Clark Fork River near Alberton. RICK AND SUSIE GRAETZ

The Clark Fork River west of Drummond near Bearmouth. RICK AND SUSIE GRAETZ

from Garrison down, it keeps a steady northwest course. Ten miles beyond Garrison, the river picks up what flow Gold Creek has to offer. Gold Creek is important in the annals of Montana history as in 1858 the first recorded gold strike was made here. The short-term settlement of American Fork resulted.

The Clark Fork passes within shouting distance of the ranching community of Drummond. At this point, flanked at a distance by the Flint Creek Mountains and the Garnet Range, the river soon finds the valley closing in on it. Along the way, on its north side, it passes Bearmouth and Bear Gulch. Unsightly dredge piles along Bear Creek are a reminder that this was once a booming mining camp; Garnet, now a preserved ghost town up in the Garnet Range, is reached through this canyon.

One hundred and two miles into its journey, the river connects with Rock Creek, a blue-ribbon trout stream arriving from the south. A bit farther and just above Missoula, the Blackfoot River enters.

It is at this junction in July 1806, Meriwether Lewis on his return trip from the coast, made a left turn off of the Clark Fork and headed east up the Blackfoot following a short-cut to the "great falls," that the Indians had informed him of the past summer.

According to the Nez Perce with whom the Corps of Discovery spent time, a path along the Clark Fork to the Blackfoot River (*"Cokahlarishkit"* or *"the river of the road to the buffaloe."*). From there, *"they informed us that it is not far from the dividing ridge* (Continental Divide) *between the waters of this and the Missouri rivers."*

After the Blackfoot, the river squeezes through the tight Hellgate Canyon and enters the hub of five big valleys — Missoula. Here the river splices the university town, then quickly leaves the openness of the valley to hug the east flank of the Bitterroot Range. After reaching Frenchtown, the river will meander through gorges and narrow passageways in between the Bitterroot Range on the west and the Salish and Cabinet Mountains to the east.

This is Montana's logging country and on its journey, the Clark Fork River moves by small timber based communities such as Alberton, Superior and St. Regis. At St. Regis, taking in the small flow of the St. Regis River, coming off of the Bitterroot Divide, it abruptly makes a U turn for about 21air miles and then at Paradise, begins its northwest flow again. At Thompson Falls, a dam forces the river into becoming a lake. Once free of the dam, it continues to widen for the next 20 miles where it encounters the Noxon Dam. Seven miles down from Noxon, the intriguing Bull River, coming out of the Bull River Valley from the north, adds more water in the area of the magnificent Cabinet Gorge. Twelve miles down from its confluence with the Bull, the Clark Fork River takes leave of Montana.

MISSOULA

Commanding center stage at the convergence of five great valleys, the Mission, the Missoula, the Blackfoot, the Hellgate, and the Bitterroot is the tree covered community ofMissoula.

Long before it became a white settlement, Salish Indians, detecting an ominous presence, called it "Lmisuletiku" from two words meaning "cold" and "water. This was the description of the canyon where they could expect an ambush by the Blackfeet as they traveled east to hunt buffalo. The canyon in turn, derived its current name "Hellgate" or "gates of hell" from French-Canadian trappers who experienced the same dangers and saw bodies of Salish who had been killed by the Blackfeet.

The first white man to inhabit the place was thought to be David Pattee who moved over from the Bitterroot Valley in 1858. But the first white men to visit the future town site were Meriwether Lewis and his Corps of Discovery on their way back to the "great falls" of the Missouri in 1806. According to Lewis's journal, they camped along the Clark Fork about where Rattlesnake Creek joins it.

In 1860, Christopher Higgins, and Francis Worden, launched a trading post at the confluence of the Bitterroot and Clark Fork rivers and called the settlement Hellgate.

The Mullen Road construction, working its way from Walla Walla, Washington to Fort Benton, Montana, reached the Rattlesnake and Clark Fork junction in 1863. Today's Front Street takes the same route. Higgins and Worden, seeing the more lucrative commercial prospects of being close to the Mullen Road, partnered with David Pattee to construct a flourmill, sawmill and a store there. Hellgate was abandoned and Missoula was born.

Even though the first Montana strike was at Gold Creek (1858), fewer than 60 miles away, and other southwest Montana discoveries were made between 1862 and 1865, Missoula did not acquire "gold fever." Rather, after Worden, Higgins and Pattee formed the Missoula Mills Company with their sawmill, her destiny lay in the forests.

Once the land had been "discovered," settlers began arriving to take up residence. Many French joined Pattee to farm and settled Frenchtown in 1864.

To ensure the town's protection should the Flathead (Salish) ever turn hostile, in 1877, the US government built Fort Missoula a few miles west of Hellgate Canyon. But owing to the friendliness of the Salish, there was no danger of this happening.

The forerunner of the Missoula Mercantile Company was established in 1873, and the Missoula National Bank was funded with $50,000 the same year.

In the 1970s, John Toole wrote, "... Missoula, like all of Montana, yearned for a railroad. Finally, the Northern Pacific reached Missoula in 1883."

"Missoula put on the wildest celebration in its history. Higgins Avenue was cleared of vehicles. Saloons rolled out barrels of whiskey, hung tin cups from the side, and dispensed the beverage free. Soldiers from Fort Missoula dragged a cannon and fired cannonballs down Higgins Avenue. John Rankin, father of the famous female politician, Jeanette Rankin, was leaning against the barrel of the cannon as the soldiers fired it. The explosion tossed him 20 feet into the air. He suffered a slight loss of hearing in one ear as a result. The Butte Miner newspaper described the behavior of Missoulians on this date as disgusting. This from Butte?"

The completion of railroads through Montana is considered to be the most important economic event in the state's history. It opened up Western Montana's timber to the nation and helped cement Missoula's well-being. The town soon became the hub of Montana's timber industry.

The mining industry grew rapidly, especially in Butte. Lumber was a hot commodity. Touted as the world's biggest and best sawmill at the time, the Blackfoot Lumber Co. was built outside of Missoula, at Bonner, to meet this need.

Missoula's early years as a logging headquarters were as violent and colorful as any cow town or mining camp. Saloons and hurdy-gurdy houses grew up in Bonner and Missoula to service the loggers who came out of snow bound isolation in the woods, where they had had no whiskey, no women, no comforts and no entertainment.

Timber-rich forests assured a solid industrial base and Missoula's population skyrocketed. It was during this period, that according to John Toole, "William A. Clark, the Copper King was, to say the least, influential in Montana in the 1890s. He always regarded his home as Deerlodge. In the early '90s, he inquired of the Deerlodge city fathers, which state institution they would like to have, the State University or the State Penitentiary. Deerlodge chose the state penitentiary on the grounds that the enrollment would probably be larger and economic activity greater. Higher education was a rather dim concept in the minds of people of Montana in the 1890s. Missoula was left with the University."

Now it was more than just a crossroads trade center, the town had character. Owing to the University, Missoula is known today as one of the state's most politically and culturally diverse communities.

After the US Forest Service established its regional headquarters in Missoula, the School of Forestry at the University, became a center for forest and game management research.

Other than the educational, cultural, sports and entertainment benefits supplied by the University, its enrollment of nearly 12,000, and the number of professors and support employees needed to run the school, adds largely to the financial health of the community.

Surrounded by national forests, mountains, and rivers, locals and travelers alike come to satisfy a love of woods and water. They can hike the "M" trail that zig zags its way up Mount Sentinel behind the University, offering a panoramic view of the city below. Convenient too is the 61,000-acre Rattlesnake National Wilderness and Recreation Area. Those who lack the time or ability to hike, hunt, bike, fish or float can enjoy Missoula's addictive environment at one of the state's most attractive urban parks stretching along the Clark Fork River it passes by the University and through downtown Missoula.

It has only been a little over a century since the white man settled in Missoula, but a great deal of history and growth has occurred in a relatively short time.

—RICK AND SUSIE GRAETZ

The University of Montana campus. RICK AND SUSIE GRAETZ

KALISPELL

Unlike many of the state's other major communities, when Montana celebrated statehood in 1889, Kalispell had not yet been formed. Those celebrating in the northern Flathead Valley did so in the small town of Demersville and the even smaller settlement of Ashley.

Strategically located at the navigable end of the Flathead River above Flathead Lake, Demersville served as the only community in the northern portion of the expansive Flathead Valley that could receive freight from the lake steamboats. In 1890, Demersville had the only bank in the area and had grown to also include a town hall, newspaper, mercantile and several saloons.

Having become one of the wealthiest men in the Montana territory by moving freight up the Missouri River from St. Louis to Fort Benton and then on to western and central Montana communities by horse, mule and oxen-drawn freight wagons, Charles Conrad was developing plans to change all of that. When old friend and railroad entrepreneur James Hill told Conrad that the Great Northern rail lines were to be built through the valley north of Demersville, Conrad took options on six of the areas farms and set about developing plans for a town about seven miles north of Flathead Lake. If the railroad's arrival in Montana in 1890 signaled the beginning of the end for Conrad's freighting business, it created the possibility of even greater riches to the west in the northern Flathead Valley. Located along the Flathead River near the confluence of the Stillwater and Whitefish rivers, Conrad named the town Kalispell after an Indian word for "prairie above the lake." As word spread of the pending arrival of the railroad, others began moving to the area to purchase property and to start businesses in the new community.

The announcement that the rail center was going to be built in nearby Kalispell was a death knell for Demersville. By the end of 1891, the entire town moved lock, stock and barrel the four miles upriver to join its growing neighbor. Kalispell then had 400 residents, 23 saloons, half a dozen gaming parlors and honky-tonks, two Chinese restaurants, two laundries and four general stores.

On Dec. 31, 1891, the railroad completed its route into Kalispell, an event marked with bands, bunting and the driving of a silver spike; the next day, the first Great Northern Railway locomotive pulled into town.

With the train arriving on a regular basis, Kalispell thrived — and so did Conrad. In a still-standing example of his wealth, Conrad built a 26-room, 13,000-square-foot Norman style mansion for his family. The Conrad Mansion became the setting for Kalispell's New Years balls and other gala events. It remains today as an example of Conrad's wealth.

Conrad's mansion wasn't the only construction happening in Kalispell. The community's first school opened in 1894 and by the turn of the 20th Century, the Carnegie Library Building was being built.

In 1904, just two years after the death of the town's founder, residents received news that because of the twisty, steep path to Kalispell, the main rail line was being moved to follow a more gradual route through nearby Whitefish. Concern was thick that Kalispell would go the way of Demersville.

Taking stock, the residents looked around and discovered that their town had the largest operating bank in northwest Montana, it was the Flathead County seat and an estimated 40 sawmills operated nearby. An interest in tourism in the Flathead and the nearby presence of the Glacier Forest Preserve (which soon would become Glacier National Park) promised the continuing growth of another industry. It quickly became clear that Kalispell wasn't going anywhere.

Today, Kalispell is known as the gateway to nearby Glacier National Park and remains the hub of the northern Flathead Valley with something more than 14,000 residents. The community now features more than 20 parks, three golf courses, the Flathead Valley Community College, a regional medical center and numerous historical buildings open for tours — including the still spectacular mansion that Conrad built.

—GRANT SASEK

FLATHEAD LAKE

On March 1, 1812, David Thompson, famed explorer and fur trader, crested a hill near present day Polson …"we alighted on the top of Bare Knowl, commanding a very extensive View of the Lake and Country far around." Thompson saw an immense, crystal clear lake stretching north towards glistening white mountain tops. On both sides of this wide body of water, dense conifer forests dominated the shoreline. On the east, the slopes rose quickly, culminating in jagged snow-covered peaks thousands of feet above the valley floor. Today, these heights are called the Mission Mountains. The gentle rises he noted above the west side of the lake are the Salish Mountains. Thompson was the first white man to view a site that still holds today's travelers in awe … Flathead Lake.

The blue waters of this western Montana gem fill a huge basin scoured out by a massive and deep glacier that moved down the Rocky Mountain Trench from Canada about 12,000 years ago. When the progress of the ice halted, a terminal moraine built up at the site of present day Polson and formed a natural dam creating Flathead Lake.

This, the largest body of freshwater west of the nation's heartland, stretches north and south for 27 miles and averages seven miles in width. Its 185 miles of shoreline are washed by water collected from mountain snows, lakes and springs that feed the three forks of the Flathead River, before they empty into the lake.

The beauty of the place attracted white settlers and by the 1880s, estimates had the scattered population of the Flathead Valley at 2,000 people. From

Flathead Lake near Bigfork. RICK AND SUSIE GRAETZ

1885 to 1930, steamboats carrying passengers and freight plied the waters of the grand lake, as it was difficult to negotiate the irregular shores. The steamers traveled back and forth from Demersville (four miles south of Kalispell on the Flathead River and now only a memory) to Polson. A one-way trip took from three to four hours. Completion of the road along the west shore ended the steamboat business.

Compared to other parts of Montana, towns along the lake came late. Polson was the first settlement. In 1880, it was called Lambert's Landing after Harry Lambert who had opened a store there. After the site started growing, and an actual town was established, it was named for David Polson, a rancher who lived in the Mission Valley to the south. The post office was opened in 1898.

Somers, founded in 1901 as a mill town, served as a central point for large logging operations until about 1948 when the Somers Lumber Company closed. Bigfork was platted in 1901 by Everit Sliter, and named because the Swan River, a fork of the Flathead River, flows into Flathead Lake at this point.

In October 1891, the formation of the Flathead Reservation (formerly the Jocko Reservation) brought together the areas three original Indian Nations as the Confederated Salish and Kootenai tribes. The southern half of Flathead Lake is part of the reservation.

Say "the Flathead" and sweet cherries come to mind. Their delicate white blossoms in May signify spring as much as their green branches laden with ruby red fruit do summer. The micro-climate of this part of the valley is conducive to cherries growth. More moderate weather than the rest of

Montana and few rapid temperature changes protect the crop. As spring comes to the state, killing frosts are common, but along the lakeshore, the water heats slowly and retards the arrival of spring, thus ensuring the cherry blossoms won't bud too early and be claimed by frost. Warmer water in the fall, after the summer heating, shelters the trees from an early freeze that would destroy them.

Wildhorse Island, rising 850 feet above the water in the Big Arm area, is Flathead's most prominent landmark. Only a few wild horses still roam this Montana State Park; a herd of bighorn sheep (80–90 in number) is now the main wildlife species. Eagles, owls, geese and osprey also spend time on the island. Aside from Wildhorse, five other state parks and several fishing access points are found along the perimeter of the lake.

Although Flathead is a natural lake, Kerr Dam, installed in 1939 several miles downstream from where the lake lets out, controls water levels. From late May until sometime in November, the water level remains at full pool, then drops by as much as eight to nine feet during winter. This is necessary to meet power demands and to protect property from winter storms and ice movement. Levels remain low until June so as to allow room to hold runoff from melting mountain snow pack.

Placid water in the morning and whitecaps in the afternoon is a common situation on the lake. Storms capable of destroying docks and boats are not uncommon. Boaters going out in the open need to know the weather forecast and pay heed to lake wind warnings. Sailors find plenty of natural power to propel their boats on the big lake.

Sightings of the legendary Flathead Lake Monster have been the source of folk tales for more than 100 years. Some try to explain the strange wakes moving slowly along the water with no boat in sight as being caused by a giant sturgeon. But then who knows?

—RICK AND SUSIE GRAETZ

THE NORTH FORK OF THE FLATHEAD

A rare setting ... the ice sculptured peaks and valleys of Glacier National Park tower above its eastern edge; larch covered hills, wildlands and the high country of the Whitefish Range climb gradually on the west; and a river tumbles through it all ... The North Fork of the Flathead.

This wilderness gem begins its run south from water collected 50 miles north of the border in the mountains of British Columbia. After entering Montana, it forms Glacier National Park's western perimeter for 58 miles before joining the Flathead's Middle Fork at Blankenship Bridge below West Glacier. Fed by melting snows from the Whitefish Range, Glacier's peaks and the crystal clear discharge from Kintla, Bowman, Quartz and Logging lakes, its volume increases dramatically along the way.

Access, for the few and far between folks living in this wild piece of geography, is via the North Fork Road, a mixed stretch of minor pavement and major gravel, extending 65 miles north from Columbia Falls. In the winter, the way is plowed to within five miles of the Canadian line. John Frederick, unofficial mayor of Polebridge, the "capital of the North Fork," estimates about 85 full-time residents are spread throughout the unelectrified valley, 25 of them live in town. In summer, the population explodes to 300.

No matter the season, the topography is splendid. A particularly spectacular fall show takes place sometime in mid to late October. The sight of yellow and deep orange larch trees against a blue sky and snow-covered peaks makes for an idyllic panorama.

This is Glacier National Park's least developed area. The Inside North Fork Road, across the river from the main route and commencing at Fish Creek, is Glacier's oldest, having been constructed in 1901 when oil was discovered near Kintla Lake.

A sizable portion of the North Fork was "cleared" by the 1988 Red Bench Fire, which scorched about 10,000 acres of Forest Service and private lands and 27,500 acres within the Park. On August 23rd, a lightening strike in the Red Meadow drainage on the west side of the river started the burn. September 6th, a cold front with high winds kicked the flames into gear necessitating the town of Polebridge and the ranger station to be evacuated. On September 10th, heavy rains significantly quiet the inferno and December snows finally end it.

The fire and the wildness of the area have created outstanding wildlife habitat. Ample spring rain, summer showers and deep winter snows ensure

The metropolitan center of the North Fork. RICK AND SUSIE GRAETZ

that trees grow tall in the timbered places. One of the densest populations of grizzly bears in the lower 48 states makes a living here. Mountain lions, black bears, elk, deer, wolves and eagles, to name a few, are some of the other critters that find sanctuary in this North Fork country. The howling of wolves, the call of the coyote and the bugle of elk in the fall add to the area's mystique.

The North Fork's greatest value lies within its incredibly diverse wildlife population and the fact that it is a main watershed for Flathead Lake. Fire and development are the two greatest threats to this untamed place. In the summer of 2003, searing temperatures and high winds pushed fires through the valley and mountainsides. Several homes and thousands of acres were burned.

In 1976, the North Fork was classified as a Scenic River under the National Wild and Scenic River Act. This ensured the banks of the river would be protected from development.

—RICK AND SUSIE GRAETZ

GLACIER NATIONAL PARK AND ITS MOUNTAINS

Of all of Montana's mountain ranges, the peaks of Glacier National Park are undeniably the most beautiful. The area serves as a living textbook of the forces of glaciation and erosion. Glaciers of ice ages past did their finest work here.

Essentially these awesome mountains are built from an enormous slab of sedimentary rock that came here from elsewhere during geologic history. Like the Bob Marshall Wilderness ranges to the south, this northern extension of the Lewis Overthrust (a geographic term meaning older rocks sliding up and over younger ones in this particular area) was pushed eastward by incredible forces within the earth, leaving behind the trenches that became the Flathead and North Fork Valleys. Estimates are that they were moved about 35 to 50 miles from their original location to form Glacier's summits.

An estimated 37 active alpine glaciers, clinging to high cirques and north facing headwalls, are scattered throughout this 1,538-square-mile preserve. The largest, 430-acre Blackfoot, 217-acre Grinnell and 220-acre Sperry, are visited by hundreds of trekkers every year. These and the other ice fields throughout the peaks, are not remnants of past ice ages, but rather formed in recent years. At the current rate of warming and melt, it is estimated that all of them could be gone by the year 2030. At one time, glaciers filled most of the area's valleys to the depths of 3,000 feet and spread out far beyond the mountains.

The force and cutting power of the ice left behind over 200 lakes, countless waterfalls, towering rock walls 3,000–4,000 feet high and magnificent U-shaped valleys. It is these results that gave the park its name.

Glacier is divided into two ranges ... the eastern 65-mile-long Lewis Range and the 35-mile-long Livingston Range to the west. The loftiest summit in

Bear grass frame Mt. Reynolds, Glacier National Park. RICK AND SUSIE GRAETZ

the park, 10,466-foot Mount Cleveland is in the Lewis group. Kintla Peak at 10,101 feet is the tallest of the Livingston apexes.

Although not as high as southern Montana's mountains, the relief makes these massifs seem taller. Cleveland's north face, rising 6,700 feet in four miles has the distinction of being Montana's steepest vertical ascent. Other prominent peaks are 9,380-foot Mount St. Nicholas, a distinctive towering point visible from Hwy 2 in the southwest, and three summits near Logan Pass ... 9,157-foot Mt. Reynolds, 8,764-foot Mt. Clements and 9,604-foot Going-To-The-Sun Mountain.

The only road to cross the park is the narrow and winding, but stunning, Going-To-The-Sun Highway. Completed in 1932 after 11 years of construction, this scenic byway, and engineering marvel, gives access to some of the same type of scenery that backcountry wanderer's experience. It is usually open from mid-June until late September. Deep snows and drifts, which by spring pile to depths of 80 feet and more, block the route the rest of the year.

Nearly all of Glacier, though, is wilderness backcountry, and 700 miles of hiking trails lead to some of the grandest sights on the North American continent. A few of the most favored walks are the routes out of southern Waterton Lake up to Hole-In-The-Wall; Boulder Pass and Kintla Lake; the North Circle footpath out of Many Glacier leading over Stoney Indian Pass and to Granite Park; the Sperry Glacier and Gunsight Lake Trail and a couple out of Two Medicine Lake. Backcountry permits are required for overnight use and are easily obtained from any Glacier Park ranger station and at St. Mary and Apgar.

Nearly two-thirds of the park is covered with thick evergreen forests. On the west side, in the area of McDonald Lake, plentiful moisture allows for the tall western red cedars to thrive. Heavy forests on the slopes of the big peaks in the northern part of the park are remote and provide excellent grizzly bear habitat. Most other big game animals call this entire terrain home … black bear, deer, elk, bighorn sheep, mountain goats, cougars, and all the small critters make a good living here.

The park's almost overpowering etched landscape has long held great spiritual importance to the Blackfeet, Salish and Kootenai people. Fur trappers first visited here in the early 1800s, prospectors appeared in 1895 for unsuccessful mining attempts, and tourists began arriving in the late 1890s. Owing to the efforts of people like George Bird Grinnell who felt this special landscape should be preserved, it was designated, in 1910, as the nation's tenth National Park.

—RICK AND SUSIE GRAETZ

BOB MARSHALL COUNTRY

West of Augusta, Choteau, Bynum and Dupuyer, the spectacular towering walls of the Rocky Mountain Front abruptly terminate the Montana prairie. For one hundred ten miles, these craggy limestone barriers serve as the eastern rampart of the Bob Marshall Country. From Ear Mountain, a prominent Front Range peak, an eagle flies 60 miles before reaching the slopes of the equally impressive Swan Range, "The Bob's" western flank.

Glacier National Park and Marias Pass form the northern border, and the valley of the Blackfoot River is the southern terminus of this eco-system. Its longest axis from West Glacier south to Rogers Pass is 140 miles. The area may be circled by highway, a 380-mile journey, but not a single road crosses it.

On August 16, 1940, the Secretary of Agriculture officially designated the Bob Marshall Wilderness. This very unique and extraordinary place was named in honor of a young, wealthy, easterner whose life passion was to set aside land for wilderness and to educate people about the necessity to preserve and protect the wild country for future generations. A tireless outdoorsman, who often logged 30 to 50-mile dayhikes, Marshall lobbied for, and changed many US Forest Service regulations regarding wilderness.

It is a land of incredible diversity and a scaled down version of what the western American wilderness once was. Windswept prairie ridges, deep canyons, soaring cliffs, dense forests, wild rivers, lush meadows and a diverse wildlife population ... all are part of this, the gem of the nation's wilderness system.

Big in size, grandeur and legend, Bob Marshall Country comprises the contiguous 1.5 million-acre Bob Marshall, Great Bear and Scapegoat Wilderness areas and one million acres of surrounding wildlands. It is home

The Chinese Wall, Bob Marshall Wilderness. RICK AND SUSIE GRAETZ

to almost every big game species found in North America, including the endangered grizzly bear. Bald and golden eagles take flight from its precipitous canyon walls and timber wolves still roam here. The Continental Divide is its backbone.

From its interior and high country are born two of Montana's blue ribbon streams, the South Fork and Middle Fork of the Flathead. The South Fork gets its start on the southern boundary of the wilderness as the Danaher River, and the Middle Fork commences as a trickle via Strawberry Creek at Badger Pass along the Divide.

Other major streams and rivers emanate from this primitive country... the Sun River, draining the area on the east side of the Divide; the South Fork of Two Medicine River, meandering north toward Glacier Park; Birch Creek, flowing east from the Divide to the prairie; Badger Creek, rising from peaks of the Front Range and surging eastward; and the Dearborn River, making its headwaters above the east wall of Scapegoat Mountain and rushing southeast to the Missouri River.

This mountain country is steeped in history acted out by Indians and early-day trappers. Its passes and river valleys served as passageways for Indians to the west seeking the bison on the prairie lands beyond the mountain wall. The Blackfeet Nation controlled the lands that border the peaks on the east, and its warriors moved into the mountains to ambush tribes heading toward the plains.

Indians frequented Medicine Springs at the confluence of the North Fork and South Fork of the Sun, to the west of today's Gibson Lake. Pictographs

194

were evident in this area. Atop Half Dome Crag, west of Heart Butte, Native Americans sought visions. The Great North Trail, used by prehistoric man and by Indian tribes in recent history, follows the Rocky Mountain Front. Travois tracks and tepee rings are still discernible.

Mountain ranges of this big country have a distinct northwest-southwest axis and are separated by long river valleys, some carved by glaciers.

The Rocky Mountain Front, with its great relief and towering limestone walls rising from the prairie, is the eastern-most uprise. It stands out as the best known of the ranges, not only because of its geographic location and beauty, but also because of controversy over oil and gas exploration.

Valleys of the Two Medicine, Sun and Dearborn rivers separate the Rocky Mountain Front from the Continental Divide Range. The reefs, peaks and ridges of stone, including Scapegoat Mountain and the Chinese Wall, that reach to the sky here, represent the essence of wilderness for many people.

For some, a backpack or horsepack trip to the Chinese Wall is a lifetime goal. And why not! It is a most unusual and magnificent formation. This 13-mile-long escarpment rises immediately 1,000 feet above its east side then slopes for several miles westward down to the White River. To view it from Larch Hill Pass at the north end is a memorable experience.

Spotted Bear River, the Middle Fork of the Flathead, the White River and other waterways come between the Divide and a central group of mountains. The Flathead Range and Great Northern Mountain, east of Hungry Horse Lake, are in the north. Further south Silvertip Mountain and the Flathead Alps, a cluster of peaks near the Chinese Wall, are prominent sentinels and perhaps some of the most remote and rugged wildlands in Montana.

The wide valleys of the South Fork of the Flathead and the Danaher set apart the central range from the western-most mountains of the Bob Marshall, the Swan Range. The Swan Peaks, and adjoining apexes to the south and east, including those near the town of Lincoln, represent the largest of the summit masses of the wilderness.

Compared to other Montana mountains, the peaks of the Bob Marshall are not high — none top 10,000 feet. Red Mountain at 9,411 feet is the loftiest. However, it is relief that counts; these mountains start at a low elevation giving the impression that they are taller than many others. Heavy snow loads, especially on the Swan Range and the peaks just south of Glacier Park, have helped maintain a few high cirque glaciers. Small alpine ice fields, existing on the slopes of Swan Peak, Holland Peak and Great Northern Mountain, are remnants of the large valley glaciers that helped sculpture the wilderness.

This pristine country is known for its mixture of big grassy meadows and dense forest. Ponderosa pine, larch, Douglas fir lodgepole pine, aspen and cottonwoods dominate the tree cover. Small stands of large cedars are found near Swan Peak. Abundant wildflower displays are also a hallmark of the Bob Marshall lands. Meadows along the east side of the Chinese Wall and Scapegoat

Danaher Meadows and River, Bob Marshall. RICK AND SUSIE GRAETZ

Mountain present some of the most beautiful beargrass spectacles in Montana.

Virtually all the terrain of the wilderness country and surrounding land is under US Forest Service control and is accessible to the public. The sharp rise of the Swan Range and an absence of numerous canyons limit access on the west, but all other areas are reached easily by roads to or near the wilderness boundary. Many outfitters and guides offer horseback trips for sightseeing, hunting, fishing and floating. Backpacking, snowshoeing and skiing are probably the most intimate ways to explore this big land. An excellent trail system provides routes in all directions. The roads that lead into, or near the wilderness boundary, provide a great sampling of what is beyond the trailhead in the backcountry, especially on the Rocky Mountain Front. Convenient Forest Service campgrounds are for the enjoyment of those not able to, or not desiring to visit or camp in the wilderness.

"The Bob" may be visited any time of the year, but spring, with its melting snows and high run-offs, is perhaps the least desirable time. By mid-June most of the smaller streams can be crossed. The bigger waterways are still running fast and deep until about the second week in July.

The heaviest use is from early July until early September. From then until late November hunters are plentiful. Travel without skis or snowshoes, becomes difficult, if not impossible, after mid-November.

The Bob Marshall Country offers a myriad of wilderness experiences. For me, it has created a priceless collection of memories ... standing atop the Chinese Wall with a fresh west wind blowing in my face ... seeing a full moon illuminating snow covered Silvertip Mountain ... storm clouds lifting to unveil the sheer face of the Swan Range ... peaceful walks through Big River Meadows ... observing hundreds of elk graze on the slopes above the North Fork of the Sun ... skiing untracked deep powder near Circle Creek ... picking wild strawberries along the South Fork of Birch Creek ... fly fishing the wild South Fork of the Flathead ... watching lightning bolts strike the rocks around me on top of Scapegoat Mountain ... virtually swimming in a sea of beargrass along Halfmoon Creek ... standing on the summit of Mount Wright at forty below zero viewing countless rainbows floating in the ice-crystal-filled air of the valleys below ... gazing in awe at the incredible expanse of wild country stretched out before me from the top of Rocky Mountain Peak and seeing the Rocky Mountain Front in spring.

This untamed land is many things to many people. Most of all, it is a chance to experience wilderness at its best. One visit will convince almost anyone that wilderness is worth saving. The Bob Marshall Country is indeed a national treasure. Thanks to the foresight of early-day conservationists, these mountains, canyons, rivers and valleys will forever remain wild and free.
—RICK AND SUSIE GRAETZ

THE MISSION MOUNTAINS

It hits you at once, this very dramatic view of the Mission Mountains, a 7,000-foot vertical rise from the town of St. Ignatius to the top of 9,880-foot McDonald Peak. This abrupt skyward reach suddenly appears as US Hwy 93 crests a steep hill northeast of Ravalli.

On the north, at Bigfork, these Missions begin their gradual ascent as forested hills, looking much the same as many of the other lower mountains of the western part of the state. But as they flow south, the elevation increases dramatically. Here the summits soar far above timberline, culminating in spectacular jagged peaks, some cradling glaciers on their north side. Along the west slope, the relief is the greatest found anywhere in the state — upward of 6,000 to 7,000 feet from the southern Mission Valley floor.

On the Swan Valley side, heavily timbered, gradually rising foothills allow only occasional glimpses of the tallest peaks.

The topography of the Missions is a compact version of Glacier National Park. The high country landscape is a mix of nearly 200 aqua blue lakes, cascading waterfalls, glacial fed streams, perennial snowfields, ice carved ridges and peaks and colorful sedimentary rocks. Most of Montana's large animals — mountain lions, lynx, goats, elk, deer and moose, as well as the grizzly — call this alpine country home. Marmots, pikas, ptarmigans, wolverines, eagles, hawks and an array of other small critters share it with them.

As on many of western Montana's mountains, larch, or tamarack, is a dominant tree. In autumn, they splash the slopes with yellow and gold color

The Mission Mountains by Pablo. RICK AND SUSIE GRAETZ

then lose their needles by winter. In spring, the new growth creates a lacy light green contrast with the darker conifers.

Place names fit the beauty of the terrain: Daughter of the Lake Mountain, Pass of the Winds, Angels Bathing Pool, Lake of the Stars, Grey Wolf Peak, Turquoise Lake and Sunrise Crags, to name a few.

The southern half of this spectacular mountain chain enjoys designated wildlands status — the Mission Mountain Wilderness and the contiguous Mission Mountain Tribal Wilderness (the first Indian preserve in the nation). The Confederated Salish and Kootenai Tribes have also assigned a portion of their wilderness as The McDonald Peak Grizzly Bear Conservation Zone. It is off limits to human use from July 15 until Oct. 1.

This 10,000-acre seasonal closure allows the big bears to remain undisturbed in these higher elevations in order to gain weight prior to winter denning. During the summer, they feast on army cutworm moths that concentrate in large numbers on the talus slopes throughout the region, and on ladybugs found on the summit environs of McDonald Peak.

Enforcing the no-people use is taken seriously by the Tribal wildlife wardens as well as Forest Service backcountry rangers. Their conscientious protection of this small area has allowed the grizzly population to remain stable. From 12 to 17 bears, including females with cubs, are observed each year.

Heavy snows and avalanche danger makes foot and ski travel impractical from mid-October through June. Access to the range is tough from the west; few trails exist and the going is very steep. On the east, quite a few roads lead to several trailheads. The lofty areas are somewhat farther in through these eastern drainages than they are from the west side, but the walking is easier, although hiking anywhere in these mountains is rugged.

For motorized visitors, the best view of the Mission Mountains is to follow US Hwy 93 from St. Ignatius to Polson, then Hwy 35 to Bigfork via the east side of Flathead Lake. Circle the range by heading east from Bigfork to the Swan Valley, then go south on Hwy 83 to Clearwater Junction.

The Forest Service publishes a topographical Mission Mountain map (it delineates the Grizzly Conservation Zone) and lists the USGS 7.5 minute maps you'll need for trekking. If you can't find it, call the Flathead National Forest. A tribal counsel conservation permit (available at most local stores) is required for any hiking and camping in the Tribal Wilderness area.
—RICK AND SUSIE GRAETZ

GLACIAL LAKE MISSOULA AND ITS MANY FLOODS

The glaciers of the last ice age approached their maximum spread about 15,000 years ago. Ice moving south out of British Columbia came down the Purcell Valley into the northern Idaho panhandle, where it blocked the Clark Fork River at the present site of Pend d'Oreille Lake. Ice spread east and west along the river valley to make a dam approximately 30 miles across. It impounded the river near the Montana line to make Glacial Lake Missoula.

At its maximum filling, Glacial Lake Missoula flooded the drainage basin of the Clark Fork River to an elevation of about 4,200 feet. The water reached a depth of as much as 2,000 feet at the ice dam. At that level, the lake contained approximately 530 cubic miles of water, about half as much as Lake Michigan. And its surface area reached about 2,900 square miles. It was one of the largest ice dammed lakes of the last ice age.

The map view of Glacial Lake Missoula shows an outline so complexly embayed that it suggests old lace. The shoreline faithfully follows every stream, tributary stream, and tributary of a tributary. The larger streams make long octopus arms that sprawl large distances.

The largest of those arms is the Bitterroot valley. At its maximum filling, the level of its highest shoreline, Glacial Lake Missoula flooded the Bitterroot Valley into the area between Sula and Darby — which was then under about 250 feet of water.

Lake water was about 1,000 feet deep at Missoula, even deeper in the western part of the Missoula Valley. Evaro, on Hwy 93 just north of the Missoula Valley, was only shallowly submerged.

Lake water flooded the Mission Valley to an average depth of about 1,000 feet. But that water reached only as far north as Polson, where it lapped against the enormous glacier that filled the Flathead Valley. At times, the lower end of that glacier floated, and calved off icebergs that drifted on the lake. Those melting icebergs dropped occasional large rocks that are easy to recognize because they are not partially buried, but perch on top of the ground.

Another large arm of Glacial Lake Missoula flooded up the Blackfoot River about as far as Clearwater Junction, but not as far as Ovando. The Swan Valley did not participate because it was full of ice. But lake water did flood the Potomac and Clearwater valleys.

One of the longest fingers of water followed the valley of the Clark Fork River beyond Drummond, about as far east as Garrison Junction, almost to the north end of the Deer Lodge Valley.

The narrow valley of the Clark Fork River below Missoula made the longest finger of Glacial Lake Missoula. It cuts northwest across western Montana to the eastern edge of the former ice dam about at the Idaho line, east of Sandpoint. All the water once stored in all of the branches of Glacial Lake Missoula flowed through that valley every time the lake drained. J.T. Pardee, the geologist who taught us most of what we know about Glacial Lake Missoula, estimated in 1942 that the volume of water that flowed down that valley when the lake was draining reached 9.6 cubic miles of water per hour. Many skeptical geologists have checked that estimate since 1942, and arrived at a similar result. That volume amounts to more than ten times the Combined flow of all the rivers in the world. Remember that when you drive along Hwy 200.

Ice floats because it is about ten percent less dense than water. Ice dams float when the water behind them reaches a depth more than 90 percent the height of the ice. The ice dam in northern Idaho shattered into swarms of icebergs when it floated. A wall of water as much as 2,000 feet high swept down the southern end of the Purcell Valley, Rathdrum Prairie, and dumped into Glacial Lake Columbia.

Glacial Lake Columbia was behind glacial ice at the north end of Grand Coulee. It flooded the valley of the Spokane River west to Grand Coulee and Rathdrum prairie north almost to Pend Oreille Lake. About 300 feet of water filled the Spokane Valley. Overflow through Grand Coulee maintained its surface at a level too low to float its ice dam.

The sudden arrival of Glacial Lake Missoula must have started Glacial Lake Columbia rocking in a series of great seiches like the big waves small children start rocking back and forth in the bathtub. Every one of those enormous splashes sent several hundred feet of water surging down Grand Coulee and all the many lesser stream valleys that drained away from the southern margin of Glacial Lake Columbia.

—DAVE ALT

GARNET GHOST TOWN

It's quiet now, especially when heavy snows descend on the Garnet Mountain Range. A century ago, though, Garnet was a boisterous place, going full blast even in the harsh winter months. Its main link to the lower elevations was a rough and somewhat torturous road that led south along Bear Creek to Bearmouth on the Clark Fork between Drummond and Missoula.

The old town is part of a mining district that covered an extensive area of these mountains. Placer gold was first discovered in 1865 on Bear Creek's lower reaches, giving birth to short-lived Beartown. Garnet, site of the "mother lode," didn't come along until 1895, 30 years after the first placer diggings.

Gold is heavy and usually filters down to bedrock. At Bear Creek, bedrock was, in some places, 50 feet below ground level. Getting to the treasure was difficult; Bear Gulch was tight, hemmed in by rock walls rising more than 1,000 feet above the creek bottom, and water drained into the shafts as they became deeper. The initial prospectors toiled arduously to take the fortune in gold that came from the Bear.

The miners prevailed and once all the Bear Creek claims were connected, one could walk ten miles through the trenches of the gulch without coming to the surface. The men who worked these claims were called "Bear Town Toughs" and took on a bear-like appearance with beards, bowed legs and a stooped back.

Before Garnet came into being, an estimated 5,000 people populated the nearby camps including Reynolds City, Ten Mile on Ten Mile Creek and Top O'Deep on Deep Creek above Beartown. Within three years, though, much of the placer gold played out and by 1868 folks were leaving. Silver discoveries elsewhere in Montana were beckoning them.

However, in 1893, the Sherman Silver Purchase Act was repealed, resulting in the closure of silver mines and thousands of men were put out of work. As the unemployed miners searched for new jobs, the Garnet Mountains came back into focus.

In 1895, at the head of First Chance Gulch and the Garnet townsite, Dr. Armistead Mitchell constructed a stamp mill to crush ore; a town was born.

The new community first took on Mitchell's name, but in 1897 it was changed to Garnet for the brown garnet found along the contact zone of granodiorite and limestone rocks of the area. The road up First Chance Gulch, a steep ravine rising from just above Beartown, came to be called "China Grade" by locals, owing to the many Chinese workers who lived along the way.

Sam Ritchey found rich ore in his Nancy Hanks Mine, just above the town's main street. A new gold rush, centered around hard rock mining, was now under way and by January of 1898, the town boasted 1,000 residents, a school, four hotels, a doctor's office, 13 saloons and four stores, among other enterprises. Twenty mines were in operation.

More interested in getting the riches out of the ground than planning sturdy houses, the town was shabbily and hurriedly built. Often times, people's homes were located on mining claims and constructed on corners of piled rock without foundations. It wasn't unusual for someone to come home to see a mineshaft being started in their front yard.

Traveling the steep "China Grade" was a definite adventure. Heavily loaded ore wagons would sometimes give way and the race between horse and wagon, as to which would get to the bottom first, was on. In the 1960s, Walt Moore who erected many of the historic signs in and around Beartown, spoke of the many harrowing events he experienced on this route, as well as escapades trying to navigate the narrow wet rocky road that followed the old placer trenches along Bear Creek.

Gold isn't forever, and during the early 1900s the yield began to diminish. It also became too expensive to continue mining. By 1905, many of the mines were abandoned and only 150 people were left living in Garnet. A 1912 fire destroyed many of the buildings, further adding to the decline.

All told, by 1917, based on $16 an ounce, approximately $950,000 worth of the yellow metal had been extracted from the Garnet claims. Today's prices in the $300 per ounce range would make the value $18 million.

In the mid-30s, when the price of gold rose to $32 an ounce, Garnet briefly came back to life and some of the former mines and dumps were re-worked. World War II took the workers away again and Garnet became a ghost town for good.

In the ensuing years, the buildings deteriorated; heavy winter snows and vandalism took their toll. In 1971, the Bureau of Land Management stepped in to save the town. The federal agency formed a partnership with the non-profit Missoula based Garnet Preservation Association, and together they have done a masterful job in keeping this great piece of Montana's heritage intact. Their management plan states, "... a minimalist approach will be used in the preservation of historic buildings and structures ... Any changes shall not be so extensive so as to create a false sense of historical development." As a result of their hard work, today Garnet is Montana's best-preserved ghost town.

—RICK AND SUSIE GRAETZ

SOUTHWEST MONTANA

DELINEATING ANY REGION IS SUBJECTIVE. THE WRITINGS IN THIS SECTION TAKE in the landscape from Lolo Pass on the Idaho border through the university town of Missoula, then east along Interstate 90 and the Clark Fork River to Garrison Junction and Hwy 12 over MacDonald Pass to Helena. From there, the boundary extends in a slightly southeasterly direction, including the Big Belt Mountains on the way to Bozeman where it turns sharply to the right following along the Gallatin Range crest to West Yellowstone. The south and west lines of demarcation trace the Bitterroot Mountains, making up the Montana/Idaho border. Everything in between is fair game.

In the simplest of terms, this is an intermountain region of mountain ranges interspersed with broad flat sagebrush covered valleys. The peaks are lofty and

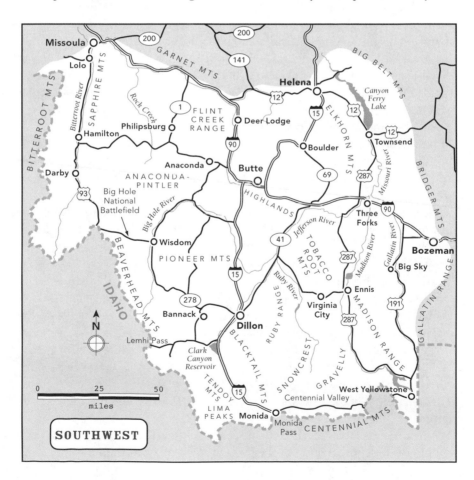

bulky. Many summits top 11,000 feet and a countless number exceed 10,000 feet. The Madison Range alone has 120 pinnacles reaching beyond 10,000 feet, including the highest peak in Montana outside the Beartooth Mountains — 11,316-foot Hilgard Peak. And 11,141-foot Eighteen Mile Peak, the top crag on Montana's Continental Divide ascends in the Beaverhead Range, in the extreme southwest corner of the state. Because of their distance from the center of some of the valleys, the summits appear to be less tall than they really are.

The Continental Divide snakes through southwestern Montana and features some of the state's great wilderness areas — the Lee Metcalf, Anaconda-Pintler, Gates of the Mountains, Welcome Creek and the Bitterroot-Selway.

The forests are less dense than northwest Montana's timber and the climate is drier. However, temperatures are among the coldest in the state and nation. Minus 50 degrees is not uncommon in a place like the Big Hole Valley, and the former mining town of Bannack has recorded 62 degrees below zero. The coldest temperature ever recorded nationally, 70 degrees below zero, was on Roger's Pass near Helena.

Southwest Montana is a gathering place for the waters that form the three main forks of the Missouri River. The Jefferson and Gallatin rivers both get their start in southwest Montana, and the Madison's birthplace in Yellowstone National Park is only a few miles beyond in the eastern frontier. The most distant waters of the Missouri come down off the Continental Divide, from springs that create Hellroaring Creek in the eastern edge of the Centennial Mountains.

Although the Three Forks was a crossroad and gathering place for many of Indian nations, unlike the Montana prairie, the southwest corner wasn't a beehive of Native American activity.

Having acquired horses by the 1750s, the Shoshone people lived and wandered throughout a huge segment of the state. This advantage over other tribes allowed them to dominate the prairie lands, considered prime bison hunting grounds. When the Blackfeet obtained guns, they forced the Shoshone into Idaho. The tribe lived there, but hunted in southwest Montana as they passed through on their way to seek the bison.

Southwest Montana was important to Lewis and Clark's Expedition. The Hidatsa who ranged to the Rockies from their homelands near today's Bismarck, N.D., had kidnapped Sacajawea, a Shoshone and one of the Corps of Discovery's most valuable members, at the three forks of the Missouri when she was only ten-years old. The Hidatsa were responsible for giving Lewis and Clark valuable information to help them on their trek westward, when they spent the winter of 1804–1805 at the Mandan and Hidatsa camps. They met the abducted Shoshone woman, now 15 or 16 and married to a fur trapper, while there.

When the explorers reached the three forks, they were anxious to find her people to trade for the horses they would need to cross the mountains. As

Haystacks mimic the mountains. Big Hole Valley. RICK AND SUSIE GRAETZ

they traveled up "Jefferson's River," Sacajawea recognized Beaverhead Rock, a limestone hill between Twin Bridges and Dillon, on the now Beaverhead River, a sign they were nearing Shoshone territory. Continuing past Dillon to the site of today's Clark Canyon Reservoir, at a point where the now Red Rock River and Horse Prairie Creek join (under the waters of the artificial lake), they met and made their trading arrangements with the Shoshone. Due to this piece of good luck, the place was dubbed "Camp Fortunate."

On Aug. 12, 1805, Meriwether Lewis topped Lemhi Pass and became the first known white man to cross the Continental Divide.

Following quickly on the heels of Lewis and Clark, fur trappers flocked to what would become Montana Territory and to this province of the state. But they were not settlers, and in their passing, left behind a negative legacy that included degradation of the natives and the depletion of resources that saw the profits flow to only a few.

Steeped in white history, gold was the basis of the first settlements in this southwest country. It was Montana's most mineralized region, a result of a molten intrusion — a batholith, in geologic terms. The Idaho and Boulder batholiths in southwestern Montana are mostly in the form of granite. Extensive in size, wherever the igneous rock of the batholiths contacts sedimentary rocks such as limestone, treasures from the earth are stored.

The first gold "colors" were found in 1852, in southwest Montana by a French Canadian half-breed (Métis), nicknamed Benetsee. Granville Stuart, who went on to become "the Father of Montana," heard of the find and prospected Benetsee Creek — known today as Gold Creek. Stuart and his partners made Montana's first gold strike here in May of 1858. Then in July of 1862, the first major discovery at Grasshopper Creek gave birth to Montana's initial Territorial Capital, Bannack.

Alder Gulch at Virginia City was next on the hit parade. This May 1863 strike was even bigger than Grasshopper Creek. Virginia City grew so quickly that it took the Territorial Capital from Bannack in the spring of 1865.

Helena, in the form of "Last Chance," followed with its own gold strike in 1864. It became the Territorial Capital designation in 1875 and the capital of Montana when statehood was granted in 1889.

As word of these and other discoveries reached the eastern United States and Europe, would-be miners crowded onto the steamboats coming up the Missouri River to Fort Benton, then ventured overland to the gold camps of southwest Montana. Others trailed north from the fields of Colorado, Nevada and California.

Many other boomtowns grew out of the frantic search for the yellow metal, as well as from silver discoveries. Granite, Elkhorn, Confederate Gulch, Diamond City, Montana City, Garnet, Horse Prairie, Southern Cross, Pony and Marysville were but a few of the legendary camps. Philipsburg, with the now deserted town of Granite, became Montana's richest silver mining district.

While gold was king from the 1860s to the 1880s, by 1890, it began taking a secondary role to copper.

Butte was born from gold when a prospector discovered the stuff in 1865 on Silver Bow Creek, but it took silver, then copper to fuel its growth. Considered one of the most prolific mining districts in the world, it earned the title "richest hill on earth."

The thousands of fortune seekers who had stampeded into southwestern Montana created a demand for meat and other agricultural products. During the 1860s, the Beaverhead, Madison, Big Hole and Deer Lodge valleys were the state's most important livestock havens. The same families have owned some of these cattle outfits, still in operation in the big valleys, for many generations. In 1862, Conrad Kohrs bought a ranch established by a Metis fur trader named Johnny Grant in the Deer Lodge Valley. It became one of the largest cattle empires in the state. Today it is the Grant Kohrs Ranch National Historic Site.

To support the need for wheat and produce, the Gallatin and Bitterroot valleys evolved into productive farming regions. In the late 1860s, three flour mills were in operation in the Gallatin. Now, this agricultural land is fast disappearing — in the Gallatin by sprawl from Bozeman and in the Bitterroot from an influx of people moving into the smaller outlying communities and up nearly every gulch.

Southwest Montana experienced the most colorful, yet darkest political eras in the state's history — the 1890s into the early years of the 1900s. Graft and corruption were rampant. Butte bred the so-called war of the Copper

Kings between Marcus Daly and W. A. Clark, which lasted 12 years. Daly kept Clark from getting elected to the US Senate and Clark helped prevent Daly's town of Anaconda from becoming Montana's capital. Daly's Anaconda Mine, sold to the Amalgamated Copper Trusts, grew into the large octopus called the Anaconda Company. "The Company," a potent force in Montana and beyond, dominated politics and newspapers well into the 1950s.

Dillon, the human cornerstone of the outlying southwest corner of the state, in 1880 became a northern rail terminus for the Utah and Northern rail line heading to Butte. The town is now the seat of Beaverhead, Montana's largest county and home to Western Montana College.

Of all of the southwestern valleys, the Big Hole is the best-known. The legendary fly-fishing Big Hole River wanders through its flat, wide and fertile bottomland. At an elevation of 6,000 feet above sea level, the weather patterns can be unpredictable. In summer, the meadows are wet from extensive irrigation and winter brings ample snow and bitter temperatures.

Here history abounds. In 1877, the infamous Big Hole Battle between the US Army and the Nez Perce was fought near Wisdom. Col. John Gibbons and his men attacked the tired and unsuspecting Indians at dawn. Initially, the fighting was up-close, with soldiers shooting into tepees, killing many women and children. Tactical errors by the U.S. Army allowed the Nez Perce to inflict major damage, and later in the day, to gain the upper hand. Under cover of darkness, the surviving Indians moved out leaving a crippled and ineffective enemy behind. The press dubbed the battle "the most gallant Indian fight of modern times."

And Jackson Hot Springs still bubbles out, just as it did on July 7, 1806, when Captain William Clark found and used the scalding waters to cook his dinner.

For the most part, the physical geography of southwest Montana has changed little with the passage of time. In Butte, in Anaconda and in the ghosts of former towns, remnants of the mining era stand silent. Cattle graze, hay is cut and old trails are still used. But the immensity of the quiet valleys and mountains still swallow most signs of human intrusion.

Southwest Montana is far more than this short synopsis. The essays that follow explore the region further.

—RICK AND SUSIE GRAETZ

BITTERROOT RANGE BELOW LOLO PASS

In the Northwest Montana chapter, we followed the Bitterroot Range and the Montana Idaho border south from the Cabinet Gorge. From Lolo Pass, forty miles west of Missoula, trhe southern segment of the range begins and is assigned to Southwest Montana. For an overall discussion of the range, read the Bitterroot essay in the Northwest section.

At Lolo Pass, some of Montana's most rugged summits, ranging from 9,000–10,000 feet, including 10,157-foot Trapper Peak, begin their climb to the sky. Towering jagged pinnacles, precipitous walls, and a series of long U-shaped glacial carved canyons make up the Montana side of the landscape. This is the section most people associate with the Bitterroots. Extending to Lost Trail Pass, much of it is included in the 1.25 million-acre Selway-Bitterroot Wilderness.

No roads penetrate the wilderness segment, but trails reaching magnificent scenery are plentiful. And this undisturbed place provides habitat for one of the largest elk herds in the world.

South of the joining of the Continental and Bitterroot divides, the peaks of the Beaverhead section are less rugged than those to the north, but they are higher and more massive. Many are over 10,000 feet, including 10,620-foot Homer Youngs, rising above the Big Hole Valley. The mountains to the west of the valley are part of the proposed West Big Hole Wilderness. For the most part they are unroaded and footpaths lead to more than 30 high country lakes.

Somewhat lower peaks south of the Big Hole watershed allow for a few roads to touch the Beaverhead crest. Lemhi Pass, the route Lewis and Clark used to complete their journey to the Pacific crosses the divide here. After the Lemhi passage, the tops sweep upward again reaching 11,141 feet at Eighteen Mile Peak, the highest apex on Montana's part of the Continental Divide. Italian Peak, the southern most point in Montana, tops out at 10,998 feet. These mountains look down on some of the state's least populated space,

Trapper Peak, Bitterroot Range south of Hamilton. RICK AND SUSIE GRAETZ

Eighteenmile Peak area on the lower SE Montana/Idaho border. RICK AND SUSIE GRAETZ

the Big Sheep and Nicholia Basin. In the mid 1800s, pioneers and gold seekers crossed rough passes leading into this sagebrush terrain on their way to the gold fields further to the north. One of these, Bannack Pass, was the crossing for the Bannack Freight Road established in 1862. The route still exists today.

Much of this snowy area is roadless, including the proposed Italian Peaks wilderness. Several trails provide access.

On the east edge of the basin and just beyond Four Eyes Canyon, the Lima Peaks — Garfield Mountain Roadless Area — Red Conglomerate Peak Complex completes the Beaverheads. Most of these summits exceed 10,000 feet and then scale down eastward to 6,870-foot Monida Pass.

Barren windswept foothills east of Monida lead the way back up again to the heights. The Centennial Mountains reaching to 9,000 feet and higher, carry the final 40-mile stretch of the Montana/Idaho border and the Montana segment of the Continental Divide. Below their north face, the Centennial Valley and Red Rocks Lake National Wildlife Refuge, home to the Trumpeter Swan, spread out. Red Rock Pass, the eastern gateway to the Red Rocks terminates the rise of the Bitterroot Mountains.

—RICK AND SUSIE GRAETZ

SAPPHIRE RANGE

Seemingly towering above the University of Montana campus, Mount Sentinel's actual rise is only 5,158 feet. To the folks in Missoula, it is just the U of M's mountain with the big M on it. But in the scheme of Montana geography, this big "hill" is the northern most point of the Sapphire Range, an 85-mile-long massif that forms the eastern perimeter of the Bitterroot Valley. On the south, part of the Sapphire's boundary terminates with the East Fork of the Bitterroot River while the rest of the summits of the southern edge butt up against the Anaconda-Pintlers. Upper Willow Creek and Rock Creek separate the Sapphires from the John Long Mountains on the east. The range is about 50 miles across at its widest points.

By Montana standards, these mountains aren't very high. None of the summits match the rugged Bitterroots off to the west. Many of its tops and ridgelines exceed 8,000 feet, and Kent Peak, at just a bit over 9,000 feet, is the tallest.

Although the Sapphires have ample roads and logged-over areas, they are also blessed with at least 320,000 roadless acres, plus 29,235 acres of designated wilderness ensuring plenty of opportunities for solitude. The roadless places are still awaiting a wilderness bill from Congress to protect them permanently.

The Welcome Creek Wilderness, a lower elevation forest, was established in 1978. Situated in the northern end of the Sapphires, it extends east from the Bitterroot watershed divide to Rock Creek Canyon. Full of old growth stands of lodge pole pine and a plentiful supply of wildlife; its highest point is 7,720-foot Welcome Peak. Thirty miles of trails encourage exploration of this wild country.

At 103,172 acres, Stoney Mountain is the largest of the roadless areas. According to Bill Cunningham in his book Wild Montana, no mountain named Stoney exists within, or anywhere near, this piece of ground. Easily reached from the Skalkaho Pass, as well as from other points along Rock Creek, 73 miles of trails crisscross the landscape. Its highest mountain, and one well worth climbing for the view, is 8,656-foot Dome Shaped Mountain, rising above Stoney Lake. The 25,000-acre Skalkaho Game Preserve, a great place to watch wildlife, especially elk, goats, and deer, is included in the Stoney Mountain area.

Fifty miles of trails provide access throughout the 77,000-acre Quigg, the second largest roadless area. Footpaths leaving from the west bank of Rock Creek lead to 8,419-foot Quigg and 8,480-foot East Quigg peaks. Ridgetop hiking, distance views and few people characterize this wild land.

Rock Creek, one of Montana's famous blue ribbon trout streams, slices through the northeast reaches of the Sapphires. It surges for 50 miles from the confluence of its middle and west forks to the Clark Fork River, 25 miles east of Missoula. After the forks join, this beautiful river wanders through open prairie-like topography. Here the flow is somewhat gentle, accelerating when its waters reach the deeper canyons within the mountains. A gravel and dirt road follows Rock Creek from the Clark Fork Valley to Hwy 38, the Skalkaho Hwy.

Climbing steeply out of the Bitterroot Valley a few miles south of Hamilton, the scenic Skalkaho Hwy crosses the heart of the Sapphires for 50 miles to its junction with Hwy 1 in the Flint Creek Valley south of Phillipsburg. Below, and just west of 7,250-foot Skalkaho Pass, Skalkaho Falls presents quite a show. This route provides a good look at some very diverse southwestern Montana terrain ranging from the precipitous west side to the gentler east slope where the road follows the upper stretch of Rock Creek. Several Forest Service campgrounds are found along the way.

Named for the valuable stones found here, these mountains are well worth a visit. The Montana Atlas and Gazetteer is a good map for guidance. To cover the area with the necessary Forest Service sheets, you will need the maps of the Lolo, Bitterroot and Deer Lodge-Beaverhead National forests.
—RICK AND SUSIE GRAETZ

BITTERROOT RIVER

Though its length is short in comparison to other major Montana rivers, the landscape the Bitterroot River flows through is long on beauty and historical significance. Guarding it on the west is the abruptly rising Bitterroot Range, the lower profiled, forest-covered Sapphires Mountains look down from the east. The surrounding valley is one of the fastest growing regions in the state.

The West and East forks of the Bitterroot, rushing out of opposite mountain ranges, join near the small hamlet of Conner to create the river named for Montana's state flower. From the beginning of its flow, it heads north and covers about 80 water miles (only 65 or so by air) until it gives up its identity to the Clark Fork River at Missoula. The gradient is relatively gentle, as only 900 feet of elevation is lost.

The East Fork of the Bitterroot comes off of the Continental Divide in the Anaconda Pintler Wilderness well to the east of the valley. Near Sula, it meanders through historic Ross's Hole. The hole, as trappers called high mountain valleys, was a gathering place for Indians and later trappers. Named for Alexander Ross, a mountain man, who along with his party was trapped in the Bitterroot headwaters by snow in 1823, it also was a place of significance to the Expedition of Lewis and Clark.

There is a great deal of controversy among professional and amateur scholars alike as to the exact interpretation of the two Captains' journals. According to Stephen Ambrose in *Undaunted Courage*, "The confusion of creeks and

Bitterroot River near Lolo. RICK AND SUSIE GRAETZ

ravines cutting through the steep mountainsides has made the route the expedition used one of the most disputed of the entire journey." So suffice to say they may have stayed on the Bitterroot Divide for a while before dropping down on Sept. 4, 1805 near the East Fork of the Bitterroot River and Sula at today's Ross's Hole. Here they met the Salish, (the Captains called them Flathead), who were on their way to the three forks to meet Cameahwait (Sacajawea's brother) and his Shoshone people to hunt buffalo. Clark estimated the encampment to be *"a nation of 33 Lodges about 80 men 400 Total and at least 500 horses."*

Ridding themselves of some of the lesser desirable steeds they had traded for in mid-August with the Shoshone, the Corps upgraded their herd by purchasing 11 *"ellegant horses"* and *"exchanged 7 for which we gave a fiew articles of merchendize."*

Leaving the Salish on Sept. 6, they met and followed the East Fork of the Bitterroot River, camping a few miles northwest of Sula. At first, the Captains called the present Bitterroot *"Flathead river,"* then soon thereafter renamed it *"Clarks river."* Meriwether Lewis, in his journal, described it as *"a handsome stream."*

The Corps would have passed the mixing spot of the East and West forks. The West Fork starts on the Bitterroot Divide and the Montana/Idaho state line southwest of Hwy 93 and Lost Trail Pass. On its way to the valley, it fills in Painted Rocks Lake, a reservoir named for the Indian pictographs on the rocks along the west side. Farther down the West Fork, Alta — the nation's first Forest Service Ranger station — still stands. Passing Conner, the East fork meets its counterpart and the Bitterroot Rivers is propelled forward.

On Sept. 7, 1805, the Corps of Discovery followed the Bitterroot River on a relatively easy course. The men had a close view of the seemingly insurmountable Bitterroot Range to the west, and as Sergeant Patrick Gass so aptly put it, *"the most terrible mountains I ever beheld."* Noticing snow on the peaks, they wondered if winter was making an early approach. Camp that night was near today's Grantsdale on the east side of the river. On Sept. 8, their night's stay was close to Stevensville on the right riverbank where numerous streams enter the Bitterroot.

It was at the confluence of the Bitterroot River and Lolo Creek, that they established one of their better-known camps, *"travellers rest."*

Lewis's journal entry of Sept. 9, 1805, reads, *"Set out at 7 A M. this morning and proceeded down and the Flathead (Bitterroot) river leaving it on our left, the country in the valley of the this river is generally a prarie and from five to 6 miles wide,"* continuing downriver and eventually crossing to the west side *"encamped on a large creek (Lolo Creek) which falls in on the West as our guide informs us that we should leave the river at this place and the weather appearing settled and fair I determined to hault the next day to rest the horses and take some scelestial Observations. we called this Creek 'Travellers rest'."* The spot is located about one mile up from the creek's junction with the Bitterroot River by the town of Lolo.

The explorers returned here on June 30, 1806, after having spent the winter at rainy "Fort Clatsop" on the Oregon Coast. It was at *"Traveler rest"* that the leaders would split, with Lewis following a new route east and Clark retracing some of their steps to the three forks. From there he was to survey fresh country — the Yellowstone River. Parting day was July 3, 1806.

Dressed in its finest, the Bitterroot Valley was preparing to face summer. The array of colorful wildflowers, blending with the new mint green of the cottonwoods and aspens, was offset by the glistening white of the snow-covered Bitterroot Range. Amid this splendor, Clark traveled to the headwaters of the Bitterroot River. His trail passed familiar sights from the previous September and led to a crossing of the Continental Divide near Gibbons Pass, to the north of Lost Trail and Chief Joseph passes.

Clark wrote of July 3, 1806, *"we colected our horses and after brackfast I took My leave of Capt Lewis and the Indians with (19) men interpreter Shabono & his wife & child ... we proceeded on through the Vally of Clarks (Bitterroot) river on the West Side ... This evening we Crossed 10 Streams 8 of which were large Creeks which Comes roleing their Currents with Velocity into the river. those Creeks Take their rise in the mountains to the West (Bitterroot Range) which mountains is at this time covered with Snow ... Some snow is to be Seen on the high points and hollows of the mountains to the East of us (Sapphire Range) ... we encamped on the north side of a large creek (Blodgett Creek north a few miles from Hamilton)."*

Even after all of this time in the wilderness, Captain Clark was as patriotic as ever and couldn't forget the 4th of July. *"This being the day of the decleration of Independence of the United States and a Day commonly Scelebrated by my Country I had every disposition to Selebrate this day and therefore halted early and partook of a Sumptious Dinner of a fat Saddle of venison and Mush of Cows."* With that done, it was back on the trail, fording the numerous creeks coming out of the Bitterroots. After first passing by Hamilton and later Darby, their camp that night was close to the confluence of the West and East forks of the Bitterroot.

Long before Lewis and Clark came through the Bitterroot Valley, Native Americans used it as a thoroughfare and a place to hunt. The Salish had their name for the waterway prior to the Captains' christening it. They called the northern part of the river "Place of the Bitterroot," after the pink flowering plant they sought for its bitter tasting roots. A favorite source of food for the native people, Lewis brought samples back to St. Louis, introducing this new species to the world.

Roberta Cheney in her book, Names on the Face of Montana, has a couple of more name tags listed. "The Flatheads (Salish) called the plant "Spet-lm" ... "plant with bitter tasting root." She also says "the original (Indian) name of the river was Spet-lm-suelko ... the Water of the Bitterroot."

Missoula took root at the place where the Bitterroot's course is spent and it rendezvous with the Clark Fork. Two men whose names are etched in the history of the area, Worden and Higgins, put up a trading post and the small village of Hellgate, this predecessor to Missoula, was open for business.

Darby, Hamilton, Stevensville, Florence and Lolo, as well as other valley towns, all claim the Bitterroot and tout it in their promotions. Unsightly sprawl from the north is rapidly invading the valley, but the river fights to hold its grace passing by groves of cottonwoods, farms and pastures land and represents the plant that became Montana state flower in 1895.

—RICK AND SUSIE GRAETZ

HELENA

Beauty abounds in all of Montana's towns. That's just the nature of this piece of the Northern Rockies and Great Plains and it's hard to go wrong. But to many, the capital town — Helena — is in the finest setting of any Montana community.

The town's location just off the east slope of the Continental Divide provides a vista for sunsets that can set fire to the sky. One evening a couple years ago, the atmosphere seemed to be preparing itself for a grand spectacle. Out over MacDonald Pass, a red disc began its fading ritual. Overhead, the cloud stuffed sky gave way to a clearing on the west, making room for the setting sun to spread its light. We reckoned it would be worth the effort to climb several hundred feet up Mount Helena's north slope to get the full effect of the promised performance.

As the sun made its exit, bits of orange, yellow, red and purple tinted the western horizon; but the anticipated flame of color didn't spread. Instead, a soft brilliance of gold illuminated the clouds and washed over the town and surrounding mountains and hills. The richness and warmth intensified, filled the air and held. No cameras at hand, the vision etched in our memories, we sat in awe … what a beautiful place, this town called Helena.

On a more recent ascent of Mount Helena, we sat comfortably on a north-extending ridge that falls out just below the cave-pocked limestone cliffs. With note pads in hand, we tried see if we could tell Helena's story from our lofty perch.

At this vantage point, it's obvious the Prickly Pear is no small valley. Looking toward the northern horizon, it's anywhere from 10 to 15 miles across, and from the west flank of the Spokane Hills, 17 miles are covered before the valley constricts to take Hwy 12 up MacDonald Pass and over the Continental Divide.

On July 19, 1805, Captain William Clark of the Corps of Discovery wrote in his journal "… *my feet are verry much brused & cut walking over the flint, & constantly stuck full of Prickley pear thorns, I puled out seventeen by the light of the fire tonight …*" From this miserable happening came the name Prickly Pear Valley, sometimes called the Helena Valley.

But long before Lewis and Clark laid eyes on the Helena area, the great Indian Nations, migrating from the west on their way to the bison hunting grounds on the prairie, found a plentiful food supply here. The Blackfeet / Piegan people called the valley Tona, or "game pocket."

Our description commences as far to the left as possible where a combination of springs and runoff, above the old mining camp of Rimini, give Ten Mile Creek its start. From this rugged village, it flows out of the mountains arriving at the capital city from the west, skirting Helena's southwest side, then reaches into the middle of the valley. Somewhere near the dilapidated Mountain View School, it connects with Prickly Pear Creek.

Looking out from this ridge on July 14, 1864, one would have noticed four men making their way down Ten Mile Creek (the route of today's Hwy 12) into the valley. Heading up what is now the main street of Helena, the Four Georgians, as they were mistakenly called, set up camp and immediately began panning the stream gravels for gold. The rest is history — "Last Chance Gulch and Camp" was born. In late October, citizens of this rapidly growing settlement, feeling the title "Last Chance" was too daunting, wanted a new name. Ideas were bantered, and finally John Summerville came up with the name Heleena in honor of a town in Minnesota. The two Es remained until 1882, when it finally became Helena.

Just north of where the "Four Georgians" entered the valley are the Scratchgravel Hills — an isolated grouping of rises dressed in a mixture of

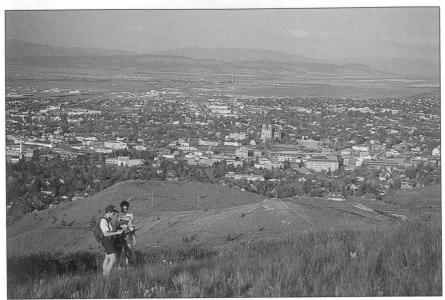

Helena from the Prairie Trail on city park Mt. Helena. RICK AND SUSIE GRAETZ

open parkland and ponderosa pine. Prospectors raked and plowed the landscape's thin layer of gravel to collect gold nuggets. The method was called scratching the gravel and the name stuck to the area.

Hidden in the forests of the Continental Divide are two mountain gaps leading into Helena, MacDonald Pass (Hwy 12) to the far left and Mullen Pass on its right. In 1870, a man named Dundhy built a toll road over MacDonald. His use of log corduroying to cover the muddy spots made travel easier for horse-drawn stagecoaches and therefore, it became the main route to and from the capital city. The name came from Alexander MacDonald, who managed the tollgate. Mullen Pass was named for Lt. John Mullen who, in the early 1860s was in charge of building the military road between Fort Benton and Walla Walla, Washington. The road ascended the pass from somewhere on the north side of the Prickly Pear Valley.

Moving you eyes a bit more to the right, the big dark tree covered bulk of 8,293-foot Nevada Mountain roadless area comes in to view. This island of dense stands of lodge pole pine straddles the Continental Divide and provides high-quality elk habitat. Black Mountain, at 8,338 feet is just a couple of miles away and blends in with Nevada Mountain.

Moving north along the horizon, the Great Divide ski area and the heavily mined district and historic town of Marysville, one of the state's leading producers of gold, are partially visible with field glasses. The Drumlummon Mine at Marysville, established by Thomas Cruse, had an output of almost $50 million worth of the precious yellow metal.

Now, look straight north toward a gap in the hills. North Pass and the North Hills usher Interstate Highway 15 out of the valley, onto the Sieben Flats through Wolf Creek Canyon then to Great Falls. In 1860, the pass carried the Mullen wagon road into the Prickly Pear Valley, where several years later, other trails, coming from Virginia City and Bozeman, connected to it.

Rising beyond the North Pass, 6,792-foot Beartooth Mountain, also called the Sleeping Giant, stands out. An outlier of the Big Belts, this was land Captain Clark covered while Lewis was on the river.

According to Lewis and Clark scholar and mapmaker Robert Bergantino, on July 19, 1805, "Clark probably left the Missouri River near Holter Dam and continued south-southeast to Falls Gulch. He then followed that gulch to Towhead Gulch and down that to Hilger Valley. Clark's camp appears to be south of the summit of the pass on Towhead Gulch about two miles west of the Sleeping Giant."

On July 19, Lewis's contingent passed through what is now the Gates of the Mountains Recreation Area, which extends between Lower Holter and Upper Holter lakes. It skirts through the northern edge of the Beartooth Game Range and the Gates of the Mountains Wilderness. He was just a few miles east of Clark.

In Lewis's words, "... this evening we entered much the most remarkable clifts that we have yet seen. these clifts rise from the waters edge on either side perpendicularly to the hight of about 1200 feet ... for the distance of 5 3/4 miles ... the river appears to have woarn a passage just the width of it's channel or 150 yds. it is deep from side to side ... from the singular appearance of this place I called it the gates of the rocky mountains."

While Lewis worked his way through the "Gates," Clark, upon leaving Towhead Gulch, followed an old Indian road, which took him from the Sieben Flats area past the Hilger Ranch to the south end of Upper Holter Lake. There, he crossed the hilly lands to the east of North Pass and traversed the east side of Lake Helena where he "passed a hansome valley watered by a large creek," (Ordway Creek to them and now Prickly Pear Creek, which connects Lake Helena to Hauser Lake) resting for the night near today's Lakeside on Hauser Lake.

Leaving the Gates of the Mountains, Lewis took in the scene of today's Prickly Pear Valley. "... the hills retreated from the river and the valley became wider than we have seen since we entered the mountains." His journal that night of June 20, 1805, went on to say. "... in the evening ... we encamped ... near a spring on a high bank the prickly pears are so abundant that we could scarcely find room to lye. just above our camp the river is again closed in by the Mouts. on both sides." His camp was about one-half mile below the bridge crossing Hauser Lake on Route 280.

Most of the paths the two Captains followed can be seen from Mount Helena, especially with binoculars.

Continuing the view to the right, the Big Belts dominate the balance of the northern skyline all the way south. Their distance hides the numerous limestone canyons, gulches and lakes among them.

Lake Helena, a Bureau of Reclamation project, is visible, but a succession of Missouri River dam-caused lakes — Hauser, Upper Holter and Lower Holter — are hidden. Hauser Dam was completed in 1911 and Lower Holter Dam in 1918. They were named after two Helena mining tycoons and businessmen.

The Big Belt Mountains separate the Helena Valley from the Smith River Valley to the east and on the prairie to the north. Within the Belts is Montana's smallest wilderness area, the 28,562-acre Gates of the Mountains Wilderness. If you have a map, you'll be able to pick out two of the more prominent mountains, 7,443-foot Candle Mountain, and the highest peak in the wilderness, 7,980-foot Moors Mountain. In the view field, they are directly above Lake Helena.

Just beyond the wilderness, 7,813-foot Hogback Mountain, shows its long ridge. Visible from the Mount Helena position, the highest summits in the Belts' range, from the closest to the farthest trailing off to the south are … Boulder Mountain at 8,819 feet, Mt. Baldy at 9,478 feet and 9,504-foot Mt. Edith. Baldy and Edith are the first to pick up snow in the early fall and the last to loose it in the summer.

As far to the right and south as possible, Prickly Pear Creek begins in the Manley Park area on the north side of Crow and Elkhorn peaks. The creek leaves the Elkhorn Mountains near Jefferson City then runs northward, passing Clancy and Montana City. It splits East Helena before easing through the valley to meet Ten Mile Creek. Together they flow as Prickly Pear Creek, first into Lake Helena, then through the expanded channel of Prickly Pear Creek, joining the Missouri in its form as Hauser Lake.

Lowering your eyes a bit, directly in front you can see the mosaic that makes up the Helena Valley — patches of agricultural land mixed with a couple of golf courses and a bit of sprawl beyond the town limits.

Two of the most distinctive manmade landmarks, Carroll College, built on Mount Saint Charles, and the St. Helena Cathedral stand out. The incredible church, with its 230-foot-high twin spires, is a lasting legacy from Thomas Cruse. Built as a tribute and a thank you for answered prayers for his success in gold mining, it is one of the town's most visible and cherished buildings. Begun in 1908, the cathedral, patterned after the Votive Cathedral of the Sacred Heart in Vienna, Austria, wasn't completed until 1924. The first funeral held in the new church was that of its benefactor, Thomas Cruise.

At the start of the 1900s, Carroll College was the dream of Bishop John Patrick Carroll. The desire became a reality in 1909 when William Howard Taft, the nation's president, helped lay the cornerstone of St. Charles Hall. Because of the school's position on the hill, it was at first called Mount Saint Charles College after St. Charles Borromeo. In 1932, the school became

Carroll College in honor of the good Bishop.

Last Chance Gulch travels south below Mount Helena's east edge and eventually splits into three gulches — Dry Gulch on the south, Oro Fino in the middle, and Grizzly Gulch just behind Mount Helena. Beyond the commercial districts on the east and west sides of Last Chance Gulch, the grand, ornate and historic mansions from the town's gold era hold court. Mostly elegant — a few pretentious — their presence is ever indicative of the cosmopolitan lifestyle that once held sway in Helena.

To the east, behind the cathedral, is the prominent sandstone capitol building. Construction on the edifice began in 1899 and it was ready for occupancy in 1902. Also located in the capitol complex is the treasure box of Montana's archives and the people's museum — the Montana Historical Society building.

There are two natural "guardians of the gulch" — 5,355-foot Mount Ascension on the southeast edge of Helena, and our viewing post, Mount Helena at 5,460 feet on the town's west side. These two summits are part of an unnamed range of mountains that occupy an enormous parcel of ground between Helena, Butte and Deer Lodge. In the gulches below Mounts Ascension and Helena, would-be millionaires dug and scrabbled for gold. Few made much of a living out of it, but they left their heritage behind. The gold in the gulch was the catalyst, but wealth was built from other sources — freighting, banking and a myriad of other commercial ventures. At one time, Helena had 50 millionaires — far more per capita than any other town in America.

This place that grew from a "last chance" at finding gold became a bedrock for the state. The newly minted 1864 territorial capital in Bannack was quickly moved to Virginia City in 1865. Helena received the honor in 1875, and when Montana became a state on Nov. 8, 1889, Helena was the temporary capital. But a heated, statewide battle arose between the Butte area "Copper Kings" — Marcus Daly who wanted Anaconda to be chosen and William Clark who supported Helena. In October of 1894, in an election, that some say was rigged, Helena won a narrow victory.

From our perspective, the weathered copper domes of the state capitol and the new federal building can be seen. Obviously, Helena's continued growth and prosperity is based on government, both in the form of the state and federal. As of the 2000 census, 25,000 persons called Helena home.

Agriculture also plays role in keeping Helena going. And because the important decisions concerning the physical health and well being of Montana are made here, the town is a mecca for grass roots organizations.

It has been said that many of the state's other big towns have lost their Montana flavor, but not Helena. Growth has been slow and the community still maintains a quiet atmosphere that hasn't changed much with time.

A climb to any altitude on Mount Helena will convince you that this Helena is a place where time and space meld together well.

—RICK AND SUSIE GRAETZ

HELENA AND GOLD

As the story goes, by the summer of 1863, word from Montana had it that Alder Gulch was bearing chunks of gold that could be plucked from the ground by any cotton-picker. Easier pickings than California once offered.

These were radical, turbulent times with the country at war with itself, and the expanding territories also offered a place to run to, a chance to make a life, as opposed to simply living one.

Some seekers organized incredible caravans, and others trekked across the plains alone, leaving their war-torn homeland behind. Many came to find their fortune, many just came.

Every steamboat from St. Louis, Missouri to Fort Benton, Montana was said to be "weighed to the waterline" as it pushed up the Missouri River "with its cargo of human freight and supplies for the mine." All were bound for Virginia City, a crowded compound thick with thieves, killers and honorable men — but there was no telling one from the other.

Among the throng were John Cowan, John Crabb, D.J. Miller and Reginald "Bob" Stanley, typical frontier miners, who would be remembered in Helena as the "Four Georgians." Crabb came from Iowa. D.J. Miller hailed from Alabama, Reginald "Bob" Stanley from England, and only John Cowan, the last of the "Four Georgians," actually came from Georgia.

The four miners were caught, with hundreds of other fortune seekers, in the Virginia City/Alder/Bannack/Grasshopper Creek sluices, with little or nothing to do. Alder and Grasshopper gulches already were claimed and being mined. There were probably as many men in the saloons looking for a claim to jump as there were men working claims in the hills. With gold fever high the best way to lower the population of the camps was to get the word out that "good colors" — that is "gold"— had been found in a remote gulch. If one could be trusted, and if he wanted to rid the town of idle miners just before the good spring run-off, he might start a rumor while visiting Alder that some hardluck tramps had struck it rich up Kootenai way, nearly 400 miles north through treacherous mountain country laced with suspicious Indian tribes growing less patient by the day with this second migration of persistent white men.

It seems that was how the eventual Four Georgians were ushered into the Kootenai stampede.

On their way north following the rumor, they camped in the valley along the Clark Fork River, where they met a mining party returning from the Kootenai who reported the diggings to be puny.

That night — it was in May, clear and cold — the word of the failed Kootenai expedition sailed through Hellgate (Missoula) like the haunting cry of a great horned owl. Realizing they were aced out of Virginia City on a cold rumor, they all must have felt a bit foolish. Still, it took several days for the disappointment of the Kootenai bust to subside. As other prospectors headed back to Virginia City or other "secret" gulches, Cowan, Crabb, Stanley and Miller, probably about June 1, decided together to pan the Blackfoot River drainages.

Without the benefit of trails or compass, and with a waning faith in the ease of gold discovery, the four men followed the river to Nevada Creek and kept heading south and east over uncharted wilderness. Eventually, they reached the Continental Divide, south of the four-year-old Mullan Road. The cold spring rains and low fog made the wilderness trek a physical terror but when they dropped down the east slope of the Rockies and followed Ten Mile Creek to the Prickly Pear Valley, the elements didn't appear as formidable

Some 19 years later, Stanley recalled the climb down the mountain to the great basin that the powerful Piegan Indians had long considered their "tona," or game pocket. He said the miners' "gladdened eyes swept the wide expanse of beautiful plains with its threading streams fringed with green-boughed cottonwoods. Bunch grass, fresh and luxuriant, waved everywhere, and herds of antelope, in scores and hundreds, fed unmolested—those nearest turning about and facing the party, wondering what intrusion of man upon their long unmolested preserves meant."

Time would tell. But as inviting as the valley appeared, after a night's camp and a small bit of panning in the gulch between Mount Ascension and Mount Helena, the prospectors decided to leave and continue north to search the maze of drainages that cut the Dearborn, Sun, Teton and Marias rivers. A more grueling, punishing horseback expedition in the rainy season is hard to imagine.

In Montana Territory in 1864 everything was a gamble and time was the fortune seeker's currency. In this country, you can feel winter coming on even in the sweltering heat of July, and winter and defeat had to be on the their minds when they sat on the bank of the Marias River and decided to head back to the Prickly Pear Valley. If they didn't find gold, they would at least find some solace in its beauty before finally admitting failure. The prospecting was dim, the men desperate and they had begun to call that gulch in the Prickly Pear Valley their "last chance."

On the afternoon of July 14, 1864, the four wearily made their way up the gulch where they had camped six weeks earlier. "It's our last chance," one of the men said again.

They made camp farther up the gulch this time and fixed a supper. Some accounts put them on the intersection of Sixth and North Park, where the City/County Building sits. Other versions place them at Sixth and Fuller, near the Montana Club.

With the benefit of gracious light from Montana's long Arctic summer days, they moved out that evening to seek the elusive "colors."

Stanley, working alone, dug seven feet to bedrock. He panned the gravel in the small trickle of a stream and saw about four flat nuggets. He plucked one from the pan, held it up in the twilight and let it fall back into the pan. It had the sound of good weight and the ring of pure luck.

Calling for his partners, the four dug—near the Colwell Building on today's Last Chance Gulch mall—into the night. Satisfied that there was gold, the men agreed the camp would be called "Last Chance."

In the following days, these "Four Georgians" officially laid plans for the camp and the law of the land. Last Chance would be in the Rattle Snake District, which extended "three miles down, and up to the mouth of the canyon, and across from summit to summit."

They also set out to define the mining claims that would extend 200 feet up and down the gulch. They called themselves "The Discovery Party" and gave themselves first rights to the meager water supply, the best claims and limited future mineral-hunters to two mining claims. They had been around long enough and knew exactly how to establish a camp before a stampede.

With that official work done and with their provisions running short, Crabb and Cowan — a Yankee and a Confederate — set out for Alder Gulch for supplies and a whipsaw to cut sluice boxes. In a fortnight, they were back in Last Chance, and in Virginia City the Montana Post mentioned that four Georgian Confederates had struck it rich in a remote gulch to the north.

I have begun to believe that then, the location of the strike, more than the strike itself, made the businessmen of Virginia City tremble. More people were coming to the territory by the day. Last Chance had better access to Fort Benton, Silver City, Gold Creek, Hellgate (Missoula) and Montana City. The geography made it a natural. Smarter and better-financed men were looking for ways for Montana to produce for the States. Gold could facilitate financial backing but it could not be depended on to make a state's economy. California and Colorado had proved that beyond a doubt. One needed agriculture, skilled laborers, merchants and ease of transportation to keep a western city of the 1860s alive. The Prickly Pear Valley offered it all.

Judge Lyman E. Munson made his way to Helena in 1865, via the Missouri River. He arrived on a Sunday and saw the town. More than 100 houses were already built and 100 more were under construction. Rent was $200 a month, lodging hard to come by and wages terribly low. Already, speculators were buying and selling claims for small fortunes.

"This was a lively camp," the judge wrote in Pioneer Life in Montana. "Three thousand people were there, street spaces were blockaded with men and merchandise, ox trains, mule trains and pack trains surrounded the camp, waiting a chance to unload. The saw and hammer were busy in putting up storehouses and in constructing sluice boxes for the washing out gold, which was found in nearly every rod of its valley soil.

"Auctioneers were crying their wares, trade was lively—saloons crowded— hurdy-gurdy dance houses were in full blast—wild mustang horses, never before saddled or bridled, with Mexican riders on their backs, where no man ever sat before, were running, jumping and kicking and bucking to unhorse their riders, much to the amusement of the jeering crowd, and as exciting as a Spanish bull fight."

Bannack, Alder Gulch, Confederate Gulch, Last Chance Gulch, Park Gulch, Oro Fino Gulch, French Bar, Skelly Gulch, Greenhorn Gulch, Dry Gulch, the Scratchgravel Hills, Grizzly Gulch, Unionville, et al., owe their gold and memories to the Boulder Batholith.

In events that occurred about 200 million years ago, the continental plate crashed, the west coast crumpled like a subcompact, the earth's crust heated up tremendously. About 78 million years ago, out of the blue the Elkhorns started spewing molten rock. Then an asteroid the size of Chicago beaned the earth, throwing evolution for a loop and all the while pieces of water-borne gold were dumped into cracks of the batholith's cooling rock. Along comes a creature with no million-year credentials who has a hankering for gold just when erosion has the batholith brushing ore off its balding head like dandruff. That is the sheerest, blindest luck.

Helena's bedrock lodes of gold were formed after the batholith assaulted the earth's crust, but before the volcanoes died. Hot springs, fueled by the magma, were fiercely active. Many still dot the region and many geologists believe the batholith is still harboring deep magmatic activity.

Like a pirate's "X" marking the spot of buried treasure, hot springs can pinpoint sources of vein ore deposits. Col. Broadwater's hot springs west of Helena and the Boulder Hot Springs are two of the area's more famous ones, but the entire region is pocked with active and inactive hot springs.

The hot water circulating deep within the earth picks up its freight of elements and minerals being forced from the subterranean pressure cooker. The hot water continues to add to its cargo as it rises. The minerals are transported in solution and carried through a tortuous course of rock. Upon reaching surface-cool rock, the water temperature drops. The cooling water cannot keep the heavy gold in solution, and it is dumped along the course. Mother lodes are fissures in hard crustal rock where the cooling water's mineral freight was dumped.

Last Chance, a placer strike, is thought to have produced $170,000 in gold its first year and $10 to $35 million before it played out. Alta, near Corbin, offered up $32 million between 1883 and 1910. The Whitlatch-Union Mine in Unionville produced $6 million in gold over 40 years. Tommy Cruse's Drumlummon Mine in Marysville, earned Helena a magnificent cathedral.

When the building boom struck Helena in the late 1880s the Helena newspapers regularly ran short news items on the discovery of gold nuggets during excavation work. In 1917, after a spring deluge, a bank president found "a gold nugget as big as a marble" in front of the Placer Hotel. The find prompted what the papers called "a placer mining bonanza" along the curbs, streets and gutters of Helena. In 1948, gold was found by workmen digging a new elevator shaft for the Placer Hotel. But by then, with only $1.75 in paying dust in every cubic yard of dirt, "We don't have time to mess with gold," was the final word from a hotel official.

During the 1970's urban renewal spree, excavated downtown building sites were successfully sluiced for gold. In the spring of 1985, after a deluge washed tons of eroded soil from the gulches, a friend who lives on Davis Street, on the lower reaches of Dry Gulch, sifted the flood sediments in his basement and found paying quantities of gold dust.

—TOM PALMER

BIG BELT MOUNTAINS

Looking out from the rise of the town of Helena, across the Prickly Pear Valley, the northeast and eastern horizon is dominated by most of the 80-mile length of the Big Belt Mountains. Survey this skyline from the top of Mount Helena and you'll see the entire massif.

Helena, East Helena and Townsend folks claim this uplift as their own and easily recognize its many distinct high points. Whether peacefully resting on his lofty bed of green, shaking the valley with his thunderous snores or resting under a coverlet of snow, the beloved Sleeping Giant, or 6,792-foot Beartooth Mountain as the maps label it, rules the northern horizon. Across the Missouri River Canyon from this sentinel, two of the most prominent peaks in the Gates of the Mountains Wilderness, 7,443-foot Candle Mountain and 7,980-foot Moore's Mountain are clearly visible. Then comes the unmistakable long Hogback Ridge at 7,813 feet. Looking a bit farther south, 8,942-foot Boulder Baldy and 8,810-foot Boulder Mountain jut up above the surrounding forest. To the east near Townsend, the regal beauty of the two monarchs of the range, 9,467-foot Mount Baldy and 9,480-foot Mount Edith, is reflected in the mirror of Canyon Ferry Lake.

Folks in White Sulphur Springs and the Smith River Valley who contemplate these mountains from their gentler sunrise side, declare some ownership as well.

Lewis and Clark duly noted the stretch of the Missouri River slicing through the Big Belts. Clark came first, camping on the night of July 18, 1805, in the hills west of today's Ming Bar. The next day he continued through the mountains beyond the Sleeping Giant and out into what is now the Helena or Prickly Pear Valley, just to the east of the interstate. On July 19, he stopped for the evening near present-day Lakeside.

Lewis and his contingent, following on the water and behind Clark, spent the night of the 18th, a short distance downriver from today's upper Holter Lake. On July 19, 1805, he wrote in his journal, "... *this evening we entered the most remarkable clifts that we have yet seen. these clifts rise from the waters edge on either side perpendicularly to the hight of 1200 feet. every object here wears a dark and gloomy aspect. the towering and projecting rocks in many places seem ready to tumble on us. the river appears to have forced it's way through this immence body of solid rock for the distance of 5 3/4 Miles and where it makes it's exit below has th[r]own on either side vast collumns of rocks mountains high. the river appears to have woarn a passage just the width of it's channel or 150 yds. it is deep from side to side nor is there in the 1st 3 Miles of this distance a spot except one of a few yards in extent on which a man could rest the soal of his foot. it was late in the evening before I entered this place and was obliged to continue my rout untill sometime after dark before I found a place sufficiently large to encamp my small party...from the singular appearance of this place I called it the gates of the rocky mountains".*

Somewhat flooded today by the backed up waters of Holter Lake, these Gates of the Mountains are just as magnificent as when the Corps of Discovery first beheld them.

Western Montana was founded on placer gold, and the Big Belts lent a hand. While the better known Last Chance Gulch gave birth to Helena, in 1864, former Confederate soldiers discovered gold in a steep narrow canyon heading east of today's Canyon Ferry Lake and christened the area Confederate Gulch.

Diamond City, its "capital," was supposedly so-named because the paths in the snow between the four original cabins formed a diamond pattern. Sprouting almost overnight, by 1867, an estimated 10,000 people were living in the town and throughout the gulch. In 1870 though, the good times and the gold played out; virtually nothing remains today.

Canyon Ferry Lake, Big Belt Mountains. RICK AND SUSIE GRAETZ

Natural features and recreation opportunities abound in the Big Belts. Dry and not as lofty as other Montana ranges, they do provide an excellent system of trails and great wildlife habitat. And since the snow leaves these mountains early, it's a popular destination for spring hiking.

On and below the northern slopes of the Belts, the 32,318-acre Beartooth Game Range offers a haven for almost every big game animal found in Montana. Osprey frequent its river border and a sizable elk herd roams freely. The reserve rolls out in what seems like gentle country, but the eastern boundary along Shellrock Ridge rises in an impressive bit of relief, almost 4,288 feet above its lowest point. Managed by the Montana Department of Fish Wildlife and Parks, the range is accessed from Holter Lake.

This wildlife sanctuary is contiguous to the very rugged 28,562-acre Gates of the Mountains Wilderness. Picturesque limestone escarpments that plunge precipitously and steep forested mountainsides are hallmarks of Montana's smallest wilderness area. Fifty-two miles of maintained trails amble throughout. Candle Mountain, an easy climb from the favorite backpacking destination of Bear Prairie, provides amazing views of the far-reaching landscape.

From its southwest corner, a 16-mile footpath leads through Refrigerator Canyon across to Meriwether Landing on the Missouri River — a simple day-trip for some hearty souls, others usually overnight in Bear Prairie. Throughout the warm months, a tour boat stops at the landing and will ferry campers to Upper Holter Lake for a fee. Hikers and horseback riders should be aware that water and horse feed in the Gates of the Mountains Wilderness is scarce.

The road to the Duck Creek Pass area, northeast of Townsend and above the east side of Canyon Ferry Lake, opens up a beautiful and different part of the range. From the pass, one trail heads north to the ridgeline between the two-miles-apart summits of Boulder Mountain and Boulder Baldy. This easy to reach place is part of the 30,000-acre Camas Creek Roadless Area.

Walking south from Duck Creek Pass, it's possible to follow a high divide leading to the summit of Mt. Baldy, then it's four miles farther to Mt. Edith where mountain goats frequent the tundra-like terrain. Other trails descend into Birch Creek Basin, the glacial cirque below the north face of the two peaks. A dozen lakes, reached via horseback and hiking paths, are scattered throughout this roadless enclave. Granite spires, called The Needles, tower above one of the lakes.

For those with a desire for motorized recreation, the Big Belts offer ample routes. Roads in two different directions from York, one via Trout Creek to Vigilante Campground and the other to Beaver Creek and the southern fringe of the Gates of the Mountains Wilderness, as well as Hogback Ridge, show the most spectacular scenery. The towering limestone walls and pinnacles are awesome. Numerous hiking trails emanate from the roads.

Smooth and deep, the Missouri river flows from Upper Holter to Holter Lake on the north perimeter of the range and gives watercraft access to the Belts. A tour boat operates through the Gates of the Mountains from the marina on Upper Holter.

Major fires have also visited the Big Belt Mountains, including one of the most infamous infernos in Montana's history, the Mann Gulch Fire. Adjacent to the big wall Lewis dubbed *"gates of the rocky mountains"* and a short way downstream from Meriwether Campground, Mann Gulch ascends steeply from the Missouri River's east side. It was here on Aug. 5, 1949, that a lightning ignited wildfire over-ran a crew of 16 smokejumpers, trapping them in the narrow gulch. Only three survived. Norman Maclean's book "Young Men and Fire" details the sad tragedy.

On Nov. 13, 1990, during an unusual dry period for that time of the year, a discarded cigarette caused almost 80 percent of the Beartooth Game Range to burn. And in the summer of 2000, more than 29,000 acres in Cave Gulch and the Magpie Creek Road east of Canyon Ferry Lake went up in flames. At almost the same time, a large fire burning in the southern fringes of the range, in the vicinity of Deep Creek Canyon, scorched 10,000-plus acres of Forest Service Land on both sides of the road over Deep Creek Pass from Townsend to White Sulphur Springs.

The Helena National Forest map has complete coverage of the Big Belts. It also lists the USGS topo maps needed for specific locations.

The precipitous forested slopes, high bare ridges, lake basins, nearly vertical jagged limestone escarpments and narrow steep gulches in the canyons of the Big Belts, are a treasure. Their easy access is inviting. Enjoy them and help protect them.

—RICK AND SUSIE GRAETZ

BUTTE, AMERICA 59701

Brought to life by the glitter of gold, silver and copper, Butte America (as it is endearingly called) is testament to the myriad folks who beginning in 1864, found their way to Silver Bow Creek and Butte City where they worked hard first looking for gold, then in the 1880s, mining copious quantities of silver and later extracting the nations largest deposit of copper; all in hopes of a better, more prosperous existence. With a persevering character and backbone formed over time by the rise and fall of enormous companies and immense fortunes made and lost, this "can do" town is as tough and tenacious as the miners, smeltermen and all the others who refused to never give up.

Nestled in the Summit Valley in the shadow of the Continental Divide, Butte resides in the middle of the Boulder Batholith that stretches from south of Helena to north of Dillon. Shaped by molten lava more than 60 million years ago, it is the cause and source of the rich mineral deposits found here.

Butte below Montana Tech looking at the Continental Divide. RICK AND SUSIE GRAETZ

Soil that once covered the batholith has long since eroded, exposing huge rock out-croppings in bizarre shapes and sizes. These soft-edged granite boulders litter the surrounding mountainsides, giving them an unworldly appearance.

The town of Butte was built on top of what was once referred to as the "Richest Hill on Earth." When Thomas Edison invented the light bulb in 1872, the need for copper wire skyrocketed; so, when Marcus Daly's Anaconda Mine struck the largest copper deposit in the world in 1882, an era of unbelievable wealth, power and politics was born in Montana. Shortly, a mean spirited competition arose when a politically ambitious banker and businessman named William Clark came to own the productive Travona Mine; he and Daly began to vie for influence over state and federal government to guarantee their continued weight and control on matters pertaining to their businesses. In 1888, Marcus openly destroyed Clark's chance at a Congressional seat and the War of the Copper Kings was on. Each owned a newspaper or two and used them shamelessly to promote their own policies or to damage anyone who got in their way (including each other). Their most outrageous dispute occurred over the choice for the permanent location of Montana's State Capital. Daly wanted Anaconda and Clark was determined it should be Helena. When the dust settled and the votes were counted, William Clark had won his revenge.

Along with the expansion of copper mining came the establishment of unions. To quote Steve Devitt from his book Butte The Town And The People, "… the workers of Butte created one of the longest-lived power bases of organized labor in the United States ... The history ... was written in Butte — in blood." Originally, the miners banded together to ensure health and safety issues were dealt with; later, they battled with the monumental Anaconda Mining Company as it tried to break their unions. So powerful was the Company, it at one time owned every major newspaper in Montana except the Great Falls Tribune and as the biggest client of Montana Power, caused the energy company to locate in Butte.

Gaping a mile wide on the hillside above downtown Butte is the infamous open-pit copper mine the "Berkley Pit." This was the Anaconda Company's solution to the high cost of hard rock underground mining. As the pit grew so did its appetite. Neighborhoods and small towns were sacrificed to appease the strip-mining gods. The uptown butte business district was spared the same fate when the mining was halted in 1982. Today, much of the area's historic buildings have fallen into disrepair, been damaged by fire or dismantled. Another result of the "Pit" was a business and population drift out onto the "Flats" south of town. Sitting at more than a mile high, the Butte of today is a cleaner, healthier, though not so wealthy place.

The good days brought accomplishments for the town and its folks, but when the mighty giants fell (Anaconda Company, ARCO, Montana Power and lately Touch America), they fell hard, leaving workers, their families and the community to struggle. Time and again Butte folk have picked themselves up and moved forward.

There are so many positive aspects to Butte — the magnificent Victorian and Beaux Arts architecture it inherited, the MSU College of Mineral Science and Technology, the towering 90-foot Our Lady of the Rockies standing guard from atop the Continental Divide, the magnificent county courthouse that rivals the Montana state capitol building, the Olympic speed skating training center, but most important is its people. There is a sense of spirit, pride and honesty in Butte folks not seen elsewhere. For instance, if you ate at Gamers Restaurant, you were expected to add up your bill, pay for it at the unmonitored cash register and to make your own change. The proprietor, Carl Rowan, was never cheated.

Butte America has the most diverse ethnic history of all Montana towns. Nearly 60 different nationalities found a home and their niche in the newly born wild and rambunctious mining town. Although each has contributed to the character of the community, the Irish are most linked with its personality. From the earliest times, they were represented in every level of Butte society. They worked not only as miners and laborers, but also as professionals, politicians and clergy and formed a tight-knit community. They were some of the wealthiest and most influential of the town's citizens — like "Con" Kelly, head of the Anaconda and the Montana Power companies, and the most noted and powerful Butte Irishman of all was Marcus Daly, who made no secret of his preference to hire fellow Irish. Now, more than a hundred years later you can scan the local telephone book and find the names that originated in Ireland still out number the others.

On the Butte America web site, George Everett rationalizes the significance of being Irish. "How important Irish roots became in Butte is illustrated by the story of an Arab rug merchant named Mohammed Akara who changed his last name in court to Murphy 'for business reasons.'"

The definitive expression of Butte's Irishness culminates every March 17th, when nearly 30,000 Montanans gather in Butte to commemorate St. Patrick's Day, and to celebrate that they too, if only for the day, are Irish.

To be a Montanan is special; to be from Butte is great.

Ah, but to be Irish and from Butte is the best!

—RICK AND SUSIE GRAETZ

ANACONDA PINTLER WILDERNESS

Butte and Anaconda folks consider this wilderness mountain range and the surrounding forestlands straddling the Great Divide to be their own. They hunt, fish, hike, climb, horsepack and enjoy the numerous roads and trails that reach the area. The Pintlers, as they are often called, are visible on all sides from lower elevations such as Georgetown Lake out of Anaconda; the biggest peaks are most evident heading northeast out of Wisdom along the Big Hole River.

While not as popular as many of the other wilderness areas in Montana, the Anaconda-Pintler is every bit as rugged and beautiful as the rest. Fifty miles of the Continental Divide bisect it and summits rising to more than 10,000 feet define its upper reaches.

The 157,874-acre Anaconda-Pintler Wilderness is part of a much larger undeveloped complex of approximately 368,000 acres. Unprotected National Forest roadless lands encircle the designated wilderness and are an integral part of the overall ecosystem. Included in this yet-to-be safeguarded domain is a northern spur off of the Continental Divide in the Pintlers, which connects to the crest of the Sapphire Range. As such, it is a key biological corridor for wildlife migration, including elk, moose, bears, bighorn sheep, and mountain goats.

The Anaconda Pintlers, coupled with 117,000 acres of unroaded country in the Sapphires (part of a wilderness study area), comprise a vast, unbroken landscape that remains wild and free, from the Skalkaho Road on the north to the Big Hole Valley along the southern perimeter. And many of Montana's big critters call this terrain home.

Two of the nation's legendary trout streams, Rock Creek and the Big Hole River, gather some of their headwaters from the Pintler high country. Cutthroat and rainbow trout are found in most of the lakes and streams.

Crisscrossed with many good trails that ascend into the cirques, hanging

Warren Peak, Anaconda-Pintler Wilderness. RICK AND SUSIE GRAETZ

valleys and numerous, beautiful high lakes, this area is an excellent choice for adventure.

In many places in Montana, the Continental Divide Trail actually approximates the Divide. Not so in the Anaconda Range; here the mountains are far too rugged. When encountering this segment, hikers need to walk well below the continental watershed. Some trails, such as the Hi-Line path out of Maloney Basin, have a semblance of following the Divide, but not for long.

West Goat Peak, at 10,793 feet, is the highest point in the range. Its twin, 10,399-foot East Goat Peak, rises just east of the Divide. The Lost Lakes are cradled in glacial cirques on the northeast facing slopes of the two mountains.

These summits and the surrounding high country are best reached via a trail up La Marche Creek, on the east side of the range and just off of the Big Hole River bottoms. The route splits when it reaches the alpine zone and will take a hiker over the Continental Divide through Cutaway Pass. Here also is a chance to trek cross-country along some of the ridgelines into Maloney Basin on the west side of the Divide. Black Bear Meadows and 10,463-foot Warren Peak are at the head of this basin.

Perhaps the greatest concentration of high lakes is in an east-west alignment just below the Continental Divide and centered around 9,498-foot West Pintler and 9,329-foot East Pintler peaks. A road to Pintler Lake from the Big Hole Valley ends at a trailhead pointing into this area.

High country lakes stay frozen into July and streams can remain bank-full and fast moving before then. Summer is the best time to visit, but the upper reaches of the Anaconda Pintlers put on a beautiful show in the fall, when the larch begin to turn orange. Snow comes early and approach roads allow for a long backcountry skiing season.

You need not be a hiker, climber or horseback rider to enjoy this landscape; there is something for everyone here. Forest Service roads meander into many areas and campgrounds along the perimeter of this wild country. An Interagency Visitors/Travel Map, available at ranger stations, especially those in southwest Montana, is an invaluable tool for road travel in the area. A very good Forest Service Anaconda-Pintler Wilderness map outlines the trail system. The Pintlers are on two forests; for information contact the Beaverhead-Deer Lodge National Forest in Dillon and Bitterroot National Forest out of Hamilton. The most popular access towns are Anaconda, Philipsburg, Wisdom and Wise River.

—RICK AND SUSIE GRAETZ

DILLON

The community of Dillon stands surrounded by the Beaverhead Mountains in southwestern Montana because that is where, in 1880, the laying of the railroad tracks came to a stop.

Sidney Dillon, president of the Utah and Northern Railroad (later the Union Pacific), was building rail from Utah to Butte when his ambitious venture was dead ended just 60 miles south of its goal by an obstinate rancher who refused to sell a right of way across his property.

Accompanying the construction crews as they layed track northward was a pre-packaged assembly of canvas and wood buildings. Called Terminus, the portable town served as the rail workers' home away from home.

Unable to proceed toward Butte, Terminus and the workers remained "ship wrecked" in the Beaverhead Valley through the winter of 1880–81, and while there, entrepreneurs opened businesses to better serve the crews. Later that summer, after Dillon received his needed right of way, the rail workers and Terminus moved northward, leaving behind the framework of a permanent community.

Now void of a name, the new town became Dillon in honor of the man who caused its start, and many of the streets paralleling the railroad tracks were named after Terminus businessmen.

Some of Montana's first herds of cattle and flocks of sheep could be found in the Beaverhead Valley. These farmers and ranchers had arrived in the area even before the railroad. Once Dillon was established, the more successful of those pioneers soon began building new homes in town that properly reflected their prosperity.

But prior to all of this excitement, the Shoshone Indians claimed the land. And on Aug. 13, 1805, while Meriwether Lewis and his men from the Corps of Discovery traveled ahead on land in search of the Shoshone, Captain

William Clark left the Beaverhead River he and his men had been struggling up, and climbed *"a high Point of Limestone rocks,"* where he took compass readings to the course of the *"Wisdom river* (Big Hole), *Beaver head hill, gap at the place the river passes thro' a mountain* (Rattlesnake Cliffs)." Called Clark's Lookout, it is on the north edge of Dillon and is one of only two places along the Expedition's route where you can stand on the exact spot Clark did (the other is Pompey's Pillar, east of Billings).

Over the years, Dillon has grown into a city of about 4,000 people and has become an economic and cultural center for southwestern Montana. It is the county seat for Beaverhead County (a tract of land larger than Rhode Island and Connecticut combined), home to Western Montana College of the University of Montana and the Beaverhead County Museum. Agriculture, mining and government services are among the community's major industries. The area's scenic mountains, valleys and Beaverhead River and the historically significant role they played in the Lewis and Clark Expedition, along with excellent fishing and hunting, contribute to Dillon's economy by luring a steady flow of tourists.

—GRANT SASEK

BANNACK, GOLD AND MONTANA TERRITORY

Exactly where, when, and which Indian tribes were first in Montana is up for debate. The state's history hadn't been penned until 1805. Up to that time, oral chronology was passed down and often one account differed from another. Historians though, have pieced together enough information to conclude that prior to 1600, the wide sagebrush cloaked valleys and big mountains of southwest Montana were empty of human settlement. Sometime near 1700, the Shoshone with the advantage of having horses, came into Montana and dominated a wide piece of territory extending from the far western reaches of the Bitterroot Mountains to well out on the high plains. Then several bands of the Blackfeet Nation drifted to the Montana prairie from Canada. Acquiring horses and guns, they proved to be the stronger warriors and drove the Shoshone to the state's southwest corner.

Pushed into a smaller range, the Snake people, as the Shoshone were often called, and their allies the Bannocks and Sheepeaters, chose to live in the region that would become Idaho, crossing back over the passes of today's Beaverhead Range into the southwest province to hunt. With the exception of well-worn native trails and migratory camps, signs of human presence remained minimal; the Native Americans were easy on the land. Soon though, all this would change.

As Lewis and Clark and their Corps of Discovery struggled westward across the state on foot and upriver by boat, they were anxious to find the Shoshone and trade for horses to get them over the high mountain passes of the Rockies.

Bannack. RICK AND SUSIE GRAETZ

Mid-August 1805, nearly four months into their Montana trek, the Expedition was following today's Beaverhead River (Jefferson's River to them), when Meriwether Lewis noted information passed to him by Capt. Clark that *"... at the distance a of 6 mi. by water they passed the entrance of a bold creek on Stard. side 10 yds wide ... which we call Willard's Creek after Alexander Willard one of our party."* Fifty-seven years later, the name would change to Grasshopper Creek and with that alteration, the silence of this place disappear.

Fur trappers, following in the Corps of Discovery's footsteps, left no settlements, only problems for the Indians in their wake. Later, as the gold fields in Colorado and California began losing their luster, prospectors' attention turned north to Idaho.

One man was instrumental in adding Montana to the gold-seekers' travel itinerary and inadvertently, to the founding of Bannack. His story is worth following. A twist of fate led Granville Stuart, referred to by his son-in-law as "the history of Montana" and who is considered to be the father of our state, to his destiny with the future Montana. In 1857, Granville was mining in Yreka, California with his brother James and cousin Reece Anderson when they decided to return to Iowa to visit family.

Commencing their trek on July 14, 1857, instead of crossing Utah, the group made a detour north to Malad Creek, in today's Idaho, some 240 miles north of Salt Lake City where Brigham Young had "declared the state of Desert (Utah), free and independent of the United States." It was under martial law and all non-Mormons in the territory were in danger of being killed.

During their stay in Idaho, Granville overheard rumors of possible placer gold near the Deer Lodge Valley in what was then Dakota Territory (seven years later to become Montana Territory).

On Sept. 11, 1857, the group packed their bags and lit out north. Later, Stuart wrote in his book Prospecting for Gold ".... We crossed to the Rocky Mountain Divide on the tenth day of October 1857, where the station (railroad) called Monida is now ... As soon as we had crossed the Divide a wonderful change appeared in the country. Instead of the gray sagebrush covered plains of Snake river; we saw smooth rounded hills and sloping bench land covered with yellow bunch grass that waved in the wind like a field of grain. A beautiful little clear stream ran northwest on its way to join the Missouri river. This is now known as Red Rock Creek. ... On the 24th of October we left Sage Creek and crossed the rather high ridge of Blacktail Deer Creek. ... Having arrived at our destination, the Beaverhead Valley, we chose as a camping place a spot in the valley at the mouth of Blacktail Deer Creek. (at its confluence with the Beaverhead River and about where Dillon is today — there were other people staying there as well) ... We all lived in elk skin Indian lodges and were very comfortable ... Fifteen miles further down the Beaverhead at the mouth of the Stinking Water (Ruby River) was another camp of mountain men."

One of those men was Robert Hereford, a trader on the various emigrant trails. Paul C. Phillips, who edited much of Stuart's works, surmised that it was Hereford who told Stuart of possible gold near Deer Lodge. Stuart wrote, while spending part of the winter in the Big Hole Valley, "... we resolved to go over to Deer Lodge where game was said to be abundant ... We were also actuated by a desire to investigate the reported finding of float gold by a Red river half-breed named Benetsee, in the lower end of Deer Lodge, 1852."

On April 4, 1858, they moved to the Deer Lodge Valley and eventually joined up with Thomas Adams. On May 2, 1858, the Stuarts, Anderson and Adams set out for Benetsee Creek (Gold Creek). Granville recorded, "... We followed it up the Creek about five miles (probably from where it empties into the Clark Fork) carefully searching for any prospect or evidence of prospecting but found nothing. Near the bank of the Creek at the foot of the mountain (Flint Creek Range south of the village of Gold Creek) we sunk a hole of about five feet deep and found ten cents in fine gold to the pan of sand and gravel. This convinced us that there were rich gold mines in this vicinity, but as we had no tools or provisions we could not do too much prospecting. This prospect hole dug by us was the first prospecting for gold done in what is now Montana and this is the account of the first real discovery of gold within the state."

Being unprepared to work the area, they left the country and didn't return until the warm months of 1860, when they founded the small camp of American Fork (nothing is left of it). Granville wrote to his other brother

Thomas in Colorado, urging him to join them. Through that bit of correspondence, word got out to the "Pike's Peakers," as the Colorado prospectors there were called, that Montana had gold.

A Colorado party, led by John White, was working its way through southwest Montana while aiming for Idaho. Coming to Lewis and Clark's Willard Creek, they headed up the gulch to try their luck. On July 28, 1862, panning the gravels of what they called Grasshopper Creek owing to the dense population of "hoppers," the prospectors found a bonanza. The place of discovery came to be called Whites Bar and the "Grasshopper Diggings." The sound of "Eureka!!" echoed through every mining camp in the west and was carried by the prevailing winds to the east, setting off a genuine gold rush to Montana, and a dramatic change throughout the southwestern part of Big Sky Country.

White had partners, but he is the only one remembered, partially because his name was left on the landscape. A year-and-a-half after the strike, he was murdered.

As author Dorothy Johnson said, "This was the best kind of a discovery ... free gold in the dirt and gravel of the streambed, gold that a man could wash out with crude equipment — with no more than the gold pan if that was all he had."

Later, the more difficult types of mining began ... first quartz or hard rock mining, then dredging, but those operations took capital. The placer gold that was initially removed was "what the Grasshopper diggings were all about." Placer is defined as an alluvial, marine or glacial deposit containing particles of valuable minerals, especially gold.

This earliest strike was about three miles down from where the gold camp of Bannack, named for the Bannock Indians, would grow. When the name was submitted to Washington, D.C, for the post office on November 21, 1863, the O was mistakenly changed to an A.

By the fall of 1862, up to 500 people had moved into Grasshopper Creek. As usual, the first to come claimed the most promising ground.

In early September, a freight wagon coming from Utah and heading for the Deer Lodge Valley made a detour on its way north. The freighters knew of the strike and probably felt they could sell the goods in Bannack just as well. This move probably helped many of the miners make it through the cold months. It is estimated that by the time winter halted work, $700,000 worth of gold had been collected along Grasshopper Creek.

Dr. Dave Alt, author and professor of geology at the University of Montana, explains why gold was found in Grasshopper Creek and the surrounding gulches.

"At Bannack, as in many gold mining districts, much of the production came fast and early from bonanza deposits in stream placers. Early miners working the gravels in the streambed skimmed the cream off the district, leaving the hardest work and leanest pickings for those who came later. That happens because streams concentrate gold as though they were naturals sluice boxes. The process is really quite simple.

"When bedrock that contains gold, the so-called mother lode, breaks down into soil, the gold remains in the soil as flecks or nuggets of native metal. Then the process of erosion moves the soil down slope and dumps it, gold and all, into the stream. However, metallic gold is much denser than any other mineral and therefore tends to lag behind as the running water washes all the lighter minerals downstream. Occasionally, great floods that shift the entire streambed at once permit particles of gold to settle through the mass of moving gravel to the bedrock surface beneath. There they lodge against the irregularities, exactly as they do against the riffles in a sluice box."

The early gold miners were never satisfied with just a placer deposit. They all lived with the conviction that far greater wealth must exist in the bedrock. In fact, the bedrock deposits are generally much leaner than those in the streambed and more difficult to work. Bannack was no exception.

At first glance, Bannack must have seemed an unlikely place to look for an ore body. The pebbles and boulders along the creek are limestone, a kind of rock that rarely contains gold. And since there is no gold in Grasshopper Creek upstream from Bannack, and very little downstream, the bedrock gold source must lie in the cliffs above the area.

On each side of Grasshopper Creek and a few hundred feet above its level, the limestone canyon walls contain large masses of granite that probably intruded the limestone as molten magma at a time of widespread volcanic activity in southwestern Montana. When that happened, the limestone that

Hotel Meade, home to the ghost of a young girl named Dorothy. RICK AND SUSIE GRAETZ

now forms a high ridge was buried thousands of feet below the surface. Erosion has since exposed the limestone, and Grasshopper Creek cut the canyon right between the two bodies of intrusive granite.

Molten granite magma reacts with limestone to form a wide variety of minerals, which crystallize in the contact zone between the two rocks. That zone, which may be anywhere from a few feet to a few hundred feet thick, makes a kind of shell around the outside of the granite intrusion, separating it from the limestone. Prospectors have long known that contact zones around granite intrusions, especially those in limestone, are likely to contain any of several different kinds of ore bodies, including deposits of gold. The early miners at Bannack must have learned that lesson well. Before the summer of 1862 ended, they had found the gold in the contact zone and staked claims around the margins of the granite intrusive on both sides of Grasshopper Creek.

When winter arrived, the camp wasn't exactly what could be labeled a town. Those who came first had no intention of staying. Get the gold and move onto another place was the mantra. So what "buildings" were there, held no resemblance to permanency.

Lean-to shelters, wikiups, tents, tepees and some rudimentary cabins made up the "homes." The "roads" were a mass of mud when it rained or the snow melted. And it was terribly cold. Bannack is known for low temperatures, in 1989, the now deserted town recorded 62 degrees below zero.

By spring 1863, 3,000 people found their way to Bannack. And another 2,000 were living up and down the gulch in four other settlements — Marysville, Bon Accord, New Jerusalem and Dogtown.

Granville Stuart felt Bannack was the place to be. But instead of digging for gold, he and his brother had commercial possibilities on their minds. In November 1862, they arrived in town — James to open a store and Granville a meat business with the cattle he drove to Grasshopper Creek. Granville didn't stay long though. By April 1863, he had closed his business, sold everything except some land and a couple of houses and returned to the Deer Lodge Valley, which seemed more appealing to him.

Would be miners and prospectors weren't the only individuals to come to Bannack. Like the Stuart brothers, others chose to sell supplies and services to those working claims. Quickly, Bannack's streets were lined with saloons, stables, meat markets, general stores and hotels. Houses of prostitution, dance halls, a bowling alley and a brewery added to the mix, as did doctor's and lawyer's offices. Tailors, carpenters and blacksmiths were also part of economic development in Montana's first capital. And with several wagon roads leading out of Bannack in all directions, freighting became an occupation; folks needed supplies. It was expensive to live there, owing to the isolation, though there seemed to be enough gold to pay the going rates.

Bannack came on fast and furious. Though the heady period didn't last long — by 1865 it had already started to wane — much was packed into those infant years. For starters, in that abbreviated span, Bannack was part of three Territories — first Dakota, then Idaho and on May 26, 1864, Montana Territory.

Sidney Edgerton, originally posted to Bannack as Chief Justice of Idaho Territory, was the only representative of organized government in the mining districts of Montana. Sent to Washington by the people in Bannack and Virginia City, he was the lead individual in securing Montana Territory as a separate entity from Idaho. Edgerton's friendship with President Abraham Lincoln led to his appointment as the first Governor of Montana Territory on June 27, 1864. Facing the job of creating a government for the Territory, his first order of business was to name Bannack as the "capital." The choice was simple — Bannack was where Edgerton lived and he didn't want to move.

With the naming of the new political division, a legislature was needed — another task for the governor. Clarke Spence in his book Territorial Politics and Government in Montana 1864–89 lists Edgerton's challenges. "...His main concern was the infant Montana, a lusty but undisciplined babe, yet to be nurtured to political adulthood. It fell to Edgerton, as the first governor, to take the preliminary steps ... to breathe life into the machinery of self-government. From his office in a curtained-off corner of his log cabin, which also doubled as a residence and at times a schoolroom, the new chief executive outlined judicial districts, commissioned county officers, named Bannack as the temporary capital ... and ordered a census taken. Edgerton proceeded to establish districts from which members of the Legislative Council and House would be selected, and to call a general election for October 24, 1864, to elect not only these representatives, but a delegate to Congress as well."

At noon on December 12, 1864, with the convening of the 20 newly elected representatives, presided over by Governor Sidney Edgerton, Bannack experienced the first meeting ever of the Montana Territorial Legislature. After a joint session, the House reconvened in a two-story log building and the Council (future Senate) in a smaller structure nearby.

Along with the riches, business opportunities and new political identity, there was also a darker side to those days. Bannack, like most all of the mining camps, was a rough and sometime dangerous place. Drunkeness, fights, robberies, killings and the like were often the order of the day.

Having been in San Quentin Prison in 1859, the infamous Henry Plummer came to town in the winter of 1862–1863. Gaining the trust of the Bannack people, he was elected by the Miner's Court, in essence the law of the community, to serve as sheriff. Immediately, Plummer organized a group of his followers, approximately 25 in number, into a gang named the Innocents, because they agreed to always plead their innocence in the unlikely event of their arrest. Under the protection of Sheriff Plummer, this band of vicious thugs set out to terrorize Bannack and other gold camps. In eight months, it is estimated they "legally" robbed and murdered more than 100 people.

Playtime outside the school/Masonic Temple, Bannack. RICK AND SUSIE GRAETZ

Folks became afraid to travel and didn't even feel safe in their homes. As the lawlessness increased, and the jail remained empty, it soon became apparent to some that perhaps their own sheriff was involved with the gang.

On December 23, 1863, the first Vigilante Committee was organized. Its members included men from both Virginia City and Bannack. Virginia City had come to life in the spring of 1863. During the next 42 days, Vigilantes went as far as Hellgate (Missoula) in pursuit of members of Plummer's gang. By the end of January, they had executed 24 of the outlaws, including Henry Plummer, and banished or silenced the remainder.

Mary Edgerton, the governor's wife, wrote on Jan. 17, 1864, "... there was a Vigilance Committee formed at Virginia City and a number of these highway men were hanged. Before they were hung, they made confessions and implicated many others. Their confession was that there was a regularly formed band of them and that the sheriff of this district was the captain."

By 1865, the news was not good for Bannack. The once easy to find treasure was playing out, folks were leaving, and then, on Feb. 7, 1865, the town lost its capital status to Virginia City, site of the biggest gold strike ever in Montana at Alder Gulch on May 26, 1863.

Although not as big of a rush as before, placer mining did pick up again in the spring of 1866. Since water was needed to flush out the placer deposits, the first miners in the gulch ignored gravel that was too far from the creek. Now, ditches were built to extend the workings beyond the streambed. Prospectors could access more rich earth by sluicing the hillside and upper gulches.

Gold mining could now go on for several more years. But working manually didn't allow the deposits on the bedrock, which was anywhere from 10 to 50 feet beneath the gravel, to be reached. A mere sluice box and shovel wouldn't do.

According to Dave Alt, "During the spring of 1895, the first gold dredge in the United States, an electrically driven model, started work at Bannack. Another followed in the fall of the same year and two more machines arrived in 1896." Eventually, five dredges labored in Bannack.

A gold dredge sits on a barge and uses a long chain of steel buckets mounted on a conveyor belt to scoop the gravel bed of the stream down to bedrock. The gravel is then flushed through sluices to recover the gold and the leftover gravel is dumped. As it bites its way along, the barge floats on a small lake of its own making. Ponds created by this method of mining are still visible on Bannack's south side. The landscape is covered with dredging piles of discarded rocks they "forgot" to reclaim.

It didn't take long for the dredges to remove most of the remaining deep placer gold from the Grasshopper Creek area. In some places bedrock was too deep even for the dredges to get to, making it a possibility that some rich deposits might still exist, but out of reach, owing to the expense of recovering them.

Although hard-rock mining continued to take place down from the town site, once the dredges ceased, the population dwindled again. Remnants of the mines and parts of the mills that crushed the ore out of the rock and earth, still stand as silent reminders of Bannack's last fling at gold mining.

As the price of gold plummeted and the mines closed (during World War II all non-essential mining was prohibited), there was no longer a stream of income to support the folks left in Bannack. By the late 1940s, most of the citizens were gone. No longer were there stores to buy groceries in, doctors to visit, a school to attend or post office to pick up mail. Soon, Bannack was abandoned, and the first Territorial Capital of Montana gained ghost town status.

But this was not a place that would crumble and sink into the dust. Concerned people in southwest Montana joined together to preserve what was left. Apparently a mining company that owned much of Bannack went belly-up, and a generous man by the name of Chan Stallings, a long-time Bannack resident, bid for the property at a sheriff's auction. Stallings then made it possible for the Beaverhead County Museum to attain segments of the town. In 1954, the Museum Association donated Bannack, ghosts and all, to the people of Montana with the stipulation that this cherished giant of Montana history could never become a tourist mecca with trinket shops and bars.

Today, more than 50 of the original buildings remain and thanks to the leadership and caring of the Montana Fish Wildlife and Parks, and the non-profit Bannack Association, this wonderful place is preserved for all to gather in a part of their heritage.

—RICK AND SUSIE GRAETZ

RED ROCKS LAKE NATIONAL WILDLIFE REFUGE AND THE CENTENNIAL VALLEY

From Monida's cluster of old buildings, just off Interstate 15 and Monida Pass, a dirt road winds its way through windswept hills before easing down into southwest Montana's high and remote Centennial Valley.

If it weren't for one of the gems of the National Wildlife Refuge system ... Red Rock Lake NWR, very few travelers would make their way through this nearly 40-mile-long valley.

Cattlemen first ventured into the place in 1876, establishing what are now some of the oldest ranches in the state. In the 1880s, determined Yellowstone National Park tourists coming from Salt Lake City, Utah, traveled by train to Monida and then endured a two-day stagecoach trip through the valley to the Park. It was necessary to overnight at Lakeview, now the headquarters for the Refuge.

During the homestead era of the early 1900s, Lakeview, and the surrounding area, was home to almost 400 people. The town had stores, saloons and a hotel. The drought years and Great Depression, coupled with the struggle against tough winters, ended the hopes of most of the population. Many of the homesteads were bought out as land was acquired for the wildlife reserve.

The landscape and most of the activities of this 6,600-foot-high, broad and flat basin haven't changed much in the last hundred years. Multi-generational ranches still carry out the business of raising livestock in a beautiful setting, and wildlife are protected and abound. Today The Nature Conservancy of Montana and other like-minded groups are working with locals to see that ranching remains a viable lifestyle for their heirs and to protect the rural integrity of the valley.

Peaks of the 10,000-foot Centennial Mountains and the Continental Divide, rise abruptly on the valley's southern flank. The 9,000- and 10,000-foot summits of the Gravelly and Snowcrest ranges guard the drainage's north side. The most distant tributary of the Missouri River, Red Rock Creek, gathers waters from smaller streams, then enters Upper and Lower Red Rock lakes before flowing out as Red Rock River on its way, via Lima and Clark Canyon reservoirs, to the Beaverhead River.

Marshes, meadows, a creek, sand hills and the two lakes make up the almost 45,000-acre Red Rock Lake National Wildlife Refuge, of which 32,350 acres are designated wilderness. In the 1930s, the 66 trumpeter swans living here were thought to be the last of their breed. This almost extinct population led to the creation of the Refuge. Now, approximately 110 trumpeters abide in the wetlands in the summer and about 25 stay through the winter in the warm open-water springs created by geothermal activity.

A myriad of other wildlife call this wondrous valley home. Moose, mule deer, elk, pronghorn antelope, 260 species of birds, lynx, grizzlies, black

Red Rocks Lake, safe haven for wild trumpeter swans. RICK AND SUSIE GRAETZ

bear and wolves reside, frequent and pass through the country. The riparian areas and sagebrush covered flats and hills provide habitat for the densest breeding population of peregrine falcons and ferruginous hawks in Montana. Grayling and west slope cutthroat trout live in Red Rock Creek..

Sand dunes found on the northern perimeter of the refuge are remains of the floor of a glacial lake that once occupied the valley. Winds from the southwest and west blew the sand into hilly formations. The breezes also carried seeds with them and now plants found nowhere else in Montana grow in the sandy soil.

To be consistent with wilderness values, the US Fish and Wildlife Service manages their lands in the valley, as primitive and wild, (without many amenities). Thus providing as much solitude and isolation as possible, for the benefit of wildlife as well as for enjoyment by humans.

June and August are best for observing the greatest diversity of wildlife. July usually has mosquito and biting fly problems. The month of May can be excellent as birds are returning, but the weather may be cold and the land muddy. Early fall is also a pleasant time to explore the region, from late November to the first part of April, the valley roads are usually blocked by snow.

Aside from the Monida access, a route from the Henry's Lake area (west of West Yellowstone) over 7,000-foot Red Rock Pass is also usable. Be sure to fill your gas tank before heading into the Centennial Valley; services are not available.

—RICK AND SUSIE GRAETZ

VIRGINIA CITY

Returning home to Bannack from a gold-searching trip in the Yellowstone Valley, six tired prospectors were captured by the Crow Indians. Had it not been for the quick thinking of one of them, their consequent good luck wouldn't have come about.

Showing no fear and trying to prove to the captors he had special powers, Bill Fairweather placed a rattlesnake in his shirt. Impressed, the natives freed them.

For whatever reason, on May 26, 1863, the group paused in their journey to pan the gravels of Alder Creek. Before dark each of the men had enough "colors" in their pans to convince them that they had made a major find.

While replenishing supplies in Bannack, they caused a bit of attention and 200 other would-be, hopeful miners followed them back to Alder Gulch, spawning the beginning of Virginia City. This proved to be the largest of all of Montana's gold strikes.

Long before these treasure-hunting intruders came along, Indian tribes lived in and traveled this country. The Shoshone were here before 1600; the Cree and the Bannocks and Sheepeaters came later. The Native Americans didn't make life easy for the first miners. Trails were closed and would-be settlers were attacked on their way west.

Eventually, many of the Indians in southwest Montana made an effort to get along with whites, though the favor wasn't necessarily returned.

Madison County Commissioner James Fergus, in 1863 said, "There is no doubt that the Indians have murdered and plundered a great many whites, but so far as my experience goes during the past winter, the whites have been the aggressors and the Indians have behaved, themselves by far the most civilized people. Many of the rowdies here think it's fine-fun to shoot an Indian."

In July 1862, news spread of Montana's initial big strike when prospector, John White, discovered gold in Grasshopper Creek. Bannack was born and on May 26, 1864, it became Montana's first Territorial Capital. The inaugural Territorial Legislature met there in December 1864, but the town's political role was short lived.

By 1865, realizing that the gold in Bannack was playing out, the politicians moved the capital to Virginia City in Alder Gulch, a distinction it would hold for ten years. All of the records and furniture for the seat of government were hauled from Bannack across the mountains by wagon, although no building was ever constructed in Virginia City to house the territorial government.

Growth came quickly. On June 16, 1863, a miner's court, which was in essence the initial government of the town, incorporated Virginia City, making it the first such city in the state. Fort Benton, established in 1883, holds the distinction of being Montana's oldest continuing settlement.

Virginia City. RICK AND SUSIE GRAETZ

Before a year was over, an estimated 7,000 people were crowded into the narrow mountain gulch, and soon the population skyrocketed to more than 10,000. Other camp/towns along the 14-mile canyon sprang up.

Of these other places, Nevada City, just a couple of miles down the road, was the most prominent, claiming 2,000 citizens. The other camps, Summit, Junction City, Central City, Union City and Adobe Town were much smaller. Only the sites of these latter places exist today. But none of the settlements came close to the civilized presence of Virginia City.

As commercial activity boomed to major proportions, more stately buildings grew from the original wikiups and tents the first miners used. Freight wagons loaded with supplies rolled in from the steamboats at Fort Benton, and via the Bannack Trail from Corinne, Utah, and a trail from Walla Walla, Washington.

Culture also came in the form of the Montana and the People's Theater and the Lyceum, a literary club. The founding of The Montana Post in Virginia City gave the state its first newspaper.

Growth and wealth in Bannack and Virginia City also attracted all sorts of ne'r-do-wells. Both places were as rough as any movie ever made the west look. Led by the infamous Sheriff Henry Plummer, the outlaws controlled life in the mining communities.

Robberies and murders were so prevalent that the victimized citizens organized, and taking the law into their own hands, dispensed what became known as "frontier justice."

As with the other camps, the placer gold didn't last forever and shortly, Virginia City began its decline. By the late 1860s, the population had dropped to about 2,000 and by 1890 to only 600 people remained.

In 1875, several controversial votes turned over the seat of Territorial government to the thriving town of Helena, formerly Last Chance Gulch. In the early 1900s, a short-lived new life was given to Virginia City with the dredging of gold in the gulch. By 1937, though, this activity, too, had ended.

Today's Virginia City, with its 158 people, is a stable, tourist oriented community serving as the county seat of Madison County and an important link to Montana's heritage. Views of the past have been well preserved here through the magnificent restoration of its buildings.

Years ago, Charlie and Sue Bovey, ranchers from the Great Falls area, began a long-term love affair with this southwest Montana community, one that grew into the first major, privately funded preservation program in the nation. The work they did is of monumental proportions and has preserved Virginia City's 1860s look. Nearly all of the town's buildings are original; none has been brought in from elsewhere.

The Virginia City Players, the oldest continuing summer-stock theater operating west of the Mississippi, persists in its quest to draw and entertain visitors just as its predecessors' performances for the miners did more than a hundred years ago.

A stunning, authentically restored 1910 No. 12 Baldwin steam locomotive trundles the scant 1.5 miles on the Alder Gulch Short Line to Nevada City. Operated on weekends by volunteer engineers, this mechanical work of art adds to the pioneer town atmosphere and attracts train buffs of all ages. The sound of the steam being released and the whistle blowing always causes excitement. During the week, a gasoline-powered engine moves the cars. Much of the credit for the success of the railroad goes to John Larkin of Michigan.

Only a dozen or so of Nevada City's original buildings remain. What prevails here now is also a result of the magic of the Boveys.

In the 1950s, in order to create the realistic look of an early-day Montana gold camp and save historic buildings, The Boveys had many period edifices from the late 1800s moved here from other parts of the state and Wyoming. The structures are so well laid out that to the uninitiated, it appears that Nevada City is a town everyone exited at once, leaving the buildings behind in good standing.

The state of Montana, through the Heritage Commission, owns the Bovey assets in Virginia City and all of Nevada City — a total of 248 buildings. The job of preserving and continuing the restoration is now in the hands of the Montana Heritage Commission, a branch of the Montana Historical Society. The Commission received a $1 million grant from the National Park Service for building stabilization. The first project, the Sauerbier Blacksmith Shop, was recently completed. Another million-dollar grant, this one from Ruth

McFarland, built the McFarland Curatorial Center, a state-of-the-art preservation and restoration center.

The lure of exploring one of the cradles of Montana history makes Alder Gulch a place well worth spending several days in. Its physical setting between the Tobacco Root Mountains and Gravelly Range are an added attraction. Public roads approach scenic sites and signs of yesterday are everywhere.

The gulch and Virginia City come alive in the summer, but the quiet of fall, coupled with that season's gold and orange also makes it a good time to see this Montana treasure.

—RICK ADN SUSIE GRAETZ

BIG HOLE VALLEY

Legendary for its fishing, haystacks, tough winters, and mosquitoes, southwest Montana's Big Hole Valley with its pungent sagebrush smell, is still the real west. Fifty below zero weather and deep snow keep the riffraff out. This sparsely populated country is home to some of the largest and oldest working cow outfits in Montana.

Sprawling in a most beautiful setting, its east and north sides touch the Pioneer Mountains. The Bitterroot and Anaconda ranges, topped by the Continental Divide rise to the west. At fifteen to 20 miles across, about 50 miles long, and 6,000 feet in elevation, the Big Hole is Montana's highest and broadest valley. The generally accepted north-south boundary stretches from Big Hole Pass to Fishtrap.

The centerpiece of this corner of southwest Montana is the Big Hole River. Headwatering in the high country via many tributaries around the southern fringes of the basin, it meanders for 113 miles before joining with the Beaverhead River, just below Twin Bridges, to form the Jefferson River, one of the three forks of the Missouri. En route, waters from numerous lakes and streams, pouring from the surrounding mountains, feed it and help create a blue ribbon fishery. The rare arctic grayling is found in her upper reaches; brook trout and mountain whitefish inhabit the braided channels of the stretch occupying the Big Hole Valley.

For the most part, time has passed by quietly in this crescent shaped valley. Though just a short way to the south, in 1862, at Grasshopper Creek, Montana's first major gold strike was made and raucous Bannack was born.

One major and violent bit of history did occurred here. On August 9, 1877, the US Army ambushed the peaceful Nez Perce Indians. Miraculously, although many of their numbers were killed in the surprise attack, the Nez Perce under the leadership of Chief Joseph, were able to hold off the enemy and escape. The site, west of Wisdom, is now the Big Hole Battlefield National Monument.

Lewis and Clark first encountered the Big Hole River in August 1805 and named it Wisdom River in honor of President Thomas Jefferson. Clark

Main street of Wisdom, Big Hole Valley. RICK AND SUSIE GRAETZ

returned to the valley on July 6, 1806 as the Expedition was heading back to St. Louis. At the site of today's Jackson, they found a spring (the original is still there) hot enough to cook a small piece of meat in five minutes. Clark christened the area "Hot Springs Valley." Local Indians called it "Land of Big Snows." Early-day mountain men referred to all mountain valleys as holes. Ranchers who first moved into these bottomlands in the 1880s, elected to call their new home Big Hole Valley ... Lewis and Clark's and the Indian's designations went by the wayside.

Today, Wisdom, population 135, and Jackson with 58 people, are the mainstays of this ranching domain. Wisdom, first known as "The Crossings" because two roads, one leading to Idaho and the other to the Bitterroot, intersected here, has its collection of saloons, eateries and a general store. After the post office was established in 1884, the town folk revived the name Wisdom. Jackson, 19 miles upstream came into being in 1896 and named for the first postmaster, boasts of Jackson Hot Springs with its lodge and artesian fed hot plunge.

In 1910, a local cattleman invented the "Beaver Slide Stacker." A device, still in use, that carries hay up its sloping side and then drops it forming stacks ... a hallmark of the Big Hole Valley and reason the place is sometimes called the "Land of 10,000 Haystacks."

As a result of the expanded Homestead Act of 1912, a population increase slowly took place in the valley. New folks began fencing out the ranchers to the south who had summered their cattle in the area since the 1870s. Tensions escalated to just short of range-war status. The 1920's depression and fierce winters eventually thinned out the ranks of the homesteaders.

The Big Hole River draws fisherman from all over, but the area offers far more than fly-casting opportunities. The surrounding wilderness has many hiking trails, easy mountains to climb, and dependable winter snows make for excellent cross-country skiing.

—RICK AND SUSIE GRAETZ

THREE FORKS OF THE MISSOURI RIVER

A labyrinth of channels, willow bottoms, islands and a general mix of wetlands interact to piece together the headwaters of the Missouri River.

From here, the point where the three forks (the Jefferson, Gallatin and Madison rivers) join as one, the great Missouri River begins an odyssey, heading forth as the starring role in the creation of a state. As a route of western expansion, the Missouri River had few equals. Missouri Headwaters State Park at the three forks, gathers in and documents well the river's illustrious past in the chronology of our Montana, through interpretive signs and displays.

History was vivid at the union of the three rivers. Long before whites trespassed, this place was a natural crossroad, camping spot, hunting area, meeting location and battleground for the natives, including the Hidatsa, Blackfeet, Shoshone and Crow. Much blood was shed at the Missouri's birthplace. Today, faint pictographs, the only physical evidence of the passing of the indigenous cultures at the forks, are found in a small cave.

Captains Meriwether Lewis and William Clark, with their fellow explorers, were the first documented white travelers to witness the area. By the time they reached the headwaters, the Corps of Discovery had already spent three months in what would become Montana. Time was running short, and anxious to trade for horses to enable them to cross the mountains, they had hoped to have encountered the Shoshone Indians by now.

July 25, 1805, Captain Clark, in spite of feet painfully blistered and ravaged with prickly pear thorns, was traveling overland and a couple of days ahead of Lewis, when he arrived at the joining of the three rivers. Quickly choosing to explore the *"North fork"* (soon to be named Jefferson's River), which in his estimation, was the route to the Columbia, he left a note for Lewis and spent the next two days in search of the Shoshone. Contracting *"a high fever & akeing in all my bones."* Finding no sign of the Natives, he reluctantly turned back, crossed over to the middle fork (to be named the Madison) and camped for the night explaining, *"I continue to be verry unwell fever verry high."*

Clark spent the nights of July 25 and 26 at two separate camps on *"Philosophy River"* (Willow Creek) near the present village of Willow Creek, just a few miles southwest of the Three Forks town site.

On the morning of July 27, Lewis and his men met up with Clark at the three forks. Lewis's journal entry for that night read, *"the country opens suddenly to extensive and beatifull plains and meadows which appeared to be surrounded in every direction with distant and lofty mountains; supposing this to be the Three Forks of the Missouri I halted the party."* Lewis then walked about a half mile up the Gallatin and *"ascended the point of a high limestone clift* (Lewis's Rock) *from whence I commanded a most perfect view of the neighbouring country."* The explorer was beholding the Spanish Peaks and Madison Range to the south, the Gallatin Range to the southeast and the Tobacco Root Mountains in his southwest view field. He could also see the Bridger Range directly to the east. In between was the lush, wide valley of the Gallatin River.

Good news came as Sacajawea recognized the area and informed them that this was the exact place her people were encamped when the Hidatsa had captured her five years earlier.

There was no question in the two leaders' minds that this was the headwaters of the Missouri. July 28, Lewis wrote, *"Both Capt. C. and myself corrisponded in opinion, with rispect, to the impropriety of calling either of these streams the Missouri and accordingly agreed to name them ... we called the S.W. Fork, that which we meant to ascend, Jefferson's river in honor of Thomas Jefferson. the Middle fork we called Madison's River in honor of James Madison, and the S. E. Fork we called Gallitin's river in honor of Albert Gallitin."*

When the Corps returned to St. Louis in September of 1806, fur trappers were already on their way to the new country. After meeting a group of

Gallatin River just before it joins the Madison and the Jefferson at the three forks of the Missouri.
RICK AND SUSIE GRAETZ

trappers heading upriver, John Colter of the Expedition left Lewis and Clark in North Dakota and return to the country he fondly recalled. In 1808, Colter and John Potts were trapping at the three forks when they encountered Blackfeet hunters and warriors. Potts was killed and Colter was given a chance to escape. The Blackfeet took his clothes and allowed him to run for his life. Grabbing a spear from his closest pursuer, Colter was able to make the kill and create a diversion. Upon reaching the Madison River, he hid among the driftwood. The Indians gave up the search and Colter began a 7-day "walk," minus clothes or footwear, to a trading post 200 miles away at the confluence of the Bighorn and Yellowstone rivers (east of modern-day Billings).

Despite this incident, Colter returned several times to the forks. In 1810, he was part of a group that established a trading post here. When Indians attacked the post and killed several traders, Colter left and vowed never to return.

By 1863, settlers had arrived in the Gallatin Valley and Gallatin City came alive on the northwest bank between where the Jefferson and Madison are already joined and the Gallatin's entrance. The goal was to make this a river "port," but the founders didn't consider, or know about, the five "great falls," well to the north, that blocked steamboat traffic. When these pioneers realized their town had no future, they abandoned it. Then in 1865, Gallatin City II was established. A ferry crossing accessed the mining camps to the west. The town served as an agricultural center until 1883 when the railroad, coming through the Gallatin Valley, passed it two miles to the south. Even before that, Bozeman's growing presence spelled the end to Gallatin City's second try. All that remains today is a skeleton of the hotel.

During Gallatin City's final years, a couple of miles to the south, Three Forks' predecessor, "An English Nobility Colony" as reported in Names on the Face of Montana — essentially a small group of cabins — sputtered along with a toll bridge that spanned the area's wetlands, as well as the Madison and Jefferson rivers. In 1882, the present town of Three Forks gained a hold. When the rails reached it, the town's future was secured.

The landscape at the headwaters has much the same appearance as when the Corps of Discovery and the fur trappers spent time here. One of Montana's historical staging areas, those periods still permeate the atmosphere of this place. And there is nothing shy about it. The Gallatin, Madison and Jefferson come in with plenty of water and power to give the Missouri an enviable starting surge — no trickles, springs or snowmelt to kick it off. At the exact place where the big Missouri goes forth, there is no mistaking it for a stream — it is clearly a major river from the get go.

—RICK AND SUSIE GRAETZ

BOZEMAN

Turn a shovel full of dirt in the Gallatin Valley today and one still finds the same rich earth pioneers encountered 140 years ago. More than the gold fields found to the west or the trail from civilization that ran past it, the city of Bozeman exists today because of the fertile soil it is built upon.

Bozeman sits at 4,795 feet at the eastern end of the semi-arid Gallatin Valley in southwestern Montana. The valley's horizons are defined by mountain ranges formed 136 million to 40 million years ago. Marking the valley's southern boundary is the Madison Range, to the northeast the Bridgers rise to meet the sky, to the west are the Horseshoe Hills and to the southwest the valley ends with the Gallatin Range. As those mountains were forming, portions of a large inland sea that had covered the valley floor began to recede, leaving behind a thick layer of productive loam over much of the land.

Then, scenic, fertile and empty of humans, the Gallatin Valley rested for thousands of years. Finally, American Indians began visiting the valley on a regular basis. The first to arrive were plateau Indians from the northwest Driven by pressure from the increasing numbers of European settlers to the east, in the late-1500s. Following soon after them in the early-1600s were members of the Sioux tribes, the Crows, and the Shoshone, or Snake.

Here, the Indians found excellent bison hunting grounds, and for more than 200 years, continued to regularly visit the valley without being hindered by the presence of whites. It wasn't until 1805 and the Lewis and Clark Expedition's arrival to the Gallatin Valley that many of the Indians received their first hint of what, or who, was to come.

More whites from "the states" were to soon follow Lewis and Clark and in the early and mid-1800s, migrations of Easterners led to Indian wars throughout the West. Those wars, in turn, led to a series of treaties that attempted to reach a peace by guaranteeing Indian tribes ownership of their important lands while ensuring that the westward flow of prospectors and pioneers could continue.

The early treaties did not stop the fighting, but despite the always-present promise of danger, prospectors and pioneers continued to move into the West. In 1851, the U.S. government signed a treaty with the Blackfeet that recognized the Gallatin Valley as Indian territory. The government's position that the valley belonged to the Indian Nations was reiterated in 1855 when the Stevens Treaty identified the Gallatin Valley and the three forks of the Missouri River as "common hunting grounds" for area Indian tribes for the following 99 years.

But by then, gold had been discovered in Gold Creek, and despite a treaty just eight-years-old, miners had formed a small town, population 25, near the three forks of the Missouri on the eastern edge of the Gallatin Valley.

Among the first to stake a claim to 160 acres near the new town of Three Forks was John Bozeman, a 28-year-old explorer and entrepreneur from

Pickens County, Georgia. Bozeman had reached Three Forks after panning for gold in the Deer Lodge Valley with early miners Granville and James Stuart. Having no liking for a miner's long hours, he filed for 160 acres near Three Forks, where he apparently also had little liking for farming. Bozeman never would put a plow to his soil — he had other plans.

Early in 1863, Bozeman was convinced that he was witnessing the beginning of a rush of prospectors into the gold fields of the western mountains and of pioneers into the fertile valleys. While in Three Forks, he began developing plans for a new wagon trail that could lead supplies, prospectors and pioneers from Utah into the mountains and valleys of Montana.

At the time, there were only two routes to the gold fields of western Montana — up the Missouri River to Fort Benton and from there on horseback to the mines or along the dry, dangerous and lengthy Oregon Trail that reached from the southern plains into Idaho and through Indian hunting grounds.

Bozeman planned to develop another, shorter trail from Utah that would leave the Oregon Trail along the North Platte River in Wyoming, travel northwest to the Bighorn and Yellowstone areas and then through the Gallatin Valley and on into Virginia City.

Bozeman believed that with time, the fertile soil found in the Gallatin Valley would be of more value than the gold fields being discovered to the west. Along with plotting a trail, he planned for a town to be built at the eastern, wetter end of the valley. That town would be the center for the agricultural industry Bozeman expected to happen. Before leaving for Utah to begin developing his trail, he convinced two other Three Forks residents, William J. Beall and Daniel E. Rouse, to start laying out the town site while he was away.

It seemed not to matter to Bozeman that his trail, and the town he intended to develop, were both on Indian hunting grounds. Despite the constant threat of Indian attack, Bozeman developed his trail. After an aborted attempt in which he was turned back by an Indian war party, finally in July 1863, with a train of 46 wagons and 89 people, he arrived in the Gallatin Valley.

In his absence, the town was plotted and in 1864 a town charter was officially formed naming the new settlement Bozeman. From the beginning, John Bozeman was his town's greatest advocate — and a staunch believer that the soil, not gold, would be responsible for its success. To help that success along, Bozeman talked businessmen Thomas Cover and P. W. McAdow into building a flourmill, and convinced G. W. A. and Elizabeth Frazier to open a hotel. In a sign of things to come, farms west of Bozeman diverted the first water to irrigate crops.

That year, Bozeman also convinced a brave, or foolhardy, rancher to move a large herd of cattle from Texas to the Gallatin Valley. Because the animals were to be driven through Indian hunting grounds, both Indian tribes and the U.S. Army opposed the plan. But despite a refusal by the Army to offer any protection, Nelson Story pushed his herd northward, often at night to avoid Indian war parties, and arrived in the Gallatin Valley with 3,000 cattle and enough supplies to open a general store. This event is pointed to as the beginning of Montana's cattle industry.

Despite the slow but steady growth of the new town, hostile Indians still lingered in, and fought around, the valley. Attacks continued along the trail and in the spring of 1865, full scale war broke out between a force of unified tribal warriors and settlers and soldiers. The next year, just three years after he had brought his first wagon train up the trail, Sioux and Cheyenne Indians successfully closed it to most traffic. In 1867, John Bozeman died at the hands of Indians on the trail he had blazed.

Bozeman's premature death caused an uproar among the residents of his growing town and the U.S. Army responded by establishing Fort Ellis nearby. Along with offering a sense of safety, the fort also immediately became a market for produce raised on nearby farms. Now, Bozeman quickly replaced the western goldfields as the destination for those who managed to get through the blocked Bozeman Trail.

The closure of the trail was made official with the Fort Laramie Treaty of 1868, in which the United States government agreed that it had been illegally constructed through Indian lands. Closed or not, settlers continued to use the trail at increasing rates, and while the Indian harassment persisted, eventually the Army reopened the route.

In 1883, when residents stood alongside the new tracks to celebrate the arrival of the first Northern Pacific Railway locomotive, freight wagon trains, stagecoaches and a telegraph had already connected Bozeman to Helena and points east. The town had brickyards and new brick buildings were replacing earlier downtown wooden structures, a stately county courthouse marked the community as the Gallatin County seat, there were two hotels and two boarding houses, a bank, schoolhouse, a couple of doctors and several churches.

That same year, the Bozeman Chronicle began publishing once a week; in 1884, the Rocky Mountain Telephone Company introduced phones to the community and in 1886, the Bozeman Electric Company began providing a dependable source of power. In November 1889, when Montana became the 41st state, there were more than 2,000 residents in Bozeman to commemorate the occasion.

Among Bozeman's residents in the 1890s was Nelson Story, the man responsible for moving the cattle from Texas to Montana three decades earlier. Story is credited with helping sway the 1893 decision to locate Montana's new land-grant college in Bozeman. First known as the Agricultural College of the State of Montana, the school was renamed The Montana College of Agriculture before receiving the name it now goes by, Montana State University. By the turn of the 20th Century, Bozeman not only had a college, it also had an opera house, symphony and library.

But while the town grew, the farmers had less success. With crops limited mostly to grain, disease made them vulnerable to being wiped out, and when they tried sugar beets, that crop failed because of the short growing season. In 1911, the first fields of peas were planted, grew just fine and two years later, 17,000 acres in the Gallatin Valley were dedicated to this crop.

During World War I, the harvest was significant enough to prompt the building of the Bozeman Canning Company. During the war, most of the peas were shipped to soldiers overseas. The pea industry lasted until 1961, but continues to be honored each summer with the Sweet Pea Festival.

In the late-1930s another, still thriving, industry was started in the Gallatin Valley when the owner of a dude ranch opened a ski hill in Gallatin Canyon. Two decades later, the larger, better-planned Bridger Bowl would open in the Bridger Mountains. Today, skiing and other winter sports remain a significant industry for Bozeman and are pointed to as one of the reasons for the community's continual expansion.

In 1940, 8,665 people called Bozeman home. By 1960, that number had climbed to 13,400. In the 1970s, the community prepared for even more growth by building a new airport terminal. Between 1980 and 1990, Gallatin County saw the fastest population increases in the state, jumping from 42,865 to 50,465 residents within the decade. And the escalation continues.

Bozeman's agricultural college has grown into a respected university and the extraordinary Museum of the Rockies has earned a reputation as one of the premier cultural sites in the Rocky Mountains. The town's scenic setting, artistic culture and nearby ski hills also have caught the eye of affluent out-of-staters and Bozeman has become a popular destination for those wanting to escape the hustle of larger cities.

One hundred and forty years ago, John Bozeman believed a town built around agriculture would be more stable and successful than one built around a gold boom. Today, his city of Bozeman seems to be proving him to be correct.

—GRANT SASEK

GALLATIN RANGE

The Gallatin Range, one of Montana's great hiking areas, is the northern-most extension of the Greater Yellowstone Eco-system. At one time, it was covered by lava from volcanic activity in Yellowstone National Park.

These summits, rising to more than 10,000 feet, are bordered by the Gallatin Canyon to the west and the Yellowstone River and the Paradise Valley on the east. Bozeman and the Gallatin Valley form the northern boundary. The massif extends into Yellowstone National Park as it heads south. It's 60 miles long and consists of 263,440 acres of wild country; 155,000 acres have been placed in Wilderness Study status.

Porcupine Creek, Gallatin Range near Big Sky. RICK AND SUSIE GRAETZ

Wildlife managers consider its peaks and the meadows to be some of America's very best elk country and essential as a wintering and calving range for the large north Yellowstone elk herd. It is also some of Yellowstone's most suitable grizzly habitat and provides an irreplaceable home for moose, big horn sheep, mountain goat, mule deer, mountain lion, black bear, lynx and wolverines.

The balance of the range is a mix of deep canyons, lower summits and a huge expanse of largely roadless, alpine and subalpine terrain.

A most unusual 25,980-acre area, known as the Gallatin Petrified Forest, is found on the west side of this southwest Montana uplift. Many of the trees were petrified in their standing position. Some stumps are thought to be almost a million years old.

Waters pouring from the crest of the range such as Tipi Creek, Buffalo Horn Creek, Porcupine Creek, Squaw Creek, Rock Creek, Big Creek and Tom Miner Creek are well known and have been long-time favorite haunts of folks from Bozeman, West Yellowstone and other surrounding communities.

Numerous trails penetrate and cross this place of beauty. One of the most popular destinations is the Hyalite Peaks, reached via the Hyalite Canyon Road out of Bozeman. From here it is possible to access many other trails that go southeast and west. Peaks such as Hyalite and Blackmore are relatively easy climbs.

Buffalo Horn Trail leads to Ramshorn Peak and Lake and takes off at the 320 Ranch about 45 miles south of Bozeman in the Gallatin Canyon. The public road crosses private land so stay on the road. The trail begins at the road's end. It's a gradual uphill trek of six miles to the lake. Ramshorn Peak at 10,269 feet is a worthwhile climb.

And from here, you can connect with the Porcupine Trail to make a point-to-point trip. Or you can cross the mountains via the Rock Creek and Deep Creek trails that lead toward Paradise Valley. For a long, but spectacular hike, you can stay north along the crest to Hyalite Peak.

About 25 miles south of Livingston off Hwy 89, it's about four miles to the Big Creek trailhead and a 12-mile walk to Windy Pass. The trail then descends to the Gallatin Canyon on the west side of the range.

Just south of Big Creek, Tom Miner Creek Trail is also a popular route into the southern reaches of this roadless country.

Much of the Gallatin Range is suitable for back country skiing, but the most frequented areas are in the southern parts and Yellowstone National Park. The valleys are wider here and access to the upper reaches is easier.

The Gallatin National Forest map is a good one to use as a starter and from there you can determine which of the USGS Topographic Maps you'll need.

THE MADISON RANGE

Twenty miles beyond Bozeman, Montana's second highest mountain range, the Madison, begins its climb from the Gallatin Canyon. It then heads south for almost 50 miles before abruptly dropping off at Hebgen and Quake lakes, near Yellowstone National Park. Along the way, the east flank waters are sent into the Gallatin River and snowmelt from its western slopes adds to the flow of the Madison River.

Six peaks top 11,000 feet, including 11,316-foot Hilgard, the highest in Montana outside of the Beartooth. Almost 120 of the apexes are higher than 10,000 feet and 74 of those are unnamed. The range comprises several groupings ... the Spanish Peaks; Fan, Lone, Cedar and Sphinx mountains; the Taylor Peaks; the Hilgard area; and the Monument Peaks. Rugged east-west canyons starting below the Madison divide separate them. Lush meadows and high open grassy basins characterize the terrain surrounding the summits.

Much of the high country splendor complex is in the federally protected Lee Metcalf Wilderness.

On the range's north end, in the Spanish Peaks, 25 points reach over 10,000 feet. Gallatin, at 11,105 feet, is the highest. Extensive glaciation is evident in this very rugged high country. One of Montana's greatest elevation gains is found on the northwest side, the rise from Bear Trap Canyon and Cowboy's Heaven on the Madison River to the crest of the Spanish Peaks is 6,500 feet. Bear Trap Canyon consists of 6,000 acres of BLM Wilderness and possibly the most exciting and challenging white water in Montana.

The Fan and Lone Mountain area is the only place in this Madison chain where a road reaches and crosses the hydrological divide. A private byway

Hilgard Lake and Peak, Madison Range. RICK AND SUSIE GRAETZ

leading from Big Sky Resort area passes through Jack Creek and the Moonlight Basin Development on its way to Ennis. This drainage also separates the Spanish Peaks segment of the Lee Metcalf Wilderness from its southern extension. Just south of Lone Mountain and Big Sky, the distinct form of the 10,876-foot Sphinx marks the skyline.

Below the Sphinx, the Taylor Peaks with 11,256-foot Koch Peak accentuate one of the least visited regions of the Madison Range. Just to the south of 11,202-foot Imp Peak and the Taylor summits, the basins of the Hilgard Peaks present one of Montana's most beautiful alpine displays. Of the more than 70 lakes that grace the Madison Range, most of them are found in these southern reaches. This segment of the mountains, as well as the Spanish Peaks, receives heavy use, especially from horse parties. And as it is some of the areas roughest landscape, with significant altitude gains, hikers earn their way.

The Monument Peak area is set apart from the main range in the southeast corner of the uplift. In essence, it is an island of wilderness separated from the Taylor-Hilgard region by the Cabin Creek Special Management Area. The Cabin Creek drainage has been open to motorized use but has become an embarrassment to Forest Service field personnel owing to a lack of regulations enforcement from the Gallatin National Forest Supervisor's office. Misuse of the land has come to the point where responsible motorized enthusiasts will not enter the place.

The Lee Metcalf Wilderness, named after one of Montana's greatest US Senators, makes up 254,944 acres of the range. Metcalf was a tireless supporter of protecting Montana's wild lands. His passing left a void in American conservation that has not yet been filled. He represented our State in the US Congress for more than 25 years and emerged as a giant in the struggle to preserve a portion of the Nation's heritage. Without him, much of our treasured wilderness would have long ago been destroyed. He was a man to match Montana's mountains.

Forest Service maps of the Gallatin and Beaverhead National Forest outline the more detailed US Geological Survey Topographical Maps you'll need to visit the area. Access points are many, but the most popular ones go into the Spanish Peaks from the north or into the Hilgard Peaks from the south. This is primarily a warm season backpacking and horse travel area since in the winter, the possibility of avalanches in the upper reaches is extreme, making backcountry travel dangerous.

Tundra and very fragile land take up much of the high country. Users should be aware of this and participate in low impact camping. The majority of the upper-most lakes show no sign of use; look at them and then pitch your tent elsewhere. Wilderness rangers, hikers and horse people have, in spite of significant visitation, kept this Madison Range wilderness pristine.

—RICK AND SUSIE GRAETZ

MADISON RIVER CANYON EARTHQUAKE AREA

With a full moon illuminating the countryside, the vacationers who filled the resorts and campgrounds in the Hebgen Lake area the night of August 17, 1959, were enjoying an especially pleasant and quiet summer evening.

Then at about 11:37 pm, the ground began to pitch and tremble; a major 7.5 earthquake was underway and the mood of the night changed! Man-made structures moved, split apart and some even collapsed. Folks, shaken awake, rushed outside wondering what had happened; stunned by the shock, they could only stare in disbelief. The lake began to slosh back and forth like a tidal wave. The first few breakers, estimated to be 20 feet high, were large enough to flow over the dam. This seiche ("saysh") action as it is called, continued for the next 11½ hours.

A few miles downstream, in the Madison Canyon near the filled-to-capacity Rock Creek campground, part of the mountainside was shattered by the major tremor, and for a few brief seconds hung poised over the unsuspecting campers. Most assumed the shaking of their tents and trailers was caused by bears; to those who got up to investigate, in the clear moonlight everything seemed normal. Suddenly, the entire mountainside across the river began to fall away. As the campers tried to flee, the avalanche, with a terrible roaring and grinding noise, crushed and buried people, cars and trailers. Survivors tell of being knocked down by a violent air blast and some were then engulfed by a huge wave of water displaced from the Madison River.

In the subsequent dust-filled stillness, the only sounds were the cries of the injured and the anxious calls of separated families.

As the night wore on, clouds gathered and masked the moon. What had begun as a cheerful summer night turned, in the space of seconds, into a time of terror, trauma and frustration. Those uninjured in the catastrophe, worked in the pitch-black darkness to rescue the trapped and wounded. The earth constantly trembled beneath their feet as repeated aftershocks shook the area and boulders and rock falls continued to tumble down the mountainsides. When daylight finally dawned, the immensity of the landslide became apparent.

About a one-mile-long section of the north-facing flank of a mountain, whose crest was about 1,300 feet above the river floor, had broken loose, and the entire mass moved across the canyon as a sheet. Estimates were it was moving about 100 mph when it engulfed the camp. The momentum of the slide was such that its front rode about 400 feet up the opposite canyon wall. The nearly 38 million cubic yards of rock that slid could have paved a three-foot deep, two-lane highway from Montana to New York.

Once the valley was blocked, the waves that crested Hebgen Dam, plus the water, which is normally released through the spillway, were impounded on the east side of the slide and Earthquake Lake, now known as Quake Lake, began to form.

Chilled and dazed, the fortunate survivors huddled on the slopes like war refugees, stranded with no way to call for help. Escape routes were blocked. Beside the enormous landslide sealing the lower end of the canyon, parts of the highway skirting the north edge of Hebgen Lake were either buried by landslides, under water or entirely broken up.

Communication lines were out. First reports of the disaster came from a ham radio operator in the badly damaged town of West Yellowstone, who had little knowledge of what happened in the Madison Canyon. All it was known for sure was that there was chaos, a threat of floods and trapped people desperately in need of help.

Before sunrise, rescue units for many agencies in Idaho and Montana were on the move. In the early morning light, a plane made a reconnaissance flight and Forest Service smoke jumpers parachuted into the canyon to give first aid and to set up communications. Men on foot, horseback and in helicopters moved in to give assistance. There were many outstanding acts of brotherhood and mutual help. Rescue workers treated the injured and evacuate them to nearby towns and ranches, where volunteers provided food and shelter. By evening, a bulldozed road had been built; the immediate emergency was over, and all who wished to leave were able to get out of the canyon.

Before all was stilled in the canyon and surrounding terrain, some 370 aftershocks were recorded. No one had known how many people were ensconced in and near the Rock Creek campground prior to the disaster and it would be a long time afterward until the toll on human life could be

Earthquake slide. RICK AND SUSIE GRAETZ

established. Twenty-eight people were killed, 19 of them entombed beneath the landslide.

After the quake, when Hebgen Lake quieted, it became apparent that the north shore had actually dropped 19 feet causing docks, beaches and cabins to be submerged. By contrast, the south shore was elevated; stranded boats and docks were common sights and immense areas of lake bottom were exposed here. Near the lake, two parallel segments of the Hebgen Lake fault block broke the ground with one side stretching eight miles and rising 22 feet in places, creating a cliff-like earthquake scarp.

The 721-foot-long Hebgen Dam built in 1915, rises 87 feet above the river floor. The ground on which it rests dropped about 10 feet during the main tremor, this and other events that night subjected the dam to stresses for which it was not designed. Though it did not fail, the structure was heavily damaged. The concrete core was cracked in at least four places and was tilted and twisted out of line.

The Corps of Engineers came in to study the landslide to prevent the rising waters of the newly created lake from cutting through the natural dam and flooding the downriver Madison Valley. By August 31, Quake Lake was five miles long, 150 feet deep and rising by nine feet daily. On September 9, only 22 days after the quake, a one-mile-long spillway was finished just as the waters were reaching the top of the dam. A huge flood was averted.

The epicenter of the quake was around Duck Creek on the east edge of Hebgen Lake; however, most of the damage moved in a westerly direction.

The simple explanation for the cause of the earthquake is that huge fault blocks of rock, some 15 miles long, abruptly slumped and tilted beneath Hebgen Lake and the Madison River Canyon. To understand this process further requires a study of the underground hot spots and caldera activity in nearby Yellowstone National Park as it is all related. A fascinating book to read on this subject is Windows Into The Earth by Robert B. Smith and Lee J. Siegel.

Yellowstone National Park itself shared in this night of terror, although not to the extent of the Madison Canyon. Out in the wilderness that night, in the Fire Hole River's geyser basin, more-than-normal amounts of hot water started belching up. Numerous geysers, some dormant for many years, sent water skyward. Others erupted with more activity than usual. Old Faithful's rhythm and force changed and placid hot springs became angry, exploding with steam, water and mud. When the earth finally began to shake, landslides obstructed some park roads.

In the Park's venerable Old Faithful Inn, the evening's festivities came to an abrupt end. Guests poured out of shaking buildings and thousands of cars, trucks and buses streamed out of the park in the face of the sharpest earthquake ever registered in the Rockies.

Today, hundreds of cormorants are often seen perched on the limbs of dead snags jutting out of Quake Lake along the highway. Perhaps the area has become a resting and fishing stop on these large, black bird's migration route. A drive through the canyon will show the power of Mother Nature as there are still signs of the damage done to the landscape. The US Forest Service administers a visitor's center atop the rubble of the giant slide at Quake Lake.

Quake Lake, Madison Canyon. RICK AND SUSIE GRAETZ

Called the Earthquake Lake Center, it is located on Hwy 287, twenty-seven miles from West Yellowstone. The building is open from Memorial Day until mid-September. During the off-season, interpretive signs are reached by parking at the gate and walking up the road.

—RICK AND SUSIE GRAETZ

MOUNTAIN NOTES

Pioneer Mountains

One of only six ranges in the state with summits over 11,000 feet, the Pioneers are separated into east and west by the Wise River, and bordered on three sides by the U-shaped channel of the Big Hole River. Dillon is off to the southeast, and Wisdom and the Big Hole Valley guard the range to the west. The East Pioneers are the highest and most glaciated of the two sets of ranges. Tweedy Peak, at 11,154 feet, and Torrey, at 11,147 feet, are the two highest summits. Many trails crisscross this seldom-visited group of mountains. The West Pioneers are more rounded than their eastern counterparts, but are no less wild.

More than 80 lakes dot the upper reaches. And an approximately 500-year-old stand of lodgepole pine, one of the oldest known, survives here.

Ruby Mountains

A 15-mile-long range southwest of Virginia City and 15 miles east of Dillon. Ruby Point, 9,391 feet is the highest point. More than half of this dry country lies above 8,000 feet.

Blacktail Mountains

This range extends 20 miles southeast of Dillon, and boasts several 8,000-foot peaks. A 12-mile-long plateau, dissected by deep timbered canyons with shear headwalls and cliffs, dominates much of the Blacktails. The central part of the plateau, Blacktail Mountain, contains a barely discernible high point of 9,477 feet.

Snowcrest Range

A little known but beautiful mountain complex, the Snowcrest is separated from the Gravellys to the east by the relatively narrow canyon of the Ruby River. Sunset Peak, at 10,581 feet, is its highest reach. It's a mix of alpine meadows, sagebrush foothills, dense timber and wooded windswept ridges. Both the Gravellys and the Snowcrest border the Centennial Valley and Red Rock Lakes National Wildlife Refuge to the south. Several other peaks in this 25-mile-long range soar above 10,000 feet, including 10,220-foot Antone Peak and 10,486-foot Olson Peak. Several other summits come close to, or exceed, 10,000 feet. Trails interlace this range that can be reached from Dillon or Sheridan.

Red Conglomerate Peak, Lima Peaks. RICK AND SUSIE GRAETZ

Tendoy Mountains

The Tendoys stretch northward just beyond Lima for 30 miles and receive heavy motorized use, although an almost 70,000-acre eastern segment, extending for 20 miles along the crest of the range, is roadless. Dixon Mountain, at 9,674 feet, is the most prominent and highest landmark in the Tendoys. Sourdough Peak, at 9,571 feet, is the second-highest summit.

Lima Peaks

Just northwest of Monida Pass and the Montana/Idaho line, the Lima Peaks, or the Garfield Peaks as they're sometimes called, soar to more than 10,000 feet high. Garfield Mountain, at 10,961 feet, towers above dry grassland. The landscape in these parts is about 80 percent void of trees. Glaciers have carved cirques out of the north face of the range. Little Sheep Creek separates these southwest Montana points from the main range of the Bitterroot/Beaverhead Mountains and the Red Conglomerate Peaks on the Continental Divide and the Montana/Idaho state line.

Tobacco Root Mountains

Southeast of Butte, the Tobacco Roots are a tight cluster of 10,000-foot peaks, with numerous lakes and extensive signs of past mining activity. Twenty-eight pinnacles reach beyond 10,000 feet. Mount Jefferson, at 10,600 feet, is the highest summit.

Gravelly Range

The Gravellys are a rolling plateau-like range to the south of Virginia City and just west of the Madison Range and Madison River. At 10,545 feet, Black Butte, the highest summit, is a distinctive landmark stretching above sub alpine grassland.

The Lionhead Mountains

Some folks consider the Lionheads to be a southern extension of the Madison Range, but the steep canyon of the Madison River and Quake Lake separated them. Others call these the Henry's Lake Mountains. They are west of West Yellowstone and contain peaks over 10,000 feet including their highest, 10,600-foot Sheep Point. Most of the Lionhead is in Idaho. Nine sub alpine lakes sparkle among some of the high cirques.

Flint Creek Range

With just one peak exceeding 10,000 feet (10,168-foot Mt. Powell), the Flint Creeks are the 13th-highest range in the state. The loftiest summits are all clustered in one roadless area near Powell. Many other crests exceed 8,000–9,000 feet. Deer Lodge and the Clark Fork River Valley are on the east with the Philipsburg area to the west. The range is 25 miles long and has many remains of early mining, including buildings of the old silver town, Granite.

Discovery Basin Ski Area is in the southwest corner, just above Georgetown Lake.

John Long Mountains

Rock Creek separates the John Longs from the Sapphires on the west, and the Flint Creek Valley near Philipsburg forms their eastern perimeter. They are 30 miles long and have very few summits over 7,000 feet. An 8,468-foot point just east of Quigg Peak is the highest top. Black Pine, at 7,937 feet, and Pine Ridge, at 7,932 feet, are two other high areas.

The Highlands

Butte's mountains are prominent from the mining city, especially for cars coming down the hill on I-15 from Elk Park into the city. Table Mountain, a plateau-like summit at 10,223 feet, is their highest point.

Elkhorn Mountains

These are Helena's hunting grounds and a wild landscape enjoying designation as a "special wildlife management unit," owing to its large elk population. They're considered to be the most productive elk habitat in Montana. A ridge connects the two highest summits, Crow Peak, at 9,414 feet, and Elkhorn Peak, at 9,381 feet. Several other peaks are over 8,000 feet. Although not considered a true ghost town, as a few people still live there, the town of Elkhorn is a remnant of a colorful mining past. The McClellan and Beaver Creek area, closest to Helena, are the wildest parts of the range.

The Bridger Range

North of Bozeman, and west across the Shields Valley from the Crazies, the 25-mile-long Bridger Range rises to its highest summit, 9,665-foot Sacajawea Peak. The Bridgers are best known for having one of the best powder skiing areas in Montana, Bridger Bowl.

Much of this chain is a long steep ridgeline, but in its north, near Sacajawea, some good hiking is possible.

Unnamed Mountains

There is no official name for the wide expanse of mountains that extends from Lincoln and the Blackfoot Valley, in the north, to Butte and Elk Park in the south. The Helmville and Deer Lodge valleys form their western boundary, and the valley of Prickly Pear Creek and the Boulder Valley guard the east. The Helena Valley is in its northeast corner. The Continental Divide meanders through it. Some maps have their own monikers for certain parts of it, such as the Deer Lodge Mountains on the east and the Boulder Mountains farther in.

For a lack of better name, we'll call them Montana's Heritage Mountains, as they have remnants of almost all of Montana's past — including logging, mining, early-day skiing and untouched wildlands. Highway 12 at MacDonald Pass crosses them in the center, and I-15 skirts their southern end on its way from Helena to Butte.

There are roadless areas such as Nevada Mountain, Blackfoot Meadows and the Sheep Head region. The old backroad passes of Fletcher and Stemple cross it in the northeast, and the Great Divide Ski Area slopes downward from Mt. Belmont.

Black Mountain, Nevada Mountain and Thunderbolt Peaks are all over 8,000 feet.

—RICK AND SUSIE GRAETZ

THE ROCKY MOUNTAIN FRONT
AND GOLDEN TRIANGLE

"I am a resident, you might almost say a product, of the Rocky Mountain Front, "the front" as we have come to call it. It is a strip of land just east of the Continental Divide and includes an edge of the plains, the higher bench lands, the foothills and then the great jagged wall of the mountains.

At the age of 89, living on the front, I have come to feel a part of what has gone before, kin to dinosaur and buffalo and departed Indians that lived here. When I step out of doors and hear a small crunch underfoot I sometimes suspect I may be treading on the dusted bones of duckbill or bison or red man killed in the hunt.

I look to the north and the south, where the foothills rise, east to the great jagged roll of the high plains and west to mountains and my vision site of Ear Mountain and good medicine lies all around."
A.B. GUTHRIE, JR. FROM *MONTANA A PHOTOGRAPHIC CELEBRATION VOL. 3*

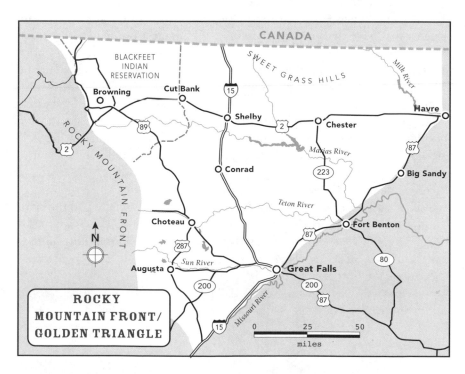

THE ROCKY MOUNTAIN FRONT

BEYOND THE REACH OF RECORDED HISTORY, PEOPLE MIGRATING SOUTH FROM WHAT is now Alaska into what became Montana established a passageway (now known as The Old North Trail) along the eastern flank of an imposing natural barrier. The first white travelers heading westward across the northern prairie gazed at glistening peaks ahead of them, a commanding sight they called the "shining mountains." Today, we refer to this 120-mile north/south stretch of one of the most spectacular pieces of geography on the continent as the Rocky Mountain Front.

This is where the plains end and the mountains begin. No transition zone of slowly rising foothills ... the mountain wall wastes no space in making its presence felt. And what a presence! The spectacular mountains of The Front, rising 2,000 to 4,000 feet above the plains, are the gates to the wildlands beyond.

The softer side of the landscape flows to the east. Rippling rounded hills are interspersed with buttes, river bottoms, flatland, clusters of deciduous and conifer trees and wetlands. When coupled with the powerful massif that halts its sweep on the west, the blend is what has inspired people to love and cherish this place.

The Front is also alive and rich with wildlife, making a home for many species that have disappeared elsewhere. The largest population of grizzly bear and wolverine south of Canada roam here, along with sizable numbers of bighorn sheep. This is the only place in the lower 48 states where the big bears still venture out to the prairie they roamed when Lewis and Clark explored Montana. Gray wolves frequent the northern canyons of the Front. West slope cutthroat trout, for the most part found only west of the Continental Divide, inhabit some of the streams of the region. The reefs and soaring walls provide sanctuary for bald and golden eagles and both prairie and peregrine falcons. The southern reaches serve as wintering ground for the huge Sun River elk herd as well as deer and antelope.

Most insignificant of the inhabitants of The Front in relation to the space they occupy is the human species. Hard up against the rise of the mountains, widely separated ranches and a scattering of isolated houses dot the open expanse. A few structures have worked their way into the canyon openings. Otherwise, the immediate Rocky Mountain Front is free of extensive people presence. Even the towns, set well to the east of the mountains, are unobtrusive. They are pleasant, small communities: Augusta, Choteau, Bynum, Pendroy, Dupuyer, Heart Butte and East Glacier, spaced over 152 miles of highway.

To understand the infinite value of this majestic piece of our state, probe its roads and trails in all seasons. In the long light of a summer evening, watch as all the details of the heights slowly fade, leaving a purple silhouette on the horizon. Catch the rich first light of a rising sun on Castle Reef or Ear Mountain. In autumn, marvel at the delicate gold of the aspens and cottonwoods in the canyons of the Teton River. On a bright January day, from the high point of the highway between Augusta and Choteau, scan the white immensity of what lies before you. And on a late May or June evening, inhale the intoxicating aroma of wildflowers that blanket the undulating hills.

There are several good locations to access the Front. In the north, from Dupuyer on US 89, a route leads west to Swift Reservoir and the north and south forks of Birch Creek, entryways to The Bob Marshall and Great Bear Wilderness areas. Seven miles north of Choteau, also on highway 89, a road heads towards The Front and the south and north forks of the Teton River. The route splits just before the mountains, with one following the South Fork and the other the North Fork past Teton Pass Ski Area (try it next winter) to the West Fork of the Teton. As these roads penetrate deeper into the landscape than most others, it is an ideal place to experience the uniqueness of the area.

Augusta on US 287 provides easy entry into the southern Front. One byway goes west to the Sun River Canyon and Gibson Reservoir and another to Benchmark, a favorite horse route into "The Bob." Highway 435 extending west and south of Augusta, points to Bean Lake and the Dearborn Canyon.

—RICK AND SUSIE GRAETZ

Rocky Mountain Front out of Dupuyer. RICK AND SUSIE GRAETZ

Sawtooth Ridge, Rocky Mountain Front. RICK AND SUSIE GRAETZ

A WINTER MORNING ON THE FRONT

No matter the season, the Rocky Mountain Front, where the swell of the prairie ends abruptly against the wall of the Northern Rockies, presents a grand sight. In the depths of winter though, the early morning hours just might show off its radiance best.

In mid February a few years back, we were making our way in the dark to one of the Front's landmarks, Sawtooth Reef, the serrated towering limestone over thrust that guards the Sun River Canyon. Frigid temperatures made us question our mission, but a brilliant night sky had promised an unobstructed sunrise. As a pre-dawn rising wind whipped a small ground blizzard across the iced landscape, the sky dropped its cloak of darkness and the subzero air was cleared of any haze. We had arrived on time for the performance.

At first, a pale pink and red hue bathed the snow and bare rocks on the upper reaches of Sawtooth Mountain. This initial kindling started a fire-like display. A brilliant orange and red flame took over, spread into a nearly neon pink, intensified and held. Unreal colors, so beautiful yet difficult to describe, we hoped would be preserved in our photos.

As the "fire" spread to the lower ground, the sky extinguished the stars, the scene took on a more balanced perspective and this bit of prairie and mountains was displayed in an unearthly spectacle. The winter sun seems to allow that rich first illumination to last a bit longer than the warmer months.

Gradually, the stronger light of the sun took over, chasing the pinks from

the landscape, leaving a brilliant, diamond sparkle to the snow, highlighting the rough, jagged ridge of Sawtooth against a fierce blue sky. We gave the occurrence a standing ovation!
—RICK AND SUSIE GRAETZ

OVERTHRUST BELT

Not unlike an ocean swell crashing upon a 1,000-foot-high natural sea wall, west of Hwy 287 between Augusta and Browning, the wave of the Montana prairie rolling toward the sunset abruptly terminates up against the magnificent limestone reefs of the Rocky Mountain Front.

Here is the western rampart of the wildlands of the Bob Marshall Country as well as the eastern fringe of what geologist refer to as the Overthrust Belt.

The formation extends, in various forms, through Wyoming and Montana and into Canada. However, our Overthrust, from Montana Hwy 200 to Marias Pass, is unique, not only in terms of splendor and as a wildlife haven, but also in its geologic makeup. From a distance, it appears as one great wall backed by loftier peaks. Fly west over it, or climb one of the summits, and you will note a succession of high ridges and deep valleys with a north-south orientation. The ridges slope down toward the west while their eastern faces are sheer cliffs. The crests are made of erosion resistant material, but the underlying rock of the valleys wears away more easily, hence cavernous valleys have been etched between the crest lines.

Sun River Canyon, west of Augusta, is perhaps the best place to observe this masterful work. A canyon road enters the mountains through a spectacular gorge cut out of the Madison limestone by the Sun River. Between the mouth of the canyon and Gibson Dam, four distinct ridges show a textbook example of overthrust faulting, a process where older rock formations slide over younger ones along the surface of their layers.

Trails heading up the Dearborn River and Elk Creek, both southwest of Augusta, also take foot travelers into the inner sanctum of this awesome bit of geology. These routes, like the Sun River Canyon Road, knife through a succession of tilted beds of gray limestone rock. Auto byways following the North and South Forks of the Teton west of Choteau, not only expose the Overthrust Belt, but also lead into some of the Front's most stunning scenery … the Teton High Peaks.

In the case of Montana's Overthrust Belt, while the mountains were building on the west, sand and mud was being deposited on the floor of the inland sea that once covered the prairie. When the salt water left, the sediments eventually lithified into shale. Geologists feel the older rocks now on the Front were forced upwards in a slanted position and then thrust eastward over the younger sea-layered material. Exactly where the movement started isn't quite understood, but there is no doubt they arrived from well into the Bob Marshall Wilderness

Overthrust Belt, Hannan Gulch, Rocky Mountain Front. RICK AND SUSIE GRAETZ

(the 13-mile-long Chinese Wall in the heart of the "Bob" is a hunk of the Overthrust) and perhaps beyond. The aged rock of the reefs, as opposed to the relative youth of the underlying stratum, dictates this. More proof lies in the fact that the exposed slabs farther west are progressively older.

How about the possibilities of finding oil and gas along Montana's Rocky Mountain Front? Fossil fuels such as oil, gas and coal are associated with sedimentary rocks (limestone, composed mostly of calcite, a mineralized form of calcium carbonate, is a sediment). However geologist estimate that because of the magnitude of the forces in the earth involved in the formation of this area, much of the oil either seeped out through cracks and faults or was cooked by the unimaginable heat. Gas quantities are estimated to be small and no more than a few months supply based on the nation's current energy demands. Exploring for fossil fuels is always a gamble but in the case of Montana's Front, it's doubtful much of anything is under this beautiful surface.

The Front's abundant wildlife, including legendary elk and bighorn sheep populations, live in harmony with the traditional uses of the land. Ranches are big, undisturbed spaces vast and human presence and activity is unobtrusive. The towns … Augusta, Choteau, Bynum, Dupuyer, Heart Butte and Browning are set well east of the mountains. Quiet roads leading into several of the Rocky Mountain Front canyons allow visitors to view a mostly unmarred terrain and marvel at this stupendous bit of landscape.

—RICK AND SUSIE GRAETZ

ROCKY MOUNTAIN FRONT WILDLIFE

In 1941, legendary forest ranger Ellers Koch noted, "The South Fork of the Flathead and the Sun River area is today considered excellent game country. Deer, elk and goats are relatively abundant. Yet in the fall of 1905 and again in 1906, I rode for a month with a pack outfit through the wildest part of that country with a rifle on my saddle, and with exception of one goat, I never saw or got a shot at a single big game animal, though grouse were fairly abundant."

In 1907, the Great Falls Tribune estimated only 300 elk in the entire Sun River region. It stated that big horn sheep were "too few to count" and "deer were a remnant."

This Sun River drainage is part of Montana's magnificent Rocky Mountain Front, where the sprawl of the Montana prairie ends and the mountains begin. Many liken this place and the entire Front to the world famous Serengeti of Africa, owing to its abundance of wildlife. It wasn't always so, though, as evidenced by the quotes above.

Alarmed by disappearing wildlife, an organization of conservationists, public land managers, hunters and ranchers joined together in 1913 to persuade the Montana legislature to establish the Sun River Game Preserve. Thus began the restoration of a viable wildlife population for the Rocky Mountain Front.

In the 1930s, the Forest Service did its part by protecting three primitive areas in the headwater lands of the Flathead and Sun rivers. In August 1940, the three regions were joined together with other acreage to become a piece of the fabled Bob Marshall Wilderness.

These wilderness areas, coupled with the creation of the Sun River Game Preserve and the enforcement of hunting laws, led to a rapid recovery of the elk population.

More elk, however, meant possible conflicts with livestock. Realizing that the elk needed winter habitat outside of the high wilderness terrain, cattlemen, along with Montana sportsmen, formed the Sun River Conservation Council to ensure there would be room for the animals.

In 1947, the Montana Department of Fish and Game, with the continued cooperation of ranchers, established the Sun River Game Range west of Augusta on the eastern edge of the rise of the mountains. In time, four more Front wildlife preserves were set aside. The Ear Mountain and Blackleaf wildlife management areas, west of Choteau, and owned by the state, are two of these special places. The Nature Conservancy's Pine Butte Preserve and the Boone and Crockett's Theodore Roosevelt Memorial Ranch are the others. Deer, elk and other wildlife now gather here when the onset of winter causes them to leave their high country summer range.

The Conservancy's Pine Butte Preserve also has provided a safe haven for grizzly bears. This is the only place in the lower 48 states where the big silvertips still venture to the plains for food and to raise their young. In Lewis and Clark's time, the grizzly was a prairie animal.

In 1972, the Scapegoat Wilderness, formerly the Lincoln Back Country, was created and added to the Bob Marshall Wilderness. The Great Bear Wilderness, contiguous to "the Bob's" northern fringe, was designated in 1978. These undeveloped wilderness additions further enhanced Rocky Mountain Front wildlife.

Elk have come back strong, with more than 3,000 head thought to make a living here. They are the second biggest migratory elk herd in the nation. The bighorn sheep population on the Front is now considered one of the largest in North America and deer roam here by the thousands. Rocky Mountain goats, native to the area, are thriving from the Front west to the Continental Divide. All this is owed to the care and concern of those who worked in cooperation for the benefit of the wildlife.

Today people realize the protection of the environment not only benefits the area's wildlife, but also the economic health of the region's small communities — Augusta, Choteau, Bynum, Dupyer and Browning.

We can't though, take this success for granted and assume it will always be so; there are threats. On Aug. 28, 1997, the Forest Service held a courageous position under the leadership of Gloria Flora, then Supervisor of the Lewis and Clark National Forest, when she signed an order that put the public lands of the Rocky Mountain Front controlled by the Lewis and Clark National Forest off limits to oil and gas exploration and development activities for at least 10 to 15 years.

Bizarre plans are presently being hatched in boardrooms beyond Montana to go after what small deposits of natural gas may underlay this national treasure. Through the ages, so many contingencies have worked together to take care of the Front, and we have come so far in this quest, that to consider endangering the sacred ground seems unconscionable.

In this ever-changing political climate, on behalf of the wildlife, we need to keep a constant vigil. And here's something to remember; Gene Sentz of Choteau and a fierce guardian of the Front, heard this about a Montana old-timer. The man told his congressman, "There are certain places on earth which should be left alone, even if solid gold were beneath it ... the Rocky Mountain Front is such a place." So be it.

—RICK AND SUSIE GRAETZ

MARIAS RIVER

In any dissertation of Montana's rivers, the Marias deserves coverage because of its historical significance as it posed a temporary obstacle and question mark for the Corps of Discovery when they first passed through the state in the spring summer of 1805.

Marias River. RICK AND SUSIE GRAETZ

South of Cut Bank and north of Valier, in a rugged broken part of the prairie, where badlands and sandstone formations prevail, Cut Bank Creek and the Two Medicine River join forces to jumpstart the Marias. The Two Medicine River begins deep in the Rocky Mountain Front in an area sacred to the Blackfeet Nation. Cut Bank Creek also takes its initial waters from the Rocky Mountain Front, just off of the Hudson Bay Divide in Glacier National Park.

June 8, 1805, Meriwether Lewis named the Marias in honor of his cousin, Maria Wood, hence Marias River.

Lewis's cousin's river flows for approximately 170 miles twisting and turning through deep canyons and a magnificent prairie landscape toward the Missouri. Unfortunately, 20 of those miles are contained in Lake Elwell by Tiber Dam. The last 80 miles though, flow unrestricted through a landscape many folks consider a lesser version of the white rocks section of the Missouri in the Upper Missouri Breaks National Monument.

Two miles before its end, the Marias takes in the Teton River, itself a product of the Rocky Mountain Front. Together they flow under the US Hwy 87 bridge at Loma and turn over their waters to the Missouri.

June 2, 1805 … Lewis and Clark began a ten-day stay at the then meeting of the Missouri and Marias rivers. In 1950, a flood diverted the course of the Marias forcing it to enter the Missouri nearly one mile farther upstream, thereby altering a physical location in history. The former channel is still visible.

Up until June 2, 1805, the information supplied by the Hidatsa Indians to the Expedition proved to be most accurate. On that date however, the Corps encountered something not shown on the crude maps they possessed. The Missouri they had been following for so many months appeared now to split into a north and south fork. The Indians had made no mention of another major waterway, after the Milk River, coming from the north. They only specified that the explorers would meet a great waterfall, and then soon thereafter the river would enter the mountains.

The two leaders were fairly sure the south fork was the Missouri, but the crew was convinced otherwise. Joseph Whitehouse, a member of the Corps, noted in his journal on June 3, *"our officers and all the men differ in their opinions which river to take."* Characteristic of their excellent leadership, the Captains agreed to explore both branches so all would be assured.

Lewis on June 3, 1805, scripted, *"to this end an investigation of both streams was the first thing to be done ... Capt. C. & myself stroled out it to the top of the hights in the fork of these rivers from whence we had an extensive and most inchanting view ... to the south we saw a range of lofty mountains"* (most likely the Highwoods, east of Great Falls).

The *"top of the hights"* the Captains climbed is now marked as Decision Point and is reached via a dirt road just south of Loma. Below this spot and closer to the river, the Expedition built caches, storing supplies and the red pirogue, to be retrieved on their homeward journey.

Upon completion of their separate inquiries, the two Captains agreed to the south fork being the correct path and thus the Expedition proceeded forward.

—RICK AND SUSIE GRAETZ

AUGUSTA

This northern Lewis and Clark County community is defined by the spectacular Rocky Mountain Front ... the vast range of rolling prairie leading west towards the abrupt beginnings of the Northern Rockies and the wildlands beyond. Ranching, wildlife and outdoor recreation are the catalysts that make the town work.

In between first downs at the Augusta Elk's Homecoming football game, we visited with Frank Dellwo about the place. With a population of only 300, the folks here have many tasks to perform. Not only does Frank have chain duty for the high school football games, but he also keeps score for basketball, takes part in community affairs, is a full time rancher and with his dad, Gordon, has operated the Buckhorn Bar for 41 years.

Typically, most of the ranches in these parts have multi-generational ownership; and like the Dellwo family, many who came to the region in the 1930s, first worked for large ranchers before establishing their own places.

Augusta is part of the big Sun River country. Meriwether Lewis of the Lewis and Clark Expedition passed through in 1806. The Blackfeet Indians they encountered called it the Sun, Medicine River, owing to the medicinal deposits and hot springs found several miles upriver from where it pours out of the mountains.

Cattle began appearing in 1862 during the open range days. Historical accounts report at one time, about 42,000 head were grazing near the future townsite of Augusta.

While the cattle operations hold sway today, according to Bert Artz who heads up the Nilan Irrigation Project, there was a period when almost 70,000 sheep grazed the area. This business began dying out in the late 1940s.

In 1871, the Augusta township was surveyed, but it wasn't until 1883 that Phil Mannix built the first post office and store. He was named postmaster in June of 1884. The most accepted version of the origin of the town's name is that Augusta Hogan was the first white child born here and the settlement was given his moniker.

By 1901, Augusta was well established as an agricultural center. Then in April of that year, a disastrous fire broke out and within a short period of time the entire business section burned to the ground. The Lewis and Clark County News stated "the fire occurred on Thursday and some said that on Friday, Augusta became the most moral town in the state, having three churches and no standing saloons or dance halls."

Between 1914 and the early 1920s, during the height of the homestead era, Augusta reached its population and commercial peak.

The Bureau of Reclamation played a major role in helping intensify agriculture in the Sun River region. In 1908 they constructed the Willow Creek Reservoir and some time after 1915, the Pishkin Reservoir was built. The largest project, Gibson Dam, holding back the Sun River, was completed in 1929.

These man-made lakes, along with the creation of the Bob Marshall Wilderness in August of 1940, and the establishment of the Sun River Game Range and Wildlife Management Area in 1947, have aided in making the Augusta region a recreation hunting and fishing mecca. Trails heading up the various forks of the Sun River, Elk Creek and the Dearborn River, lead into the Scapegoat and Bob Marshall Wilderness areas. Many dude ranches and outfitters operate out of here.

Frank Dellwo has seen many changes in his time. Most notably, the purchasing of small ranches by bigger outfits. The new owners employ fewer folks and often supplies and equipment are purchased out of the area thereby impacting the local economy. But the upside, Dellow says, is that the land has been kept in production and many of the old ranches are staying intact.

While Augusta is in no danger of drying up and blowing away, both Dellwo and Walsh are unhappy to see that the high school, now made up of 42 students, is shrinking. And in fact, with only nine players on a six-man football team, and five of them graduating, the program most likely will go by the wayside next year.

And then there's the Augusta American Legion Rodeo, the oldest rodeo in Montana and one of the most popular. This one-day, last weekend in June contest has been filling the streets with locals, cowboys and tourists for more than 65 years.

With magnificent views of one of America's great pieces of terrain, along with chances to view the huge Sun River Elk herd, visitors and recreationists will always find their way to this town.

—RICK AND SUSIE GRAETZ

CHOTEAU

Entitled the "Front Porch of the Rockies!" and indeed it is. Choteau sits approximately 20 miles to the east of one of the great American landscapes … the abrupt collision of the Northern Rocky Mountains and the prairie … Montana's Rocky Mountain Front. The 1,900 folks living here own bragging rights to residing amid some of the finest outdoor opportunities and scenery anywhere.

The place has a story that goes back in time to the dinosaurs and ancient travelers. Paleontologists, including Jack Horner, of MSU's Museum of the Rockies, have discovered dinosaur-nesting grounds on the appropriately named Egg Mountain just west of town. This finding of a vegetarian, nurturing, prehistoric animal challenges the old vicious, voracious carnivore image that had been held of these creatures. The approximately 8,000-year-old Great North Trail, leading from the Arctic to Central America, and used by the first people to enter North America, as well as Indian tribes that arrived in what would become Montana, is still visible in places along the base of the mountains to the west.

Records indicate in 1854, James Body was probably the first white man to explore this area. In 1859, Jesuit priests established a short-lived mission three miles south of today's Choteau. Cattle ranching got its start in 1853 when James Gibson brought livestock into the country. And Isacc Hamilton and A.B Hazlett opened a trading post on the Teton River in 1865, stocking it with goods brought by steamboats to Fort Benton.

The town's strongest roots come from "the Old Agency." From 1855 until 1869, the Blackfeet Indian Agency was located at Fort Benton. Native hostilities forced the US Government to move it. In December 1868, Captain Nat Pope, the Blackfeet agent, with the aid of some of the chiefs, selected a site three and one-half miles northwest of present day Choteau. Originally called "Four People" or "Four Persons", as four Cree Indians were killed there in 1857, it eventually it took on the name Old Agency. The post closed in 1876.

In 1883, Hamilton and Hazlett platted the new town of Choteau. Apparently, it still retained the monicker "Old Agency" until officially dubbed Choteau in 1893. The name is a misspelling of the Chouteau family name. Pierre Chouteau, Sr. was the head of the American Fur Company, the dominant trading outfit on the upper Missouri River. The Choteau inhabitants preferred to keep the incorrect spelling so as to distinguish their city from Chouteau County. The town of Choteau is the seat of Teton County, while Fort Benton is the seat of Chouteau County.

Life in this gentle community revolves around ranching and farming. Drawing on one of the region's biggest crops — barley, Malt Montana, a budding business, could be a supplier of the key ingredient for making beer. The US Forest Service's Rocky Mountain ranger station is located on the north end of town. The Old Trail Museum, exhibiting fossils, dinosaur bones and items of Choteau's history offers paleontology workshops. And a myriad of other businesses including a movie theater, hospital, eateries, various shops, gas stations, motels and a highly respected weekly community newspaper, The Choteau Acantha, mix together to create an inviting atmosphere. Built around the old (1906) County Courthouse at the head of Main Street, the town has a prosperous look to it.

It's the landscape that attracts people to this place. On the west, beyond the Rocky Mountain Front, the peaks, rivers and forests of one of the nation's great pieces of wild country sprawls out — the contiguous Bob Marshall and Great Bear wilderness areas. One of the main routes into "The Bob," the Headquarters Pass Trail, takes off at the terminus of the South Fork of the Teton Road, about 35 miles from the center of town.

Teton County is one of the few places left where grizzly bears still venture out to the prairie as they did in the days of Lewis and Clark, before the march of civilization forced them into the mountains. The Nature Conservancy of Montana's Pine Butte Swamp Preserve, a magnificent stretch of prairie wetlands, between the Front and Choteau, serves as spring habitat for these big bears.

Twelve miles to the southeast, Freezeout Lake Wildlife Management Area provides nesting grounds for waterfowl and a rest stop for thousands of migrating birds. Pelicans, geese, hawks, and tundra swan are amongst the winged critters that frequent its waters and sky.

Pishkun Reservoir, southwest of Choteau, is popular for rainbow trout and northern pike. The South and North forks of the Teton River, tumbling out of the high country to the prairie, are fished for rainbow, brook and brown trout.

The North Fork and South Fork Teton roads open up numerous hiking and cross country ski routes into the backcountry and display spectacular mountain scenery. And Teton Pass Ski Area off the North Fork of the Teton Road is perhaps one of the most scenic downhill ski areas in the state.

Choteau is one of the most perfectly placed towns. No wonder those who call it home have such a great sense of ownership and feel the responsibility to take good care of the landscape.

—RICK AND SUSIE GRAETZ

TRIPLE DIVIDE PEAK

We hate to throw cold water on the celebrity status of any of our majestic Montana mountains, but recent studies have caused us to review a long-held belief. It's widely understood that Triple Divide Peak on the Continental Divide in southern Glacier National Park is so named because it sends waters to three oceans, one of only two such apexes in all of North America to do so.

Waters draining from the west side of the peak clearly enter the Pacific Ocean through Nyack Creek and the Flathead, Clarks Fork and Columbia rivers. By way of Atlantic Creek, North Fork Cut Bank Creek, the Marias River and other tributaries flowing into the Missouri and on to the Mississippi River and the Gulf of Mexico, the Atlantic Ocean receives Triple Divide's east flank runoff. This is all well documented.

Now here's the rub. Popular belief holds that snowmelt and raindrops falling on the northern gradient of Triple Divide Peak, entering Hudson Bay Creek, help fill St. Mary's Lake, which empties into the St. Mary's River, which leads through the Saskatchewan River system north and northeast to Hudson Bay, eventually ending up in the Arctic Ocean.

However, currents show that Hudson Bay is part of the Atlantic Ocean. Tidal exchanges occur through deep straits connecting the Bay to the Atlantic. The inlets leading to the Arctic Ocean are shallow; therefore Hudson Bay most likely does not add to the Arctic and perhaps it is the other way around.

If this is all true, that would leave only one mountain — Snow Dome, a high ice-covered peak on the north side of the Columbia Ice Fields in Jasper National Park, Canada — to truly hold the distinction. With this massif, it is certain waters reach the Pacific via the Columbia River system; to the Atlantic from Hudson's Bay (assuming again that Hudson's Bay is part of the Atlantic as Jasper National Park folks believe); and all precipitation and melt on the north side drains to the Athabasca Glacier (a tongue of the Columbia Ice Fields), which forms the Athabasca River, which in turn pours into the McKenzie River flowing north through the Yukon and finally emptying into the Arctic Ocean.

An interesting question to ponder: If Hudson Bay could be proven to discharge into the Arctic Ocean and not the Atlantic, then Montana's Triple Divide Peak would be the only peak truly launching waters to three oceans. As it is, this Glacier National Park summit does flow in three directions but apparently not to three seas. J. Gordon Edwards' book, *A Climbers Guide to Glacier National Park*, states that waters from the peak go to the Pacific, Atlantic and North Atlantic; no mention of the Arctic Ocean. Canadian geographers feel the same way, including Dr. Derald G. Smith, Professor of Geography and chair of the Department of Earth Science at The University of Calgary.

—RICK AND SUSIE GRAETZ

GOLDEN TRIANGLE

U NDULATING RIBBONS OF STRIP FARMING FLOW SEEMINGLY FOREVER ACROSS THE uncluttered landscape of Montana's Golden Triangle — so named because of the shape of this particularly fertile land mass and the color of wheat ready for harvest. An inverted triangle with Great Falls at the bottom balancing point, the eastern boundary slants upward to the northeast following Hwy 87 through Havre and beyond toward the Canadian border, where it makes a sharp left turn and heads directly west through the Blackfeet Reservation to US Hwy 89. Along the viewscape of the phenomenal Rocky Mountain Front, the final leg of the triangle follows Hwy 89 southeast down through Browning, then Choteau, ending back at Great Falls.

During the last Ice Age, a continental ice sheet bulldozed its way south out of Canada scouring much of this region. The glaciers scraped and buffed the topography, rendering it generally flat and gently rolling, suiting it for the large machinery essential to grain production. The receding ice left rich soils in the form of glacial till.

Growing half of Montana's wheat, this is the most productive and prosperous of the state's non-irrigated farming areas. High-quality, well-drained soils create ideal conditions for dryland wheat production.

Within the Golden Triangle, both spring and winter wheat are grown. Winter wheat, the most desirable to plant as the yield per acre is greater, is planted in October and harvested in late August. The hope here is with good moisture the seeds will germinate in the fall, go dormant over the winter and be covered with snow to protect them from the winds and the cold. If all goes well, when the warm weather arrives the crop already has a strong head start. Where it is too frigid, or if the grower is not much of a gambler and less willing to take a chance on the weather, spring wheat is put in the ground in May and cut in mid-September.

Strip farming, the practice of alternating wide planted and unplanted lanes of land, is common to this region. Each sowing season, the use of the lanes is rotated. If a field sits fallow for one year, it retains moisture allowing for a healthier crop the next year. Notice that the fields are usually plowed at right angles to the prevailing wind to minimize wind erosion.

Silos or grain elevators are a sign of the bounty of grain growing in this area. These "sentinels of the prairie" are found in almost every town large or small. And indeed some of the towns are small; they struggle economically and continue to lose population.

Great Falls, Cutbank, Conrad and Havre are the largest of the communities. Others such as Rudyard, Chester and Valier have downsized greatly since the

The town of Chester is surrounded by wheat fields. RICK AND SUSIE GRAETZ

end of the homestead era. At one time, from about 1909 to 1918, this region boasted a much larger population as the area experienced heavier than usual rain and grand harvests. The small towns prospered, as did the railroad that brought the folks here in the first place. Then the drought, beginning in 1918, left the land dry and barren. Shortly afterward the Depression weighed in and the country began to empty out. Those who did manage to stay on are the backbone of this region of now mostly large operations.

Along the Hi-line, or northern plateau of the triangle, communities are more closely spaced, this harkening back to the railroads and their grain elevators or collection depots for the harvest. The trains picked up in nearly every community. Today it is different.

Small elevators have lost out to economies of scale and pricing. Most that were in business 20 years ago have shifted ownership to larger companies and many are used only for storage. Farmers seeking better prices began trucking their harvest to larger elevators, thereby hurting the smaller operations. And the railroads offer the best tariff when they can load 110 car units in one place.

Large shuttle elevators as they are called, feature a one-mile-long circle of track on one side of the elevator so the hopper cars can be rapidly loaded, usually in one day. This efficiency allows for better transportation rates.

Fort Benton, on the eastern edge of this band of wheat, provided excitement for the area in the last half of the nineteenth century. First, the era of steamboats brought almost every character known to the old west through the country; then later, in the 1860s until about 1883, the Whoop-Up Trail, built on the smuggling of guns and whiskey, as well as commercial freight, perked up with new trade opportunities. It pulled out of the Missouri bottoms, followed the Teton west, crossed the Marias River Ridge and aimed northwest, passing through today's Shelby into Canada's Bow River Valley and Fort McLeod. The legend of the Old West was extended through the Golden Triangle.

Aside from cultivation, another common site throughout the Golden Triangle are the granite boulders that clearly are not part of the sedimentary rock found in the area. Thousands of rocks, some the size of cars, were brought in by the ice from Northern Manitoba. Geologically they are called glacial erratics. If you examine some of them closely, they feature smooth, polished, marble-like edges and often are surrounded by a trench. The millions of bison that once inhabited the grasslands of northern Montana used these as rubbing rocks to help scrape the loose fur from their hides.

Saline seep can be found throughout the Great Plains of Montana, but it is especially notable in the Golden Triangle. The underlying bedrock of the region is composed of an impermeable layer of shale. When the ground becomes saturated, the water absorbs salt from the soil. This saline solution flows along the bedrock, finds an area to escape, puddles and evaporates; the salts left behind create the look of a snow patch where nothing will grow.

Today, the average size of the area's farms is approximately 2,500 acres; with a movement toward larger holdings, this average will increase. As most of the farms are multi-generational, there is a great deal of history, pride and loyalty to the land.

Following an unfolding strip of highway, it is quite a sight to come upon a rise and be greeted by an endless, swaying field of ripe, golden grain. Beneath a summer blue sky, the sun bleached stalks of wheat toss their heavy, seed-laden heads as they dance to the rhythm of the wind. Sometimes frenzied, more often seductive, always mesmerizing, the land's sheer beauty catches you by surprise. You shake your head and nod, and understand a little better what it is that makes folks love this part of the country.

—RICK AND SUSIE GRAETZ

GREAT FALLS

With the Missouri River at its side, and the magnificent Rocky Mountain Front next door, the city of Great Falls has a lot going for it. History, natural wonders, and a strong sense of who it is, gives this city of 55,000 folks a strut your stuff attitude.

Lewis and Clark were the first known white explorers to catch sight of the "great falls" — a series of rapids and five breathtaking waterfalls on the Missouri River — when they arrived here in the summer of 1805. Lewis's journal entries expound on the beauty of the "great falls," and the name was a natural for the future town.

It took the Expedition one month to make the portage around the falls. Before the party left, they celebrated the Fourth of July at the present site of Giant Springs State Park, one of the largest fresh water springs in the world and home to the Roe River, the shortest river in the world.

Enter Paris Gibson, a young man who came west in May of 1882. Seeing the potential for the harnessing of the waterpower of the falls, he implored railroad tycoon James Hill to make Great Falls a stop on his line. Copper was a hot commodity in Butte and there would be a need for electricity.

Unlike many other western cities, Great Falls was architecturally planned. Gibson saw to it that the streets were laid out in a precise, arrow-straight pattern, with consecutively numbered avenues paralleling north and south off of Central Avenue, and street numbers heading east and west of the Civic Center. A firm believer in beauty and open space, he set aside an unheard of 886 acres for city parks and insisted that elm, ash, and fir trees were planted on every street and boulevard. The result is a city that is easy to find your way around and with a feeling of substance and roots thanks to the tree shaded streets and neighborhood parks.

Once the dams were built (five), the nickname "Electric City seemed appropriate.

Modern culture has grown out of the history of Great Falls, first in the life and works of western artist Charles M. Russell, the legendary cowboy who made Great Falls his home. The world-class museum that bears his name holds the world's largest collection of his art and artifacts.

His studio, built in 1903, is on the Museum grounds and is open year round. It is said that Charlie never finished a painting anywhere else. Also on the grounds is the original home he and his wife Nancy built in 1900.

Located on a bluff overlooking the Missouri River, the Lewis & Clark National Historic Trail Interpretive Center features the Expedition's portage around the Great Falls of the Missouri and focuses on the life of the Plains Indians who lived in the area.

A wonderful accessory to the city is the River's Edge Trail — 5 miles of scenic, paved trail that follows the Missouri River from Gibson Park (downtown Great Falls) past the Lewis and Clark Interpretive Center toward Giant Springs State Park.

Malmstom Air Force Base on the east edge of the city, has been an economic boost to the community since its inception in 1942. Since 1961, has primarily been involved with different aspects of the minutemen missiles. In 1999, Malmstrom was named the best Air Force installation in the continental United States.

—RICK AND SUSIE GRAETZ

SWEET GRASS HILLS

On a clear day you can see them from 75 miles or more away ... three high natural monuments rising above the vast prairie north of Shelby and Chester. Together they are the Sweetgrass Hills; separately maps call them buttes ... West, Gold and East buttes. They are, though, true mountains ... isolated rises of igneous rock. And although they look like volcanoes, it is doubtful they ever spewed lava.

West and East buttes are just under 7,000 feet high and Gold, or Middle Butte, reaches 6,512 feet above sea level. Their relief over the surrounding strip farms and grasslands averages about 3,500 feet.

Blackfeet Indians and other Plains tribes have used the Hills for centuries as sacred sites to seek visions and for other religious purposes. They called them Katoysix, meaning "a place of sweet pine" and burned the trees for ceremonies. Some believe that whites incorrectly translated the meaning of the Indian word when giving a name to these monoliths. Another story gives the credit to the sweet smelling grasses growing on the mountainsides.

Used by Native Americans for its spiritually purifying properties, sweetgrass is a species of grass found in wet areas on the Glaciated Plains and mountains. It is one of the most widely used plants for incense. When burned as a blessing, it brought benevolent powers to Montana Indians.

A survey leader of the International Boundary Expedition (the Sweetgrass Hills are hard up against the Canadian border) noted in 1874 that gold bearing

East Butte, Sweet Grass Hills. RICK AND SUSIE GRAETZ

quartz was showing in the area. In 1885 some prospectors made a strike at Middle Butte and the short-lived town of Gold Butte was born. The US Government, in a blatant disregard for a treaty that ceded these lands to the Blackfeet tribe, allowed 100 miners into the area. Needless to say the Indians lost their claim.

Cattlemen also discovered the rich grass below the three uplifts and large ranches were established. Cowboy artist Charlie Russell and a partner operated the Lazy KY outfit in these hills.

The Homestead Era of the early 1900s came to this part of the Montana high plains; however, severe drought and falling farm prices forced most of the homesteaders to give-up by 1920. In the early 1920s though, oil was discovered around the buttes. Kevin and Sunburst, just to the west of West Butte came to life and the economy of the area received a boost. Sunburst was so named because the sun appears to "burst" over the Sweetgrass Hills just to the east.

Today, with the exception of scattered public lands, most of the Hills' landscape is private. Oil production is now minimal, gold is panned by hobbyists and agriculture is the mainstay of the economy.

Roads lead from Shelby and Chester, forty miles away, to each of the buttes. A public campground sits just south of the "capital of the Hills," Whitlash, a quiet community of twenty people. No saloon here, just a church, school and community hall.

It's a beautiful place, this Sweetgrass country, especially in the spring and summer. East and West buttes have lodgepole, Douglas fir, ponderosa pine and limber pine interspersed with flower filled meadows and aspen trees on them, while Gold Butte is covered with open grassy terrain. Springs flow from all sides of the mountains and feed the aquifer that provides water for 250 ranches and farms.

Elk, deer, owls, hawks and eagles are among the wildlife inhabitants of this sparsely populated land.

The picturesque towns of Chester and Shelby on Highway 2 offer lodging, meals and easy access to the myriad of dirt roads leading to the Hills. The route to Whitlash is gravel, but some of the other roads are tough to handle when it's wet. In dry weather a passenger car will get you into these sentinels of the border. A BLM map Sweetgrass Hills — Montana/Alberta is the most useful to use in finding your way here. The Montana Atlas and Gazetteer will also work.

The Sweetgrass Hills, while still considered sacred by the Blackfeet, are beloved landmarks to the folks who live and work within their far ranging sight. And they are protective of them, not only for their beauty, but also because they provide liquid gold ... water. As seasonal storms sweep across the prairie, their thunder filled clouds collide with and obscure the buttes. Morning sunrises silhouette them against glorious orange and yellow skies. Their appearance on the horizon is a signal to the locals that home is near.

—RICK AND SUSIE GRAETZ

FORT BENTON

Rising from a sandstone bluff north of town, Signal Point was once used by spotters to sight steamboats chugging up river eight miles away. Word then went out to the townsfolk that a steamboat was "round the bend!" Today from the Signal Point and other places on this high perch, one can get a great view of the big Missouri, historic Fort Benton, the Bear Paw Mountains to the northeast and the Highwoods on the southeast horizon.

The Corps of Discovery, led by Captains Lewis and Clark, passed by the area on July 13, 1805, after having camped downstream about eight miles.

In 1845, Alexander Culbertson of the American Fur Company established Fort Lewis, a trading post three miles up from today's Fort Benton. Ice jams and floods made reaching it in winter and spring difficult, so the post's log buildings were dismantled and floated to the present day site in the spring of 1847. The first residents, though, arrived at the new location in autumn 1846, essentially giving birth to Montana. This, the oldest continuing settlement in the state, was at the head of navigation on the lifeline to Montana Territory — the Missouri River.

Fort Clay was the initial name of the new structure. But on Christmas day 1850, the name was changed to Fort Benton in honor of Senator Thomas Hart Benton, a patron of the American Fur Company. It soon became a boisterous "old west" town of legend. As Winfield Stocking wrote, "Although it continued to be a mere village in size, in a commercial way it was the Chicago of the plains. It was the door through which all the gold hunters, adventurers, speculators, traders, land-seekers, big game hunters, fugitives from justice, desperadoes and all the bad Indians on the top of the earth entered the Northwest." A sign on the levee states that the street along the river was "The bloodiest block in the west."

The Missouri River Steamboat Era, lasting from 1859 until 1888, gave this riverbank community new life at a time when the fur trade was dwindling. On July 2, 1860, the Chippewa from St. Louis became the first boat to dock. One tried in 1859 but didn't make it. Throughout this colorful period, an average of 20 boats a year steamed up the Missouri toward Fort Benton. An estimated 600 boats arrived between 1860 and 1888.

Gold discoveries in western Montana created a rush that attracted would-be miners to the territory. Missouri steamboats were the most practical way to get here; an estimated 10,000 people made the journey along with countless tons of freight. The trip to Fort Benton from St. Louis took 60 days and cost about $150.

From the time the ice melted in the spring until the river froze in the fall, the levee was piled with goods headed for the gold camps of southwest Montana. "All trails lead out of Benton" was a familiar statement in those days. The settlement was the anchor of the 625-mile-long Mullan Road, that

The historic Grand Union Hotel, Fort Benton. RICK AND SUSIE GRAETZ

when completed in 1862, led to Walla Walla, Washington. Travelers heading out of town used stage lines and bull and mule trains.

A Canadian trade boom resulted in the establishment of the 240-mile-long Whoop-Up Trail pointing north out of town to Fort McLeod, Alberta. According to Fort Benton historian and author, Jack Lepley, from 1874 to 1883, up to 50 percent of Fort Benton's business came as a result of this path to Canada. Although plenty of legitimate commerce was carried out, the transportation of illegal whiskey over this dangerous, adventurous route is what made it famous. When the rails of the Canadian Pacific reached Calgary, use of the Whoop-Up Trail was no longer needed.

In September 1887, the railroad's arrival at Fort Benton, signaled the end of the era of river trade. As the river port quieted, agriculture stepped in to become the mainstay of the economy; and that is still the case today.

Fort Benton is one of the most fascinating and prettiest towns in Montana to visit, especially when seen in the spring, summer and fall. The cottonwood-lined Missouri River flows peacefully along a well-maintained levee area of commercial buildings and old homes. It's hard to imagine that this quiet agricultural town was as boisterous and raucous as the stories tell. But the sights and sounds of history are part of what makes Fort Benton so special today. The townsfolk have gone out of their way to preserve important reminders of a way of life.

Remains of the adobe fort buildings, two museums — the Museum of the Northern Great Plains and the Museum of the Upper Missouri — restored homes, a levee with a keelboat and interpretive signs and a bridge that has spanned the Missouri since 1888 add to a pleasant walking tour under massive and stately cottonwoods. You can see the firehouse, built in 1883, and learn of the story of "Old Shep," a legendary Fort Benton collie. And the Bureau of Land Management maintains a good river visitors center. Here you can obtain information on floating the river, as well as learning of outfitters who will guide you, and of places that rent canoes.

Then there is Fort Benton's pride and joy, the newly refurbished Grand Union, Montana's oldest operating hotel. This historic landmark was originally opened on Nov. 1,1882, and as one of the levee signs says, "US Army officers, Canadian Mounties, trappers, miners, traders, river captains, stockman, missionaries, Indian agents and road agents rubbed shoulders in the Grand Union's lobby, spacious dining room and adjourned to its well stocked-bar for the relaxation due the frontiersman at a weary journey's end."

Although the hotel did operate fairly consistently from 1882 to 1983, it was essentially just a shell when Jim and Cheryl Gagnon bought it and embarked on their dream to restore the building to its former glory, and to preserve as much of the historic value as possible.

What a magnificent job they've done. The lobby and the staircase are still the same, but the hotel rooms are now comfortable and luxurious mixture of what's new and old, so that everything works in this modern era.

This is a town and a place that every Montanan should visit at least once. If you were born here, it is part of your heritage.

—RICK AND SUSIE GRAETZ

HAVRE

In April 1887, railroad tycoon James Hill gathered together a large workforce and began laying rail from Minot, N.D. westward into the expansive plains of eastern Montana. Seven months later, workers for his St. Paul, Minneapolis and Manitoba Railroad (St. P.M. & M) reached Great Falls with 545 miles of new track behind them. The next year, Hill connected his line with the Northern Pacific Railroad in Helena and the Union Pacific in Butte.

Those hundreds of miles of rail line through a mostly empty Montana required terminals and railroad shops, and in turn, those facilities needed dependable sources of water. In north central Montana, near a small creek that flowed into the Milk River, Hill believed he had found what he needed. But, the creek was named Bull Hook and the ramshackle community that had sprung up next to nearby Fort Assinniboine was named Bull Hook Bottoms. That would have to change. Bull Hook Bottoms wasn't a name to attract businessmen or settlers, and around 1890, it was changed to Havre. Legend has it the new name was to honor the first homesteaders in the area, who were from LeHavre, France.

Bull Hook Creek turned out to be less than dependable, but Havre's rail station was situated in a perfect location to service Hill's locomotives — especially after he made the decision in 1893, to create the Great Northern Railroad by extending his lines westward and connecting with the Northern Pacific. Soon, Havre's rail shops would become the largest on Hill's lines west of St. Paul.

In January 1904, as the railroad and a developing agricultural industry were prompting Havre to grow, fire burned much of the town to the ground. Until the downtown was rebuilt, businessmen moved underground and set up shop. Portions of this subterranean commerce district are open for tours giving a unique window into the town's past.

Over the years, the local economy remained dependant on agriculture and the railroad. Never one to let an opportunity slip by, during Prohibition, taking advantage of its close proximity to the Canadian border, Havre become a natural hub for rum running, a profitable but short-lived industry.

With more than 9,600 residents in 2000, Havre became the largest city along the Hi-Line and a commercial center for smaller towns in the area. Settled within sight of the gentle Bear Paw Mountains, it is home to Montana State University-Northern and it is also the headquarters for the Montana Division of the Burlington Northern Santa Fe Railroad. An exciting historic and cultural discovery is the nearby Wahkpa Chu'gn Archaeology Site, a large prehistoric Indian bison kill site more than 2,000 years old.

—GRANT SASEK

THE BEAR PAW MOUNTAINS

A Geography/Geographic History of Montana is the title of a course I taught at the University of Montana in Missoula. In an recent essay assignment, one of my students came up with interesting "name tag" information on these north central Montana mountains that seems to have several variations

Kirsten Kuka, of Havre wrote in her paper. "The official name of the mountains of the area has been a controversy. Lewis and Clark called them the 'North Mountains,' the Gros Ventre tribe called the peaks, 'Many Buttes' and other Native tribes referred to the range as the 'Mountains of the Bear.' More variations on the name are, 'Bears Paw Mountains' and 'Bear's Paw Mountains.' Jim Magera, a local historian of Havre, found that the original settlers titled them the 'Bear Paw Mountains.' Most geological and official government documents agree, and refer to the range by this original title."

Kirsten adds, "The name comes from a Cree Legend. As the fable goes, the Creator set aside the mountains as a place no man could enter. It was a time of great starvation. A young hunter returned home with only one rabbit, which was certainly not enough to feed his family. The hunter's mother-in-law was very upset because he wasn't properly providing for the family. She asked him to go to the sacred area in the mountains to get food. The friends of the hunter warned him that the Chief of Bears resided in the mountains, and he would kill anyone who entered. The hunter was desperate though, so he went to the sacred place. The Chief of Bears pinned the hunter to the ground, and was going to kill him. The Creator shouted to the bear to release the hunter, but the bear refused. The Creator struck the bear's paw with a lightning bolt and the hunter was released. The paw became Mount Sentinel. The bear was then turned to stone, and he became Box Elder Butte. The bear's friends were also turned to stone because they were associated with him. They became the remaining mountains in the Bear Paw Range."

From a distance, this north central Montana range appears as an unbroken mass. Entering, you realize it is a 50-mile span of separate buttes and peaks. Most of the high points are grassy and interspersed with scattered timber stands.

The Rocky Boy's Reservation, home of the Chippewa and Cree people, borders the Bear Paw on the west and the Fort Belknap Reservation of the Assiniboine and Gros Ventre nations defines the east edge. Big Sandy, Havre and Chinook are nearby.

Baldy at 6,916 feet is the highest summit and only a few of the peaks exceed 6,000. Relief ranges from 1,000 to 3,000 feet. Many of the rises are former volcanoes.

The land hasn't and doesn't changed much, except for a short spell between about 1910 to 1925 when homesteaders, filing on free 160- and 360-acre sites, flocked to Havre and Hill County. Shortly, almost every gulch had at least one cabin. Drought and depression, and the reality that the area was not suited for farming, soon forced the new arrivals out. Today, several large ranches such as the 100-year-old IX Ranch and the one operated by Cowan and Sons claim a large portion of the territory.

Cleveland, with a population of four, is the "capital" of the Bear Paw. The Cleveland Bar (formerly the post office) and a few assorted buildings, including the Cleveland School (five students) make up the "town." It came to be in 1892, just prior to the homestead era and never exceeded 100 residents. There are no signs left of several other nearby communities such as Rattlesnake and Maddox. Lloyd, just west of Cleveland, still has a post office that opens a few days a week. In the southwest sector, Warrick no longer has a post office, but hosts a one-teacher school.

With the exception of a few sections of state land, most of the Bear Paw terrain is private. But, plenty of public roads honeycomb this collection of buttes. It's pleasant country and easy on the eyes. Nothing to overwhelm you, just prairie hill beauty.

At 10,000 acres, Beaver Creek, the largest county park in the nation, stretches for 17 miles into the Bear Paw south of Havre. Originally part of the old Fort Assiniboine Military Reservation, which was abandoned in 1911, it was taken over by Hill County in 1947.

In the Bear Paw Mountains. RICK AND SUSIE GRAETZ

The park offers respite from the summer heat with hiking, fishing, and swimming in a mountain setting of grasslands, pine, aspen and cottonwoods. Trout are found in Beaver Creek, Bear Paws Lake and Lower Beaver Creek Lake. And many species of wildlife including bobcat, beaver, coyote, grouse, deer, fox, beaver, eagles and hawks call it home.

This Great Plains oasis also serves as a winter playground for ice fishing, Nordic skiing, snowshoeing and sledding. Strict rules keep the place quiet and clean. About seven miles south of Beaver Creek Park, the Bear's Paw Ski Bowl has a 900-foot vertical drop and double chair lift.

The Bear's Paw Battlefield, a national historic park managed by the National Park Service is between Chinook and Cleveland on county road 240. This is where in the fall of 1877, Chief Joseph and his Nez Perce people were forced to end their heroic flight from persecution by the US Army.

In spite of being badly outnumbered, the Nez Perce made a valiant stand. Heavy casualties were suffered on both sides. After six days of fighting, his people hungry and cold, Chief Joseph surrendered and called to his camp, "... hear me my chiefs, I am tired; my heart is sick and sad. From where the sun now stands, I will fight no more forever."

Robert Lucke, a long-known Havre historian, has produced an excellent map with trails and routes you can follow to explore this seldom-visited area. The BLM Rocky Boy and Winifred maps cover the entire area.

—RICK AND SUSIE GRAETZ

NORTH CENTRAL
AND NORTHEAST MONTANA

EW PEOPLE, AND PERHAPS THE MOST MAGNIFICENT PRAIRIE COUNTRY IN THE nation, best describe this province of Montana. Its western bounds follow Hwy 87 from Fort Benton, through Havre to Canada. The U.S. Canadian line, the 49th parallel of latitude, defines the north. The southern demarcation is a bit jagged. It stays on the southern fringe of the Missouri River Breaks to US Hwy 91, then abruptly points south before turning east to follow the "Lonesome Highway 200" to North Dakota.

In both its liquid form and frozen, water shaped the physical geography in this territory. Ice sheets advancing out of Canada slid into northern Montana from the east edge of the Blackfeet Reservation by Glacier National Park, across to North Dakota. These natural bulldozers gouged and scraped the land, carrying and pushing rocks and soils. They "borrowed" boulders, called glacial erratics — some as large as a cars — from northern Saskatchewan and Manitoba, Canada, more than 500 miles away, and presented them to northern Montana on permanent loan. Thousands are scattered across the prairie.

Sitting atop a butte off the west side of the Bear Paw Mountains, 1,000 feet above the prairie, an abundance of these "kidnapped" glacial erratics illustrate

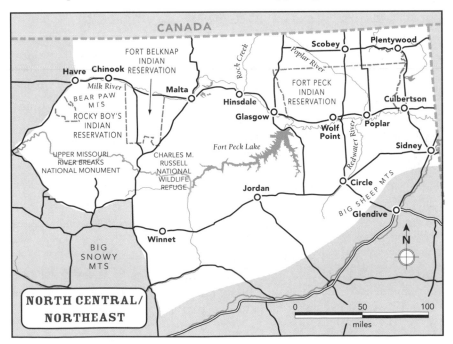

Northeastern farm scene near Bainville. RICK AND SUSIE GRAETZ

how thick the ice was. The Bear Paw and Little Rocky mountains and Sweetgrass Hills weren't covered and became islands in a sea of ice.

The glaciers scoured the landscape, subdued it and laid down rich soils of glacial till in the areas that grow wheat and barley, especially the far northeast corner of this region. Land south of the Missouri escaped the ice and has much coarser topography and poorer soils.

As the centerpiece of north central and northeast Montana, the Missouri River opened the state to human habitation. As a route of western expansion, it had few equals. The river holds forth in an incredible landscape. Breaks, heading toward the river from both the north and south, are rough terrain cut by water — a labyrinth of coulees and gullies between high ridges. Some of the ridges are void of trees while others grow in an open forest, usually of ponderosa pine, especially deeper into the Breaks.

Badlands, another prominent feature of a the Missouri River Breaks and widespread places of Montana east of the mountains, are miniature deserts, void of vegetation and created by fire. They represent very fragile and beautiful terrain.

The Upper Missouri River Breaks National Monument guards a large portion of the Missouri River, extending 149 miles from Fort Benton down to the Fred Robinson Bridge. Designated as a Wild and Scenic River in October 1976, by then President Gerald Ford, in January 2001, President Bill Clinton expanded its size and gave it Monument status. The river breaks and badlands landscape bears a diverse vegetation, including groves of cottonwoods, ash, box elder, willows, conifers, grasses, sagebrush, greasewood and low lying riparian growth.

Extending downriver from the edge of the Upper Missouri River Breaks Monument is the crown jewel of the nation's wildlife refuge system, the 1.1 million-acre Charles M. Russell National Wildlife refuge. Surrounded by more than 2 million acres of BLM land, the CMR extends from 10 miles before the Fred Robinson Bridge and US 191, for about 145 miles to Fort Peck Dam.

While dry land farming dominates the land west of Hwy 87 in the "Golden Triangle," land use changes heading east. The uneven and varied landscape has less cultivation and more grazing, with large ranch operations dominating the economy. More gravel and dirt roads exist than paved byways. There are fewer people here than anywhere else in the state, and they're well spaced.

The "Big Dry" comes by its name honestly. When the sun is through baking the land around Jordan, the wind comes in to extract its share of what little moisture is left. This translates to an arid landscape with mostly livestock outfits working the land.

Amid the breaks north and northeast of Jordan, hidden beneath the sandy soil in the Hell Creek formation, is one of the world's richest fossil beds. Since 1902, several major dinosaur discoveries have been made in the area, including the first complete T-Rex.

Population loss is the rule throughout most of north central and northeast Montana. Examples are the Garfield and Petroleum county areas. Garfield lost 20 percent from 1990 to 2000 and Petroleum lost 5 percent in the same period. Together they have 1,772 people. As of February 2003, Garfield

Iron Stake Ridge, CMR National Wildlife Refuge, Missouri River. RICK AND SUSIE GRAETZ

County had 1,279 people and 82,326 head of sheep and cattle, a 64-to-1 ratio. Some places though, especially the bigger communities like Sidney and Glasgow, are holding their own.

This is a unique corner of Montana with great physical assets. The pieces to follow will take you through the landscape, including the wildlife refuges and Indian reservations.

—RICK AND SUSIE GRAETZ

MILK RIVER

When discussing the waterways of Montana it is important to include the internationally flavored, 538-mile-long Milk River. It pulls its waters from the front range of the Rockies by way of three main tributaries, the North, Middle and South forks tumbling off of the Hudson Bay Divide in Glacier National Park on the western perimeter of the Blackfeet Indian Nation. Initially, the Milk is a product of the confluence of the Middle and South forks directly north of Browning just below Canada. From this point, out in the middle of Blackfeet Reservation rangeland, it wiggles northeastward until it crosses the Canadian line, 47 miles after its start. In Canada, it will pick up its North Fork.

After experiencing 167 Canadian miles, the Milk decides to return stateside north of the Hi-Line town of Rudyard. Thirty miles later, it enters the long and narrow Fresno Reservoir just west of Havre. This basin will greatly control the tempo of the river from here down. After slipping out of its confinements, it meanders through Havre and follows US Hwy 2 eastward, continually switching from one side of the highway to the other.

Though sluggish, brown-colored and lacking beauty, the Milk River, through numerous diversion dams provides much needed irrigation on the northern Montana prairie. While the river its self doesn't have the splendor of some its peers, the prairie country it visits is quite beautiful.

After Havre, Chinook, Harlem and Dodson get a glimpse of the waterway. Between Harlem and Dodson, on US Hwy 2, it forms the northern boundary of the Fort Belknap Indian Reservation, home to the Assinboine and Gros Ventre nations. Beyond Fort Belkanp, the town of Malta cradles the river. At this ranching community, the Milk makes a short run to the north and then begins a southeastward direction, passing Hinsdale and Glasgow on its way to the Missouri River, just down from the Fort Peck Dam.

As the waters of the Missouri are flowing clean through the spillways of Fork Peck, the muddiness of the Milk provides a very distinct contrast where they meet.

Lewis and Clark make mention of the Milk in their journals. It was one of the landmarks the Hidatsa Indians had told them to look for on their way west. The Indians called the Milk "the River that scolds all others" On May 8, 1805, Meriwether Lewis noted "… *the water of this river posseses a peculiar whiteness, being about the colour of a cup of tea with the admixture of a tabelspoonfull of milk. from the colour of it's water we called it Milk river. we think it possible that this may be the river called by the Minitares* (Hidatsa) *'the river that scolds at all others'..."* Lewis also noted the Milk River Hills that rise almost 700 feet above the floodplain of the Milk and Missouri.

MALTA

US Hwy 191 climbs a steep grade out of the Missouri River bottoms north of Fred Robinson Bridge. As it gains the upper extent of the river breaks, a far-reaching, high plains landscape sprawls towards Canada 125 miles to the north. The Little Rockies rise directly ahead and a rough, rolling prairie flows off to the east. You're heading through historic landscape, once the domain of the nomadic Plains tribes, toward the valley of the Milk River and the ranching and farming community of Malta.

Between 1870 and 1900, this was the setting for the true "Old West" and Malta might well be considered its capital. Trappers, cattlemen, cowboys, and all manners of outlaws wandered through here. Cattle drives up from Texas brought the herds to winter on the region's rich grasslands between the Missouri and Canada. It was once the focal point of a vast beef empire and was founded to serve the area ranches. Big cow outfits held sway; names like Phillips, Coburn, Matador and Phelps are all etched in Montana's history.

Indians called the future town site "The Big Bend" as the Milk River turns in a half-circle near here. The first "citizen" was Robert M. Trafton out of Minnesota, who came to collect the bleached bones of slaughtered bison.

In 1885, Trafton established a trading post a few miles to the west of what would eventually become the seat of Phillips County. The westward building Great Northern Railroad reached Siding 54 on August 13, 1887, and Trafton moved his store to the new town site in anticipation of increased business. Cowboys and other solitary souls inhabiting these high plains of north-central Montana needed a Saturday night destination; Malta became that place. And it was as wild as any western movie could depict!

The newly minted community needed a proper name. Railroad agents gathering in Minneapolis, blindfolded an employee and had him point his finger to a spot on the globe. Thus Siding 54 was named Malta after an island in the Mediterranean Sea.

The railroad helped the ranchers thrive, even after the days of the open range came to an end. In 1910, through the Homestead Act, thousands of would-be farmers flocked to the area. Malta prospered even more as harvests were bountiful, but the drought starting in 1918 and the Great Depression of the 1930s put an end to the dreams of most homesteaders, forcing them to leave. While farming is important to Malta today, it is still primarily considered cow country.

Modern day Malta is a far cry from its raucous beginnings. This now quiet agricultural center is presently home to 2,100 folks. After a decline due to agricultural downturns, it appears that the population has now leveled off.

Anne Boothe, Executive Director of the Phillips County Economic Growth Council and the Chamber of Commerce Manager, is an optimistic Malta booster. She cites many positive achievements of the community in spite of problems with the farm and ranch economy, the loss of jobs from mining in the Little Rockies and the destruction by fire of the high school on Christmas Eve 1995.

As for the fire, the community, with the help of insurance money, went to work and a bigger and better school was built. Boothe points out that the farming economy has the potential for improving as cattle prices are up, and lessons learned in tough times, have helped people to be better farmers. Alternate crops, like chickpeas and lentils, are being planted instead of just wheat.

Citizens felt that empty buildings on Front Street shouldn't be allowed, so a community owned, clothing store called "Family Matters" was started. This has been an investment in the overall commonwealth, not just in one store.

A state-of-the-art movie theater with surround sound is joined by a healthy variety of other businesses, including a lumberyard, bulk plant, three banks, plenty of eateries and several motels.

Then there is tourism. Malta is a great base camp to explore some of the most unique prairie environment in Montana. To the south there is the immense Charles M. Russell National Wildlife Refuge, the spectacular Missouri River Breaks, Fort Peck Lake and its 1,600 miles of shoreline, the Little Rocky Mountains with their colorful mining history and the Fort Belknap Indian Reservation home to the Assiniboine and Gros Ventre nations.

Seven miles east of town, Bowdoin National Wildlife Refuge is a premiere haven for waterfowl. It lies in the central flyway of one of the great winged creature migration routes of North America. Beyond Bowdoin, Nelson Reservoir offers good boating and fishing.

Back roads leading north of town to Loring, a small picturesque community six miles from the port of Morgan and the Canadian border, pass through scenic river breaks of Little Cottonwood and Cottonwood creeks as well as segments of the Milk River bottoms.

You won't see many people as you wander through this land, but you'll hear the sounds of history and you'll probably encounter plenty of deer and antelope.

—RICK AND SUSIE GRAETZ

BOWDOIN NATIONAL WILDLIFE REFUGE

Fifteen thousand years ago, after leaving its home base in northern Canada, a runaway continental ice sheet passed through these parts scouring the landscape and moving the Missouri River 50 miles to the south. The lakes that now make up the Bowdoin National Wildlife Refuge were once a horseshoe bend of the pre-glacier Missouri.

This north central Montana wildlife haven, seven miles east of Malta, is part of a once incredibly rich animal kingdom frequented by the plains tribes, including the Blackfeet, Cree, Gros Ventres and the Assiniboine nations. They hunted and gathered roots, berries and herbs here. Tepee rings found on the refuge are evidence of their passing.

In 1936, recognizing the wildlife values of the area, the US Government established the Refuge under the joint management of the US Bureau of Reclamation and the US Fish and Wildlife Service. In February 1972, the USFWS took over sole jurisdiction.

Prior to the establishment of the sanctuary, water levels of Lake Bowdoin and the surrounding ponds fluctuated wildly between spring runoff and the dry summers. The shallow water remaining through the summer months was hot and stagnant and frequently became infested with botulism, killing thousands of birds every season.

To help solve this problem, the Fish and Wildlife Service established a system of dikes designed to hold spring runoff and keep water levels as high as possible. An evaporation loss rate of 36–40 inches each year doesn't help the situation especially in drought years. A Milk River diversion at Dodson, about 25 miles to the west, reaches the refuge by way of a viaduct. Although they don't always get as much volume as they want, Refuge managers rely on their Milk River water rights to ensure adequate flow is available. Water levels still fluctuate, just not as dramatically.

Vanishing water creates alkaline deposits, another management issue on the refuge. Salts … sodium, calcium, magnesium and potassium are leached from water when it dissipates in the warm dry air, leaving a white alkaline or salt residue on the earth. In the dry months, winds blow away the salts. In a strong gale, it may appear that the lakebeds are on fire as the light colored accumulations fill the air. During the time of high water, the alkaline buildup is flushed out. If it weren't for nature's compensating actions, the closed lake basins of Bowdoin would eventually become useless to wildlife.

Good management has created one of the best nature viewing areas in Montana. More than 230 different species of birds and waterfowl have been identified. Bowdoin is also considered Montana's prime place to see pronghorn antelope in their natural habitat. Big game hunting is not allowed so the herd has natural age distribution; big animals are evident.

Bowdoin's upland native grasses are considered to be of extremely high quality as evidenced by the presence of the Sprague's Pipit and the Baird's Sparrow; birds that choose only the best.

Along with Medicine Lake NWR, Bowdoin has the largest colony of white pelicans in Montana. Some of us who float prairie waterways call these birds "the river's Air Force." With their enormous black-tipped wingspans, they silently fly in "military-like" formation. At Bowdoin, they congregate and nest on the Pelican Islands.

Some years, in order to accommodate a growing population of nesting Canada geese, the Refuge managers create artificial islands. In winter, mounds of dirt are piled on the thick ice and then spring melt allows the new "land" to form.

Habitat is defined as a place that provides a living creature with everything needed for survival and the piping plovers find this haven to be good for their needs. However, at times it's necessary to provide a man-made lair for these small birds. A sandy shoreline is too bare, so pebbles are spread on a beach to help camouflage the aerie from predators.

Bigger animals especially need adequate cover and they find it here in the form of shelterbelts made up of tall grasses, shrubs and cattails. These protected areas also provide food for the many birds and mammals that remain throughout the cold months.

The names of all the neighbors who live here throughout the warm days are too numerous to mention. Included though in the population are double-crested cormorants, whitetail deer, great blue herons, ring-necked pheasants, sandpipers, sharp-tailed grouse, coyotes, osprey, an occasional bald eagle, all kinds of hawks, falcons, numerous ducks, tundra swan, loons, owls, the yellow-rump warbler and the yellow-billed Cuckoo.

From the time the "transient residents" arrive for the summer until they gather in autumn to begin their southern sojourn, constant chatter fills the air; there is much to "talk" about and do as new life is created.

Early morning and late afternoon in the spring and fall are the best times to visit the Bowdoin National Wildlife Refuge. Its 15,500 acres can be seen via a 15-mile circular route. This special natural community is easily reached from Malta.

—RICK AND SUSIE GRAETZ

THE LITTLE ROCKIES

Indians migrating through this territory north of the Missouri River called them "the island mountains." From a distance, they resemble atolls rising from the prairie sea of north central Montana. Although not very lofty (the highest point is 5,720-foot Antoine Butte), they reach 2,500 feet above the surrounding plains and can be seen from 75 miles away. To the people in towns like Roy and Malta, this 50-square mile mass of igneous and sedimentary rock is a favored landmark.

Catholic church, Zortman in the Little Rockies. RICK AND SUSIE GRAETZ

Much of early-day Montana can be described as being the Wild West, but the Little Rocky Mountains and the country rolling south into the Missouri Breaks was perhaps the epitome of the Old West etched on movie screens. A little over 100 years ago, the characters of those times ... cattle barons, gold seekers, outlaws, cowboys, vigilantes, rustlers and horse thieves went about their ways here. And before they were forced off the land, the free-roaming Plains Indians hunted enormous bison herds that passed in the shadow of these mountains.

Gold brought the white man into the gulches of the uprises of Montana. There are records of an 1852 gold find, but mining didn't begin on any scale until the finding of "color" in southwest Montana in 1884.

In 1893, Pike Landusky hit it big in a canyon near the site of the town named after him. At about the same time, gold was also found to the northeast in Ruby Gulch. Here, Pete Zortman established a mill to extract the precious metal from the ore. The town that grew up below the bonanza took on his name.

One of the Little Rockies most written about happenings involved a bar room killing. Pike Landusky, himself a legend, met his end at the hand of Harvey "Kid" Curry, one of the wild Curry Brothers Gang, who frequented the Little Rockies. The stories vary, but the shooting supposedly took place in 1894 during a Christmas celebration in Jew Jake's Saloon. This event started "Kid" Curry on the outlaw trail for real as he joined up with the likes of Butch Cassidy and the Sundance Kid. A hideout in the badlands south of the mountains kept them safe from "the long arm of the law."

The Little Rockies' beginning as a roaring, almost lawless frontier outpost fueled by the shiny nuggets of small placer claims, soon evolved into a rich mining district. This mineral extraction business culminated in 1979 with the development of a large mine by Pegasus Gold. In 1998 though, bankruptcy shut it down; today reclamation of the mine is underway.

Most of the land in the Little Rocky Mountains is part of the Fort Belknap Indian Reservation, home to the Assiniboine and Gros Ventre tribes. The Gros Ventres live along the mountains in the Hays-Lodgepole area, while the Assiniboine have settled at Fort Belknap Agency along the Milk River to the north.

Though they did use it for vision quests, early-day Indian tribes feared the island range as they believed bad spirits lived there. Eagle Child and Mission Peak were, and still are, sacred points to the Gros Ventres. Tribal medicine men climbed them to fast and meditate. Legend has it that no one ever stayed beyond three days ... terrifying visions forced them to retreat.

Today, the tribes are working on developing the tourism potential of the mountain segment of their reservation. When mining reclamation is completed, a road will be constructed crossing the Little Rockies (it was there in the past) connecting Zortman (off the Reservation) with Mission Canyon on the southwest side of the range.

Zortman is the "capital" of the non-reservation part of the Little Rockies. The picturesque Catholic Church on the mountainside overlooking town was built by the Whitcomb family in 1911. This historic little white building, used today by several religions, is a favorite wedding chapel for locals and visitors alike. "Main Street" features a cellblock from the first jail as well as two of the original settlement buildings, the Miner's Club and Kalal's Bar. A side trip to the old wooded cemetery is both peaceful and interesting. Hard economic times, owing to the closing of the Pegasus mine, have not thwarted community spirit; while preserving its history, the town is also looking toward new opportunities. The Little Rockies' blend of trees and water, prairie, river breaks and mountain scenery coupled with a colorful past, is viewed as a very good, long lasting asset to be celebrated. Hiking trails will be developed, rock climbing is gaining popularity, gold panning is a major activity (rubies and garnets are also found) and hunting on the land beyond the mountains is being promoted.

On the flat land surrounding the Little Rockies, ranching continues to be the main economic factor. Old time outfits like the Matador Ranch keep the tradition alive.

—RICK AND SUSIE GRAETZ

GLASGOW AND FORT PECK

On May 8, 1805, the first "tourists" to this region, the Lewis and Clark Expedition, camped at the confluence of the Milk and Missouri rivers, about 18 miles southeast of present-day Glasgow. Lewis explored the Milk for about three miles and wrote, *"The water of this river possessed a peculiar whiteness, being about the colour of a cup of tea admixture of a tablespoon full of milk. From the colour of its water, we called it Milk River."*

Glasgow, in the Milk River Valley, came to be in 1887 as the Great Northern Railroad was pushing its way west. It was originally called Siding 45 ... the 45th rail siding west of Minot, N.D. Four or five tents made up the first structures.

A spin of the globe by a blindfolded railroad clerk in Minneapolis determined the town's name. Stopping the motion, his finger came to rest on Glasgow, Scotland. Hence, the name Glasgow, Montana. Many other eastern Montana railway towns such as Zurich, Malta, Harlem and Hinsdale owe their titles to this unimaginative process.

Originating as a place for the railroad to pick up livestock and grain, Glasgow remained a quiet agricultural community for a long period. In the fall of 1933, its lifestyle changed abruptly as men, desperate for work, jammed into the town to build Fort Peck Dam. Used as the primary trade and transport depot for the dam project, Glasgow was on its way to becoming one of the busiest places in northeast Montana. While most of the workers lived in and around the construction area, many stayed in Glasgow. The project brought in up to 11,000 workers, plus their families. Estimates are that there were 50,000 people in the area during the construction peak.

Adding immensely to local prosperity and growth was the arrival of the Glasgow Air Force Base in the late 1950s, only to have it close in 1969. While the base existed, almost 16,000 people lived between it and Glasgow. Stan Sonsteng of the Glasgow Courier remembers that at 5 p.m. during the low light of winter, he could observe a steady stream of lights on the road leading to the facility from town.

The folks of Glasgow have managed to make a go of it in spite of the ups and downs from the drought and depression of the '20s and '30s, through the base closure and recent slumps in the agricultural economy. Like much of eastern Montana, this is a place where people have deep roots and love where they live. Today this town of 3,500 people is a regional livestock center and a gateway to the eastern end of the CMR and Fort Peck Lake.

A visit to the Valley County Pioneer Museum gives an insight into the integrity and determination of those who settled and continue to live here.

Leaving Glasgow, it's about 18 miles to Fort Peck and Fort Peck Lake. With almost 1,600 miles of shoreline, it is the largest body of water in Montana.

Plains Indians once roamed this country following enormous bison herds.

Fort Peck Lake and Dam. RICK AND SUSIE GRAETZ

The places where they camped along the river, and later the area Lewis and Clark walked, are now well under the waters of Fort Peck Lake.

Fort Peck Dam is one of the largest earth-filled river impediments in the world. Its original purpose was not only to control floods, but also to create jobs in a depression-saddled economy. Completed in 1940, at the time, the undertaking was the nation's largest public works project.

The work spawned shanty boomtowns that were scattered around the development area — Square Deal, New Deal, Park Grove, Delano Heights and Wheeler. These places disappeared almost as quickly as they grew. Some, including New Deal, are now covered by deep waters of the lake. Today, all that's left of any of them, except for Fort Peck, is the rebuilt Buckhorn Bar; the original burned down in 1983.

With the commencement of the dam project, the orderly development of the Fort Peck town site, planned and built by the Army Corps of Engineers to house its employees, began in the fall of 1933. A neat and tidy community, it invites you to stay in the 1930-style Fort Peck Hotel (the rooms were remodeled in 1993), visit the Fort Peck Interpretive Center and Museum to view its collection of Indian artifacts and fossils uncovered during the construction of the dam, and if you're there between June and September, be sure to attend the Fort Peck Summer Theatre. Built in 1934 as a movie house for the dam workers, it was kept open 24 hours a day to entertain the round the clock work shifts.

Fort Peck Lake is treasured for its size and outdoor opportunities. Six recreation areas within a few miles of the dam provide access for water sports, fishing and hunting. The Montana Governor's Cup Walleye Fishing Tournament is a nationally recognized event held the second weekend in July.

Fort Peck Lake is surrounded by the eastern unit of the Charles M. Russell National Wildlife Refuge. Roads lead out of Fort Peck and Glasgow to scenic and recreation points on the Lake and Refuge. As most of them are only passable in dry weather, check in with the CMR Field Station in Fort Peck.
—RICK AND SUSIE GRAETZ

PLENTYWOOD TO SCOBEY

Idyllic prairie town ... clean, orderly, and picturesque, describes Scobey. Known as the center of one of Montana's most productive grain-growing regions; surrounded by low hills and buttes, it occupies a small space in the broad Poplar River Valley. Like so many places in northeast Montana, the town began late in the first decade of the 20th Century, primarily as a result of the railroad and the accompanying homestead era. Early on, two competing railroads—the Great Northern and the Soo Line, running parallel to and seven miles apart from each other, were vying for the abundant agricultural products gathered in the area ... at least until the years of drought and depression came along.

Incorporated in 1916, Scobey was named for Major Charles Scobey, a then agent at the Fort Peck Indian Reservation. Known in its earlier days as "One-eyed Molly's House of Pleasure," the distinctive Daniels County Courthouse, built about 1913 on Scobey's main street, is on the National Register of Historic Places.

Pioneer Town, a re-creation of an early 1900s homestead hamlet and one of the finest museums of its kind, is Scobey's featured attraction. Forty-two original structures, some 100 years old, have been brought to the site. Many, falling into disrepair, were to be torn down; most came from nearby towns such as Whitetail.

To see Pioneer Town and the nearby geography requires a couple days well worth spending.

After finishing up in Scobey, head east on Route 5. It's only 43 miles to Plentywood, but at the least, take all day to get there.

When the Great Northern and other railroads first came through the northern prairie, sidings and depots were established about every six miles and small communities grew up around them. Most have long since disappeared and others are ghosts of their former selves. First en route, you'll encounter Madoc and its two grain elevators. You can only imagine eager homesteaders pulling up with their ample wagonloads of harvested wheat.

Next down the road comes Flaxville. At one time, the only crop grown in the area was flax, so the name came easily. First called Boyer, it was located a little more than two miles to the southwest. When the railroad arrived, the

Big Muddy country north of Scobey on road to Plentywood. RICK AND SUSIE GRAETZ

place was moved to its current location and the named changed. On the west edge of town, Duck Stamp dollars have helped establish a waterfowl production area. A group of grain elevators, a saloon and an antique store make up much of the local economic development.

From Flaxville take a seven-mile side trip north on County Road 511 to Whitetail, at onetime a stop on the Soo Line.

Between Flaxville and Scobey, the terrain is undulating and wheat fields are prevalent. Beyond Flaxville, you'll enter a mix of badlands topography, coulees and shallow canyons ... cow country. The landscape along the way is quite scenic.

Redstone, east of Flaxville, was established somewhere around 1900. It took its name from the red shale in the area. "Dutch Henry," a notorious outlaw leader, had one of his camps nearby. The no longer functioning, colorful Westland Oil Co. Service Station and its antique pumps greets your arrival. Just down Main Street, a new post office stands out.

South from Redstone, in the vicinity of Eagle Creek and Eagle Nest Butte, the Wood Mountain and Moose Mountain trails come close to each other. Both of these historic paths lead into Canada. The Moose Route started at Wolf Point and snaked northeast leaving the United States in the area of Port Raymond, north of Plentywood. The Wood Mountain Trail began by Fort Union, near present day Sidney, and crossed the border northwest of Scobey. The Assiniboine and Sioux used both, as did other early day wanderers.

Poke around some of the back roads near Redstone, especially in the badlands of Big Muddy Creek to the north. The Outlaw Trail, named by Butch Cassidy and used to move stolen horses and cattle to Canada, wandered through the coulees of the Big Muddy. Cassidy had a "rest station" in the vicinity.

Beyond Redstone, Hwy 5 eases into the valley of Big Muddy Creek heading east towards Plentywood.

The landscape around these parts hardly indicates that there is wood to be found. In the open range days, several cowboys from the nearby Diamond Ranch outfit were attempting to build a buffalo chip fire. The notorious outlaw leader Old Dutch Henry told them, "If you go a couple of miles up this creek, you'll find plenty wood." Following his advice, they found an abundance of fuel and named this creek, that reaches the Big Muddy Creek just west of the present-day town, Plentywood. In1912, the moniker was passed on from the creek to the emerging settlement developed by the railroads and an influx of homesteaders.

Main street is very appealing and compact, with an assortment of businesses that belong in the heart of any community ... a drug store, hardware store, clothing shop, cafe, newspaper office, at least one saloon and a couple of banks. The Sheridan County Courthouse is at the head of this commercial thoroughfare. The fairgrounds stand out on the south edge of town.

A collection of early-day memorabilia at the Sheridan County Museum will give you insight into all that came before in this distant part of Montana. You'll find it by the fairgrounds.

After defeating Custer at the Battle of the Little Big Horn in June of 1876, Sitting Bull traveled north, crossed the U.S. border and sought refuge in Canada for five years. Then in July 1891, at the site of present-day Plentywood, he and his Sioux band "surrendered" to the US Army.

This now quiet corner of Montana, between Scobey and Plentywood, hides a very wild and colorful past. Daniels (Scobey) and Sheridan (Plentywood) counties were once part of Valley County. A stock inspector noted in his files that, "Valley County is the most lawless and crookeddest country in the union and the Big Muddy is the worst of it. It has Indians, outlaws, horse and cattle rustlers, bootleggers, homesteaders, baseball rivalries, newspaper wars, political battles, communists and car thieves."

The Outlaw Trail crossed into Canada north of Plentywood. Rustlers moved their stolen cattle and horses along this passage. Butch Cassidy named the trail and established a rest station in the Big Muddy Valley.

Outlaw enterprises took place in the late 1800s and early 1900s. The latter part of the homestead era and then the roaring '20s brought on other activities. The newly arrived "sodbusters" weren't pleased with either major political party, so they formed the leftist Farmer-Labor Party and held sway in most local elections. It was reported that in 1930, more than 300 folks in Sheridan County voted a full communist ticket. Quite a contrast from the staunch conservatism that prevails today. By 1928, things started to quiet down, and the communists as well as the Klu Klux Klan, which was active for a period, began disappearing.

Today, the future of the area, as well as the present, revolves around agriculture with its roller coaster prices, the Conservation Reserve Program, and unpredictable weather. It's a part of Montana's great heritage; when you traverse through, try and picture it 70 to 100 years ago.

East of Plentywood the ecologically important prairie pothole country breaks off from seemingly endless stretches of cultivated land. This is a critical breeding/migrating area for North American wetland and grassland birds. The Nature Conservancy of Montana through their Comertown Pothole Preserve, easements, and cooperation with the Fish and Wildlife Service has protected a total of 2,425 acres, allowing endangered species, such as the piping plover, a chance to recover. If the warm season is wet enough, wildflowers cover the green hills and birdsong echoes across the many ponds.

Westby, on the sunrise fringe of this area and once part of North Dakota, is as far as you can go in northeast Montana. This farm village boasts of the state's most frigid average winter temperature. Far from the range of warming chinook winds, it latches onto cold air from the north and keeps it for a while.

From Plentywood follow Route16 twenty-two miles south to Medicine Lake National Wildlife Refuge.

—RICK AND SUSIE GRAETZ

MEDICINE LAKE NATIONAL WILDLIFE REFUGE

Mid-May, 5:00 a.m., the lifting fog, a product of a cold night, is catching the first light of a mellow sunrise ... the tall grass and reeds take on a gold and orange hue while the surrounding water gathers all the colors of the sky transforming its surface into a pastel painting. The crisp air is noisy, as the entire neighborhood chats in profusion. Grouse, performing their mating ritual, add a distinct sound of to the excitement.

The previous weeks saw a raucous homecoming ... a tradition carried out each year as tens of thousands of geese, ducks and birds fill the spring sky on their way back to northeast Montana's Medicine Lake National Wildlife Refuge. This prairie oasis, bordered by seemingly endless stretches of wheat fields witnesses one of the great wildlife spectacles in America.

Just 22 miles south of Plentywood, Medicine Lake is located above the former channel of the Missouri River. Before the last ice age, the river ran north to Hudson Bay. A glacier moving out of Canada forced it to turn south. When the massive flow of ice receded, it left a blanket of glacial till, resulting in rocky, rolling hills interspersed with numerous wetlands, marshes and ponds.

Medicine Lake is the largest of these bodies of water and depends upon summer thunderstorms, winter snowmelt, the flow of Big Muddy Creek

Medicine Lake National Wildlife Refuge. RICK AND SUSIE GRAETZ

reaching the area from the north, and Lake Creek coming from the northeast for its water. The name is derived from medicinal herbs and roots Indians gathered around its shores. An exploration of the surrounding higher terrain shows tepee rings and other signs of early-day use.

Set aside in 1935 via a presidential order, MLNWR has grown from an original 23,700 acres to 31,660 acres. Part of the landscape, 11,360 acres, is preserved as the Medicine Lake Wilderness Area. It includes the main lake and the unique sand hills in the southeast section. Management of this national treasure is entrusted to the good hands of the US Fish and Wildlife Service.

More than 100,000 migrating waterfowl make Medicine Lake their warm weather habitat. Great blue herons, white pelicans, geese, grebes, and ten different species of ducks share this prairie ecosystem with countless other birds. Each year, as many as 30,000 ducklings are produced. Every fall, more than 10,000 sandhill cranes spend a week here. Foxes, raccoons, pheasants and deer also populate the area.

The refuge boasts the largest pelican rookery in Montana and third largest in the nation. These magnificent birds have a nine-foot wingspan and nest on the big island in the middle of Medicine Lake. More than 2,000 white pelicans are born each season.

The piping plover, a rare bird, actively breeds in the wetlands. Their flute-like call is one of the great sounds of nature.

Geese are the first to arrive; showing up in February and March, they set up their territory and prepare for nesting even before the ice melts. It's usually late April before Medicine Lake thaws, just in time for the summer dwellers to show up. All the winged creatures leave by around the first of November when the lakes begin to freeze. Coulees that drain towards the lake offer shelter for the animals that stay throughout the long cold months. Winter at Medicine Lake is quiet, as ice and snow dominate the landscape and temperatures can plummet to 50 degrees below zero.

It's an easy place to see. Refuge headquarters is about two miles to the east of the highway on the western edge up the lake. An observation tower, rising 100 feet above the office, offers a great view of virtually the entire wildlife haven. A self-guided 14-mile-long tour route leads to other view points, including Medicine Lake Overlook to the east of the refuge's buildings. In the southwest corner, off of Hwy 16, a road goes to a day-use area and some high hills that also afford excellent views of the lakes and surrounding prairie country.

As you tour the refuge, you'll note some cultivated areas. Farmers plant grain fields on several hundred acres each spring. The refuge keeps about one-quarter of the potential harvest and then lets it stand as a wildlife food source. This practice helps to keep birds and animals out of the local fields.

Although wildlife is there throughout the summer, May, June and October are the best months to see Medicine Lake. July and August can get quite hot. Montana's warmest temperature on record was documented here when the thermometer reached 117 degrees on July 5, 1937.

—RICK AND SUSIE GRAETZ

LONESOME HIGHWAY 200

From the center of the state at Lewistown, it is 262 miles to Sidney and just a few miles farther to the Dakota line. At night you can drive 50 miles or more and never see another vehicle. Fly over it at after dark and you rarely notice a light. This far-flung portion of Hwy 200 traverses Montana's loneliest stretch of geography.

But loneliness is this huge swath of landscape's greatest asset. For what it lacks in civilization, it makes up for in the grandeur of the prairie and the echoes of history. Montana Hwy 200, originating at the Idaho border in the northwest part of our state, is your trail across this great section of America.

Departing Lewistown with the compass pointing towards the sunrise, the road climbs through the western foothills of the forest covered Judith Mountains, an island uplift in the vast sea of Montana's Northern Great Plains. Atop the pass, to the south you get a glimpse of the elongated mass of the Big and Little Snowy mountains. The view-shed to the northwest brings out the lower lying North and South Moccasins. Gravitating down the east slope of the pass, the northern reaches of the Judiths, marked by the distinct form of Black Butte, are tailing off towards your left. Few ranches are visible on the way to Hwy 200's junction with Hwy 19, coming in from the north. Here, the small community of Grass Range is just one mile down the road. A busy café and gas station sit on the edge of town.

For a worthy side trip — assuming that you have several days to complete the journey, head north on Hwy 19 towards Malta. It's 39 miles straight ahead to the Missouri River crossing and the western end of the 1.1 million-acre Charles M. Russell National Wildlife Refuge. The folks at the Sand Creek Wildlife Station at the top of the hill on the south side of the river can give you plenty of information on what to see and do in this wildlife haven. Camp at the James Kipp Recreation site off the Fred Robinson Bridge for the night.

When your adventure here is finished, head back south to Hwy 200. Once again moving eastward, it is 23 miles to Winnett, seat of Petroleum County. With the establishment of a Post Office in 1912, Winnett officially became a town and grew on the homestead rush and the discovery of one of the richest pockets of oil at Cat Creek in 1920. The demise of the same events emptied the community. Gas and food are available and it is worth stopping in to visit this place that in its heyday was rollicking and prosperous.

Fifteen miles beyond Winnett you will pass over the storied Musselshell River. Roads from here and Winnett lead into the Missouri River Breaks and the CMR Wildlife Refuge.

McDonald Creek edges the south flank of Hwy 200 beyond Winnett and empties into the Musselshell. The country along the way consists of a river bottom with pine-covered bluffs to the south and north. After crossing the Musselshell River, the road climbs through high hills with a mixture of sagebrush and an open forest of ponderosa and juniper pines. Up until now, you have been gradually descending from a high plateau that began at the foot of the Northern Rocky Mountains. Lewistown sits at an elevation of 3,963 feet, while Sidney is 1,931 feet above sea level.

At milepost 160, an historic sign points out the one-time location of Fort Musselshell on the Missouri River about 35 miles to the north. In the 1860s and 1870s, the fort served as a trading post and stopping place for Missouri River steamboats. The River Crow and Gros Ventre Indians also traded here. The sign points out that other tribes, namely the Assiniboine and Sioux, regarded "this Post as an amusement center where bands of ambitious braves could lie in ambush and get target practice on careless whites."

This was a lawless land. Errant cowboys and outlaws considered the rancher's four-footed inventory to be fair game. In 1884, Granville Stuart, often considered the grandfather of Montana, disposed of the cattle and horse rustlers holed up along the Musselshell, especially at its mouth with the Missouri, by subjecting them to vigilante justice carried out by "Stuart's Stranglers."

At one time, this area served as a river passage point for migrating bison herds that thundered by the millions across the very land the highway now bisects. On a day when the wind is still, listen and you might hear the shouts of the Indian hunters as they pursued these mighty animals. Indeed, every mile of the way suggests a story of the Plains Indians who frequented this segment of eastern Montana.

At about milepost 166, you reach the high point of this stretch of Hwy 200. From the crest, the prairie seems to stretch forever in all directions; broken up by buttes, and coulees, it is anything but flat. An outline of the mountains you left behind is silhouetted against the sunset.

The topography to the north of your route is made up of some of the most spectacular river breaks in the nation. The Missouri River cuts a swath through land that rises to a thousand feet above it. All you view is part of the CMR. Though you rarely see buildings, ranching and grazing dominate here. Some of Montana's most historic ranches such as the Bar N and the Mill Iron claimed the land.

The distance from Winnett to Jordan is about 70 miles. As the road aims to Jordan from these high pine covered hills, it slowly drops through a prairie of sagebrush, coulees and the occasional clump of cottonwoods, where perennial springs in an otherwise dry land keep the trees healthy. Since there might not be another tree for miles, one wonders how the seeds got to these solitary forests in the first place.

From here eastward, the road often undulates like a roller coaster. Occasional tracks head north or south, and if it's dry, they are worth exploring. Twenty-one miles from the Musselshell, you reach the small town of Sand Springs with its general store, school, post office and a couple of houses.

In the early 1900s, Sand Springs was considered for the County Seat of Garfield County. At that time, and before the depression, it had two grocery stores, a newspaper, a garage, hotel and a flourmill. Its population is now down to about five and serves 35 postal customers and at this writing there are anywhere from three to five students attending the school.

From milepost 202 and beyond, Smokey Butte, looking like an old volcano or a teepee with a somewhat flat top, stands out to the north. Stories have it, Indians used to send smoke signals atop here that could be observed for long distances.

About 12 miles before reaching Jordan, you will cross Big Dry Creek, a bit of water that lends its name to a landscape often termed "the Big Dry." Late 1800's photographer L.A. Huffman called it "the Big Open" and National Geographic labeled it "Jordan Country."

The independent town of Jordan rises from the banks of Big Dry Creek and straddles Montana Hwy 200. If the weather is warm you will likely see the daily card game going on outside of the fire station. If you're not into touring the local watering holes, the Jordan Drug with its genuine operating old fashion soda fountain, is a good place to stop and wet your whistle. There are a couple of places to stay and Jordan should be your camp for at least a couple of nights.

Downtown Jordan, a daily ritual when the sun shines. RICK AND SUSIE GRAETZ

This seat of Garfield County is an entry to some of the most remote and beautiful deep river canyons, badlands and prairie wilderness in the west. The most rugged of the terrain is part of the CMR Wildlife Refuge. The road to Hell Creek State Park, on Fort Peck Lake, 26 miles north of Jordan passes through stately piney buttes and high rises that offer excellent views of some of upper reaches of the Missouri River Breaks, Devil's Creek, Snow Creek and Crooked Creek all north of Jordan are worthwhile places to visit. The Haxby Road east of Jordan leads far out to the badlands and into the breaks.

Jordan houses a field station for the Charles M. Russell National Wildlife Refuge. It's on the west end of town. Stop and inquire here about road conditions, maps and other pertinent information.

Leaving Jordan, once again moving eastward on Hwy 200, you will cover 37 miles through a landscape often dominated with badlands before arriving at the junction with Hwy 24 leading north towards Fort Peck and Glasgow. Travel slowly through here and pull off whenever possible and enjoy the view. The early morning and late afternoon light brings out the life and character of the sandstone sculptures.

Badlands are mini-desserts formed when the vegetation cover is destroyed, usually by wild fire or overgrazing. Water runs off the underlying clay surface and soft bedrock. Erosion starts, gullies are formed and seeds of potential new growth of plants and grasses are washed away or are unable to take hold in the hardened soil. Heavy spring and summer downpours accelerate the process. Steep slopes are etched quickly, and seemingly smooth surface alluvial deposits stand out below them. Soon the entire disrupted area is void of green growth.

These badlands and the breaks to the north contain some of the richest fossil beds on earth. A sign in Jordan reads, "Many of the most complete dinosaurs on display in the world were gathered here in Garfield County. The first Tyrannosaurus Rex skeleton came out of these hills in 1902. In fact, four of the six Tyrannosauruses found in the world are from Garfield County."

Hwy 24 offers a scenic side trip. If you would like, spend the night at Fort Peck in the historic old hotel or camp in one of the numerous campgrounds. Several access roads lead into the Big Dry Arm section of Fort Peck Lake and the eastern perimeter of the CMR. Badlands, hills and coulees are abundant all the way north. The Sand Arroyo Badlands are of particular interest. Please remember, these side routes are only passable when it is dry.

Back on the main trail, Hwy 200, the country opens and one notices an absence of sagebrush and evidence of sod busting. At about milepost 267, a side road leads south to the quiet settlement of Brockway. During the homestead era, life was good here. Today, the train station sits along a rail bed void of tracks and spaces exist where buildings once stood on the carefully laid out streets. A silent reminder of the past.

The Redwater River runs through Brockway and parallels Hwy 200 to Circle. Take a gander at the scenic Redwater River Canyon to the south of town. Inquire at Circle or Brockway for directions.

The environment after Brockway and on to Circle and the Redwater River Valley displays softer rolling high plains and grasslands. Near Circle, crops become more expansive and undulate across the hills in pleasing geometric patterns. The rough austere terrain has faded out.

The old time "cow town" of Circle, picked up it's name from the Circle Brand, one of Montana's earliest ranches. Today, the town is still very farm and ranch orientated. Spend some time here and drop in on another authentic ice cream and soda fountain at Chapin's Drug for a milkshake. Also, be sure to visit the McCone County Pioneer Museum on the west end of town.

At Circle, just to confuse you, the road we have been following branches off with Hwy 200S going southeast to Glendive and the main Hwy 200 continuing northeast towards Sidney, which is our destination.

To the south of Circle and on the way to Richey, the sandstone bluffs of the Big and Little Sheep mountains come into view. Proving that the pioneers had a sense of humor, these somewhat vertically challenged "mountains" were named after the Audubon sheep living there. Sadly, early homesteaders eliminated the herds of handsome animals and they live on in name only.

Be sure to stop and visit the Richey Historical museum for a look at what the local homesteading lifestyle was like.

From Circle to Sidney and the Lower Yellowstone River Valley, you'll travel 72 miles. As you near the Yellowstone, land farmed with sugar beets, wheat, corn and other crops are evident. The road also skirts Fox Lake Wildlife Management Area. Stop and see what critters have taken up residence.

In 1888, the friendly and inviting community of Sidney was named for Sidney Walters, the young son of a local pioneer family. Sometimes called the Sunrise City, with 5,000 people, it is the largest town in northeast Montana.

Stay here overnight and explore some of the badlands and breaks of the Yellowstone River just south of town, as well as historic Fort Union to the north. This is also "Confluence Country," the meeting of the Missouri and Yellowstone rivers. Some of Montana's earliest recorded history was played out here on the eastern fringes of our state. From the 1830s to the 1850s, the place held supremacy over the fur trade business of the Upper Missouri River, and north of Sidney, on April 27 1805, Lewis and Clark and their Corps of Discovery crossed into what would become Montana Territory.

This is the eastern end of your journey and you are once again in the arms of civilization. Whether you picnic in one of the lovely treed parks, play a round of golf or tour the outlying area, don't miss the Mondak Heritage Center. A combination art gallery, gift shop, library and reference facility and wonderful local history exhibit. A stop here will give you a better understanding of the sites you encountered along "Lonesome Hwy 200," which once you get to know it, isn't so lonesome after all.

—RICK AND SUSIE GRAETZ

JORDAN COUNTRY

Late 1800's photographer L. A. Huffman called it "The Big Open," National Geographic termed it "Jordan Country" and others refer to the sparsely populated country south of Fort Peck Lake as "The Big Dry." The small ranching town of Jordan is the heart of this scenic territory.

Rising from the banks of Big Dry Creek and straddling MT Hwy 200, Jordan was founded in about 1896 by Arthur Jordan. He asked that the town take the name of a friend from Miles City who was also named Jordan. The first residence was Arthur Jordan's tent. Later, he established a post office and store for this fledgling cow town.

Jordan and the surrounding expanse of rangeland is still very much cowboy country and the place retains an old west flavor. False-front buildings on main street haven't changed much since the communities earliest days ... some are over 80 years old.

This seat of Garfield County is your entry to some of the most remote and beautiful mix of deep river canyons, badlands and prairie wilderness in the west. The most rugged of the terrain is part of the 1.1 million-acre Charles M. Russell Wildlife Refuge, which surrounds Fort Peck Lake in a 200-mile-long strip. And wildlife abounds out here ... antelope, elk, mule deer, whitetail deer, wild turkeys, sage grouse and numerous waterfowl make these wildlands their home. Before heading into this inviting region, it's best to travel beyond Jordan to get an overview of the landscape to the east and northeast of the town.

From Jordan, drive east on MT 200 toward Circle. Fifteen miles out, you'll enter a ten-mile stretch of very spectacular views of red and yellow colored buttes, badlands and distant vistas. Farther yet, 36 miles from town, you'll encounter Hwy 24 pointing north, which parallels the Dry Arm section and eastern edge of Fort Peck Lake. If you'd like to camp, put a boat in the water, or just see the lake, take advantage of the recreation areas along the its length; there are several and they are well marked. The Sand Arroyo badlands found here are fascinating. Remember, most of the roads to these places are only passable when it is dry.

After your visit to Dry Arm, stay in Jordan a couple of days or camp in the Missouri Breaks. There are many roads and trails throughout this river wilderness, but before striking out, inquire at the Charles M. Russell Wildlife Refuge office in town. They can advise you on conditions and regulations on the Refuge and the best routes to follow. Understanding the roads and knowing the weather forecast will add to the success of your trip. Getting hung up in the gumbo created by wet weather is not a pleasant surprise.

The terrain east and north of Jordan is famous among paleontologists for its fantastic fossil beds. Dinosaurs and pre-historic creatures once roamed here. In 1904, a Tyrannosaurus Rex was discovered in the Hell Creek Formation. See the dinosaur display in the museum while in town.

Hell Creek State Park, on Fort Peck Lake, 26 miles north of Jordan is a popular area. On the way there you'll go through the stately piney buttes and high rises on the road that offer excellent views of some of the upper reaches of the Missouri Breaks and the CMR Refuge. Devil's Creek, Snow Creek and Crooked Creek, all north of Jordan, are worthwhile places to explore. The Haxby Road east of Jordan reaches a long way out through the badlands and into the breaks.

This is a place that will amaze you ... it is truly uncommon and one of the most fantastic wilderness regions of America.

—RICK AND SUSIE GRAETZ

FIRST T-REX DISCOVERY

We have penned a considerable amount on the Missouri River Breaks, especially on the landscape north of the Missouri between Malta and Glasgow and south of it down to Jordan. All of our previous readings led us to believe William Hornaday of the American Museum of Natural History uncovered the first complete T-Rex skeleton while hunting in one of the deep coulees of Snow Creek north of Jordan. Recently, Robert Hurley, a Glasgow attorney, sent an interesting note explaining that Hornaday had nothing to do with this discovery; actually, it was a Garfield County rancher who spotted the remains. Rather than try and reiterate ourselves what Mr. Hurley wrote, we present his correspondence and other information on the subject.

"Mr. and Mrs. Graetz, The March 20th Great Falls Tribune carried your article about the Missouri Breaks, and you suggested that in 1902, William Hornaday of the American Museum of Natural History descended into a canyon and uncovered one of the world's first intact T-Rex fossils.

"… I am not a paleontologist. However, I do suggest there may be some confusion here. My longtime friend, Lawrence "Hoolie" Edwards has often told me the story about the finding of the first T-Rex at Haxby, an old-time Post Office north of Jordan … Hoolie has explained how his father met Dr. Barnum Brown (not William Hornaday) of the American Museum of Natural History in New York; they talked about hunting in northeast Montana; they talked about the dinosaur bones that Hoolie's father, George Edwards, had found near the Edwards ranch; and about 1902, if I am recalling my dates correctly, Dr. Brown arranged with Hoolie's father to come to Glasgow and to take a ride with a team of horses from Glasgow to the Edwards ranch, where George Edwards personally led Dr. Brown to the so-called first and most famous T-Rex skeleton, which was not down a canyon, but at the surface on a bluff near Haxby, Montana.

"I respectfully suggest that you may have confused William Hornaday with Barnum Brown, who gets credit for "discovering" this fossil.

"And neither Brown nor Hornaday nor any other museum official should have taken credit for discovering this T-Rex — George Edwards had discovered it and led Dr. Brown right to it. If I am recalling correctly, Hoolie's quotation of the 'so-called discovery' was to the effect that Brown didn't even get his shoes dirty — he rode right up to the discovery on the buggy or wagon, directed by George Edwards.

"I suggest this is another of the instances where Montana history glorifies the wrong discoverer ... Sincerely, Robert Hurley"

Our interest was peaked. So we sent the missive to our good friend Doug Smith, the Sheridan County planner and a respected archaeologist/historian/geologist. Doug felt Robert Hurley was substantially correct, but in doing some research, he found a letter in his files from the above mentioned Dr. Barnum Brown to a woman in Circle, Montana explaining where he claimed the T-Rex was found. Brown's letter dated March 12, 1953 in part reads as follows.

"Dear Miss Wischmann: ... Your letter of March 2nd was forwarded to me ... I believe practically all of the specimens I found for the American Museum came from Garfield County and few if any from the present McCone County, the boundary of which was established after I worked that region.

"I started work in the badlands of the Missouri River in the Spring of 1902 with Jordan on Big Dry Creek as headquarters and I continued working the region each summer until 1909.

"My first discovery of a dinosaur was the skeleton of Tyrannosaurus Rex at the old Max Sieber buffalo cabin on Hell Creek 16 miles Northwest of Jordan.

This skeleton we sold to the Carnegie Museum of Pittsburgh when it was feared Germany might bomb New York City and destroy Museum specimens.

"The second T-Rex skeleton now mounted in the American Museum I found on the John Willis ranch on the Big Dry which I think was also Garfield County … You might also enquire of Art Vail, sheep man, if still living for all nearby ranch people were interested in my work and most helpful … It is very difficult to trust one's memory in a very active career."

So now we took Robert Hurley's advice to contact Lawrence "Hoolie" Edwards and get the details directly, "so you aren't reporting second or third hand."

Hoolie Edwards, an "old-time cowboy" living at the end of a road, 52 miles into the Breaks from Jordan, told us, Dr. Brown is correct on the location of the second find, but that the skeleton of the first T-Rex found by his father in 1902, was 15 miles from the buffalo cabin where Brown claimed to have made his discovery.

It would seem to make sense that a local rancher working the untracked badlands of the Missouri Breaks on a daily basis would be more apt to uncover something of this nature than a scientist from New York. After reviewing the evidence, we concur with Hurley, Smith and "Hoolie" Edwards that the evidence seems to point to George Edwards as the person who located the initial T-Rex.

As for Hornaday, Smith tells us he was "the guy from the Smithsonian who collected some of the last Buffalo from the same area as the T-rex find and had them stuffed."

—RICK AND SUSIE GRAETZ

NORTHEAST MOUNTAIN NOTES

Blue Mountain
This high point just off of the North Dakota line between Sidney and Glendive is 800 feet higher than the remote prairie it overlooks. At a whopping 3,084 feet in elevation, it is the tallest point in northeastern Montana.

Sheep Mountains
The Little and Big Sheep mountains are a series of hills and eroded badlands between Circle and Glendive. Their highest point at 3,625 feet is no more than 300 feet above the adjacent country.

—RICK AND SUSIE GRAETZ

CENTRAL MONTANA

THE CENTER OF BIG SKY COUNTRY DEFINES ITS NORTHERN FLANK WITH THE Missouri River Breaks, then points south to the Yellowstone/Missouri Divide, only a short distance north of the Yellowstone River. On the west, the Castle, Belts and Highwoods are the boundary. From there, stretching toward the sunrise, its eastern perimeter follows the Musselshell River after it makes its turn at the "Big Bend" near Melstone, to the Missouri River.

Central Montana has experienced virtually every stage of Montana's history, from the times of the nomadic Plains Indians through the Lewis and Clark Expedition, which opened the area to fur traders, prospectors, cattlemen, outlaws, vigilantes, railroads and homesteaders. Today, it epitomizes much of what the Real Montana it is famous for — small population, open space, intact ranches and farms and a dominant rural way of life.

The largest community — Lewistown with the 6,000 folks who choose to live there — is plopped right on top of Montana's geographic center, and brags of having one of the nation's purest water supplies. The liquid, clarified as it flows through the limestone rock of the Big Snowy Mountains, gushes out of the ground just south of town at Big Springs.

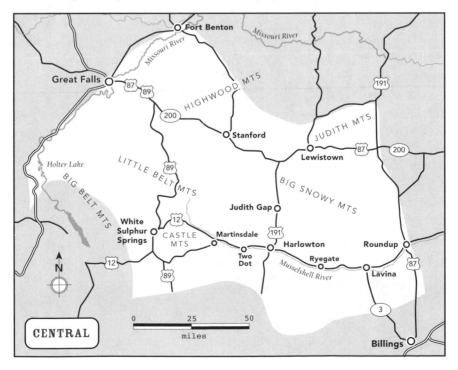

This Montana province is also the gathering place of the prairie island ranges: the Big and Little Snowy, Highwood, Judith, North and South Moccasin, Bull, Little Belt and Castle mountains. In addition, the northern peaks of the Crazy Mountains are part of central Montana. All are weather producers for the Central Territory, hatching some of the state's heaviest spring snowfalls and severe summer thunderstorms. Showers are frequent over them, and the grass, as the proverb states, seems to be greener on their side of the fence than in other parts of the state.

Outside Lewistown's south door sit the Big Snowy Mountains — the pride of this part of the state. Ascending in an elongated mass from the ocean of prairie lands of central Montana, a perch on their crest, 8,681-foot Great House Peak, looks out on the farthest-reaching views in Big Sky country. On a day when the air is clear, a hiker can survey a 300-mile span from the Sweetgrass Hills near Shelby in the northwest, to the Beartooth and Pryor mountains below the Yellowstone River to the south and southeast.

Mining and the search for gold played a major role in bringing people to the Judith, Little Belts, Moccasins and other high terrain. In 1880, gold was discovered in the northern segment of the Judith Mountains, establishing the current-day semi-ghost town of Maiden, which at one time had a population of 6,000. Now silent, Gilt Edge on the southeast side, was another of the boisterous Judith gold camps. When the ore played out, as it did elsewhere in the state, remnants of these and other gold camps such as Kendall in the North Moccasin Mountains, attest to the once flourishing human presence in these parts.

Old trails traversed central Montana. First there was the Musselshell, leading from the confluence of the Musselshell and Missouri rivers to the south, then westward. Arriving on steamboats, passengers and freight were loaded onto stagecoaches and wagons, which then followed the trail toward Helena through the Musselshell Valley. In 1874, the Carroll Trail, out of the old town of Carroll north of Lewistown on the Missouri River, took over as the main route.

This course, used by the Indians and settlers, crossed Judith Gap, a wide, windy blizzard-prone pass that after leaving the Missouri Breaks led from the Judith Basin near Lewistown to the Musselshell Valley at Harlowton. Later, the Great Northern and Montana railways put down tracks through Judith Gap.

In the 1870s, western Montana stockmen could see the value of moving their herds to the nutritious tall — and free — grass of central and eastern Montana. Granville Stuart, who is often called "the father of Montana," was one of the first to realize this. He the built headquarters for his and his partner's cattle empire — the DHS ranch — at the base of the north side of the Judith Mountains near Lewistown.

In the days of the open range, the Judith Basin Cattle Pool was one of the largest of the early open range outfits. Investors purchased cattle and hired cowboys to run the pool. Utica, near the Judith River and on the east side of the Little Belt Mountains, was a center for this activity and the place where cowboy artist Charlie Russell began his career by sketching on a piece of cardboard, a dying cow depicting the terrible winter of 1876–1877.

Here, the Judith River drains the Little Belt and Judith mountains then flows into the Missouri River just west and north of Lewistown. Captain William Clark of the Corps of Discovery named the attractive river for his girlfriend in Virginia.

Bison once owned the Musselshell Valley. But it was here, in about 1888, an unknown person killed possibly the last wild bison in Montana. The valley was also the last stand of the bison and Indian trading posts.

By 1875, there were an estimated 10,000 head of cattle in the valley. Like the Judith Basin cattlemen, ranchers here also organized; their outfit was the Musselshell Association. Cowboys gathered all of the herds in the entire 150 miles of the valley then moved the cattle along the range into strategically placed corrals. Eventually, the herds were sorted by brand. A single roundup could employ 60 men and use 300 head of horses.

Sheep, especially in the upper Musselshell and in the Martinsdale region, were just as important as cows.

Like the Judith Basin, the Musselshell is very historic with old ranches, big cottonwoods, sandstone and outcroppings of cliffs. A great blend of mostly undisturbed landscape, ranches and small communities are well spaced.

The Milwaukee Railroad, which took over the Montana Railway, helped build the communities of the Musselshell. Roundup grew out of their need for coal for the steam locomotives, with the ore being mined in the nearby Bull Mountains. The Milwaukee has long since gone, although Roundup and other Musselshell Valley communities still hang on with an agricultural based economy.

Central Montana's major river is the Musselshell. Born from waters in the Castle, Crazy and Little Belt mountains, it heads east to Melstone then abruptly turns north to the Missouri River, meeting it at the UL Bend on the Charles M. Russell National Wildlife Refuge.

The island mountains of this region of Montana can be seen from great distances, but another major central Montana landform also is visible from many points. Created by volcanic activity, Square Butte, north of Stanford and an outlier of the Highwood Mountains, is a big igneous block with a slightly tilted top and steep sides rising from cultivated fields. In geologic language, Square Butte is a laccolith, formed when molten rock squirted up through a dike and formed a bubble, or blister, under the sediment. Erosion eventually removed the sediments. Most of the known laccoliths in North America are found in north central Montana.

The essays that trail this summary will take you well into the center of Montana.

—RICK AND SUSIE GRAETZ

MUSSELSHELL RIVER VALLEY

"The trail ran up a creek which kept getting smaller as we went along . Then it went over a low range of hills. When we came to the top of the hill, we could see that we were coming to our promised land at last . As we stood up there, Balboa gazing on the Pacific did not have anything on us. The Musselshell country was a beautiful land. A person could stand in the same place and see buffalo, deer and elk, all at the same time without turning his head."

ANDREW GARCIA FROM *TOUGH TRIP THROUGH PARADISE — MONTANA IN 1878–1879*

Launched by springs and creeks on the eastern fringe of the Northern Rocky Mountains, the North and South forks of the Musselshell River pour out of the Crazies, Castles and Little Belts cutting their way through the last ridges and hills of Montana's mountainous province before joining and forming the Musselshell River.

Bonding of the tributaries takes place in a mixture of wetlands and pasture that spreads onto a prairie landscape heading toward the sunrise and the beginnings of Montana east of the mountains. From this simple start, the Musselshell will twist and turn for 364 miles through the heart of Montana, a landscape short on human presence and long on gentle beauty.

The river's past was only yesterday and its annals collect most all the chapters of our state's bygones. It ran the gauntlet from the natives and the first explorers and exploiters to the days of the prospector, the big sheep and cattle empires, the coming of the railroad and the arrival and demise of the homesteaders.

Its final thrust empties into the Missouri River, in a place that witnessed centuries of passage by the original claimants to the land ... the great Indian Nations and Montana's initial days of white history. Long before the white invaders came into the Musselshell, the indigenous clans prized the valley as prime hunting territory. No one tribe controlled the Musselshell, instead it was shared or fought over. The River Crow settled in for a while, but were forced to move south with the formation of the Crow Reservation in 1868.

Indians gave the legendary river its name. As the Hidatsa and Mandan described the landmarks Meriwether Lewis and William Clark should look for on their journey west, they told of the freshwater mussels to be found in a river the explorers would meet after *"the river that scolds all others"* (the Milk River). Clark wrote in his journal *"The Minetarres (Hidatsa) inform us that this river heads in the 1st of the rocky Mountains & passes through a broken Countrey its head at no great distance from the Yellow Stone River."* How accurately they described the location of the Musselshell! Lewis called it *"Shell river"* or *"Muscle Shell,"* and so penned it on May 21, 1805; the moniker took hold — albeit with a different spelling. Hal Stearns, in his book The

The Musselshell River north of Melstone. RICK AND SUSIE GRAETZ

Upper Musselshell Valley of Montana, states W.W. DeLacy, a mapmaker of note in the 1860s, spelled it "Musclshell" and that "this spelling persisted until November 1879. From that time on, the river and valley were spelled Musselshell." Stearns speculates that it was the US Post Office that changed the lettering of the name.

Cattle and sheep were the catalyst to advance settlement of the Musselshell Valley. Ranchers came together to take advantage of free grass amid an unfenced land. The Musselshell Association (an organization of cattlemen) gathered all of the herds in the entire 150 miles of the valley. The cowboys moved the cattle along the range into strategically placed corrals, then eventually brought them together and sorted the herds out by brand. A single roundup could have 60 men and 300 head of horses.

Sheep, especially in the Martinsdale region, were just as important as cows and actually appeared on the range before the bovines, having been brought in during 1876. Throughout the time of unfettered land in the Musselshell, the big cattle outfits, in an out-of-character move, shared the range with the huge sheep ranches.

Railroads came next in the line of succession to bring people to the valley. First there were the smaller lines … the Jawbone and Montana railroads, then the big one — the Milwaukee, with which the history and fortunes of the Musselshell Valley were inextricably linked for more than 70 years. The Chicago, Milwaukee & St. Paul Railroad Company was an established Midwest transport business. In 1905, management determined a need to expand westward to Seattle and tweaked its name to Chicago, Milwaukee, St. Paul & Pacific; in Montana it remained the "Milwaukee Road." Tracks began entering the state from South Dakota in 1906. One of the main objectives of the route was the agriculturally significant Musselshell Valley, which lay between the Great Northern and Northern Pacific realm. The Milwaukee reached the valley in 1908. Rails of the Jawbone, or Montana Road, owned by Richard Harlow were already in place along part of the planned way. The carrier first leased, then bought Harlow's right-of-way.

The Milwaukee line ran along the Musselshell River between Melstone and Martinsdale, then climbed through the river's South Fork over Summit and descended to the Smith River Valley. In building the route, workers moved the river's channel more than 100 times, something that could never be done today.

In 1915, the corporation announced it would electrify its engines between Harlowton and Avery, Idaho. This proved to be an efficient and less expensive way to operate. The engines that pushed the trains uphill traveled backward downhill, using both brakes as generators to recharge electricity used on inclines.

Milwaukee promotion campaigns convinced would-be settlers to move to central Montana. Towns sprang up along some of the sidings and "sodbusters" grabbed up bottomland.

A combination of the Homestead Acts, railroad "hucksterism" and years of adequate rain brought homesteaders to the Musselshell from 1900 through 1917. Then a series of droughts commencing in 1917, followed by the Great Depression, emptied the land. Faded hopes and dreams became the order of the day throughout the Musselshell Valley. Those able to hang on left relations who are now the pillars of the communities the river touches.

The Milwaukee's struggle under a huge debt and competition from other lines forced it to end its Montana service in 1980.

Musselshell country of present is the epitome of the old and the real Montana. It is free of big towns, sprawl, interstate highways and trinket shops. Uncluttered space dominates. The populace is unobtrusive and of the land; multi-generation ranches and farms the mainstay. Cattle, sheep, canvas-topped wagons and other signs of agriculture fit in well.

Meagher, Wheatland, Golden Valley, Musselshell, Petroleum and Garfield counties all claim the river. Combined, their population in 1990 was 11,191 and as of the 2000 census it was 11,502. The towns of Roundup, White Sulphur Springs, Harlowton and Ryegate hold 37 percent of the inhabitants. Roundup, with its 1,931 citizens, is by far the largest hamlet.

Founding tributaries of the river start in high terrain and drop through a mix of forest, meadows and sage covered hillsides, then combine in level topography at 4,700 feet. From this modest elevation, the Musselshell loses altitude slowly. Descending at the average rate of about seven feet per mile of riverbed, it finds its way to the Missouri River's channel at 2,160 feet.

Embarking on an eastward course, 132 air miles will be traversed through Montana's heartland before its identity is lost to the Missouri. In doing so, it will display what many folks consider to be the most beautiful drive in the state.

Near Martinsdale, as the valley widens and the main river is sent on its way, the loftiest summits of the Crazy Mountains rise on the south. The clear profile of the eastern extremity of the Little Belt Mountains is to the north. The river takes this view a fair distance, then as the jagged Crazies and the low arc of the Little Belts begin fading in the rearview mirror, the elongated mass of the Big Snowy Mountains rise with a north bearing as an island in central Montana's high plains. Now the Musselshell is on the prairie and as it moves toward the east, these mountains soon begin disappearing below the curvature of the horizon.

The valley deepens near Ryegate and the road climbs a couple of grades opening up views of the valley and the benches above it ... the panorama sprawls across a magnificent piece of Montana.

In terms of makeup of the terrain, a common thread runs through it. Open forests of Ponderosa pine and juniper contrast against cottonwoods of the river bottoms. In some places the land opens and in others it closes in as the canyon deepens, the distant vista hidden by sandstone bluffs and low hills. Relief is kept to a minimum. And there is no doubt this is ranch country.

Beyond Roundup, the mountains are out of sight and the country spreads to even larger proportions. Here the earth and sky fuse together with no interruptions.

A tribute to the rails that made the town of Harlowton. RICK AND SUSIE GRAETZ

Geologically speaking, most of the Musselshell landscape is simple and made of sedimentary rocks — limestone outcrops in the canyon of the North Fork are followed by shale and sandstone for most of the stream's journey. Near Roundup, the river meets the Fort Union Coal formations and as it turns north at Melstone, it is just on the edge of the Williston Basin oil pools.

Headwaters

As the centerpiece of the Upper Musselshell, the Castle Mountains, a massif of 8,000-foot peaks, provide ample water to the tentacles of the river from the north as well as the south and are in essence the Musselshell's primary birthing ground. Their name was attained from ridge top spires, resembling castle turrets, which dominate the visible igneous rocks of the western fringe of the range. Some reach more than 50 feet into the sky. The sedimentary limestone of the eastern rim isn't conducive to creating steeples, but it's the contact zone of the eastside sedimentary and westside igneous rocks that allowed the development of the intense mineralization in this uplift. Old prospector trails crisscrossing the forest canyons and ridgelines are remnants of when the historic Castles boasted the largest silver and lead ore mine in Montana.

In 1885 and 1886, Lafe Hemsly and his three brothers staked mining claims in the area; 200 other settlers promptly followed. Soon, underground mining for the rich veins of silver and lead commenced and the boomtown of Castle grew. A bank, two hotels, four newspapers, a dance hall, a church, a schoolhouse, a jail and 14 saloons were some of the established structures. Calamity Jane ran one of the restaurants. A stage line provided daily service to White Sulphur Springs, Townsend and Livingston.

Hemsly's Cumberland Mine was the richest of all. In September 1891 it was responsible for a $40,000 a month payroll. The Cumberland was doing so well that a New York capital firm purchased it and about 20 other nearby properties.

By 1891 there were 1,500 to 2,000 people in the area; but almost as hastily as the town grew, it died, never to recover. Folks began leaving the area in droves when the price of bullion drastically dropped in the silver panic of 1893. Now Castle and its collection of buildings stand silent.

Miners felt a railroad from Helena would provide a less expensive and easier way to get the ore to the smelters. The line started on the Missouri River south of Townsend, crossed the mountains at Ringling, climbed to Lennep and on to Castle. By the time the rails reached the disappearing mine camp in 1896, it was far too late. Supposedly the name "Jawbone" was given to the railroad owing to the persuasive talk of its promoters. Eventually, it continued through the Musselshell Valley to Harlowton and was known as the Montana Railroad, before ownership passed to the Milwaukee.

Lee Rostad, prominent Montana author, who with her husband Phil ranches in the Upper Musselshell near the South Fork's first tide, knows the terrain well. A description, in her words, follows.

"It's good land ... a valley between the Crazy Mountains to the south and the Castle Mountains to the north. The elevation is over 6,000 in places. The divide at Loweth was the highest point on the railroad east of the Continental Divide.

"Indians camped in the valley. Later, the settlers found rock hammers when they plowed an alfalfa field and spotted teepee rings along the higher banks of the stream.

"At the western end of the basin, the summit divides the drainages between the South Fork of the Smith River and the South Fork of the Musselshell. The settlement at the top was naturally called Summit, later changed to Loweth. When the railroad was built through, Summit supported a hotel for rail workers and later passengers. Its post office operated from 1915 to 1918. The eventual name alteration was for C.F. Loweth, chief engineer on the Milwaukee Railroad. The Loweth post office was closed in 1924, but the substation for the railroad and a half dozen railroad houses remained until the 1950s. Today, Loweth consists of a brick shell that was once the substation, a Montana Power post, the shipping yards for cattle, some foundations and a couple of apple trees.

"A few miles from Loweth, Warm Spring Creek, which rises in the Castles and the Bozeman Fork Creek, which comes from the Crazies, join to form the South Fork of the Musselshell. Twenty seven miles from Loweth, the South Fork joins the North Fork at Martinsdale."

Lee adds, "The upper river tributary is predominantly Norwegian and most people are related and that adds to a way of life that is close, but often very structured as the young people work into the fabric of the community. A surprising number return after school or another career."

Distinctive for its often-photographed white Lutheran church of 1910 vintage, Lennep sits approximately halfway between Summit and Martinsdale. In 1899, the Montana Railroad gave birth to the town and it continued to serve as a station when the Milwaukee Road later bought the line. Lennep received its name from a conductor on the Jawbone Railroad who named it in honor of his hometown, Lennep, Germany. Not much is left of this once thriving place save the church, schoolhouse and a few buildings.

Passing Lennep, the South Fork enters a wider valley and meanders through the sheep grazing grounds of the old Bair family ranch, now a museum, before joining the North Fork.

Exploring the North Fork requires a visit to the town of White Sulphur Springs. Positioned west of the divide separating the drainages of the Musselshell and Smith rivers, it is physically just on the border of the Musselshell country. However, as the seat of Meagher County, which asserts ownership of all of the geography of the river's headwaters, it is entitled to be part of the Musselshell's domain.

The Musselshell River east of Ryegate. RICK AND SUSIE GRAETZ

For many years, Indians used the area's hot springs. James Brewer, a traveler on the Carroll Trail, noticed them and in 1866 built a stage stop and developed the springs for folks passing through. However, it was the successful pursuit of cattle and sheep ranching that grew the town, although the mineral waters were, and still are, a draw.

Verle and Patricia Rademacher, publishers of the Meagher County News, have been in White Sulphur Springs for 37 years. Verle feels the community is stable because of agriculture, the Forest Service and recreation opportunities. He also touts the fact that the hydrological divide east of town is the true central Montana watershed as it sends waters in all four compass directions.

The Musselshell's North Fork drifts out of the Little Belts northeast of White Sulphur Springs and just south of Lost Fork Ridge, eventually finding its way south to the Bair Reservoir where it leaves the man-made lake in an easterly flow.

West of the reservoir between mileposts 58 and 59 near the Jamison Trail off of the south side of Hwy 12, on July 5, 1866, a couple of prospectors uncovered a copper deposit. Staking their claims, they named their camp Copperopolis. Mining occurred on and off for several years but the discovery never lived up to its initial promise. All that is left today is a mine dump.

In the summer of 1867, about ten miles from Copperopolis, Fort Howie was assembled as a line of defense against the perceived threat of attacks during the so-called "Indian Wars" of 1867. Three months after completion, the fort was abandoned. Its location was east of Checkerboard in a hay meadow on the north side of the road at about milepost sixty-nine.

The North Fork touches the summer fishing retreat of Checkerboard just down from Bair Reservoir. In 1920, the Sumpter Inn was built here, then in 1945 the name was changed to Checkerboard after a stream in the area. Fifteen miles from this place, the North Fork meets its kin from the south and the Musselshell begins its surge.

The Musselshell Heads East

Martinsdale serves as a human outpost a short distance south of the confluence. The town began as Gauglersville after Frank Gaugher in 1876, when he built a store along the Carroll Trail. Richard Clendennin went into competition against Gaugher by building another store and a hotel in 1877. In 1878, the newcomer was successful in his bid for a postal route and renamed the trading post Martinsdale after Martin Maginnis (who never lived there), a territorial delegate to the US Congress. In 1899, when Richard Harlow's Jawbone Railroad came through, the town was moved two miles to its present location.

Charlie Bair, one of the most prominent men in the development of agriculture in the Musselshell, began ranching in 1891 and up until 1910, held a grazing lease in Crow Country near the Yellowstone. Somewhere in between these years he went to the gold mines of the Yukon and made his fortune promoting a machine that pressurized and heated water, a boon for mining gold in the frozen Klondike. He returned to Montana with plenty of capital.

Bair lost the reservation lease in 1910 and moved all of his operations to Martinsdale. In the '20s and '30s, he proceeded to buy large tracts of land as it became available. He also bought ownership in the Martinsdale Land and Livestock Company and became the majority shareholder. It had been estimated that at one time prior to 1920, he had more than 300,000 head of sheep, one of the largest herds in the world!

Charlie Bair passed on in 1943 in his 85th year. This individual who arrived in Montana in 1883 working for the Northern Pacific Railway as a conductor, left immense wealth and a legacy behind. His family, especially his daughters (Alberta the last surviving member of the family died in 1993 at the age of 98) were philanthropic to the hilt. Their home at Martinsdale, housing an incredible collection of antiques and artifacts, became the Bair Family Museum after Alberta's death.

Martinsdale now serves local ranchers, hunters and anglers. Some of the old buildings including the depot still remain. A bank stands out as a remnant of the homestead days. The Crazy Mountain Inn, built in 1901, has been renovated and does a lively business. Sheep once found in large numbers still graze the fields and hills surrounding the town.

Gordon Butte, just on the west edge of Martinsdale, is a prominent Musselshell landmark and perhaps the final outlier of the Northern Rockies along the river. Geologists Dave Alt and Don Hyndman call it "an outpost of the Crazy Mountains resembling a giant hockey puck." More than a mile in diameter and about 700 feet high, this "laccolith" is an almost perfectly circular intrusion of molten rock, created when a blister of magma was injected into the area's sedimentary rocks.

Two Dot, named for early-day cattleman "Two Dot Wilson," touches the Musselshell River 17 miles below Martinsdale. Wilson's brand consisted of two dots, with one on the shoulder of the animal and another on the thigh, thus making it hard for rustlers to change the mark.

Roberta Cheney, in her book "Names on the Face of Montana," relates an interesting story about Wilson. ""Two Dot" was never one for dressing up, and at one time in Chicago after he had gone there with a load of cattle, he was arrested for vagrancy because he was so dirty and unkempt. He asked the policemen to go to the bank with him and when it was verified that Wilson had just deposited more than $10,000 the policemen let him go. The incident had begun as a practical joke ... two of the cow hands Wilson brought to Chicago with him decided to play a trick on the boss and pointed him out to the police as vagrant. "Two Dot" found out about it and went the cowboys one better. He took the next train home and left them in Chicago without any money or a return ticket."

In 1900, the Montana Railroad reached Two Dot, facilitating the town's growth. As with every other Musselshell Valley town, the homestead years swelled the population and the expansion of businesses. The 1910s were heady days, until the drought changed everything.

Nineteen miles from Two Dot, Harlowton, county seat of Wheatland County, guards the river. "Harlo," as it is commonly called, is a crossroads of travel from the Yellowstone River country, the Musselshell Valley and the Judith Basin. Richard Harlow, developer of the Jawbone and the Montana Railroad, laid his tracks toward the small settlement of Merino. As an act of gratitude, the town folks changed the name to Harlowton. When the Milwaukee Railroad bought out the Montana Road, Harlowton served as the division switching point. Trains headed east had steam locomotives put in place of their electric engines, and westbound trains dropped their steamers in exchange for electric engines.

Harlowton's main street is typical of most small Montana towns, neat and orderly but with vacant buildings. Local quarries provided sandstone for storefronts constructed by immigrant stonemasons who had developed their trade in Europe. As a result, part of the downtown is preserved as an historic district.

Agriculture is now the town's bread and butter. Jerry Miller, publisher and editor of The Times-Clarion, Harlowton's paper, says that when the Milwaukee pulled out in 1980, 125 jobs were lost, but many of the workers managed to stay in the area. He considers that the town's economy should remain firm. The potential for more wind generated electrical power in the Judith Gap area is real and he would like to see restoration of the historic Graves Hotel finished, as it would attract more visitors. The grand old edifice was named for A.C. Graves, an early 1900s Harlowton promoter.

The Times-Clarion was the longtime domain of legendary Montana newspaperman and historian Hal Stearns, now of Helena, who wrote extensively on the Upper Musselshell. Stearns owned the paper from 1941 until 1973. The current publisher began working for Stearns in 1948, then bought the weekly in 1973.

Judith Gap, a broad wind-swept divide between the Big Snowy and Little Belt mountains, north of the Musselshell, carries Hwy 191 to the river valley at Harlowton. Indians following the bison used the path over this prairie pass for centuries. In the 1870s, stage and freight lines traversed the old Carroll Trail that crossed through the Gap. Later the Great Northern and Milwaukee railroads laid track over it.

Harlowton to Melstone

East of Harlowton and beyond where the road over the Judith Gap meets the Musselshell, the river edges closer to the roadway. The wide-open valley begins narrowing somewhat, the river canyon deepens and heavy cottonwood growth begins to show. Approaching Ryegate, the sandstone rimrocks the river is known for become more plentiful.

Shawmut, about 17 miles from Harlowton, is a small outpost with a collection of buildings from the early part of the 1900s, and occupies space north of the river. Named after a local rancher, it is sheep raising country.

Just beyond Shawmut and a bit south of the highway sits the former town site of Barber. Next to the railroad, it was platted in 1910 by Henry Bartz. Today, only a couple of old buildings and a church are left. But in 1920, there was a bank, a hotel, a general store, an implement store, a post office and a church. Originally, Barber was named Shawmut. When the railroad needed more land and ranchers refused to sell, the train depot was literally picked up and moved by rail eight miles to the west and the "new" Shawmut came into being. Roberta Cheney mentions in Names on the Face of Montana, that someone from the original Shawmut "quipped that they had been given a clean shave and should change the name to Barber — and so they did."

As the homesteaders left, the general store and post office stayed open until the late '50s. By the end of 1970s, only the church was still viable and remains so to this day.

Fifteen miles east of Shawmut and on the north side of the river, Ryegate — the seat of Golden Valley County — is propped up against three-mile-long sandstone bluffs. A railroad official noticed fields of rye on the then Sims-Garfield Ranch, and named the town after the crop. Ryegate holds the distinction of being home to Montana's first woman sheriff, Ruth Garfield. In 1920, when her husband was killed, she was appointed to finish his remaining two-year term. As county seat, Ryegate holds local government jobs that add some permanence lacking in other nearby towns.

Sixteen miles below Ryegate, Lavina is on the north bank of the Musselshell at the junction of Montana Hwy 3 and US Hwy 12. Hwy 3 serves as Lavina's Main Street and leads south to Billings. For a time the place was called "White City" as the residents had a penchant for painting most of the structures white. Records show two different versions of how it became Lavina. One claims it was named for the daughter of the housekeeper of an early day settler named Vance. Other historical notes say it was named for the girlfriend of Walter Burke, who was hired in 1882 by frontier merchant Thomas Power of Fort Benton, to establish a stage stop on the 220-mile road between Fort Benton and Billings.

Two prominent vintage structures, the Adams Hotel and Slayton Mercantile, are reminders of a different era in Lavina. The Adams, now closed, for many years served travelers on the trail. The Mercantile is the town's social center. Lavina's post office was opened in 1883.

Heading east of Lavina, the river is out of sight of Hwy 12 for about 10 or 12 miles. It is 23 miles from Lavina to Roundup where Highway 87 wanders up from Billings to the south. Along the way, the Bull Mountains, a coal bearing sedimentary uplift, come into view on the southeast. Coal found here was used to fuel the steam engines of the Milwaukee Railroad.

The highest points of this 50-mile-long range of low mountains are just a bit over 4,000 feet. Their sandstone benches separate the Missouri and the Yellowstone river basins and provide water to the Musselshell. Fires have ravaged the Bulls, once heavily timbered, in recent years.

"Capital of the Bulls," Roundup is the largest town on the Musselshell. Close to 2,000 folks call the place home. In 1882, just below the sandstone rimrocks, a couple built a saloon and store near where Half Breed Creek and the Musselshell meet. A post office opened in 1883.

It became known for coal and the Milwaukee Railroad, but the moniker comes from the 1880 days of the open range. A short distance west of where the town now lies, cowboys met from throughout the Musselshell to participate in their annual roundup.

When the Milwaukee Railroad made it here in 1907, the town's demeanor changed dramatically and growth took off. The unfenced, free grass times were long gone, having been ended by an influx of 1903 homesteaders, and although ranching persisted, the cowboy posture was lost for sometime to come. The company established the Republic Coal Company when it laid its tracks into Roundup. In essence it became a company town, although the actual coal mining camp of Klein was located two miles to the south.

A Milwaukee Railroad historian claimed, "The Milwaukee Road became

Roundup's modern founder, employer and provider." By 1913, 3,000 people called the area home, many of them from across the Atlantic. Mining of the hard black fuel attracted immigrants from Eastern Europe. The Europeans knew how to mine coal and became a valuable asset; their descendants add greatly to the community today.

Roundup's Musselshell Museum's historical records estimated at one time 600 miners dug enough coal to fill a railcar every 12 minutes. One vertical shaft in an area mine was dug 287 feet into the ground.

Today, coal mining, the Milwaukee Railroad and the homesteaders have departed, but a stable community lingers on.

Twenty-three miles east of Roundup, just south of Hwy 12 on the southern side of the river, is the village of Musselshell. Now a mere shadow of its former self, at onetime it was called "The Crossing" and was the only spot between Fort Maginiss near Lewistown and Fort Custer on the Yellowstone River to traverse the Musselshell.

By the 1870s, many large cattle companies drove their herds up from Texas to winter on the rich grasses in the valleys of central Montana. The crossing at Musselshell was considered the last stop on the Texas Trail. From here, the livestock spread out to the north to forage the open range.

In 1880, Larry Reed and his Crow wife built a cabin and a store near the original ford, and on the south bank, called "Lower Crossing", giving birth to what would become Musselshell. For a brief period the place was called "Reed's Crossing" A post office opened in 1883, presumably under the name Musselshell. As the town grew, newspaper accounts touted it as the "Metropolis of the Valley" and for a time it was the largest settlement along the river.

Adair Rademacher, a member of the local water board, explained that today there are only 40 water users, but at one time there were five or six saloons, two banks and two dry good stores. She points out that the Handel brothers were responsible for the fact that the town didn't get even bigger. It seems the Milwaukee Railroad was approaching the area and had asked the men to donate some of their land for a right of way. They refused and as a result, the train roundhouse for the railroad was established farther east at Melstone.

Mrs. Rademacher stated it was coal and the railroad that attracted people to the town, especially Eastern Europeans. Not only did they know how to mine coal, but also "were the only ones willing to work hard enough to lay railroad track in the hot weather experienced on the prairie of central Montana." Most of the miners worked in the Star Mine, a Bair family holding, northeast of town. The Star operated pumps night and day as some its tunnels ran under the Musselshell.

A sturdy red brick building, still enduring in Musselshell, was once the Hotel Stockwell. Built by a Mrs. Stockwell, an entrepreneur who as well as owning and running a hotel, traveled to purchase fabrics to create items to sell. Her two daughters married the Handel brothers.

The yellow firebrick school building, no longer needed as schoolhouse, was, as of July 1. 2003, given to the town to be used as a community center.

Melstone, 14 miles farther down river, was named for Melvin Stone, an Associated Press reporter who was aboard a train with the Milwaukee's president when the rails first achieved this area. The town, a beneficiary of the Handel brothers' refusal to donate land, was also more populated than Musselshell during the homestead era and height of the Milwaukee Railroad period. Kim Walker, present-day City Clerk and Treasurer, said there are approximately 129 individuals living in Melstone as of 2003, and that in 1990 the population was rated at 139.

As to the Melstone area, Mrs. Walker states, "it grows on you and you learn to love it."

Drought of the past several years has hurt this town that now relies on ranching, although cattle herds are now building back. The number of ranches, all multi-generational operations, are staying about the same; in some cases the children are returning to take over management.

Dorothy Minnie, born on a homestead 14 miles from Melstone, lived in the area for 83 years. Mrs. Minnie related when she was younger people stayed close to home, the "homesteaders didn't travel much … transportation wasn't available in the area and everyone helped each other out." Now she said, "people go to Billings, 60 miles away, for lunch." She reminisced that "as kids they didn't go to town very often and Melstone was quite big." There were many businesses including banks, at least four grocery stores, and three hotels. Once, she and her sister were sent into Melstone to get bread and Mrs. Minnie said, "We got lost getting the bread in the downtown area."

On to The UL Bend and The Missouri

Two miles east of Melstone, at the "Big Bend of the Musselshell", the river makes an abrupt turn to the north and enters landscape considerably drier than the river's course up until this point. Badlands show and the rises are mostly buttes and rock outcroppings. The view shed is extensive as the river leads into a part of Montana often called "the Big Open" and "the Big Dry." The Musselshell seems to get lost on this part of the vast prairie as it cuts a canyon through the sandstone. The only giveaway of its presence is glimpses of ribbons of cottonwoods.

According to Dorothy Minnie, this section in the earlier days was sheep, cattle, and homestead country, but she remembers it was always more arid to the north of Melstone.

As well as changing directions, the river leaves Hwy 12 trailing off to the east. County Road 500, mostly gravel for 34 miles to Hwy 200, now follows the stream from a distance. Private land must be crossed to get to the water. By late summer, this stretch of the Musselshell to its end (approximately 130 miles) is nearly dewatered. Heat, lack of rain and upstream irrigation add up to meager substance, if any, to fill the channel. White alkaline deposits often take the place of liquid flow.

Mosby, at the Hwy 200 crossing of the Musselshell, today retains only an abandoned house. In 1891, William and Mary Mosby situated their post office to the east side of the Musselshell crossing and established a ferry. In 1904, they moved farther down river to the present site and kept a ferry going until a wooden bridge was built in 1918. Since the post office was in their home, it became a center for ranch families from afar as they came to collect their mail.

Mrs. Mosby once wrote a piece for the Winnett Times. Speaking of the Musselshell and the Mosby area she noted "... it is wild, rugged, spectacularly scenic, lonesome and harsh, but it's good country — very good country. Spring ice jams on the Musselshell turn loose raging floods that cover bottom lands, and tear down fences and strew dead trees and other debris." The Lewistown News Argus paraphrased the thoughts of homesteaders from the same place: "We are 80 miles from a doctor and the dirt trails can be knee-deep in mud or belly-deep in snow before the paved highway is reached that will take people to Lewistown, Winnett or Jordan."

From Mosby, the Musselshell makes its final 74-mile run through a landscape not very often seen. Half way from its terminus it enters the crown jewel of our nation's wildlife refuge system, the 1.1 million acre Charles M. Russell National Wildlife Refuge. The canyon again narrows as the Missouri River Breaks begin.

Where the magical river ends and Fort Peck Lake and the Missouri River start is somewhat nebulous especially from the air. The Musselshell is silting in its channel and the lake segment of the Missouri in the area of U.L. Bend. Before Fort Peck Dam's 1940 completion, the free flowing Missouri carried valuable silt from the Musselshell down river to create new beds for cottonwood seedlings and built islands beneficial to wildlife.

Very quiet now, the Musselshell's terminus was a place of significance, though, in the time of cattle barons and earlier. Here vast herds of bison crossed the "big muddy" on their annual migrations, and as a major fording point for the Indians of eastern Montana, battles and skirmishes often occurred there with the white man and among themselves over hunting rights and other hostilities. A succession of fur trading posts, wood yards, military camps, ranches and homesteads at one time or another occupied the area.

The confluence was also a gathering place for horse rustlers and other outlaws. Horse stealing rings tormented ranchers in the Missouri Breaks in the late 1800s. Raiding ranches in Montana, Wyoming, the Dakotas and southern Canada, bandits drove the livestock to remote areas of the Breaks in and around the Musselshell, "worked the brands," then drove them to Canada for sale, repeating the process with stolen Canadian livestock. On the return trip, the outlaws were always on the lookout for the law and vigilantes.

One of the most famous incidents of "vigilante justice" occurred in 1884. Granville Stuart, operator of the DHS ranch, led a group of local stockmen to the Musselshell to clean out a large horse-thieving ring. Two outlaws were hanged there and two more suffered the same fate at Rocky Point upriver on the Missouri. A few days later these stockmen, who later became known as "Stuart's Stranglers," apprehended more horse thieves at an abandoned wood yard at Bates Point, 15 miles below the mouth of the Musselshell. Five outlaws were killed in the ensuing gun battle. Seven men managed to escape, but five of these were later captured by soldiers in eastern Montana and returned to the vigilantes. They were hanged from cottonwoods that grew in the broad flat bottoms of the Musselshell.

The area surrounding the joining of the Missouri and Musselshell may have been the epitome of the old and Wild West. Much has been written about it. In 1885, Peter Koch penned some of his memoirs of life he had spent at "Muscleshell" in 1869 and 1870. "From Fort Benton to the Yellowstone the country along both sides of the Missouri was as wild as when Lewis and Clark first stemmed its turbid current. It is true that a few trading posts were planted along its banks, that a number of steamboats yearly made their difficult way between and over its sand-bars to Fort Benton or Cow Island, that at rare intervals a clearing had been made around a wood-yard in one of the densely wooded points. But the steamboat passed, and when the sound of its whistle was beyond hearing no sign of its passage was left ... The trading post did not become the nucleus of a village or a center for spreading civilization. It was simply a place to accumulate robes, skins and furs.

"The center of this life on the upper part of the river was the trading post at Muscleshell. To those who landed there early in June 1869, the place presented a characteristic sight. It enjoyed at that time its greatest prosperity and formed quite a little village ... the settlement was ambitious and aspired to become a city. A town site was laid out, and hope were entertained, that a military post would be established, and that this would be made the shipping point for Montana freight instead of Fort Benton on account of the difficulties of navigation on the upper river. But all those ambitions were destined to disappointment. No military post was established (only camps). The Indian trade declined for various reasons. With the completion of the Union Pacific Railroad the river route lost importance for a time, and when it was revived not Muscleshell but Carroll was selected as the shipping point. When I left the place the Missouri had already undermined some of the houses, and to-day not a vestige is left to show where the settlement once stood."

Sadly, the Musselshell ends unceremoniously in a sluggish flow ... silting is not a pretty way to go out. And in terms of legend and notoriety, the Big Missouri that receives its meager contribution, has a far greater and widespread reputation. At this point then, the Musselshell accepts its status. But to the folks upriver, and to those who know and appreciate Montana's blend of a diverse landscape and history, the Musselshell River is every bit a grand river and a fine asset to the Missouri and Big Sky Country.

—RICK AND SUSIE GRAETZ

LEWISTOWN

Seventeen miles east of its junction with Hwy 191 on the edge of the Judith Basin, US 87 crests a hill and presents one of the most impressive views of any town in Montana. Lewistown, the centerpiece of Big Sky Country (it is the geographic center of the state), spreads out in the beautiful valley of Big Spring Creek. The gold-painted dome of the significant Fergus County Courthouse leads your eye down towards the historic buildings of Main Street.

This seat of Fergus County, is surrounded by mountains ... the Moccasins to the northwest, the Judith Mountains rise on the east and northeast and the inviting Big Snowies flank the south. Just to the north, the Missouri River cuts its way through badlands and river breaks. Big open country ... ranches, wheat fields and prairies fill in elsewhere.

Fort Sherman Trading Post, established in 1873, was the first sign a settlement might take hold here. Speculation had it that the Crow Indian Agency would be moved from its site on Mission Creek near Livingston to what would eventually become Lewistown. The relocation never took place, but the post played a part for the Carroll Road, a trail leading from the short-

The grand Fergus County Courthouse anchors downtown Lewistown. RICK AND SUSIE GRAETZ

lived settlement of Carroll, on the Missouri River, through the Big Spring Creek Valley on its way to the gold camps near Helena. Carroll was used as a port by Missouri steamboats during the low water years of 1874–75.

In 1874, Fort Sherman was eventually sold to the partnership of Reed and Bowles, who shifted the new post about two miles south of today's townsite. Only one original building is still standing. The partners split and in January 1881 Reed founded the Reed's Fort Post Office.

Camp Lewis, named for Major William H. Lewis, was built in 1874 in the present downtown. In March of 1884, a post office was opened at the camp and the place took on the name Lewistown. In August 1885, Reed's Fort and Lewistown merged and the original mail center closed. The first permanent settlers entered the area in 1879 when about 35 Metis families (a mix of Chippewa Indians and French Canadians) came here from Canada.

This central gem witnessed most of the activities that were the underpinnings of Montana. Initially it catered to wagons carrying freight from Carroll landing. In the late 1870s and early '80s, the territory witnessed ranchers driving cattle from western Montana to the open range and lush grasses of these parts. In 1880, Granville Stuart, often considered the father of the state, partnered with others to establish the sprawling DHS Ranch northeast of Lewistown. That same year, gold discovered in the Judith Mountains gave birth to the towns of Maiden and Giltedge. Kendall, in the neighboring Moccasin Mountains, came along on an 1890's strike. And even though the Indian wars were winding down, Fort McGinnis was established in 1880 on the east side of the Judith Mountains to protect settlers in the region.

Lewistown was incorporated in 1889 and the Central Montana Railway, later to be purchased by the Milwaukee Road, arrived in 1903, giving a boost to the agricultural economy of the area.

Homesteaders arrived here en masse between 1903 and 1914. In the early 1920s, though most of the newcomers in the state were forced off the land by drought and depression, many of the sodbusters that came to the Lewistown region had better luck.

After the depression years, Lewistown calmed down to the quiet and peaceful agricultural trade center of 6,500 people it is today.

The downtown area is healthy and well supported by local residents. The local paper, The News Argus, has a colorful motto: "covering central Montana like the stars."

Of Lewistown's many bragging points, the number one attraction is its ultra-pure water supply, emanating from the Big Snowy Mountains. Snow melt and rain seeping into the limestone found in these 8,000-foot peaks finds its way to the Big Springs south of town. Fifty thousand gallons per minute rise from the bubbling springs in an area that not only serves as the town's the water center, but also as a fish hatchery.

Brewery Flats, an approximately 26-acre patch of ground, formerly owned in part by the Fish and Game, occupies the bottom lands along Big Spring Creek just to the south of town. It's an open space with a trail system that also provides fishing access. Once displaced meanders have now been replaced. It's possible that in the future, acquisition of private land adjacent to the current project will bring the total protected land to approximately 110 acres.

Three parts of town as well as the Fergus County Courthouse are listed in the National Register of Historic Places. There's also a distinct style of architecture throughout created by Croatian Masons who migrated here between 1898 and 1915. For a while, Lewistown was called "the stone city." The Carnegie Library built in 1905 is a good example of this.

The Central Montana Historical Museum and Lewistown's Art Center have added to the rich culture of the area. Highlights of summer are the fair and rodeo held the last weekend in July. And the trails of the Big Snowy Mountains beckon to climbing, hiking and cave exploration experiences. From their long flat tops, the very nice landscape that is Lewistown and the center of Montana make a fine panorama.

—RICK AND SUSIE GRAETZ

THE BIG SNOWY MOUNTAINS

Colors filled the entire sky and painted the many distant mountains in all manners of red, orange and purple. Arriving at the summit of Greathouse Peak in time to experience a prolonged and glorious sunset, we received benediction and a just reward for an arduous day's hike.

These Big Snowy Mountains ascend in an elongated mass from the ocean of prairie lands of central Montana ... a distinct range with a perch that looks out on the farthest-reaching views in Big Sky Country. This unique mountain complex is located 15 miles south of Lewistown, the geographic center of the state. Instead of a rugged summit line, an eight-mile-long tundra-like meadow, over 8,200 feet high, makes up a large portion of the top. One lengthy stretch, a narrow smooth spine, is appropriately called Knife Blade Ridge. On a day when the air is clear, from the Snowies' highest point, 8,681-foot Greathouse Peak, a hiker can survey a 300-mile span from the Sweetgrass Hills, near Shelby in the northwest, to the Beartooth and Pryor Mountains below the Yellowstone River Country to the south and southeast.

These east-west aligned mountains are made of a porous limestone that allows rain and snowmelt to seep down through them into an aquifer that pours out in several springs; including Big Springs, which supplies Lewistown with its water — reportedly the purest in the nation. Deep bowl-like canyons and sparse tree cover characterizes the dry south side of the Snowies'. North face canyons are longer, have a somewhat gentler rise and are heavily forested.

In the western end of the Big Snowies, over time, caves have been etched

Lewistown (center), Judith Mts. (far right) and Moccasins (far center) from the Big Snowies.
RICK AND SUSIE GRAETZ

out of the limestone. Many smaller ones are still unexplored. The largest of the known caverns, Big Ice Cave, just below the top ridge, is a treat on hot summer days ... the temperature inside is 40 degrees cooler than outside. From a five by ten-foot entry, the cave slopes downward to a room about 100 feet long and 75 feet wide. Refrigeration comes from a heavily compacted icy snowdrift that lasts the year round. This underground wonder is accessed from Neil Creek on the southern perimeter.

Popular Crystal Lake, on the north, is reached by Rock Creek Road, off of Montana 200 west of Lewistown. From here, a trail leads to another prominent cave, Devil's Chute. A footpath off of this route also heads to the nearby Big Ice Cave. Sharp eyes will spot marine fossils in the vicinity of the caves. Just below the lake, take a three and one-half-mile trek up the East Fork of Rock Creek to the stunning Crystal Cascades, a 100-foot stair step waterfall.

Further east, Half Moon Creek Trail approaches the Snowies' divide from the north, and the Swimming Woman Canyon Trail reaches it via the southern flank. Both byways meet near Greathouse Peak and just west of 8,678-foot Old Baldy, the second highest summit. Once winter's snow banks melt, the terrain up high is dry, so backpackers planning on overnight stays along the crest need to carry all their water with them.

With the exception of the Crystal Lake area and caves, the Snowies are quietly used. Their outstanding wilderness characteristics have allowed for a 104,000-acre core area to be set-aside as a wilderness study area by the US Congress. Hawks, golden and bald eagles, moose, deer, elk, goats and bear thrive in the pristine and quiet environment of the high country of these mountains.

A factor in keeping these central Montana mountains wild has been the lack of commercial gold deposits or extensive areas of harvestable timber. The folks in Lewistown take pride in this place. They were alarmed when exploration for a possible open pit copper mine in Swimming Woman Canyon was proposed several years back. The plan has since been dropped.

For a good overview map of the area, use the Lewis and Clark National Forest Jefferson Division Visitors Map. An index for USGS topo maps for the range is available at your local outdoor shop. The Lewis and Clark National Forest ranger stations at Harlowton and Stanford manage the public land in the Big Snowy Mountains.

—RICK AND SUSIE GRAETZ

MOUNTAIN NOTES

Highwood Mountains

Used by the Blackfeet Indians as vantage points to spot bison herds, these mountains — east of Great Falls and rising to 7,000 feet, are believed to be remnants of ancient volcanoes. Their highest point is Highwood Baldy at 7,625 feet. When the Lewis and Clark Expedition first saw them in 1805, they mistakenly thought these were the Rocky Mountains.

Judith Mountains

Northeast of Lewistown, 6,400-foot Judith Peak is the tallest summit in the Judiths. A road ascends to its top and offers fantastic views of the surrounding Judith Basin country. The semi-ghost town of Maiden, once a booming gold and silver community, is also reached via this route.

In the late 1800s and early 1900s, the Judiths were heavily mined. It is almost impossible to wander through them now without stumbling upon reminders of that era.

The Mocassin Mountains

Separated into north and south segments by Warm Springs Creek, these high hills are just to the northwest of Lewistown and across the valley from the Judiths. With the exception of their apexes that are on BLM ground, the surrounding country is in private ownership. The highest points are about 5,600 feet.

Little Belt Mountains

Located southeast of Great Falls, the Little Belts are 70 miles across and 60 miles from north to south, reaching from the Smith River on the west to Judith Gap below their east side. They're known for logging, mining, Yogo sapphires and skiing; Showdown, Montana's oldest downhill ski area, is just above King's Hill Pass in the center of the massif.

A few of their broad peaks rise over 8,000'. Mount Baldy, 9,175', and Yogo Peak, 8,801', are the highest. Two of Montana's most fantastic wild places, the Middle Fork of the Judith River and the Tender Foot/Deep Creek area, are in these central Montana mountains

Little Snowy Mountains

An eastern and lower offshoot of the Big Snowy Mountains, extending 12 miles in an east west axis to the southeast of Lewistown, their highest elevation is just less than 5,800 feet.

Bull Mountains

This 50-mile-long range of low mountains and hills is just south of Roundup and north of Billings. Its highest points are just a bit over 4,000 feet. Once heavily timbered, in recent years, fires have ravaged the Bulls. Their sandstone benches separate the Missouri and the Yellowstone river basins, and provide water to the Mussellshell River. Most of this country is in private ownership, and rough public roads traverse them.

—RICK AND SUSIE GRAETZ

MISSOURI BACK COUNTRY BYWAY

Thirty-eight miles north of Lewistown, Hwy 236 rolls into the small ranching town of Winifred. Most outsiders passing through are heading 26 miles farther northwest to Judith Landing, a popular take out place for floaters coming down the Upper Missouri River Breaks National Monument.

More than just the historic Landing makes this area attractive. The Missouri Breaks National Back Country Byway points east out of Winifred via the Knox Ridge Road. It traverses through badlands, coulees, rolling prairie, and in places, overlooks the Missouri River. From its high points the horizon extends for a hundred miles or more. The Little Rockies, Judith, Bear Paws and Moccasin mountains stand out. And this part of the Missouri Breaks is rich in wildlife ... sort of an extension of the Charles M. Russell National Wildlife Refuge immediately to the east. Antelope, big horn sheep, elk, white-tailed deer, mule deer, prairie dogs, beaver, grouse and hundreds of species of birds make this terrain their home.

The best chariot to use for this circular excursion is one with all-wheel drive and high clearance. A Subaru Outback can do it. If you have a highway rig, you can still negotiate the Knox Ridge Road segment. And there is nothing wrong with doubling back ... the scenery looks different facing the other direction. Although the miles are short, (less than 100 round-trip) take at least 2 days to wander. You'll need to get out of your roadster and walk the ridges, climb the buttes and descend to the river.

The route starts in Winifred. About 12 miles out, a BLM kiosk posts interesting information about the trip ahead. Take the Knox Ridge Road to US 191 and the Fred Robinson Bridge area. Eat your lunch or camp under the big cottonwoods along the Missouri at James Kipp Recreation Area and enjoy reading the displayed historical information. The last several miles of the Knox road, before the highway, pass through the western end of the CMR National Wildlife Refuge.

For the Refuge section of this passage, you'll be atop one of the highest ridge lines in the area. Looking north, you're gazing at the Little Rockies, below you can see Two Calf and Grand islands as well as the Kendall Bottoms. Lewis and Clark camped near here on May 24, 1805.

Reversing back about seven miles from Hwy 191, a right turn on the Middle Two Calf Road takes you further into the breaks and some great view points (they all should be signed). The first one is the five-mile pitch down to Woodhawk Bottom, site of an old homestead, next the Woodhawk Trail turns north, about 2 miles beyond the bottom access, and leads to Deweese and Sunshine Ridges. These are spots that will allow you to drink in some very nice prairie and river scenery and imagine the past.

Beneath where you are sitting, and for that matter all around, Blackfeet warriors and hunters searched for their enemies and the millions of bison that trampled the ground. The Corps of Discovery walked the banks in front. If you were on this spot in 1859, you could have witnessed the Chippwea, the first steamboat to come up the Missouri, on its way to Fort Benton. And if you managed to get back to one of these ridges on September 23, 1877, and looked down on Cow Island, you would have observed the great Chief Joseph and the Nez Perce people as they encountered soldiers guarding supplies near the island; they took what they needed and burned the rest. Look up Cow Creek on the other side of the river; that was the trail the Nez Perce used in their effort to reach freedom in Canada as they fled from the pursuing US Army.

There are plenty of scenic options ... use your feet to find them. Carry plenty of water and wear sturdy leather boots as protection against the small cactus and other things that tend to stick to soft boots. And be wary of rattlesnakes; they make their living here. Only follow the Middle Two Calf Road if you have the right vehicle and don't attempt the Byway if it has been raining or rain is expected. These roads turn to gumbo when wet and you could have an unplanned extended stay.

In planning to explore this country, two BLM maps are the best ones to use: Winifred and Number 16. The Bureau of Land Management Lewistown Office manages the Byway in cooperation with the US Fish and Wildlife Service and Fergus County.

—RICK AND SUSIE GRAETZ

UPPER YELLOWSTONE RIVER

GATHERING SOME OF THE FINEST MOUNTAIN AND PRAIRIE TOPOGRAPHY ON THE planet … peaks reaching past 13,000 feet in elevation, the largest high mountain lake on the continent, dense evergreen forests, buttes, colorful badlands, deep canyons and sweet smelling sage and juniper covered hills, Montana's Yellowstone River drains a 70,000 square mile piece of the west in grand fashion. Once serving as "a moving highway" into the wilderness, this unique river mirrored the passage of millions of bison, the travels of the Corps of Discovery, creation of the nation's first national park, the foundations of a state and the unfortunate ousting of the regions first occupants … the great Indian nations.

Long stretches haven't changed since the Yellowstone's not-so-long-ago yesterdays, much of the water continues to course through clean space. Human presence has grown along the river, but for the most part it is unobtrusive. One could say this fabled waterway still represents the real Montana.

We find it fitting, that for all the beauty collected within its journey and the history represented, the Yellowstone is persistently the free spirit she was born to be. The 670-mile-long waterway remains the nation's longest undammed river, because the people of Montana, from all political persuasions, felt she was too valuable and important to flow in any other way. They demanded she be left alone!

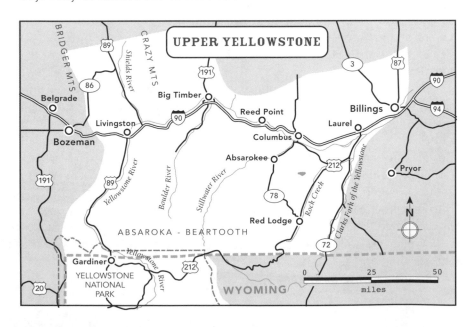

Yellowstone River in the Paradise Valley. RICK AND SUSIE GRAETZ

Thanks to this wise decision, the Yellowstone continues to distribute her rewards: diverse eco-systems follow her path, healthy stands of towering cottonwoods grow in profusion, riparian areas supporting wildlife flourish, fisheries for cold and warm water species are some of the finest in the country, a myriad of fruitful crops are nurtured on once barren land, she offers floating for all abilities and aids in the economic well being of the communities that depend on her.

The words and photography that follow are an attempt to bring all the Yellowstone River represents together. By following it from a Teton Wilderness glacier's trickle to the point where it gives up its considerable mass to the Missouri, the landscape, historical notes, wildlife, fish and towns along the way are blended together to provide what we hope will be a fascinating trip.
—RICK AND SUSIE GRAETZ

EXCERPTED FROM *MONTANA'S YELLOWSTONE RIVER — FROM THE TETON WILDERNESS TO THE MISSOURI* BY RICK AND SUSIE GRAETZ.

THE YELLOWSTONE RIVER

Millions of buffalo curried her flanks
as she shed winter's ice in the spring.
In the smoke of ten thousand campfires
she heard drumbeats and war dances ring.
On the crest of her bosom she sped Captain Clark
and Sacajawea as well.
She bisected the prairie,the plains and the mountains
from her birthplace in "John Colter's Hell."
To the traveler she whispered,"Come,follow me,"
with a wink and a toss of her head.
She tempted the trapper,gold miner and gambler
to lie down by her sinuous bed.
"Safe passage," she murmured provocatively,,
"safe passage and riches as well."
She smiled as the thread of Custer's blue line
followed her trails and then fell.
She carved out the grade for the railroads;
She took settlers to their new home.
Watered their stock,watered their fields
and let them grow crops on her loam.
Her banks were the goal of the trail herds;
her grass was the prize that they sought.
'Till the blizzard of '86 and seven,
nearly killed off the whole lot.
Don't boss her,don't cross her,let her run free
and damn you,don't dam her at all.
She's a wild old girl,let her looks not deceive you...
But we love her in spite of it all.

Yellowstone River above Hayden Valley, Yellowstone National Park. RICK AND SUSIE GRAETZ

THE YELLOWSTONE RIVER

Beginnings in the Teton Wilderness

Just off the Continental Divide, deep in Wyoming's Absaroka Range and Teton Wilderness, Younts Peak, brushes thin air at 12,156 feet. When the melt season arrives, snowfields in a cirque high up on the massif's north face and other flanks are adorned with countless rivulets. Trickling off the snow, they weave in the mountain's tundra forming into small creeks as they gather in the denser vegetation below, providing the initial waters for the North and South forks of the Yellowstone River. Beneath Younts' west wall the two branches unite to power the surge of the largest undammed, free running river in America as it commences its 670-mile-long odyssey to meet the Missouri beyond Sidney, Montana. And what a journey it makes!

From its spawning grounds 28 air miles below Yellowstone National Park's southeast corner, the fabled river enters a narrow deep canyon fighting its way down a boulder-strewn course. For about ten miles the newly formed river passes through a forest of pine, spruce and fir fitted with small meadows and willow flats. The 1988 fires that burned a great deal of acreage in Yellowstone National Park also touched this corner of the Teton Wilderness and as a result some new aspen growth is being observed. The conifer mix is changing and lodgepole is coming back in places while exhibits of wildflowers, including arnica and fireweed, are sprouting up under the burnt snags.

Numerous unnamed streams and waterfalls tumble off the Continental Divide to the west and from Thunder Mountain and volcanic cliffs on the east. Industrious beavers have created ponds in many places. The rough Continental Divide Trail follows the river on its north and east side with many small but easy creek crossings. The exception is the braided and gravelly Castle Creek where it pours over landslide and flood debris. Fording Castle on horseback is easy but a foot traveler will get wet.

Here the river is connecting with some of the nation's finest wilderness landscape … beautiful, untamed and gaining its wild soul. Far from any road, this is the gorge of the Upper Yellowstone.

Near Castle Creek the Yellowstone departs its canyon confines and embarks on a torturous meander through marshy river bottoms of the twenty-one mile long Yellowstone Meadows and Thorofare Valley. These wetlands extend from one to two miles across and the river with its islands, channels and deep pools is up to 160 feet wide in places. Lush meadows of high grass and dense willows border provide prime moose habitat as well as a summer home for the Northern Yellowstone and Jackson Hole elk herds. Cutthroat trout move upriver to spawn here in early summer attracting the king of the wilderness … the silvertip grizzly bear. Other wildlife, including bison, eagles, big horn sheep, cougars and deer are plentiful. Canada geese and sandhill cranes call out early in the morning throughout the summer and the Delta pack of the Yellowstone wolves has taken up territory here.

The trail coming from the river's headwaters and Marston Pass on the Continental Divide intersects with several other routes near Bridger Lake and Thorofare Creek. Here the Thorofare Trail takes over and heads towards Yellowstone Lake skirting and passing through the meadow's east perimeter. Fording some of the peripheral streams, especially Thorofare Creek can be tricky business. The water in these wildlands is swift, deep and cold. High runoff and lasting snowbanks make much of it impassable until mid-July … just part of the great wilderness experience this first segment of the Yellowstone River offers.

While the bottomlands the Yellowstone River occupies are spacious, the mountains on either side reaching high above them continue to be impressive. Some of the views, especially from vantage points such Hawk's Rest, about two miles south of the park boundary, combining panoramas of the river and its lofty guardians are almost unbelievable. Wyoming's 80-mile-long Absaroka Range with its 10,000 to 11,000-foot summits, including the Park's highest point … 11,358-foot Eagle Peak, form a fortress on the river's sunrise side.

Early explorers who entered this wonderland called the Absarokas "Yellowstone Mountains" and "Great Yellowstone Range." In 1885, the US Geological Survey maps gave them the name Absaroka. Referring to the moniker the Crow Indian Nation used to describe themselves. These mountains had been part of their ancestral lands; Absaroka was interpreted as referring to "children of the large beaked bird."

Part of the Absaroka Range, 10,969-foot-high Trident, a huge wall-like feature with a plateau top rises abruptly above the Thorofare Valley just as the big river enters Yellowstone NP. Three finger-like arms that extend out from the plateau westward gave the formation its name.

The Continental Divide, passing through the Absaroka Mountains, presides over the Yellowstone River's west side in its upper course. As the Divide snakes northwest it loses elevation and crosses Two Ocean Pass, an almost flat area with plenty of water. Here North and South Two Ocean creeks meet and part. One fork becomes Atlantic Creek and makes its way to the Yellowstone River, while the other drains towards the west and the Snake River. Massive Two Ocean Plateau, reaching 10,115 feet at its highest mark, now carries the Divide. The Plateau drops off to Yellowstone Lake on the north while the Continental Divide climbs to the heights west of the lake.

The historically rich Upper Yellowstone River Country fascinated and intrigued early-day trappers who often mentioned the area in their diaries. In 1807, John Colter from the Lewis & Clark Expedition was the first known fur seeker/explorer to enter the region; and it wasn't until 60 years after his first visit any serious exploration of the Park occurred. The legendary Jim Bridger, who is credited with the discovery of Two Ocean Pass, camped at today's Bridger Lake in 1830. The tales told by these mountain men of the countless diverse thermal features they saw were thought to be exaggerations. Colter's incredible, and to some unbelievable, stories of hot water pools, geysers, bubbling earth and sterile landscape, caused listeners to name the area Colter's Hell

During the fur trade era of the early 1800s to 1840, trappers established well-used routes from Jackson Hole and the Snake River to the Yellowstone Plateau. Two Ocean Pass was an easy course for them to follow — low and marshy. On the east side of the pass, they named the valley the Yellowstone River follows — "Thoroughfare." Somehow over time, the spelling was shortened to Thorofare.

In noting the separating of the waters at Two Ocean Pass in his journal, trapper Osborne Russell wrote, "One side bound for the Pacific and the other for the Atlantic Ocean. Here a trout of 12 inches in length may cross the mountains in safety." Theory has it, this was how the cutthroats made it to the upper river and Yellowstone Lake.

The Thorofare Valley terminates in the area of the Yellowstone River's "delta" as it reaches Yellowstone Lake in the Park's remote southeast region. In attaining the lake, the young waterway has traveled approximately 70 miles from its inception; by trail the distance is only about 32 miles.

The River Enters Yellowstone Lake

Six hundred and thirty thousand years ago, molten rock filled two large cavities below Yellowstone's Central Plateau. Lava, forced to the surface, formed a bulge that resulted in an incredible explosion estimated to have been 1,000 times larger than the 1980 Mt. St. Helens eruption; the future Yellowstone National Park literally blew up. The two volcanic chambers that spewed their contents collapsed, creating an enormous caldera 30 by 45 miles wide. Eventually, rhyolite lava filled much of the depression constituting the Yellowstone plateau. Later during the ice age, a 3,500-foot deep alpine glacier ice cap covered the area. As the monumental glacier moved, it most likely ground out a segment of the southeast rim of the caldera allowing Yellowstone Lake to take form.

Positioned at 7,733 feet above sea level, Yellowstone Lake stretches 20 miles north and south and 14 miles east to west giving it the distinction of being the largest high mountain lake on the North American continent. Even though the lake is frozen for more than half of the year and extremely cold in the summer, it is thought the water at some of its greatest depths is boiling. In the West Thumb area it has been measured at 320 feet deep. This grand body of water with its sweeping vistas and fir bedecked shores and coves at one moment can present a scene of serenity and calm or an ocean of chaotic white caps stirred up by a howling wind.

Trappers and the first wanderers into what would become Yellowstone Park praised the lake for its wild beauty, in summer Indians lived on its shores and sat beneath the same moon that today continues to send a seemingly endless river of sparkle across its surface and for the first serious explorations into the area viewing this splendor became the goal.

Three expeditions are credited with paving the way for the creation of Yellowstone National Park and an understanding of the wonders it held. In 1869, the Folsom, Cook, Peterson Expedition departing from Diamond City, Montana, spent 36 days exploring the region. Their greatest contribution was a more comprehensive map of the area they covered and confirmation of the future park's incredible landscape. Before setting out, David Folsom wrote in his journal, "The country around the Headwaters of the Yellowstone River, although frequently visited by prospectors and mountain men is still a veritable terra incognita … The hardy prospectors searching in this region for new diggings have hitherto failed to find gold in paying quantities but have always returned to repeat the tales of wonderful waterfalls a thousand feet in height, of innumerable hot springs of surprising magnitude … Owing to the fact that this class of men had gained a reputation for indulging in flights of fancy in recording their adventures, these reports were received with considerable incredulity until it was noted that, however much the accounts of different parties differed in detail, there was a marked coincidence in the descriptions of some of the most prominent features of the country."

The F-C-P Expedition's reports greatly influenced Henry Washburn, then Surveyor General for the Montana Territory. Just a year later in 1870, starting from Montana's capital, Washburn and his troop, during their 40 days of exploration, affixed many of the names to the Park's landmarks. The Washburn

Expedition received the main credit for discovering much of what is now Yellowstone National Park.

Washburn's account led to government financing of several inspections of the area led by Ferdinand Hayden, a geologist with the US Geological and Geographical Survey. In 1871, the first reconnaissance team including famed artist Thomas Moran as well as a photographer William H. Jackson traveled for 38 days throughout the landscape. The images, paintings, data, maps and written descriptions of the land's majestic and unique character brought back by the Hayden Survey, impressed and convinced Congress and President Ulysses Grant this place was well worth preserving.

On March 1, 1872, President Grant signed a law "... to set apart a certain track of land laying near the headwaters of the Yellowstone River as a public park ... for the benefit and enjoyment of the people." The nation received a treasure — its first national park and a long stretch of the Yellowstone River in its early run was now protected. A precedent was set and the tradition of forever preserving notable landscapes for all people begun.

Strange and interesting things occur under Yellowstone Lake's surface. In the mid-1970s, Bob Smith a University of Utah geophysicist was examining seismic activity of the lake's basin. He noted sediments on the lake bottom moved and would at times tilt upwards to the north although the river, or at this stage the water in Yellowstone Lake, flows from south to north.

The Molly Islands in the lake's southeast arm, serve as a white pelican rookery. Even in high water years, the small islands protrude and nesting is possible. One spring, during a normal water year, researchers found one of the islands completely submerged and all the young birds drowned. Apparently the tilting of the lakebed poured more water into the southeast section. The center of this action appears to be occurring just north of where the river leaves the lake at Fishing Bridge.

And the caldera has not been stable. In the 1920s, elevation benchmarks were installed in various places along the park roads. New readings taken in the mid 1970s in these places by the US Geologic Survey, showed the entire caldera had risen about 30 inches since 1923. Further studies showed it rose another 10 inches between the mid 1970s and 1984.

According to Smith, the caldera then began lowering by less than one inch a year from 1985 to 1995. This information came from using a Global Positioning System to get exact measurements. Since, it appears an uplifting is again taking place, but more so in the northwest segment of the caldera. Yellowstone Lake seems not to be affected and remains at approximately the same level. Smith calls this "the huffs and puffs of the Yellowstone Caldera" and says this can go on for "tens of thousands of years without an eruption".

The cause? Possible subsurface activity ... tectonic, hydrothermal or the movement of or cooling of molten rock, any one or all.

The lake's size as well as the surrounding beauty is what commands the attention of anyone viewing it. Sharp peaks of the Absaroka Range line the entire east shore. Mount Sheridan at 10,308 feet looms like a lofty island to the south and the more subdued highlands of the Central Plateau slope off to the west.

With all its mystery, variable conditions and grandeur, the lake also provides the Yellowstone River with a resting spot before continuing its journey connecting the mountains to the prairie.

Consider this study in contrasts. At the same time a farmer and his sons near Glendive are pumping warm irrigation water from a slow paced silt-laden river for their fields, far upstream in the Thorofare Valley a grizzly sow and her cubs are splashing through the Yellowstone Rivers cold, clear, fast moving water in search of breakfast. While aspen above the riverbanks in the headwaters quake in a cool mountain breeze, big cottonwoods downstream are providing much needed shade for floaters on the river's segment near Savage.

The River Leaves Yellowstone Lake

Leaving the vast, enchanting and interesting Yellowstone Lake, the Yellowstone River resumes its travels, cruising under Fishing Bridge before tumbling through LeHardys Rapids (created by a fault) then holding back as it lazily forms long smooth arcs in the pastoral Hayden Valley, prime grizzly bear and cutthroat trout habitat.

Geologic studies show the valley is an ancient lakebed filled with glacial and stream gravel and was probably once part of Yellowstone Lake. The glacial till contains clay that tends to clog the earth's pores and prevent water from seeping deep into the ground. This condition brings about the area's marshy surface and allows for the river's lethargic meanders.

In the Park, widespread thermal activity is found mostly to the west of the Yellowstone River, but some places along its route show off fine examples of the hot water displays that awed the mountain men. In Hayden Valley's upper stretch, Sulphur Cauldron and Mud Volcano show off. An ample groundwater supply is needed to create hot springs and geysers, something Hayden is lacking. Instead, fumaroles and mud pots flaunt their magic.

Fumaroles occur when the underlying water supply is scarce and what little there is boils away before reaching the surface, the new supply filling the void seeps in slowly, hence steam rises out of the vent instead of a spout of water. Bubbling mud pots are the outcome of the high sulfuric acid contents of the water and vapor leaching underlying rocks, breaking them down to pieces of fine clay and spitting it to the surface.

After flowing out of Hayden Valley, the river's mood changes drastically from unhurried and independent to a dynamic showoff.

As the sleepy Yellowstone River leaves the Hayden Valley, it becomes the centerpiece of one of the most spectacular scenic wonders of Yellowstone

Yellowstone River beyond Livingston. RICK AND SUSIE GRAETZ

National Park, the 20-mile-long Grand Canyon. Here the river puts on perhaps its most striking display. Suddenly squeezed between multicolored rocks and 1,200–1,500-foot deeply etched canyon walls, the now roiling water plunges 109 feet over Upper Falls, creating a deafening roar as it then plummets down the often-photographed 308-foot drop of Lower Falls.

To ensure that this amazing presentation has an audience, the Park Service has provided roads to Upper Falls and aptly named viewing spots such as Artists, Grandview and Inspiration points, each providing a different perspective to the thunderous wonder. Artist Point is perhaps the finest overall look at the Lower Falls and the impressive depths of the severe cut the Yellowstone has made through the soft rhyolite lava.

Upper Falls, while not giving the quite the grandiose performance of its downriver version, represents the start of the deepening canyon.

Brilliant yellow, red and orange hues dominate the ragged walls of the canyon. Over eons of time, this spectrum of color was created by acid steam and water rising from vents deep inside the earth. This caustic concoction carried the dissolution of minerals from heated stones to the surface and deposited it on the rocks of the canyon — a chemical process that continues today.

The most exhilarating of the vantage points is adjacent to the rim of Lower Falls. The only access to this close-up encounter to the thunderous spillway is via a precipitous footpath down the cliff wall. Back in 1889, someone wanted to install an elevator down the cliff, but the superintendent of the Park wouldn't allow it. Today, in order to experience the power of the Park's highest waterfall, you still have to earn the privilege the old fashioned way by climbing down and up again.

Near the canyon rims, spread out in the timber, are ancient visitors from Montana's Beartooth Range, 45 miles to the north. These enormous granite boulders, looking distinctly out of place in this area of lava flow, were carried over on the back of a glacier during the ice age.

From here, the Grand Canyon of the Yellowstone continues on out of sight of roads and is only visible in places from a trail on its west side, an area few people ever visit. The river passes the steep east slopes of former volcano, 10,243-foot-high Mount Washburn, before widening out about four miles up from Tower Creek's entrance and the road coming from Dunraven Pass. Here, well-defined stratums of columnar basalt flows sandwiched between glacial till give the steep faces and cliffs of the canyon the resemblance of a layer cake.

The show is not over yet. After a brief respite in the Tower section, the river once again drops rapidly roiling into the inner depths of the exceptionally wild and seldom seen Black Canyon. Floating this stretch is illegal, therefore only adventurous hikers catch a glimpse of this magnificent chasm.

As Black Canyon plays out, the Yellowstone reaches the tourist town of Gardiner, Montana, some 2,500 feet lower in elevation than Yellowstone Lake.

The handle "Yellowstone" comes from history's somewhat fuzzy recollection of the name the first known white intruders gave this waterway. For whatever reason, the national park took on the river's title. In the 1740s French Canadian trappers made a foray into what is now Montana and traveled an unknown distance up the lower Yellowstone. Noticing yellow colored stones in and along the river channel, they called it R. des Roche Jaune (spelling as appearing on 1790s maps) or in English "River of the Yellow Rock." William Clark's journal entries in 1806 referred to it as "*rochejaune*." According to Crow Tribal elder and historian, Joe Medicine Crow, long before the whites decided on a name, the Crow Indians called it "Elk River," as they often hunted the majestic animal along the river's banks.

Entering Montana

Taking leave of Wyoming and the Park, it now enters human environment, sometimes sparsely inhabited and other times a bit crowded. The wilderness of its birth and the phenomenal natural wonders of the nation's oldest national park that it has been an intricate part of have been left behind, but more adventures, wild country and beauty in view of the river lies ahead.

At this point, before the Park is no longer in sight, it is interesting to note the first superintendent Nathaniel Langford inferred the Park should belong to Montana when he stated, "… the park is only accessible from Montana. It is impossible to enter it from Wyoming … those Wyoming mountains would make the park useless to that territory."

Straddling the Yellowstone River, Gardiner serves as the northern entrance to Yellowstone National Park and host to a myriad of tourists in search of food, lodging and trinkets. On the west edge of town, an imposing basalt arch dedicated in 1903 by President Teddy Roosevelt, is a symbolic gateway welcoming all to the Park.

Johnston Gardiner, an old trapper in the Upper Yellowstone during the 1830s, is the settlements namesake. By 1883, a spur line of the Northern Pacific Railroad extended from Livingston to Cinnibar just four miles short of Gardiner. A lengthy dispute between prospector "Buckskin" Cutler and Postmaster Jim McCartney over townsite ownership held up progress for nearly 20 years. In 1902, the steel road bringing visitors to the park finally made it into town. The line was abandoned and the tracks removed in 1970.

Gardiner is a town divided. Not only by the Yellowstone River, but the southwest side of Park Street is the National Park boundary; hence the unusual setting of commercial buildings on only one side of a downtown street and an open field on the other.

West of this small burg rises the massive 10,969-foot Electric Peak. A member of the Hayden Survey party, while nearing the top, apparently encountered a lightning storm that caused his hair to stand on end, consequently the name.

Above the river's embankment, five miles to the north of Gardiner, an unusual geologic formation makes its presence known. Called the Devil's Slide, it is best described in the journal of an 1869 explorer, " At one place we noticed a slate formation having a vertical dip … It pasted through a hill which in wearing away, had left two smooth, unbroken walls, twenty feet thick, and from 20 to 80 feet in height. They were about 60 feet apart and ran parallel to each other from the bottom to the top of the hill; the space between them presented the appearance of a well traveled road." To most folks looking at it today, this configuration at the base of Cinnabar Mountain looks like a giant red tinted playground slide. The distinct color is probably the oxidation of iron in the rock.

Before heading north into Montana's serene Paradise Valley, the Yellowstone squeezes and negotiates its way through Yankee Jim Canyon for four wild roller coaster miles. This is the river's last major whitewater event.

"Yankee Jim" was Jim George who in 1872 blasted a path through the canyon's west side, opening the first road to YNP. He charged a fee to those who used it and provided a roadhouse for the visitors. In 1883, the new railroad ended his toll business. Although the Northern Pacific bought the right of way from him and used the road to lay tracks, he despised the company and was known to shake a fist at the passing trains. Some historical notes claim the NP, as part of the deal, had to build Jim a new road higher up on the hillside. The initial road and rail bed is still very clear (marked abandoned on maps) and there are signs of a crude rout further up the slope.

When President Roosevelt came to the Park via the rails in 1903, he asked to have the crusty Yankee Jim, who still resided in the area, come meet him; the reply to the invitation was, "You know where I live Teddy." At on time he loved to entertain tourists in his saloon with tall tales. Rudyard Kipling called him the biggest liar he ever met.

Old Jim's cabin was located upriver on the west side of the Yellowstone just before the canyon tightens. He lived there until he died sometime in the mid 1920s. Yankee Jim Canyon terminates where Tom Miner Creek and Basin, on the west, add runoff to the river.

Entering the appropriately named Paradise Valley, the jagged peaks of the Absaroka Mountains, part of the Absaroka-Beartooth Wilderness Area stand guard to the east, while the summits of the Gallatin Range are the backdrop to the east. The Yellowstone River gathers water from both. Courtesy of these high country borders, glaciers once inched their way down from cirques and covered the valley. Many canyons in both ranges are blocked by moraines from ice that never quite made it to the valley bottom.

Sixty miles in length, the Gallatin Range, with tops over 10,000' extends into the National Park. Considered by wildlife managers to be some of America's best elk country, it is essential wintering and calving range for the large northern Yellowstone elk herd.

The Absarokas are part of a wildland made up of the Absaroka and Beartooth Ranges that stretches eastward to the plains. Like their Wyoming relations, they were first called the Yellowstone Range until 1879 when the name for the Crow Indians was given to them. From this range, the valley's most impressive landmark, 10,921-foot Emigrant Peak holds court.

In late August 1864, a group of emigrants heading west missed Bozeman Pass and instead turned south into the Paradise. They made their way towards the peak and well into Emigrant Gulch and Creek and found placer gold.

The gulch climbs a grade in the tight canyon between the steep east face of Emigrant Peak and west flank of 10,195-foot Chico Peak. Winter, which shows early here, eventually forced them to locate lower in the canyon; Yellowstone City, a short-lived camp of 300 people was born. The gold played out in three years and the miners and their families moved on.

At the mouth of Emigrant Gulch, Old Chico, another mining camp with its nearby hot springs was built. Jim Bridger along with a band of Crow Indians wintered here in 1844. Today, the springs are the renowned Chico Hot Springs Resort that has grown from the original development of 1900.

Nelson Story, a prominent early day Montanan drove Texas cattle into the Paradise Valley in 1867 and established a sizable ranch selling beef to the miners and other settlers. It was probably Story, or one of the other first settlers to make it here, who came up with the title Paradise for this piece of the Yellowstone's way.

Known for its grand scenery, numerous spring creeks and some of the nation's best trout fishing. In its route to this point, the river has picked up clean flow mostly from wilderness and untrammeled topography. The clear blue green water is of a better quality than most other blue ribbon trout streams. The late Ray Hurley, a Livingston guide proclaimed, "the Yellowstone in this area is the Yankee Stadium of trout fishing." According to George Anderson, owner of George Anderson's Yellowstone Angler, and first rate fishermen himself, "If anyone could make that statement it was Hurley. Ray was one of the all time great Yellowstone fishing guides."

True native cutthroat trout frequent the river's deep pools and wildlife is plentiful. Geese and ducks along with deer and other critters populate the riverbanks and eagles and hawks claim the sky. As a mother takes care of her young, so too does the Yellowstone nourish and give shelter to nature.

On the north end of the valley, the river constricts through Allenspur, an abandoned railroad branch that separates Paradise Valley from the Yellowstone Valley. Engineers, oblivious to the wonders of a free flowing river, more than once had the audacity to propose this locale with its high rock walls as a dam site. Their plan was to contain the Yellowstone and flood the Paradise Valley. More rational minds have prevailed and it is extremely doubtful the scheme will ever come to fruition.

Livingston and the Big Bend of the Yellowstone

A few miles downstream at the "Big Bend," the river introduces itself to Livingston, a former frontier/railroad town and now a prominent approach to Yellowstone National Park. The "Grande Dame"of the high country now makes an abrupt turn toward the east and faces the morning sun.

From this point on, the Yellowstone River was important to the Lewis & Clark Expedition. On the return leg of their journey in 1806, the Captains split near Lolo, Montana. Lewis investigated a new route to the Great Falls on the Missouri and Clark forged his way back to the three forks of the Missouri then set out across the future Bozeman Pass and into the Yellowstone Valley coming upon the river at the "Big Bend." In all, Clark and his troops made 14 camps along the Yellowstone, five of them between present day Livingston and Billings. Indians had informed them the Yellowstone watered some of the finest land on the continent.

Clark's journal entry of July 15, 1806 after leaving the Three Forks in part notes, "... *proceeded up the branch (of the Gallatin) to the head thence over a low gap in the mountain thence across passing over a low dividing ridge (Bozeman Pass) to the head of a water course (Billman Creek) which runs into the Rochejhone, prosueing an old buffalow road keeping on the North Side of the branch to the River rochejhone at which place I arrived at 2 P M." Clark peered south into the Paradise Valley and later recorded "... The Roche passes out of a high rugid mountain (most likely he was referring to the Gallatins) covered with*

Snow ... The mountains (Absarokas) ... on the East side of the river is rocky rugid and on them are great quantities of Snow."

In 1873, when Amos Benson built a trading post, stage stop and of course a saloon on the banks of the great Yellowstone River about four miles down stream from today's Livingston, Benson's Landing was established and the area came to life. A rickety ferry rigged across the Yellowstone by another "entrepreneur" Bill Lee, carried passengers headed to the Paradise Valley and YNP.

In July 1882, railroad surveyors set up a camp called Clark City near the Big Bend. When the rails reached the town on December 1, 1882, Clark City already had six general stores, two hotels and 44 other establishments of which 30 were saloons. With a profit to the tune of $200,000 as an incentive (railroad land sales), NP officials decided the town needed to be down river a short ways. Town folks bought lots and moved. A town was platted and named for Crawford Livingston, a director of the Northern Pacific Railroad. A wild west town of legend, attracting characters like Calamity Jane, it took 30 saloons to help quench the thirst of the nearly 2,000 early residents who made Livingston the largest neighborhood on the Yellowstone.

It was the railroad that made the place work, especially when a locomotive repair shop was put into operation. Tourism and outdoor recreation soon added to its economic coffers

Livingston, built on stream gravel, may well have one of the most scenic settings of any town in Montana. With the Yellowstone River as its centerpiece, mountains rise from the edge of town on the west and south ... the Absarokas and Gallatins close by and the Bridgers and Crazy Mountains a bit off in the distance. Framed by the downtown, the 9,314-foot-high Livingston Peak, (Mt. Baldy to some — it doesn't look bald), was a vision quest site for Crow Indians.

The area has quite a reputation for considerable winds, and on Mission Flats southeast of town, a few wind turbines harvest the brisk breezes coming off Canyon Mountain to the southwest, through Bozeman Pass and the Bridgers and Bangtails on the west and northwest.

The Yellowstone Heads to the Montana Prairie

With Livingston to her back, the widening river turns towards the rising sun and begins to realize the bulk of its 70,000-square-mile drainage basin. The late Mike Malone, historian and one-time president of Montana State University, sized it up well; "The Yellowstone Basin embraces an enormous swath of the American West, a swath so large and so diverse in terrains and subregions that it seems, in some respects to be a microcosm of the West itself."

From here eastward, the river's work as a canyon cutter has ceased and it takes on a the chores of changing channels, creating braids and assisting in the regeneration of cottonwoods by providing fertile silt as a bed for the seeds.

The Yellowstone River looks well to the south for its donations. Most of her contributions come from rivers originating deep in Wyoming, among them the Bighorn, Tongue and Powder. The Shields River, just down from Livingston, is the only large flow from the north. Each tentacle not only adds more power to the torrent but also carries bits of history from Montana's origins to the mother stream.

Remaining unharnessed and ever changing with the seasons, reciting the same chants the Corps of Discovery, Crow, Cheyenne and Sioux heard, challenged by man but gloriously undefeated, she is beloved by all who take the time to know her.

A sharp mountain skyline and the close-up majestic surroundings slowly give way to an immense horizon and a landscape possessed of simple grandeur stretching seemingly forever. Sky before narrowed by tall trees and peaks, opens to an unlimited playing field for clouds, storms and all manners of pink, red, orange and purple painted fiery sunsets and rises. The mighty Yellowstone is heading to the Montana prairie.

Past the Big Bend, the waters of the Yellowstone begin a less precipitous drop than before. Initially, from its outlet at Yellowstone Lake to Gardiner, the river loses 44 feet per mile. Between Gardiner and Livingston, 811 feet in elevation is lost at a rate averaging 19 feet per mile. So far, the altitude deficiency is substantial, but from Livingston to Billings the drop is 10 feet per mile and from Billings to Sidney and the Missouri, 3.4 feet per mile. Sidney is 2,572 feet lower in elevation than Livingston. This continual, down gradient ensures a relatively rapid flow and some very good paddling. See Falcon Guide's "Paddling Montana" for details on floating the entire river.

While cutthroat trout are the prime species of fish in Yellowstone Park, various geneses of trout, including rainbow, mountain whitefish and browns, inhabit the water north of Gardiner. At Livingston, though the water temperature of the river has increased. Here, it is still considered in fishing terms as a cold water, mountain river. This definition will change as the river flows across the prairie.

About five miles east of Livingston, the Shields River, accumulating its volume from the Bridger and Crazy mountains, meets the newly sprawling Yellowstone. Named by Captain William Clark in honor of John Shields, a fellow member of the Corps of Discovery, the place also served as the Expedition's first camp on the Yellowstone. Clark noted a distinguished landmark in his journal ... the long high dark ridge, on the north side of the confluence, today's Sheep Mountain.

From this point forward, recorded history and events of the river become more vivid. Explorers and fur traders following Clark's initial foray spent a good deal of time on this the "Middle" Yellowstone River.

The landscape the "Roche Jaune" has been silently passing through witnessed long-time Indian activity when the tribes of the Northern Great

Plains followed migrating bison and made seasonal camps along her banks. As the 1880s marched forward, the quiet river soon observed clashes between the natives protecting their ground from eastern white intruders.

In the mid-1880s, with the ever-increasing white trespass onto Indian lands that would become Montana and Wyoming, treaty boundaries were set for the tribes in hopes of allowing a more peaceful coexistence between the newcomers and the original proprietors. In September 1851, the so-called Fort Laramie Treaty was signed with many of the Native nations. The Crow, who had lived in and hunted the Yellowstone country, "were given" more than 38 million acres to "keep forever." Included in this territory was much of southern Montana from the headwaters of the Yellowstone River east through the Paradise Valley, to the Powder River and north towards the Musselshell River. In essence they controlled almost all of the topography drained by the Yellowstone.

However, the white tide continued to increase without regard to the agreements. Prompted by pressure, the US government once again attempted to sign "new treaties" with the Indians in order to reduce their land. On May 7, 1868, another Fort Laramie accord was endorsed; "Crow Country" shrunk to eight million acres and a reservation was created. However, in a concession to the Indians, the objectionable and illegal Bozeman Trail that in part followed the Yellowstone from near Big Timber to Bozeman was closed. Wagon trains would no longer be allowed to pass through the region.

The first Crow Agency headquarters was established in 1868 where Mission Creek, born in the Absaroka Mountains on the south, enters the flow of the Yellowstone. Later, further reductions would continue shrink their land ownership. Today the Crow Reservation's northern perimeter is well south of the Yellowstone and encompasses only a segment of one tributary basin; the Little Bighorn and Bighorn river valleys.

From Livingston for a long haul downriver, the Crazy Mountains grab a huge piece of the northern horizon. Nowhere else in Montana is the transition from prairie to mountains so dramatic as it is with the Crazies. In a 20-mile span from the river bottoms of the Yellowstone to the pinnacle of 11,214-foot Crazy Peak, the terrain rises more than 7,000 feet. This island of mountains, the third highest range in the state, is only about 30 miles deep and 15 miles wide, but it is an imposing sentinel.

The Crow Indians used the Crazies for vision sites. It was on top of Crazy Peak that Chief Plenty Coup had his vision telling of the coming of the white man with his cattle and railroads that would destroy the bison herds and overwhelm the natives. He foresaw that the life his people knew would come to an end. To the Crow Nation these mountains they call Awaxaawippiia, are most sacred and revered and are still used for spiritual purposes.

Several colorful versions of how the Crazy Mountains received their name exist. One rendering attributed to the Crow refers to a physical description of the convoluted geology and screaming winds that roar through the canyons. Other stories are of a woman from a wagon train running off into the hills after Indians attacked her group; it is said she went mad. Another edition has it that she went insane during the trip, escaped from her party and headed for these mountains. Choose the one you like best.

However they were named, the Crazy Mountains are especially splendid in the spring when they are portrayed as a brilliant jagged mass of snow-clogged peaks surrounded by the emerald green Yellowstone Valley. It takes your breath away.

Past Mission Creek the Shields River joins in and the Yellowstone enters a constricted canyon, then makes a sharp bend to the north before rolling east again. Here, as the canyon opens, the Crazy Mountains loom large.

Springdale, the next human enclave enroute at one time boasted of nearby Hunters Hot Springs. Named after Dr. Andrew Hunter (he bestowed the name in honor of himself), who was searching for gold but stumbled across the springs instead, the hot waters were first used by the Crow Indians for healing purposes and later, by trappers and adventurers passing through for bathing. In 1883, the enterprising doctor-turned-prospector constructed a 100-room hotel and bathhouse near the springs hoping to attract tourists traveling on the newly completed Northern Pacific Railroad. Around 1900, a Butte businessman purchased the resort and built the 300-room Dakota Hotel. Shortly, the place began losing money and closed for good after a fire in the 1930s. Today, not much is left of the town, but Springdale provides excellent access to the Yellowstone River.

Continuing on, Big Timber, the county seat of Sweetgrass County, welcomes the river's arrival. The south face of the Crazy Mountains is the backdrop for this picturesque ranching community. Wide tree lined avenues and a main thoroughfare with historic structures contribute to the town's charm.

Back when Captain Clark and his group were desperately in need of watercraft to get on the Yellowstone and speed up progress, stands of large cottonwoods along Big Timber Creek beckoned them. Almost, but not quite big enough around to make canoes out of, the Corps' hopes were dashed and they remained on horseback for the time being.

A stagecoach stop at the mouth of the creek was the town's forerunner. In 1882, when the railroad showed up, the original settlement was moved and the town named Big Timber in honor of the then stately, but now gone, cottonwoods.

An abundance of delightfully scented grasses and flowers strewn across the valley, foothills and mountains to the north and south of the river, gave the county its Sweetgrass moniker. The availability of rich vegetation fueled a notable sheep industry. By the late 1800s, Big Timber was one of the nations largest wool centers. Congregating sheep from a wide area, enough of the product of these animals was collected to house Montana's first woolen mill.

A prosperous beehive industry was also a result of the flowers and grasses. Sheep and beehives along with cows are yet an important part of the landscape.

On July 17, 1806, about two miles below Big Timber, Captain William Clark encountered two streams, directly athwart of each other entering the Yellowstone. He noted them on his map as, *"South and North Rivers Across."* Following a serpentine route from the Crazies is today's Big Timber Creek while *"South River"* is now the Boulder River working its way down from the Absarokas.

Moving forward, the Yellowstone widens and finds as many as ten channels in some places and creates habitat for bank beaver, geese, ducks, eagles, hawks, owls, pelicans, deer and antelope. And in this stretch below Big Timber the river's mix of a wide and narrow valley is edged by ridges, low bluffs and hills spotted with open forests of juniper and ponderosa

The next two stops on the river tour are Greycliff, named after a local shady colored landmark and best known as the home of Prairie Dog Town State Park, and Reedpoint, a lively community with a great sense of humor.

Reedpoint's current claim to fame is the annual "Great Montana Sheep Drive." In late August, thousands of visitors crowd the miniature town's Old West-like four-block main street to view and cheer on the wooly run. Estimates are that in the mid-1920s almost 50,000 sheep ate the grass in the hills surrounding the community, but so few critters are used for this event the coordinators run the herd through town twice to afford a better effect.

Authentic and historic buildings give the town character and the Hotel Montana looks as if it came straight out of a cowboy movie. Named after area homesteaders the Reed family; at one time, Reedpoint was known for the giant vegetables grown in the area.

For almost 80 road miles since the river turned out of the Paradise Valley, the towering north wall of the Absaroka-Beartooth Mountains has been in and out of view from the Yellowstone. On a clear day their presence is visible up to 100 miles away. Nine major drainages pour out of their higher reaches, giving the Yellowstone River, between Yellowstone National Park and Billings, one third of its flow. As the single most prevailing landform along the river's entire voyage, the term "shining mountains" is appropriate to them as much as any range in the state.

And what about this entity? Two ranges separated by the Boulder River as it flows north out of the high country through a sheer canyon to the Yellowstone River make up the roof of Montana, the awesome nearly one million-acre Absaroka-Beartooth Wilderness, a wild landscape where the highest summits in the state soar above an already cloud-piercing plateau.

Glacier's, maintained by more than 400 inches of annual snowfall, fill high cirques and cling to north facing head walls of some the highest ridges and summits.

More than three-fourths of the AB is above timberline and elevated enough to have tundra soil. Together, they boast of more than 120 peaks over 10,000 feet in elevation. Twenty-nine top out at over 12,000 feet, including Montana's highest, 12,799-foot Granite Peak. An estimated 1,000 lakes are cupped within the two ranges.

Beyond Reedpoint, the river carries itself into a narrower plain surrounded by subdued hills … ranching country. Just before finding a wider berth to amble through, a Beartooth Range-born river, the Stillwater deposits its clear, cold water into the mix. Mike Sample, in his book *Fishing Montana* says "Stillwater is a misnomer … The Stillwater has less quiet water proportionally than any river in the state." He terms it a "roly-poly stream." To find its beginnings you need to go nearly 70 miles across the Beartooth to Mt. Abundance by Cooke City.

Captain Clark's journal of July 19, 1806 reads, *"passed the Rose bud river."* He was referring to the Stillwater, but mistakenly seemed to think Rose Bud was the Indian name for the stream. Crow legend has it otherwise. A revered young Indian woman died and her body was washed into the river by a violent storm. When the weather cleared a still pool had formed where her body was. Her people, feeling the place was now sacred, called it "still water;" eventually the river took on the name.

Not far downstream from the Stillwater, the Yellowstone provides river front property for Columbus, the county seat of Stillwater County. In 1875, with Crow Agency relocated to the Stillwater River near Absarokee and commercial business to be had, Horace Countryman established a stagecoach stop and trading post near current day Columbus on the old Yellowstone Trail. The establishment and settlement had several names … Eagle's Nest, Sheep Dip (for the bad whiskey sold at an Indian trading post) and Stillwater. The Northern Pacific reached here in 1882, and on January 1, 1894 they renamed it Columbus, perhaps after Christopher Columbus or for Columbus, Minnesota. They already had a Stillwater, Minnesota along their line.

The new town became well known for a sandstone quarry in the bluffs to the north. In 1899, stone from here was used for constructing the State Capitol building in Helena. Word spread and Columbus began supplying the high quality material across the state. With the retirement of some of the original stonemasons in 1910, the quarry's activity slowed. Replacements were hard to come by and stone was becoming less popular for building. Columbus has always had a strong agricultural based economy and that has kept the community going.

By the time he reached the site of today's Columbus, Captain Clark was fretting, *"time is precious as it is our wish to get back to the U states this Season."* He also had an injured man with him who couldn't ride his horse; canoes were desperately needed. *"… proceeded on about 9 miles … passed over two high points of land"* before sighting a cottonwood grove with trees large enough from which to make canoes. Halting on the north side of the Yellowstone River about two miles south of Park City, they settled in from July 19th until the morning of July 24th and dubbed the spot "*Canoe Camp.*" Here they built two 28-foot-long dugout canoes, lashing them together for stability.

The high points of land Clark described were most likely the striking long ridge of Young's Point that drops off to a cliff where the Yellowstone sweeps next to it about five miles before Park City.

Park City was founded in 1882 by a group of Wisconsin folks who couldn't afford the high real estate prices in Billings. Being the "can do" type, they decided to establish their own town and struck out about 23 miles up the Yellowstone. The growing and refining off sugar beets became the key industry bringing prosperity with it to the little town. Originally called Rimrock after the landforms in the area, their desire for gardens and trees caused them to change the name to a more fitting Park City. Now, there are some who claim it initially was called Clark City and when the Northern Pacific showed up, the railroad manager, for whatever reason wasn't too happy with this name change. So instead of building a large railroad center in Park City he chose Laurel about seven miles to the east. At least that is how one story goes; there are various versions of it.

For a while it was called Canyon Creek, then the copious amounts of laurel growing on the riverbanks won out for a name. As with other towns along the way, Laurel grew as the result of the railroad. It soon laid claim to having the largest rail yard between Minnesota and Seattle. The refining of petroleum eventually came to town and these activities coupled with the rich farmland in the valley allowed Laurel to grow steadily. Today the oil refinery just north of the river, dominates this blue-collar workingman's town.

At this point, the big stream makes a distinctive change from a mountain river to a prairie flow. The Clarks Fork of the Yellowstone approaching from the south gives up its water, and in doing so is the first tributary to introduce significant silt to the Yellowstone.

The Clarks Fork didn't start out with these intentions, its upper flow is pure and clear from places like the pristine Sky Top Lakes and glacial melt below the south face of Montana's apex, Granite Peak. As it reaches lower elevations and assumes a more gentle profile, it picks up this added burden.

This new contributor, named for Captain William Clark, has had an interesting historical past. Native Americans called the river's confluence with the Yellowstone the "Lodge where all dance." Clark's writings of July 24, 1806, mention passing " *a large council lodge … or The lodge where all danc,*" and it most likely was a Crow Sun Dance Lodge.

For centuries, Indians used a trail along the Clarks Fork. During the winter of 1806–07, John Colter, a member of the Corps of Discovery, followed the river towards the mountains, and other mountain men traveling towards the Yellowstone region also traced this water route.

The Nez Perce with their leader Chief Joseph stayed along the Clarks Fork of the Yellowstone after passing through Yellowstone Park in 1877 on their epic journey to escape from the US Army. Crossing the Yellowstone when they met it, the weary Natives then proceeded north to Laurel and up through the sandstone bluffs of Canyon Creek. A detachment of the US Cavalry caught up with them there on September 13, but the Indians turned back the soldiers and continued their march towards Canada.

After the Clarks Fork, the big river is classified as warm water and the fish inhabitants change as sauger, carp and catfish take over.

Heretofore along the Yellowstone's entire journey, mountains have been ever present. Now the horizons beyond the banks expand as the Northern Great Plains begin to claim their domain. From Columbus east, the river unifies with the prairie and its easy beauty.

Nearing Billings, the isolated Pryor Mountains are seen to the south, but for the most part, cliffs and rising and falling ranch land dominate the scenery.

The Pryors, named after Nathaniel Pryor of the Lewis and Clark Expedition, issue waters to the Yellowstone by way of the Bighorn River and Pryor Creek. Red desert, ice caves and wild horses are symbols of this most unique piece of Montana mountain country. Unlike any other place in the state, its diversity is unequaled.

The island-like Pryors are made up of two high ridges, each about 20 miles across. The northern stretch is within the boundaries of the Crow Reservation. Here, the highest points, a little over 7,300 feet, descend gradually to lower timbered buttes. Ice caves and the 31,000-acre Pryor Mountain National Wild Horse Range highlight the southern part, were summits top out over 8,700 feet. A dramatic plunge of 5,000 feet from sub alpine terrain down to a desert environment exists at the southern tip.

The Yellowstone Meets Billings

The big town/little city of Billings, a center for agriculture and regional trade and the site of Montana's largest and busiest airport, Logan Field, holds court on the banks of the Yellowstone River. Yellow-tinted rimrocks, present in various stretches along the river, tower over the Billings Valley to the north while the river brushes up against them to the south.

Coulson, established during the winter of 1876–77, preceded Billings by five years. Named after the Coulson Steamboat Co., a sawmill, trading post and ferry were put in place east of present-day Billings where the railroad bridge now crosses the river. Knowing the railroad was forging westward through the Yellowstone Valley, the founders had high hopes that their town would become a center for the Northern Pacific.

Frederick Billings, a wealthy San Francisco lawyer, land investor and philanthropist became involved with the Northern Pacific Railroad in the 1860s. He took over as president of the line in 1879 and secured the right-of-way across Montana for the company. At that time, the US government was anxious to see rails completed to the west coast. As an incentive generous land grants were awarded to the NP. For every mile of track laid, they were given alternating sections of land along the right away. The sections were 80 miles wide; and they could sell them.

Mr. Billings and other managers of the railroad tried to negotiate with the Coulson founders for land, but they were greedy and demanded too much money. As a result, a decision was made to move the railroad's midpoint a few miles upriver. At the same time, Billings became a partner in the Minnesota and Montana Land Company, which purchased more than 30,000 acres along the Yellowstone from the NP, including the ground for the new town. Billings was platted in 1882 and the founders planned commercial development along the tracks. It's interesting to note, the road paralleling the railway on the north side is called Montana Avenue and the one on the south edge Minnesota Avenue, this apparently to honor the company that made the town possible. The first train arrived on August 22, 1882 and Coulson soon became a ghost town.

Although he didn't live in Billings (his son Parmly did for a few years), the town grew under its namesake's guidance from afar. During the late 1880s, Frederick Billings was considered "one of the most influential figures in America."

Billings expanded rapidly and by 1910 had a population of 10,000. While the rails brought businesses of all kinds, the most dominant was livestock. Cattle were brought in by the thousands, and the selling and shipping of cows became an economic mainstay. In spite of its size today, the cattle and agricultural atmosphere exists, the trains continue to hustle through town and their long lonesome whistles are still heard along the banks of the Yellowstone.

Native American and white battles were part of the Yellowstone River's past, but recent years have seen skirmishes of a different sort. An on-going labor to benefit this great river is centered out of Billings where constant vigilance has been needed to keep the Yellowstone flowing free and healthy. In the 1970s the Arab oil embargo put power and mining interests' minds in motion to consider building electrical generating plants near the river, using dams and eastern Montana coal. Once on line, the plants would have taken as much as 80 percent of the Yellowstone flow in low water years, a price Montanans didn't care to pay. Opposed to using its volume for dams and power plants, the State designated the river to preserve its agricultural economic base, and for recreation, fish, wildlife and water quality. The word was out … Leave her alone!

Yet the issues continue. On one hand the Yellowstone is the only large river in the contiguous states that does not have an impoundment dam on its main stem, and it still supports a dynamic cottonwood riparian forest that is emblematic of a great diversity of aquatic and terrestrial life. On the other hand, this dynamic river has supported a vital agricultural base in southern and eastern Montana for over a century.

After heavy flooding in 1996 and 1997, conservation and economic development entities were far apart in their approaches to managing the river. Government agencies, caught unaware, had routinely approved small incremental river modifications, which over the years began to add up to the potential degradation of significant reaches of the Yellowstone. Suddenly, the diverging points-of-view reached the stage of litigation over government management of the river.

Considering the Yellowstone to be "Last Best River" in the lower 48 states and a major priority, in 1999, The Nature Conservancy of Montana established a field office in Billings. Seeing room for both reasonable development and preservation, rather than the animosity produced by litigation, TNC set about forming partnerships with other conservation organizations to develop voluntary, incentive-based programs for private landowners who were interested in protecting and restoring riparian habitat and to engage all of the players in community based discussions for problem solving.

Under the name Yellowstone Conservation Forum, TNC was a catalyst in forging an alliance with the council of all of the conservation districts along the Yellowstone, the 18 federal and state agencies that have river management responsibilities, the 11 cities and towns along the Yellowstone and the 22 involved conservation groups to raise awareness about Yellowstone River issues. The partnership hosted a roundtable meeting to focus the attention of the many state and federal government agencies on keeping the Yellowstone a natural and economically productive river. This coming together physically and intellectually created a political climate that has allowed major funding to be allocated for a joint local, state and federal comprehensive study of how management of the river affects hydrology, biology and socioeconomics.
—RICK AND SUSIE GRAETZ

TAKEN FROM *MONTANA'S YELLLOWSTONE RIVER* BY RICK AND SUSIE GRAETZ.

THE CRAZY MOUNTAINS

"It's a good country. Where a man can sit in his saddle and see … all across to the west stretch the Crazies, and, swinging in the stirrups, a man has to throw back his head to follow their abrupt shoulders up to the white crests of the peaks. A pretty clean country where a man can see a long way and have something to see."
SPIKE VAN CLEVE'S WORDS FROM FORTY YEARS' GATHERIN'S, SPEAKING OF THE VIEW FROM HIS RANCH.

Considered an island range owing to their location separate of the main Northern Rockies, the Crazy Mountains of south central Montana are more akin to the Rockies than they are to the state's other rounded and more forested isolated ranges. The valleys of the Yellowstone and Shields rivers set them well apart from the Absarokas to the south and the Bridgers on the west. They are only about 30 miles by 15 miles in size, but serve as sentinels on the horizon from many points east.

Here, the transition from prairie to mountains is dramatic. In a 20-mile span from the river bottoms of the Yellowstone to the pinnacle of Crazy Peak, the terrain rises more than 7,000 feet.

These "Crazy Woman Mountains," as the Indians sometimes called them, are crowned by 11,214-foot Crazy Peak. With 25 pinnacles soaring to more than 10,000 feet, they are the third highest range in the state. Ice, wind and water erosion sculptured them and created the more than 40 jewel-like lakes scattered amongst the sharp saw-toothed ridges and alpine basins. Today, only one ice-age remnant remains; Grasshopper Glacier clings to a north facing headwall between Cottonwood and Rock lakes on the west perimeter.

Nearly vertical slopes lead to the highest summits and windswept barren ridges. Mountain goats find this terrain to their liking and frequent the steepest areas.

The northern flanks of the Crazy Mountains are gentler, and the vegetation more lush, than the rocky and precipitous southern reaches. The historic Mussellshell River headwaters here in the north, and the Shields River begins its flow from the sheerer west ramparts. Sweet Grass Creek, heading towards the Yellowstone, rushes out of one of the deep eastern canyons.

There are several stories on how the mountains got their name. One was that a wagon train, coming through the Mussellshell Valley, was attacked by Indians. A woman's family was killed, and it is said, she ran into the mountains to haunt the Indians. Another has it that a woman settler was separated from her wagon train and wandered into these peaks. People thought that she couldn't survive without going mad so the range was dubbed the "Crazy Woman Mountains." Others claimed it was because they popped up in the middle of nowhere or because of the convoluted geologic formations found there. Take your pick.

The Crazies are significant to Native American culture. In 1847, Chief Plenty Coup, the last great chief of the Crow Nation, climbed Crazy Peak to seek a vision so he might properly lead and guide his people.

Although they do not enjoy the lasting protection wilderness status would give them, the extremely rough terrain and the attitude of local ranchers, and lately of the Forest Service, has kept this country pristine and relatively free of roads. Checkerboard ownership places a good portion of the landscape in private hands, including favorite climbing places such as Conical, Granite and Crazy peaks and Rock Lake. Some owners will give permission to enter, but most will not allow motorized use of this wild country ... foot and horse travel only! The same goes for much of the public land.

There isn't an access shortage as most of the footpaths traverse Gallatin

The east side of the Crazy Mountains. RICK AND SUSIE GRAETZ

National Forest ground. One of the most popular routes into the Crazies is reached from Hwy 191 between Big Timber and Harlowton via Big Timber Canyon. Beginning at Half Moon Campground, the trail climbs to the high areas around Conical Peak and the Twin Lakes area and then crosses a pass before lowering to Sweetgrass Creek and another trailhead. Tracks also lead to the west side of the range from Wilsall and Clyde Park. There are about 66 miles of horse and walking byways within the Crazy Mountains.

The best overall map to use is the Gallatin National Forest Visitor Map. Forest headquarters are in Bozeman. You will need it to ascertain land ownership. To find out about who to call for permission to climb in private areas phone either the Big Timber Ranger station for the east side, or the Livingston office for the west.

—RICK AND SUSIE GRAETZ

ABSAROKA-BEARTOOTH

Heading up the Yellowstone River Valley through breaks and bluffs, a formidable piece of country, appearing like a long white wall, comes into view far out on the southwest horizon. A massive uplift, the Absaroka-Beartooth Mountains, one of America's great pieces of high and wild landscapes, looms ahead.

And awesome it is ... the roof of Montana where the highest summits in the state soar above an already cloud-piercing plateau.

This land in the sky was named in part for the Absaroka people ... the Crow Indians. The Beartooth Spire (called "Na pietsay" by the Crow), and seen from the Beartooth Highway is responsible for the Beartooth moniker.

The A-B, as it is sometimes called, consists of two distinct ranges separated on the north by the Boulder River as it flows out of the mountains through a precipitous gorge to the Yellowstone River. On the south, the ranges' seam line is less definitive.

The Beartooth crags climb to the east and consist mostly of bare land above tree line. Glaciers fill high cirques and cling to north facing headwalls of some of the highest ridges and summits. More than 400 inches of annual snow helps maintain perennial snowfields and glaciers, and is the reason much of the high country is still under significant snow cover into late July.

Somewhat lower, but very rugged, and with a heavier forest cover, the Absarokas rise on the west side of the Boulder River. They see fewer visitors than the Beartooth and are more difficult to navigate.

More than three-fourths of the A-B is above timberline and elevated enough to hold tundra soil. Nine major drainages pour out of the higher reaches, giving the Yellowstone River, between Yellowstone National Park and Billings, one-third of its flow. Estimates of the number of lakes are close to 1,000.

Unroaded segments of the complex cover more than 1,135,000 acres. Most of it, 920,324 acres, is federally designated wilderness

Together, the Absaroka-Beartooth boasts of more than 120 peaks over 10,000 feet in elevation. Twenty-nine of them top 12,000 feet, including Montana's highest, 12,799-foot Granite Peak.

Owing to its elevation, this lofty terrain is scoured by wind and at times ferocious weather. Summer thunder and lightening storms accompanied by hail, can be frightening at times, and snow is possible even in July and August.

Many large, high elevation snowfields provide fertile habitat for the bloom of a microscopic algae that creates extensive patches of "pink snow." Dissolved nutrients, the energy of the sun, and carbon dioxide combine to promote reproduction and growth of the this algae.

Virtually every Montana big game animal and a myriad of little critters call this place home. The high lakes and streams are fabled for fishing. Brook trout are the most common, followed by cutthroats, rainbow, golden and graylings.

Once up in the rolling alpine landscape, a hiker gains a pristine place. Here is a most magnificent environment of glistening lakes, rushing streams, waterfalls, snow, ice and in the warm months, a wildflower display among the best in the Northern Rockies. Great views spanning idyllic mountain panoramas are everywhere. It is a world unto itself!

Numerous trails provide access along the entire fringe of the Absaroka-Beartooth. But in the high terrain, they disappear. Though these cloud-swept areas are relatively easy to negotiate, a map and compass should be used.

Absaroka-Beartooth Wilderness. RICK AND SUSIE GRAETZ

And elevation gains, as much as distance, need to be considered when planning a trip.

From the northeast, the Stillwater drainage leads to the Lake Plateau and many day trips. On the Beartooth east face, West and East Rosebud canyons head to some of the high plateaus, as well as the Granite Peak region. Near the Red Lodge area, trails follow the West Fork and Lake Fork of Rock Creek through deep canyons up toward more lakes and towering peaks.

Entrance may be gained from several points along the Beartooth Highway, especially from just below the west side of Beartooth Pass. From the Cooke City environs, trails point towards a grouping of 12,000-foot peaks. The Kersey Lake-Broadwater trailhead is popular for crossing the Beartooth to East Rosebud.

Lady of the Lake Trail and paths out of the Daisy Pass area, both near Cooke City, head to high lake fishing. Farther west in Yellowstone National Park, routes start from Slough Creek into Buffalo Plateau and some of the seldom used southern reaches of the Absaroka. East of Mammoth, Hell Roaring Creek allows for a point-to-point trip across the southern Absaroka to Slough Creek.

From Paradise Valley, the Mill Creek region has many starting points into the western perimeter of the wilderness. On the north, from the Yellowstone Valley, footpaths take off from the Boulder River and switch back to both the Beartooth and Absaroka mountains.

A Beartooth wanderer needs to be ready for cold wet weather, even in summer! For finding your way, good maps and several books are available.

The Rocky Mountain Survey Maps of the area are 15 minute in scale and have less detail than the USGS 7.5 minute sheets, but added features make them a good companion. Both are handy to have. Harrison Fagg, a climber of all the 12,000-foot-plus Beartooth peaks, published "The High Country Map," featuring climbing notes for each of the tallest summits. Forest Service maps are also available. Falcon Press has "Hiking the Beartooth," which lists many trails with detailed information on each. Montana Magazine's "Beartooth Country," is a pictorial with significant writing.

This is a fragile place that needs respect. Go prepared, keep a clean camp and enjoy some of the most spectacular mountain scenery on the continent.

GRANITE PEAK — MONTANA'S HIGHEST MOUNTAIN

It is all a mountain should be — remote and majestic. Sheer walls on all sides and crevassed glaciers flowing from its upper reaches present an awesome sight. At 12,799 feet, Montana's Granite Peak stands out as the patriarch of "the roof of Montana," the Beartooth Range of the south central part of the state.

The 1 million-acre Absaroka/Beartooth Wilderness boasts 28 peaks above 12,000 feet in elevation. Granite is one of seven of these found in a closely-grouped chain that includes Hidden Glacier — 12,377 feet, Glacier Peak — 12,351 feet, Mount Villard — 12,319 feet, Tempest Mountain — 12,478 feet, Mystic Mountain — 12,063 feet and Mount Peal — 12,002 feet.

The heights of Granite and the surrounding summits piqued the interest of early-day Beartooth explorers and mountaineers. In late July 1898, a geologist and mining engineer James Kimball, led a pioneering expedition to these big peaks. He was searching for minerals and planned to map the region between Cooke City and Nye. Bad weather disrupted the mapping, and no precious metals were found. The group did make an attempt on Granite Peak, but were stopped at the 11,447-foot level (estimated by their aneroid barometer).

Perhaps the person with the most interest in exploring the Beartooth and climbing Montana's loftiest peak was Fred Inabnit (Mount Inabnit, south of East Rosebud Lake was named in his honor). His first sojourn in these mountains was in 1907; then, in 1910, he approached Granite with the thought of scaling it. He scanned the east ridge and concluded that there had to be a better route. After crossing Granite Creek and the pass to Sky Top Drainage on the peak's east and south sides, his party was turned back by an intense August snowstorm.

Again, in 1922, Inabnit led five well-equipped climbers to Granite, approaching from the south by way of Sky Top Creek. They came within 300 feet of the top before being halted by sheer walls.

The undaunted Inabnit returned once more, in 1923, after persuading the Forest Service to participate in a joint climbing venture. From a camp on

12,799-foot Granite Peak. RICK AND SUSIE GRAETZ

Avalanche Lake, in upper Granite Creek (southeast side), the expedition split into two assault teams. They spent the first day making a reconnaissance of the mountain, and concluded that there was no easy way to the top. The next morning, Inabnit led his group into the Sky Top for another try at the south face. Forest Service legend Elers Koch took the other climbers up the east ridge. Steep walls again blocked Inabnit and his team when they heard the triumphant shouts of the rangers above, and that was how Granite Peak was first climbed that Aug. 23, 1923.

Ascending Granite today is just as exciting, and almost as challenging as it was at the turn of the century. Altitude, weather, and very rugged and precipitous terrain, place our state's highest summit and its environs among the most adventuresome areas to climb in Montana.

The peak can be approached from several points. The south side is best reached by going from Cooke City to the Sky Top Lakes. The most popular route, and the one that leads to the so-called "easiest climb" (on the east face and also to the north face) is from Fishtail to Mystic Lake and the Froze-to-Death Plateau. A trail up Phantom Creek from East Rosebud Lake is also used to get to these same places. All these routes are shown on Rocky Mountain Surveys' Alpine/Cooke City map. And you can get the more detailed 7.5-minute USGS quads at your local outdoor shop as well. Falcon Press's *Hiking Montana* has a good description of the Mystic Lake access.

There are four major routes to climb the peak: the east face route, the north face, a couple of spines on the southeast side, and the south face. The south and north faces are the most difficult. No passage on Granite offers a hands-in-the-pocket walk. All approaches and pitches are steep, requiring a great deal of physical effort. Granite Peak should never be considered as a first mountain for novice climbers unless they are accompanied by at least one experienced mountaineer. Knowledge of route finding, belaying and rappelling techniques, and the use of an ice ax, is necessary. An experienced group can do the east face without equipment — other than an ice ax needed for the snow bridge encountered part of the way up. A 150-foot length of at least a 9-mm rope, for safety purposes, would be good to have.

Granite presents many hazards, including intense rain or snowstorms that can strike at a moment's notice, high winds, slick boulders, falling rocks, and the dangers of hypothermia. Dressing properly with layers, using quality camping gear, and having some idea of the long-range weather conditions will help provide you with a great experience in spite of the inherent dangers on, and around, this very formidable mountain.

—RICK AND SUSIE GRAETZ

BEARTOOTH HIGHWAY

The elevation is noticeable, even while you're trekking on a relatively flat ridge; breathing is deeper and steps are slower. Here, at nearly 11,000 feet, one is well above the surrounding terrain. For miles in every direction, the vistas include mountains, perennial snowfields, distant forests, and grasslands. Numerous small lakes reflect passing clouds. And your lofty perch doesn't require climbing an arduous mountain footpath. This is Beartooth Pass, the high point of one of our nation's finest roadways: US Hwy 212, the Beartooth Highway.

This region has been traveled for thousands of years, and evidence of Native American use remains. The first recorded crossing of the Beartooth Plateau was in 1882 by General Philip H. Sheridan of the US Army. Later, Ed VanDyke established a better route, called the Slick Rock Trail, which started at Wolf Creek on the upper Clarks Fork and traversed the plateau before coming down the steep, talus slopes to Rock Creek. The miners and merchants from Red Lodge sought an easier route. Dr.Siegfriedt, of Bear Creek, and later O.H.P. Shelley, a Red Lodge newspaperman, championed a road over the current terrain. Congressman Scott Leavitt sponsored the Parks Approach Act and in 1931 his proposal passed Congress. By 1932, the $2.5 million construction project was under way and on June 14, 1936, the scenic highway across the Beartooth was ready for use.

This unique thoroughfare opens country usually accessible only to wilderness visitors. It traverses the alpine Beartooth Plateau and Wyoming's High Lakes Country, skirting the southern perimeter of the almost one million-acre Absaroka-Beartooth Wilderness.

The 65-mile-long Beartooth Highway heads southwest from Red Lodge, rises gradually through glacier-carved Rock Creek Canyon, then begins a very steep climb, via switchbacks, up the south wall of this drainage to the 10,000-foot Line Creek Plateau. From Beartooth Pass at 10,947 feet elevation, the road descends moderately through high, wildflower laden meadows and lakes to the conifer forests in the canyon of the Clarks Fork of the Yellowstone River, where, at 7,300 feet above sea level, it meets Wyoming's Sunlight Basin Highway and continues to its terminus at Cooke City. Yellowstone's northeast entrance is just seven miles away.

Although the highest segment of this road to the sky is in Wyoming, Montana anchors both ends.

The highway is closed when autumn blizzards become serious, often in October. Winter storms can drop more than 35 feet of snow on the high country. Frequent winds reposition the white stuff to create enormous drifts and cornices on the lee side of exposed ridges. When the road is plowed-open in late May, travelers might pass through cuts 30 to 40 feet deep. In June and July, a ski-racing camp operates atop the pass and recreational skiers and boarders can find plenty of degrees of steepness along the higher reaches of the roadway.

What makes this Beartooth Highway so special? It provides easy access to wild and remote areas, but at the same time, offers a quality experience to those wanting to stay near civilization. In most areas, you can venture 100 hundred yards off the pavement and feel you are in the heart of an untrammeled wilderness.

You'll find interesting day hikes from various points off of the Beartooth Highway. One trail is reached by following the road along Rock Creek to its end; this dirt byway passes through the Limber Pine and Parkside campgrounds west of Red Lodge. On top of the plateau at the sunrise end, look for the Beartooth Loop National Recreation Trail. West of the summit, follow trails coming from Island Lake, Beartooth Lake or from the Clay Butte Lookout Road.

Trailheads leading to the backcountry are many. The Beartooth Hikers Guide (Falcon Press) outlines trails for all abilities and Beartooth Country (Montana Magazine) is an excellent companion book.

The Custer National Forest-Beartooth Division map provides an overview of the highway and trails. For wilderness travel, use the USGS 7.5 minute maps or those produced by Rocky Mountain Surveys out of Billings. Most outdoor shops have them.

Hike these off road areas with great care ... this is tundra-like topography. The vegetation is delicate and susceptible to long-lasting damage. Avoid making fires and pack out everything you take in.

Take time to see this national treasure. If you are only passing through, allow four hours for driving and stops. Better yet, take a week.

—RICK AND SUSIE GRAETZ

LOWER YELLOWSTONE RIVER

FROM BILLINGS TO THE TONGUE RIVER

Downstream from Billings, crops such as sugar beets, corn and soybeans flourish thanks to the presence of some of Montana's most fertile soil.

Pioneer stockman, S.S. Huntley's name was given to the next town on the tour. The first hamlet was a stagecoach stop and steamboat landing on the north side of the river. Once again the railroad stuck their nose into the design of things and when the NP came through in 1882, the town was relocated across the Yellowstone.

Most folks out in these parts prefer agrarian activity to industrialization and the Reclamation Act of 1902 made it possible for the Huntley Irrigation Project to get started. The plan called for a diversion dam to be built on the Yellowstone. In 1907 when it was completed, river water flowed to more than 30,000 acres of cropland allowing Huntley and nearby Ballantine and Worden to sustain life.

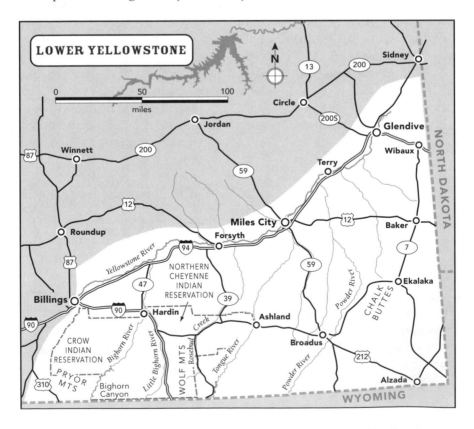

Worden was the maiden name of Senator Joe Dixon's wife. Her father was Frank Worden of Missoula fame. And Ballantine took the last name of a railroad manager.

The heavily irrigated land in and around the Huntley Project area soon gives way to more marginal agricultural country. Watered parcels are evident as the Yellowstone's flow continues east but only on select bottomlands. Dry land wheat is raised on the upper benches, but for the most part rangeland dominates.

Thirty miles below Billings stands a National Treasure. The only visible remaining evidence of the Lewis and Clark Expedition is preserved on the north wall of the 200-foot-high Pompey's Pillar. On July 25, 1806, Clark halted here, etched his name and the date in the formation's sandstone and then recorded the deed in his journal...

"at 4 P M arived at a remarkable rock Situated in an extensive bottom on the Stard. Side...this rock I ascended and from it's top had a most extensive view in every direction. This rock which I shall Call Pompy's Tower is 2oo feet high and 400 paces in secumphrance and only axcessable on one Side which is from the N. E the other parts of it being a perpendicular Clift...The Indians have made 2 piles of Stone on the top of this Tower. The nativs have ingraved on the face of this rock the figures of animals &c. near which I marked my name and the day of the month & year."

Named after Sacajawea's son Jean Baptiste Charbonneau whom Clark called Little Pomp or Little Chief, the landmark has been designated a National Monument. Captain Clark also christened a creek near this spot Baptiste Creek.

Standing on top of Pompey's Pillar, one bids farewell to the mountains. The fading blue and purple outline of the Beartooths is yet seen far to the west. The not so imposing Pryor and Bighorn ranges are discernible to the southwest. Only 20 miles of the Bighorns extend into Montana and these summits top out at 9,000 feet. The loftiest crags over 13,000 feet are in the 100-mile Wyoming stretch. To the southeast, the low rise of the 50-mile-long Wolf Mountains, separating the Crow and Northern Cheyenne reservations, are visible. The Bull Mountains, also 50 miles in length and with few points over 4,000 feet, reach above the pine studded prairie hills north of the river. From now on, the mountains that have been an ever-present connection to the river will no longer be a part of the horizon; the unobstructed sphere of the prairie now takes in all points of the compass.

The river, as it eases along towards its next tributary, the Bighorn, seems to be more active than above Pompey's Pillar in cutting its banks sending chunks of sandstone into the water

The Missouri was known for its steamboat era, but in the 1870s and 1880s, the big boats also spent time on the Yellowstone River. Steamers heading up the Yellowstone more often than not carried military personnel and freight; their main task was supplying Fort Keough (the current Miles City).

A far trickier river to navigate than the Missouri, most of the vessels only reached the mouth of the Bighorn River well east of Billings. And wood, the fuel needed to keep the steamers moving wasn't always available. Native Americans spent the winter camped along the river bottoms. When food became scarce, their large contingent of horses often resorted to eating the bark of the trees. Each winter they could girdle hundreds of cottonwoods and kill them. Those traveling the river well after the "Indian removal" noted magnificent stands of cottonwoods coming back.

Grant Marsh, who became known as the finest river pilot on the Yellowstone, was the first to give a run at the old girl. On a military reconnaissance in 1873, he brought the Far West within two miles of the mouth of the Powder River, before grinding to a halt on a reef of rocks 147 miles upriver from the Missouri-Yellowstone Confluence.

Between the towns of Custer and Bighorn, the largest subsidiary meets the Yellowstone. The Bighorn River, spilling from glaciers deep in Wyoming's Wind River Range, wanders into Montana through one of the most precipitous gorges in the Northern Rockies-Big Horn Canyon before joining the Yellowstone. Prior to the 1966 closing of the Yellowtail Dam gates, the Bighorn ran wild through this deep canyon. Now the impoundment collects silt and sends out clear, cold water creating one of the nation's great fisheries downstream.

Custer, which takes its name from Lt. Col. George Armstrong Custer is located about three miles upstream from the mixing of the Yellowstone and Bighorn rivers and Bighorn about one mile downstream. Both were much larger towns during the heyday of the Homestead Era.

A tributary of the Bighorn, the Little Bighorn (called Greasy Grass by the Crow and other tribes), was the site of the best known of all of the Indian/white battles. On June 25, 1876, the infamous Lt. Col. George Armstrong Custer led his Seventh Cavalry to defeat by the unified Teton Sioux and Northern Cheyenne forces at the "Battle of the Little Bighorn" near today's Crow Agency. His entire command was killed … more than 260 men in all.

The bodies of the dead and those wounded in other skirmishes that same day were taken to the confluence of the Bighorn and Little Bighorn to be loaded on the Far West. The steamboat, piloted by Grant Marsh, made the chancy trip of 50 miles up the Bighorn's rock strewn channel. The captain then raced his 190-foot-long boat with its human cargo down the Yellowstone to the Missouri and east to Bismark in Dakota Territory. Setting an incredible record, he covered the 710 river miles in 54 hours.

In 1807, Spanish trader Manuel Lisa built Montana's first fur post on the Yellowstone near the mouth of the Bighorn River. Owing to constant Indian troubles, it lasted only four years. And it was from Fort Manuel Lisa that John Colter set out on his astonishing winter of 1807–1808 adventure through "John Colter's Hell" and the headwaters area of the Yellowstone River.

Billings sits between the Rimrocks and the Yellowstone River. RICK AND SUSIE GRAETZ

Fur trading was brisk along a stretch of the Yellowstone from the Bighorn River to the outlet of the Tongue River at Miles City. In a span from 1807 until 1875, at one time or another, eight trading posts existed. By 1876 they were gone, victims of an industry turned unprofitable.

Sometime around 1870, situated on the banks of the Bighorn River across from Custer, the prosperous town of Junction City (for a short time it was known as Terry's Landing) came to be as a trading post. A multitude of raucous saloons helped create the epitome Wild West town attracting all manner of characters. Since the so-called "Outlaw Trail" pointed through here on its way north from Wyoming to Canada, horse rustling was an occupation for many of the residents and most of the transients. Considered "neutral ground," Junction City was a good place for them to congregate. The rustlers, respecting the property in the community, did their deeds elsewhere, while adding to the local economy with their spending.

By the early 1880s, Junction City began shrinking in size. The railroad's progress up the Yellowstone Valley was putting an end to all of the fun on the wrong side of the river. Before long, the restless waters of the Yellowstone undercut the ground and the site of a vibrant part of the past washed away.

Where the Bighorn sends its waters into the Yellowstone was once the most active and significant point on the whole river, serving both as a center for military operations and the fur trade. The ever-changing channel of the Yellowstone makes it certain the mouth of the Bighorn is not where it was during these early times. Today, the waters of both rivers pass a silent space, the buildings and clamor of a boisterous and disorderly time long since gone.

Beyond the Bighorn River, the Yellowstone's final 300 miles move in an authentic warm water environment. The transition from the icy rivulets of glacier melt high in the Wyoming wilderness, through tumbling waterfalls to a mellow, slower paced prairie flow is complete. From the mouth of the Bighorn down to Miles City, a very wide Yellowstone River splits into numerous channels; islands and gravel bars are frequent. High spring flows are constantly creating new channels and sandbars and backwaters. This high degree of activity, common to an unfettered river, creates riparian diversity and idyllic wildlife habitat. This is the way it is for much of the "prairie stretch of the river" from the Bighorn's entrance to the Missouri. Turkeys, deer and antelope tour the earth above the waters edge and bank beaver, muskrats, an occasional otter, ducks, geese and blue heron are amongst other wild inhabitants that call the embankment and water home. When they are migrating, thousands of whistling swans and sandhill cranes fill the river's airspace.

From the Bighorn River on down, the lower Yellowstone provides ideal conditions for walleye, sauger and sturgeon. And then there is the prehistoric paddlefish, which the lower Yellowstone, in addition to segments of the Missouri in central and eastern Montana, are the only places in the world outside of China's Yangtze River where these whopping fish (some weigh up to 100 pounds) live. In all, there are about 45 different species in these murky waters and unlike their cold water, up river friends with sharp eyes for finding sustenance, these fish must feel for their food with whiskers and other feelers in their not-so-clear surroundings.

By 1870 the bison had been slaughtered, Indians were being pushed to reservations, the fur trade was dying and cattlemen began moving into the Yellowstone River Valley and other points in Eastern Montana. Grass was abundant and free and fed cattle well as it had the bison for hundreds of years. They came from Western Montana and far to the south. Longhorn cattle were driven up from Texas to winter on the open Montana prairies. Cattle and sheep ranches sprouted up everywhere on the high plains of eastern Montana and especially in the Yellowstone country.

Too much of a good thing proved fatal. An overcrowded range combined with a dose of Mother Nature's revenge nearly killed the industry. The summers of 1885 and 1886 were dry and hot; very little grass grew. In November of 1886 a combination of snow, cold and thawing hit the country building a layer of ice on the ground. The animals couldn't break through to get what little grass there was. Then on Christmas Eve, heavy snowstorms began and a merciless cold with temperatures of 50 and 60 degrees below zero descended from the north. In March when the chinooks came and the freeze broke, more than 60 percent of Montana's livestock had perished. This delivered a fatal blow to the open range days along the Yellowstone. Those operators who were able to keep going changed their traditions and established ranches that still exist in the Yellowstone drainage.

On the heels of the ranchers, came the homesteaders who made perhaps the most permanent mark on the Yellowstone Valley. Their influx created overnight towns. The first Homestead Act of 1862, impractical as it was, offering only160 acres of free land to would-be farmers, attracted outsiders to the valley. It became obvious that more land was needed to survive and in 1909, Montana Senator Joe Dixon led efforts to create the 1909 Enlarged Homestead Act offering 320 acres of land, cutting ownership time from five to three years and allowed a five months absence from the stake.

From 1900 to 1918 were the expansion years for the Homestead Era in the Yellowstone Valley. Then the ample rains that had provided bountiful crops and allowed for false advertising by the railroads and land promoters, decreased. Each succeeding year became drier until finally the wind picked up and carried the plowed parched soil from countless acres into the Dakotas. Thousands of disheartened sodbusters left everything and exited Eastern Montana, allowing the prairie to reclaim itself. Farm failures caused many towns to die or become shells of their former selves. The hardiest folks who figured out away to stay joined with the ranchers who survived 1886–1887 and became the backbone behind those who call the banks of the Yellowstone River home today.

Treasure County's seat, Hysham, fronts the Yellowstone's south side about 17 miles below the town of Bighorn. It began as an NP Railroad siding in 1882 and was named after the proprietor of the Flying E cattle outfit, Charles Hysham. A town site was laid out on school teacher Ada Channel's homestead and a store opened in 1906. Looking more at home near the Alamo in Texas, the out of context Spanish style stucco Yucca Theater on Main Street is a prominent historic landmark. Giving the town character and a touch of distinction, it was built in 1931 by Dave Manning, a Montana lawmaker, who, at the time of his retirement in 1985, had served longer than any other legislator in the nation … 52 years. The Manning family donated the property to Treasure County to serve as a museum.

Forsyth is the next port of call for the ever-widening river. Picturesque and peaceful it sits beneath a backdrop of high sandstone bluffs and badlands. Known for its Neo classical courthouse, a beautiful copper domed structure, it was named after General James W. Forsyth, who in 1885 became the first military leader to arrive here on a Yellowstone steamboat.

Here again, in 1882, the Northern Pacific Railroad played a hand in building another community by establishing a division house. Rail jobs provided growth, but it wasn't until after 1901, when the Homestead Era began, that town truly enlarged. This the county seat of Rosebud County, also saw the arrival of the Milwaukee Railroad in 1908 on the opposite side of the river as it was directing its way northwest to the Musselshell Valley.

The railroad and the abundance of coal to the south in the Colstrip area keep Forsyth's economy healthy.

Farming and grazing land trade places off and on for the next ten or so river miles to Rosebud Creek and the tiny town of Rosebud. Named for the tangle of wild roses that bloom profusely along the Yellowstone and up the creek, the area holds its own place in history. In 1835, the American Fur Company built Fort Van Buren where Rosebud Creek, getting its start in the Wolf Mountains to the south, runs into the Yellowstone River. It was abandoned in 1845. Then on June 22, 1876, Lt. Col. George Custer and his ill fated men camped at the mouth of the creek before their three-day march up the Rosebud to face their destiny on the Little Bighorn River. In 1882, the Northern Pacific established a railroad siding, and livestock trailed to the area for shipping brought a town to life.

Although they were very near some of Montana's richest coal deposits, Captain Clark and his fellow floaters passing through this landscape identified the coal seams along the river's banks and wrote (the coal) *"is like that of the Missouri of an inferior quality."* Further notes for that day, July 29, 1806, included *"… great quantities of Coal in all the hills … late in the evening I arived at the enterance of a River which I take to be the 'Lazeka''*(Sioux name) or *Tongue River … I intended to encamp on an eligable Spot imediately below this river, but finding that its' water So muddy and worm and to render it very disagreeable to drink, I crossed the rochejhone and encamped on an island close to the Lard. Shore …"*Camp was on the northeastern edge of what would become Miles City.

The Yellowstone River at Miles City. RICK AND SUSIE GRAETZ

Miles City — Cattle Capital on the Yellowstone

At Miles City the Tongue River, originating as a cascading alpine stream in the Bighorn Mountains of Wyoming, joins the Yellowstone adding the abundance of silt accumulated on its journey after leaving the Tongue River Reservoir near Decker, Montana.

After the Indians' revenge against Custer in 1876, the US Army felt it necessary to build a post about two miles upstream from where the Tongue and Yellowstone rivers join. At first, the soldiers, under the leadership of General Nelson Miles, were stationed at an uncomfortable cantonment on the Tongue River.

In late 1876, Miles ordered many of the civilians whom he considered to be "loafers and coffee coolers" out of his temporary headquarters and drew a line two miles to the east, which they were not to cross. Within a couple of days the deposed but undaunted folks had set up tents for a saloon and gambling parlor; they were back in business. Named after the cantankerous and ruthless general who ousted them, the seeds for Miles City (or Miles Town) were planted. True to the spirit of the West and holding no grudges, the General was invited to a feast of whiskey and wild game in spite of his actions against the new town's folk.

Construction of Fort Keough began in 1877, it was completed a year later and General Miles was named commander. Miles City relocated (not the railroads fault this time) to the east side of the Tongue at a place where the Yellowstone River washes its north side. The Northern Pacific's tracks made it here in 1881. Although the Indian war ended shortly after the fort was finished, it lasted until the early 1900s.

Now Custer County's seat, Miles City quickly became the most prominent village in the Yellowstone Basin and an important trade center. Known as a tough town boasting of 23 saloons, a mangy mix of hide hunters, soldiers, cowboys and railroad workers made it seem lawless at times. Once it was the largest horse market in the nation and is now the home of the renown Bucking Horse Sale.

In its founding days there were over 200,000 head of cattle in the area and plenty of cowboys tending them and spending money. As the town evolved, it continued to grow in importance to the livestock industry and remains very much a cattleman's (and cattlewoman's) community. And least anyone forget where the city came from, the outstanding Range Riders Museum, dedicated to the cowboys who came to Miles City before 1910, shows off its colorful past.

Throughout its heyday, Miles City was reputed to have one of the best red-light districts in the west. Located on the edge of town, rumor has it the neighborhood was populated with beautiful, stylish women from Las Vegas and other cities. On the "fancy ladies" day off, dressed in their finery, they took to the streets shopping, getting their nails and hair done and dining out. It was said nary a respectable woman would leave her house much less show her face downtown on Wednesdays.

Main Street with its distinct western historical atmosphere was actually laid out before the town took hold. Originally, it sat on the trail between Bismark and Fort Keough (the I 90 of today) and served as the principal road to the fort. One writer called it "an artery of commerce and travel." Used by stagecoaches, bull wagons, horse riders and the businesses, the town grew up around it.

On To the Missouri

According to Vic Riggs of the Montana Department of Fish, Wildlife and Parks, ten miles downriver from Miles City, a 36-mile stretch of the Yellowstone to about Fallon changes its shape from the braided, multi-channeled river to a straighter and mostly single channel owing to a strong bedrock presence. This section has changed little since Captain Clark floated through on July 30, 1806, and wrote, *"This is by far the worst place which I have Seen on this river from the Rocky Mountains to this place ... a succession of bad shoals, interspersed with hard brown, gritty rock extending for 6 miles."* They had to lower the canoes over them by hand for fear of breaking the boats up on the rocks. Manageable in high water, normal river volume makes them a chore to descend. A bison by the rapids inspired Clark to name them Buffalo Shoals.

Thirty-seven river miles east of Miles City, the Powder River — a mile wide, an inch deep, too thin to plow and to thick to drink," enters the Yellowstone. Originating in the Snake Mountains of Wyoming, it contributes 50 percent of the Yellowstone's silt load and less than 5 percent of its water.

Camped across from the mouth of the Powder on July 30, 1806, Clark gave a similar description, *"... proceeded on at 7 Miles passed the enterance of a river the water ... is Shallow and the water very muddy and of the Colour of the banks a darkish brown. I observe great quantities of red Stone* (clinker or scoria) *thrown out of this river that from the appearance of the hills at a distance on its lower Side induced me to call this red Stone*(clinker or scoria) *river. as the water was disagreeably muddy I could not Camp on that Side below its mouth ..."*

If a landscape could ever be called open, this piece of the Yellowstone in any direction is the essence of that illustration. Roads, humans and trees are scarce; a sweeping range, badlands and uncluttered views are plentiful. And there is nothing to hold back the wind. In the summer of 1877, the steamboat Osceola was taken apart by a ferocious force. The captain wrote the owner

Forty-six river miles down from Miles City, the Yellowstone passes Terry a small ranching settlement nestled at the foot of beautifully sculpture red, beige, rust and black colored badlands. Chief Sitting Bull and his Sioux people spent the winter of 1868 near here.

Named for General Alfred Terry, the Commander of the Western Army in the late 1870s, it originated as a bison hunter's dugout in 1877. Wolfers supplying wood for passing steamboats (no wonder the land is void of trees out here…steamboats burned 30 cords of wood in a 24 hour day), were the next to contribute to the initial population and later a few homesteaders moved to the area. One, Evelyn Cameron, who came in 1893, became a notable photographer chronicling life on the southeast Montana prairie. The Cameron Gallery next to the Prairie County Historical Museum contains an exhibit of her work.

The arrival of the Milwaukee Railroad in 1907 and the hordes of eager and desperate homesteaders it brought spurred Terry's growth. As with most of the other towns in this corner of the Great Plains, the homestead bust of the 1920s caused the community to deplete its population and resources.

Across the river from town, the Terry Badlands cover an extensive area reaching north to the Big and Little Sheep mountains and the Yellowstone-Missouri divide. The Sheeps, a series of gumbo hills and eroded badlands stand no more at their tallest point than 300 feet above the adjacent country, but they are high enough to be noticed.

July 31, 1806, Clark observed the colored sandstone and the cap rock formations that have a more erosion resistant rock on top of weaker material, as well as other dry land creations in the area.

Ten miles by road from Terry, sits another old, once a much bigger, railroad related town. Fallon came to be in about in 1884 as a Northern Pacific station. Army officer and Indian agent Benjamin O'Fallon, nephew of Captain William Clark, left his name here.

The Yellowstone's next port of call is Glendive and the spectacular Makoshika State Park.

In 1854, George Gore, an Irishman with no conscience, came to southeast Montana to hunt. His traveling entourage consisted of more than 100 horses, six wagons, an arsenal of guns and ammunition, numerous dogs and 40 workers. He hired Jim Bridger as a guide and spent the next two years in the territory slaughtering grizzly bears, elk, deer, antelope and countless bison and raising the ire of Indians and white alike. While crossing a small stream that entered the Yellowstone, the greedy tourist christened it Glendive Creek (some records show Glendale was the original name) after a place in Ireland. The name Glendive, corrupted from his naming if that were the case, stuck.

It's the same story for Glendive as with most of the towns along the river, it too owes its start to the military in 1873, the railroad in 1881 and the homesteaders in the early 1900s. But other factors also occurred.

Yellowstone steamboats visiting the military establishment brought newcomers and supplies and by 1880, the town was platted. This is cattle country, and big herds were driven to Glendive to be shipped out by rail. A short-lived boom came to town in the 1950s, as underlying oil was tapped. By the 1980s much of this activity disappeared and the town settled down to the agricultural center and Montana's Paddlefish capital it is today.

Makoshika, the Indian name for this badland topography, is one of the state's best-known parks. Visible from the river, it literally starts in Glendive's backyard.

Rising above the surrounding range, the preserve covers 8,832 acres studded with pines and divided it into finger like mesas separated by mostly barren, steep, gullied slopes and coulees. A place of contrasts, the area receives more than ten inches of rain a year allowing for lush green undergrowth, but many of the south facing slopes and true badlands are sunbaked, with little or no vegetation. Dinosaurs come to mind when exploring this beautiful and exotic park. It isn't difficult to imagine ancient creatures roaming the rugged terrain. Fossils imbedded in the walls of the numerous box canyons give credence to these thoughts.

These badlands, or mini-deserts, begin forming when the vegetation cover is destroyed, usually by wildfire or overgrazing. Erosion starts, gullies are formed and seeds of potential new growth of plants and grasses are washed away or unable to take hold in the hardened soil.

Heavy spring and summer downpours accelerate the process. Steeper slopes are etched faster and seemingly smooth surfaced alluvial deposits fan out below them. Soon the entire disrupted area is void of green growth. Once well into the creation stage, they perpetuate themselves and usually become permanent. In a few instances, vegetation takes hold again in the disturbed areas and the beginnings of badlands topography is reversed.

While this carved dry-appearing country receives as much precipitation as adjacent areas, the lack of a protective shield of flora gives it an image of receiving very little moisture.

Exquisite sandstone formations are often intermingled with a badlands environment. Miniature and giant toadstools, castles and cathedrals, fine lined domes, balancing rocks, sentinel-like spires and other beautiful statues of rock add color and personality to these rain-furrowed hills while gremlins and goblins stand watch atop high cliffs. Wind erosion helps fashions them, taking away one grain of sand at a time.

Agates are another lower Yellowstone River attraction. Millions of years ago, volcanoes ruled eastern Montana. Powerful eruptions of molten lava and ash covered and destroyed more than hundreds of miles of forests. After centuries of activity, the climate cooled and rain washed silica and minerals from the surface of the land down into the labyrinths of hardened lava beds, filling the nooks and crannies with what several eons later would become Montana agates.

In those unstable geologic times, mountains were being born and layers of buried lava broken up. Driving rains eroded the debris washing it into the lower country. The Yellowstone River is the recipient of a magnitude of the alluvial gravel; and mixed amongst the rocks and stones are beautiful agate treasures waiting to be found.

The Yellowstone River near Sidney. RICK AND SUSIE GRAETZ

A few agates are found around Livingston, but down river past Pompey's Pillar, they gain in volume through to the confluence with the Missouri. The magical stones with patterns and scenes hidden inside are especially plentiful in the Glendive to Sidney area. Tom Harmon's Agate Stop and Museum in Savage is a good place to learn the history and hints on hunting these ancient gems.

Intake, Savage and Crane create small human outposts along a 52 mile-stretch of the Yellowstone. Intake was born in 1909 as a result of a diversion dam built for the Lower Yellowstone Irrigation Project. When the work was completed, there were nearly 400 miles of canals and ditches carrying Yellowstone River water to croplands including wide spread sugar beet fields. Historical notes show Savage, which also benefited from the irrigation project, was named for H.M. Savage, a railroad official. The town of Crane, close to Sidney was titled after the owners of the Crane Ranch.

From Savage to Sidney, nearing the end of its run, the river provides a popular floating stretch amidst the Elk Island and the Seven Sisters Wildlife Management areas and the state owned Crittenden Island. Elk Island, actually three islands in high water and one in low flow, is near Savage, while Crane provides access to the seven small islands named Seven Sisters that steamboat Captain Grant Marsh entitled in honor of his siblings.

Floating from Elk Island to the Seven Sisters is a great way to see this special length of the Yellowstone, home to whitetail and mule deer, upland game birds, ducks and geese and other wild critters. Rebecca Kallevig, a teacher out of Sidney, remarked it takes from five to seven hours to cover this 12-mile stretch of water. She recommends paddling hard once you put in at Elk Island in order to get into the more scenic right hand, side channel. And since the river moves slowly here, sightings of eagles, blue heron and all manners of birdlife are a strong possibility.

William Clark wrote, on August 2, 1806, about this segment where the river and life in general slows down and spreads out, the "*river wide and very much divided by islands and Sand and Mud bars ... Saw emence numbers of Elk Buffalow and wolves to day ... passed the enter ance of Several brooks on each Side.*" Clark was most likely describing Elk Island and the Seven Sisters.

According to Howard Blunt from Montana Fish Wildlife & Parks in Glendive ,the river down from Glendive with its wide bottoms crowded with islands and sandbars and cottonwoods growing in profusion, still looks very much as Clark depicted it. From Intake on down, the terrain on the river's east side becomes rugged. Badlands and river breaks intermix and ascend well above the floodplain. Juniper, small ponderosa pine and green ash give a warm color to a harsh soil. The riverbank's west fringe rise to the territory beyond is more subdued and supports a scattering of riparian areas away from the main river.

Experiencing this part of the Yellowstone by canoe or raft is best as the highway from Glendive to Sidney seldom nears the water to present a good view or a feel for it.

Sidney is about a mile west of the Yellowstone and about 14 river miles short of its marriage to the Missouri. Named in 1888 for Sidney Walters, the young son of a local pioneer family, locals like to call it the Sunrise City, as this is where the sun first greets Montana. A pleasant community dotted with expansive tree-lined city parks, with five thousand people, it is the largest town in northeast Montana. Built on hard work and determination by folks with strong ethics, Sidney has weathered disasters that have erased all signs of many other towns. At one time, it could be said the place was teeming with homesteaders purchasing supplies and building materials and aiding the economy. By the time the dust from the drought cleared, there were few customers left. To say times were tough would be an understatement. Folks pared their lives down and fought to bring prosperity back. Then, like Glendive, the oil boom and bust visited Sidney; once again it hung on. Today, sugar beets, wheat and ranching provide the dollars, and the exhibits at the highly acclaimed Mondak Heritage Center provide reminders of the rich, historical past.

A few river miles north of Sidney, the Yellowstone crosses the North Dakota line, and then abruptly changes her mind and rushes back into Montana. It has been a long journey; about 90 percent of it spent shaping and nourishing this Big Sky state we like to think she calls home. Finally, about two miles west of the border, the Yellowstone bids Montana adieu, turns toward North Dakota and stays on track for the Missouri.

Some of Montana's earliest recorded history was played out here on the eastern fringes of our state where the Yellowstone ends its run. On April 27, 1805, The Corps of Discovery, after having spent a few days at the joining of the two rivers, first entered what would become Montana Territory. Through Fort Union, this "Confluence Country," from about 1828 until 1867, held supremacy over the fur trade business of the Upper Missouri.

The original Fort Union, built in 1828 by John Jacob Astor and his American Fur Company, was located about six miles up the Missouri from the Yellowstone. A handsome, some would say royal place, it attracted famous men of the day. When the Fur Trade Era ended in 1867, the fort fell into disrepair. Much of the material was moved to aid in the expansion of Fort Buford, a military post closer to the Yellowstone's confluence. Steamboats churning up the Missouri used what wood was left to feed their hungry boilers.

Today, the Fort Union Trading Post National Historic Site has been reconstructed into an exact replica as it was in 1851, and with the natural reconfiguration of the rivers, it is about three air miles up from the joining of the waters. For anyone interested in the fabled Missouri and Yellowstone rivers this historic site should be on your trail.

The geographic history of the Yellowstone-Missouri Confluence is also worthy of note. The original site of the uniting of the rivers the Corps of Discovery witnessed is about two miles to the southwest of the current junction.

Mike Casler of Fort Union points out that the historic maps made by early scientific expeditions, show a stable confluence well after Captain Clark made his. Casler noted a huge ice jam in the 1930s caused widespread flooding in the Yellowstone Valley and along the Missouri sending both rivers out of their banks and shifting channels. The confluence itself was forced to the northeast. A Landsat image shows very clearly a meander scar indicating the former river paths and their mixing spot. On the ground you can see it near Fairview, Montana, a town just to the west of the Yellowstone whose main street is divided down the middle by the Montana-North Dakota border.

Three miles from the eastern edge of Montana and Fort Union, the big wide silt-laden Yellowstone gives up her independence to the Missouri, together forming one very formidable river. Under the flag of the Missouri, it lunges towards a rendezvous with the Mississippi River.

—RICK AND SUSIE GRAETZ Taken from Montana's Yellowstone River by Rick and Susie Graetz.

PRYOR MOUNTAINS

Red desert, ice caves and wild horses — symbols of a most unique piece of Montana's mountain country — the island-like Pryor Mountains of south central Montana.

The Pryor Mountains. RICK AND SUSIE GRAETZ

From the Yellowstone River Valley and the big-little town of Billings, these Pryors appear as hills when compared to the towering Beartooth peaks 30 miles to the west. But their looks are deceiving. The view from an airplane flying just beyond their flanks, especially along the east face, reveals a steep, rugged and high landscape.

Named after Nathaniel Pryor of the Lewis and Clark Expedition, the Pryors rise from the heart of traditional Crow Country. Still used for vision quests today, this treasured land contains sacred sights and ancestral burial grounds. In order to safeguard these cultural and religious places, the segment of the Pryors located on the Crow Indian Reservation is closed to non-tribal members.

The Pryors are made up of two high ridges, each about 20 miles across. The northern stretch is within the boundaries of the Crow Reservation; here the highest points, a little over 7,300 feet, descend gradually into lower timbered buttes.

Ice caves and the 31,000-acre Pryor Mountain National Wild Horse Range highlight the southern part where the summits top out over 8,700 feet. A dramatic plunge of 5,000 feet to a desert environment exists at the southern most tip. This area is on public ground.

An 8,500-foot-high reef of limestone with sharp drop-offs makes up most of the west side of the range. The eastern perimeter declines from wooded ridges to lower hills that are abruptly ended by the sheer walls of the Big Horn Canyon National Recreation Area, a place of reefs, mesas and deep canyons.

This raised landscape is unlike any other place in the state. Its diversity is unequaled, ranging from high desert to sub-alpine terrain in a short distance. Places such as Dry Limestone Canyon, Big Coulee and Burnt Timber Canyon, all on the western edge, and in public ownership, are textbook examples of varied vegetation and landforms in a compact area.

Twenty inches of moisture falls annually in the heights, while less than seven inches sprinkles the lower dry country. Owing to just enough precipitation and snow cover, the upper Pryor meadows display a colorful warm — weather show of wildflowers, while in the desert area, blossoms, watered by thunderstorms, show off in the spring and early summer months.

From 120 to 140 head of wild mustangs roam the protected Wild Horse Range. The origin of these horses is somewhat uncertain. Many feel they are descendants of Spanish steeds that arrived in these parts through the Indians in the early 1700s. However, the most ancient record keepers have never mentioned them in their notes. The important factor is these magnificent animals live here and run free.

Before the onslaught of early day hunting and disease wiped them out, bighorn sheep roamed the ridges. In 1972, the animals were reintroduced to the nearby Bighorn Mountains. Not too long after, they crossed the frozen Bighorn River and moved back up into the Pryors. Today, there are approximately 150 sheep making a living along the east and southern escarpment of the Pryor Mountains.

Ice caves of the Pryors are a unique feature. The largest, Big Ice Cave, is an underground chamber insulated by rock walls that allow its icy floors to remain frozen throughout the summer. It, as well as the other icebox caverns, is in the heart of the southern tier of the range. A few other caves are hidden along the southeastern edge of the Wild Horse reserve.

While some of the caves are reachable only by foot, several roads lead to the Big Ice Cave — a 4x4 outfit with clearance is needed for most of them, but one is suitable for a highway car. Driving in the Pryors is on rough dirt roads that are only passable in dry weather. Hiking is perhaps the most reliable way to explore this unusual country.

The majority of the canyons of this desert-like topography receive very little walking use. Places, such as Lost Water Canyon, run the gauntlet of a prairie eco-system and offer the foot traveler a tough, but worthwhile, wilderness experience. Crooked Creek, the largest canyon in the Pryors, is 15 miles long and can be entered on either opening, but once in, it's very difficult to get out until the other end is attained. Other highlights of these mountains are the Dry Head Overlook with its view of the Bighorn Canyon, the wildlife haven of King Canyon, the easy Commissary and Island ridge hikes and the Bear Canyon trek to Big Pryor Mountain in the heart of the uplift.

Access to most of the Pryor — Wild Horse Range/Bighorn Canyon complex is through Bridger, Montana and Lovell, Wyoming. The Bighorn Canyon

Visitor Center at Lovell is the best starting point. They can provide trail and byway information and have maps. The best map in my opinion is the BLM Billings-Bridger-Powell special recreation edition. BLM headquarters is in Billings.

Natural preservation and recreation are the primary management objectives of the three government agencies (US Forest Service, National Park Service and Bureau of Land Management) and the sovereign tribe involved with the Pryor lands. Preservation of the wildlands characteristics is also a goal of many citizen groups such as the Montana Wilderness Association.

RICK AND SUSIE GRAETZ

BIGHORN CANYON

The late afternoon sun enriched the shades of yellow and red in the sedimentary layers of the 1,000-foot-high canyon walls; below, the ribbon of water had already absorbed their shadows. On a mesa to the south, a bison herd grazed the new green grass, while remnants of winter snow offset the surrounding summits of the Bighorn and Pryor mountains. Strong winds that rose earlier in the day ceased, and an imposing silence enveloped a most beautiful landscape ... spring was showing off.

Pretty Eagle Point was my perch to view this unique and awesome chunk of Montana — the Bighorn Canyon country. This is the heart of traditional Crow Indian domain, and on that late May day, it was easy to understand why it was once used for vision quests and is still held sacred.

South of Billings, the undulating prairie is terminated by the massive uplift of the Pryor and Bighorn mountains. Eons ago, a wild river began tumbling through here carving a twisting, narrow canyon through the steep-faced limestone plateau that separates the two ranges, creating one of the most precipitous gorges in the Northern Rockies. Since 1966 though, the flow of this Bighorn River has been tamed by Yellowtail Dam and a lake now sits placidly in its place.

The terrain echoes a history of early-day tribes and fur traders. Caves found throughout the area were used for seasonal shelter and food storage. An upper route that skirts the north rim — Bad Pass Trail — was established to avoid the dangers of the river. This 48-mile path allowed passage from the lower terrain of the north end of the canyon to river bottoms near present-day Lovell, Wyoming. Parts of the trail are still discernible, but most of it is on the Crow Reservation and off limits to non-Crow people without a tribal permit.

Just beyond the dam, where the Bighorn River picks up its flow northward toward the Yellowstone, the Bozeman Trail of 1864–1868 forded the river. This pioneer road, leading from Wyoming to western Montana, was under constant attack by the Sioux and Cheyenne, as it trespassed on Indian Territory. To protect white travelers coming through, in 1866 the army built Fort C.F.

The Bighorn Canyon and River. RICK AND SUSIE GRAETZ

Smith. An 1868 treaty with the various Plains Tribes, including the Crow, closed the trail and the fort. Ruins of the ill-fated structure can still be seen.

Today, the stretch of water behind the dam, reaching upstream for 71 miles, is known as Bighorn Canyon National Recreation Area. Since the public lands extend only 75 feet beyond the high water mark, for the most part, use of the northern area is limited to the water.

From the north, an 11-mile-long road from Fort Smith climbs steeply to the plateau and leads to the OK-A-BEH Boat Landing. You can also do a three-mile hike/climb to the landing. Enroute, either by vehicle or on foot, vantage points allow for great canyon views.

The best access to the Bighorn Canyon interior and hiking trails is on the south out of Lovell, Wyoming. The paved road from here ascends north for 27 miles through high desert and the Pryor Mountain Wild Horse Range to Barry's Landing. About three miles farther, via a dirt track, the historic Lockhart Ranch is accessed. You can hike beyond the ranch for about 12 miles.

The horse range you'll pass through was established in 1968 to protect the 120 to 140 wild mustangs that inhabit this dry area. Enter their home with respect for the animals and the fragile soils.

One particular spot off of this south end road, Devil's Canyon Overlook, at 1,000 feet above the water, offers perhaps the finest view of this unique piece of geography.

Boat transportation provides access to the many side drainages of the canyon such as Big Bull Elk Creek and Black Canyon. Both headwater high up in the

Bighorn Mountains. Their sidewalls soar upward to 2,500 feet in some places. In the quiet areas, you'll most likely spot the inhabitants of this country ... bighorn sheep, bear, deer, beaver, elk, coyote, mountain lion, and rattlesnakes.
—RICK AND SUSIE GRAETZ

TONGUE RIVER

The Tongue River that eases out of its reservoir near Decker is entirely different from its beginnings as a fast-flowing stream, headwatering high in Wyoming's Bighorn Mountains, just across the Montana line. Once free of the dam, it meanders lazily on its way to meet the Yellowstone River at Miles City.

Two versions explain its name. One claims Indians described it as "crooked like the white man's tongue and couldn't be depended upon." Hence, Tongue River. Another states Native Americans named the river for a tongue shaped formation of trees and rock that appears on a mountainside near its origin. Granville Stuart, famed Montana rancher, legislator and historian, called it the "crookedest stream in Montana."

The river is part of a large, sparsely populated, unique piece of geography that includes the Tongue River-Rosebud Divide, the Tongue River breaks and a portion of the far-flung Custer National Forest. It's a rough landscape made up of coulees, buttes, breaks, ridges and colorful red shale hills.

Cottonwood river bottoms give way to open forests of juniper and pine that fill the coulees and spot the higher plateau-like terrain. Sagebrush covers the open land. Although not quite as steep, nor as deep, as the Missouri River breaks, it's rugged and picturesque.

To experience this somewhat forgotten corner of Montana, head out of Billings on the interstate to Crow Agency, then take US Hwy 212 east for 26 miles to where it reaches Hwy 314. From there go south toward Decker to the Tongue River Reservoir. On the way, you'll pass the turn off to the Rosebud Battlefield State Park. Excellent interpretive signs tell the story; it is well worth the stop to pick up this bit of Montana history.

Once you've reached the reservoir, you have two choices to get to Birney. Retrace a few miles back up Hwy 314 and turn right onto County Route 566, or follow the winding road along the lake and river to where it meets up with Route 566. Either way is scenic.

With no services in these parts, including in Birney, make sure you have plenty of gas and water before venturing out. The distances aren't great, so if you fill up in either Lame Deer or Crow Agency, you should have enough fuel.

When they're dry, most roads in the breaks are good.

From Birney it's possible to make a 50-mile loop into the Custer National Forest to Otter Creek, to Hanging Women Creek and back to Birney. Enroute, you'll meet a side road to 4,347-foot-high Poker Jim Butte Lookout. The view from the top covers much of the area and shows evidence of the 80,000-acre Otter Creek fire, which burned during the summer of 2000.

Leaving Birney, go northeast for about seven miles to where a byway turns northwest through the Northern Cheyenne Indian Reservation to Lame Deer, then back to the starting point of Hwy 212.

Not much has changed in the Tongue River landscape over time. Up until 1868, it was part of traditional Crow Indian Country. Then the Cheyenne and Sioux claimed it. The area played a notable role in the so-called Indian wars of the latter 1800s.

The Rosebud Battlefield is where on June 17, 1876, General George Cook and his Crow allies encountered a large contingent of Sioux and Cheyenne warriors. The ensuing clash is considered one of the largest battles to occur during the era of the white invasion of Indian lands. Under Chief Crazy Horse, the tribes outmaneuvered and outfought Cook. If it weren't for the Crow, Cook would have suffered the same fate as Custer experienced eight days later on the Little Big Horn River, just across the Wolf Mountains from the Rosebud.

Another fight near here, marked as the "Battle of the Butte," occurred on Jan. 8, 1877, as General Nelson Miles marched into the Tongue River area and took on Crazy Horse and his band.

After the Indians were subdued, settlers moved in and established ranches. From 1890 to 1910, considerable small-scale coal mining took place in the upper Tongue to provide fuel for railroad steam engines. Today, the large Decker and Spring Creek strip mines take out the coal.

The Tongue River west of Birney. RICK AND SUSIE GRAETZ

With the price of natural gas rising, tapping of the methane gas associated with coal is a growing activity in this region. Signs of the wells are scattered throughout the hills. Since the gas is trapped in the coal beds by water pressure, retrieving it requires pumping enormous amounts of ground water to the surface. Ranchers are understandably worried and concerned as to what this process will do to wells and aquifers. The issuance of any new permits is on hold.

The best map, Birney, Montana, is published by the Bureau of Land Management. For the Northern Cheyenne Reservation use Lame Deer Montana, also a BLM map.

The Tongue River Reservoir State Park, just north of Decker and about five miles into Montana, offers camping and warm water fishing. The lake is about 12 miles long, 250 yards wide and only ten feet deep. To spend more than a day in the Tongue River Breaks, camping out or using a camper are your options.

—RICK AND SUSIE GRAETZ

POWDER RIVER

"A mile wide, an inch deep, too thin to plow and too thick to drink" is as appropriate a portrayal today as it was when the first inhabitants described southeast Montana's Powder River. In September 1805, French explorer Francois Antoine Larocque recorded, "The current of the river is very strong and the water is so muddy that it is scarcely drinkable. The savages say that it is always thus and that is the reason that they call the river Powder, for the wind rises and carries from the slope a fine sand which obscures and dirties the water."

The Sioux, Cheyenne and Crow indians at one time used the Powder River country as their hunting grounds. After the mid-1880s, when the bison were slaughtered and the US Army forced the Indians out of their homelands, large cattle herds were driven north from Texas to graze on the rich grasses in the broad valleys of the Powder. Big cow outfits claimed huge tracts of land, until the legendary winter of 1886–87 virtually wiped out their operations.

Some of the cowhands from these initial ranches stayed on and established smaller places. At the turn of the century, they were joined by a tide of homesteaders. These would-be farmers saw their numbers severely reduced by drought and an economic depression. The steadfast ranchers and homesteaders who managed to hang on formed the backbone of the population of today's vast Powder River County.

The Powder River that once witnessed "the old West" now takes it easy as it makes lazy meanders through a quiet landscape of simple beauty. This cowboy domain of widely scattered ranches is dominated by buttes, grassy

The Powder River between Powderville and Broadus. RICK AND SUSIE GRAETZ

hills, narrow canyons, a big sky and a cafe au lait colored, cottonwood-lined waterway.

After the Powder enters Montana from its beginnings in northeast Wyoming, it covers 150 air miles (its twists and turns probably triple the surface distance) before emptying into the Yellowstone 35 miles northeast of Miles City. Broadus is the only town it encounters on its journey north. And this picturesque hamlet is a great place to stay while you explore the easily accessible and scenic river.

Named after the Broaddus family — early day settlers in the valley — one of the d's in the name was mistakenly dropped by Washington, D.C. when the local post office was chartered. George and Margaret Trautman founded the town in 1908 when they built a log cabin store. In 1919, Mrs. Trautman donated 80 acres for a town site with the stipulation that Broadus be made the county seat and the streets be "wide enough to turn a team and a wagon around on." The almost 600 folks who call Broadus home can still do that today. This county seat has a decidedly genuine western look to it.

Probe the Powder to the south of Broadus first. Ask in town how to find the road that heads down the west side of the river. It is about 36 miles of riverbend vistas to where you'll cross the Powder River and come back up on the east bank route. Wildflowers in the spring and summer and brush and leaf changes in the fall add color and diversity to the open, rolling landscape. The bottomlands are primarily private, but the hillsides above the roadway are mostly public BLM land. Take plenty of time to cover the approximately 75-mile loop, as the viewpoints are splendid.

The northern stretch of the river out of Broadus features badlands topography, especially in its upper reaches. Sunrises and sunsets here are magical in their displays. Follow the Powderville West Road for about 88 miles to Hwy 12, east of Miles City. You'll pass through Powderville, once a lively community and stage stop between Deadwood and Miles City, now consisting of only a part-time post office next to an unoccupied house. The original town was about a half mile away toward the river.
—RICK AND SUSIE GRAETZ

EKALAKA AND THE CHALK BUTTES

An historical sign on the edge of town states Ekalaka was established in 1885 by a bison hunter who set out to erect an "edifice for the eradication of ennui." His wagon became stuck in the snow and that's the point where he started the underpinnings of a community. His explanation was, "Hell, any place in Montana is a good place for a saloon." He unloaded the lumber from the wagon and commenced construction on the spot. However, the town wasn't named after this initial resident, but rather for the wife of one of the first white settlers in the area, a Sioux woman named Ijkalaka.

Although a saloonkeeper founded Ekalaka, the country grew on cattle. The first herds came through from Texas and Wyoming in the 1870s and by the 1880s, big ranch outfits were in place. The rich grasses of the area supported huge bison herds, then later were prized for cattle grazing. Sheep were also a mainstay of the early-day economy. At one time Carter County led Montana in sheep production.

If Miles City is the capital of southeast Montana's cowboy country, then Ekalaka is next in line. This Carter County seat of 450 people is the gathering spot for ranchers and other folks from a wide expanse of territory. Often this land was called "Miles City's south side," as it was south of the Yellowstone and east of the Northern Cheyenne and Crow territory.

A two-block-long Main Street encompasses, among other businesses, a couple of cafes, saloons, motels and the 6,000-square-foot Carter County Museum, housing dinosaur bones found. It's highly thought of and worth a visit.

The prairie stretching from Ekalaka in all directions is some of the most beautiful mixture of landscapes in eastern Montana. Most prominent are three sections of the far-flung Custer National Forest ... the Long Pines, Ekalaka Hills and the Chalk Buttes, and Medicine Rocks State Park.

While these places may not be mountains to folks in western Montana, they're tall landmarks out here. The highest points in most of them stretch upward nearly 700 feet above the surrounding topography.

Just southeast of Ekalaka, the Chalk Buttes are a collection of buttes and hills, with a high point of 4,140 feet. Forested up to the rims of their flat tops, they're an oasis on the nearly treeless plains that stretch out for as far as the eye can see. Like other vantage points out here, Native Americans used them for religious purposes and vision quests.

Many legends have been recorded about the area, including the story of Starvation Butte. It is said that an Indian woman climbed it and as she reached the top, her footing crumbled beneath her. Unable to return, she died of starvation. Fighting Butte was the site of a skirmish in which a hunting party of Crow Indians was chased to the top by Sioux. Backed to the steep edge of the table of rocks, the Crow were forced to leap to their deaths when the enemy set the top ablaze.

On the southern edge of town, the Ekalaka Hills are another rise of limestone. A road climbs through them to the edge of their precipitous south side where far-reaching views into Wyoming and South Dakota can be enjoyed. Their highest point is 4,111.

The Long Pines, a partially timbered island uplift in far southeast Montana, begin about 15 miles southeast of Ekalaka. Several unimproved roads lead in to the area. Ever since a 1988 fire burned a large percentage of the trees here, the roads have not been maintained. There are campsites in the Pines, but very little water, the same situation that existed in the Chalk Buttes and Ekalaka Hills. The very soft limestone surface rock soaks it up.

Capitol Rock, so called because it resembles the nation's capitol, stands out on the far eastern edge of these hills. It's a massive deposit of light colored volcanic ash. The routes leading to it require a four-wheel-drive vehicle with clearance. Perches high up on the cliffs and crags of the Long Pines, provide

The Chalk Buttes. RICK AND SUSIE GRAETZ

homes for hundreds of eagles, hawks and falcons, including the rare Merlin falcon.

Medicine Rock State Park is 12 miles to the north of Ekalaka. Sacred to the Indians, it is managed by the Montana Department of Fish, Wildlife and Parks. The park is a mix of twisted and odd-looking formations, some towering 80 feet above the prairie. Tribes gathered here each fall to call on the medicine spirits they believed lived in these rocks to protect their hunters. The Sioux name for the Medicine Rocks is "Inya-oka-la-ka", meaning "rock with hole in it." Strong winds coming from the west have over the eons continued to etch holes and other sculptures in this easily eroded sandstone.

The scenery is not the only attraction in these parts. This remote geography provides a good living for mule and white-tailed deer as well as pronghorn antelope.

—RICK AND SUSIE GRAETZ

MOUNTAIN NOTES

Bighorn Mountains

The most sacred of mountains in Crow Country, this 120-mile range has only its northernmost 20 miles in Montana.

Up to 50 miles across, the Bighorns start a gradual climb to 9,000 feet from the valley of the Little Bighorn River as a series of fissured wide ridges. The upper reaches of the Montana segment of the Bighorns are relatively flat. Relief from the bottoms of the two major canyons that split the area, Black Canyon to the east and Big Bull Elk Canyon on the west, ranges from 2,000–2,500 feet. These deep ravines drain to the Bighorn Canyon as they slice through the sheer northern edge of the range.

Wolf Mountains

On some maps, these mountains on the eastern edge of the Crow Indian Reservation south of Hardin, are split into the Rosebuds on the north and the Wolf Mountains in the south, but most maps show them as being one 50-mile-long, low-lying chain called the Wolfs. Several summits range between 5,000 feet and 5,500 feet in elevation, but most only reach 4,000 to 5,000 feet.

Dense forest interspersed with huge parklands provides good grazing and wildlife habitat. The eastern side, sloping off to the Tongue River Valley and the Northern Cheyenne Indian Reservation, has particularly beautiful wildflower shows in the spring and summer. From points on the western fringe, it's possible to look out across much of Crow Country.

The Long Pines

Just south and east of the Ekalaka Hills, south of the town of Ekalaka, the Long Pines rise to 700 feet above the surrounding landscape, and to elevations

In the Long Pines between Ekalaka and Alzeda. RICK AND SUSIE GRAETZ

close to 4,500 feet. At one time, this extreme eastern portion of the Custer National Forest had a heavy cover of ponderosa pine. Recent fires though, have taken out many of the trees and opened up the country. Capital Rock, on the Long Pines' eastern side, is a mass of white volcanic ash resembling the nation's capitol. The US Forest Service protects it as a monument, and primitive roads reach it.

—RICK AND SUSIE GRAETZ

MONTANA ...
ESSAYS ON TIME AND SPACE

THE FOREST FIRES OF 1910

EDITOR'S NOTE: IN RECENT YEARS, FROM 1988 THROUGH SUMMER 2003, MONTANA HAS EXPERIENCED SOME SEVERE FIRE SEASONS; HUGE AMOUNTS OF LAND HAVE BURNED, ESPECIALLY IN YELLOWSTONE NATIONAL PARK AND THE SOUTHERN BOB MARSHALL COUNTRY. NOTHING THOUGH DURING THIS TIME SPAN COMPARES TO THE CONFLAGRATIONS OF 1910. THIS ACCOUNT OF THAT RED SUMMER IS REPRINTED FROM THE MONTANA HISTORIAN.

> *"All hell broke loose on August 20, 1910. This day saw 300 small scattered fires, hundreds of great blazes, and a hurricane swirl together across northern Idaho, northeastern Washington and western Montana to create the greatest conflagration in the forest history of the United States."*

IT WAS ONE OF THE DRIEST SUMMERS ON RECORD. FROM THE BEGINNING OF APRIL on, there was no sign of the usual spring rains. Without this anticipated rainfall, crops dried up and the hills hardly turned green. The forests were like tinder, ready to explode at the touch of a spark. Beginning in July 1910, sporadic fires caused by severe electrical storms broke out in the woods of Montana. Idaho, Washington, and Oregon. By July 15, over 3,000 men were working as firefighters.

Senator Thomas H. Carter of Montana blamed the fires on Gifford Pinchot. Former Chief Forester Pinchot, in turn blamed Carter and other senators for opposing appropriations for fire fighting. The government plainly waited too long to put western lands under protection.

No matter who was at fault, it was sadly apparent that the Forest Service lacked funds and equipment. There were only several scattered lookout towers, and few skilled firefighters. Detection of fires usually took several days, and in vast wilderness areas that had only a few primitive trails, fires were difficult to reach. There was no reserve of fire equipment. As tools were needed, they were purchased from local stores. When these stores sold out, firefighters were forced to wait until requests arrived.

Firefighters in 1910 were paid five dollars a day plus board — good wages for that time, but the risks they took were high. All they 'had to stop an oncoming blaze was a pickax and a shovel.

Recognizing the potential of a massive fire breakout in the West, President William Taft authorized the use of Army troops for fire fighting on August

Devestation after the fires of 1910, northwest of Missoula. US FOREST SERVICE REGION ONE

8th. None of these troops arrived in time.

On August 10th high winds complicated by low humidity sent a wave of fires from Idaho over the Bitterroots into Montana. As quickly as possible, firefighters manned the scattered blazes and, by the 19th, the fire situation had improved markedly. Thinking there was no immediate threat of danger, crews relaxed. They did not get the long rest they needed. "All hell broke loose" on August 20th. In the late afternoon gale force winds of over 60 miles per hour blew from the southwest. Fire lines held for days were quickly lost and little blazes were immediately big ones. The sky turned yellow. The heat of the fires created huge, hot whirlwinds in front of the fire line.

Crossing rivers and mountain ranges, these fires combined to burn 2,595,635 acres of national forest land and 521,184 acres of non-forest land in two days. Little was spared as the fire destroyed towns, homesteads, lumber camps and anything else in its path. By the evening of August 20th, one-third of Wallace, Idaho was in ashes — over 200 buildings were burned and two lives lost. The fire completely destroyed the Montana towns of Taft, DeBorgia, Haugen and Tuscor.

"Hundreds of soldiers, farmers and laborers are already battling on the fire line. Several hundred more are hurrying to their aid and there is a crying need for at least 3,000 men in Oregon, Idaho and Montana alone . . . The government is spending $30,000 daily in an attempt to control the conflagration. Only rain to break the drought, and the cessation of the wind can save the forests."

John Stanton, a veteran fire fighter of 82 years, relating his experience in the 1910 fire, stated: "We could see the flames far away. The cook said that we should stay for supper, but it didn't look too good, so me and my buddy started for Avery, Idaho." The members of Stanton's crew who stayed, 33 of them, died in the flames or of smoke inhalation. The intense heat melted the coins in their pockets.

"Fifty Mile Front of Flames in Montana"

Ranger Edward C. Pulaski had been put in charge of a crew of about 150 men in the Placer Creek area. He was well acquainted with the drainage since he had mined there the last 25 years. When he spotted the approaching flames, he rounded up a group of 44 men and two horses, and sought shelter.

Pulaski knew the location of two old mining tunnels, one 50 feet and the other 100 feet in length, and headed the party in that general direction. With a wet gunnysack over his head, Pulaski explored the longer tunnel while the others stayed behind. Finding it safe, he herded 43 of the men and the two horses into the tunnel. One man, separated from the others, fell behind the party and was burnt beyond recognition before he could reach the tunnel.

Once in the mining tunnel, the men quickly covered the entrance with wet blankets. The overpowering heat sucked the cool air out and replaced it with scorched, unclean air. With little oxygen left in the tunnel, the men lay on their stomachs and sucked at the dampened ground.

As one man attempted to escape the almost unbearable tunnel, Pulaski ran to the entrance and threatened to shoot anyone trying to leave. Pulaski stood fast until he was overcome by the intense heat and lack of oxygen, at which time he was replaced by another crewmember. When the supporting timbers of the mine began to catch fire, the men splashed water from the stream, which flowed through the tunnel on the timbers until each man, like Pulaski, fell unconscious. It was not until three a.m. that a man managed to crawl out the entrance to find nothing but ashes and the remains of the fellow crewman. The horses were so badly burned that they were shot when help arrived at dawn.

"Ranger Joe Halm and a Party of Fifteen Unaccounted For"

Ranger Joe Halm and his men had been fighting small forest fires in vain in the St. Joe area in Idaho. On the afternoon of August 20th, a dirty, breathless man dashed forward from out of the brush, yelling, "She's coming! The whole country's afire! Grab your stuff, ranger, and let's get out of here!" With a hand on his pistol, Halm confronted his fearful crew. "Not a man leaves this camp. We'll stay by this creek and live to tell about it. I'll see you through." The men began to panic as the fire closed in and the heat became intolerable. They hastily threw water from the creek as high as they could in hopes of extinguishing small blazes. After what seemed an eternity, the fire subsided. As the chill of night set in, the men tried to dry blankets by the heat emitted from charred trees to wrap around their wet bodies.

They awoke the next morning to a smoking mass of wreckage. All were safe except for a few minor burns and injuries. Later that day, a messenger reached them as they picked through the blackened remains. Halm's crew learned then that Wallace and many other towns had burned and that they themselves had been given up as lost. Halm later commented, "Little did I know as I spoke, that our fire was but a dot on the blackened map of Idaho and Montana."

"Death Toll Increasing Every Hour."

A Saltese man, burnt badly in the Taft fire, was wrapped in cotton bandages soaked in oil and laid in a cooled freight car. To check on him, one of his friends entered the darkened car, lighting a match to see. The oil-soaked bandages ignited, and the injured man dashed from the car in flames, burning to death before anyone could remove the bandages from his body.

Con Roberts, a prospector, died when he stumbled while trying to escape the fire and lost his artificial leg. The flames consumed him as he hobbled through the forest. The rest of his party had deserted him and were located, all safe, in Avery the next morning.

Mrs. Speedy Swift was trapped at home with her baby and 12 firefighters by walls of fire on all sides. Each of them covered their body with wet gunnysacks and beat desperately at the flames until the fire passed on. Many others survived in this fashion, some seeking refuge in old mines and tunnels. Others had the chance to survive but panicked, departed from their parties and tried to outrun the blaze.

"Thousands of Refugees in and Around Missoula."

About 1,000 refugees have been brought into Missoula today. There is much distress among them. Their wants are being supplied by Missoula people and they have been given temporary homes."

The Milwaukee ran lines from Missoula to ailing cities, including Avery and Wallace, Idaho. Their crews are credited with diligent efforts that saved hundreds of lives. The trains ran through flames and over burning, weakened trestles. On the Avery route, for example, the railroad lost 16 bridges.

Once in Missoula, arrangements were made for food and lodging for the refugees. C. H. McLeod, manager of the Missoula Mercantile, opened up the company's warehouses so that supplies would be readily available. Charlie Schrage, owner of the Grand Union Pacific Hotel (now the Park Hotel) cooked breakfast for the homeless. Florence Hotel employees transported tables and chairs to the Grand Union to provide additional seating. Many private homes and businesses offered the refugees places to stay.

"Most of the visitors are cordially welcomed and all the city can do for them is done cheerfully. But there has followed in the wake of the fire, a small army of moochers and worse." A special police force was appointed by the mayor to protect the town and its residents from disorderly conduct. Beggars posed as refugees to obtain a free meal while looters took advantage of the city's state of confusion.

"Little Hope of Relief for Stricken Montana"

Although the actual fire just missed Missoula, it was near enough to scatter ashes, cinder and burning embers throughout the city. Residents of the Missoula area watered down their houses with garden hoses at night, trying to prevent their houses from igniting from the sparks. Reports from as far east as Chicago told of sightings of a huge smoke cloud. Fumes and smoke from the blaze reddened the sun in Denver and Kansas City.

"Mother Nature has come to the rescue and spread a covering of snow over the mountains and rains in the valleys. Everyone is exceedingly rejoiced."

About one a.m. on the 22nd of August, the wind dropped and the humidity changed, stopping further growth of fire size. On the night of the 23rd, there was a light general rain, aiding the weary fire crews by minimizing cinders. The first report of precipitation was from a railroad man to a reporter: "It is twenty-three degrees in Blossburg and snowing like hell." Montana received traces of snow the following morning. A good general rain basically ended the 1910 fire season on August 31 by extinguishing many of the remaining fires.

Within a period of 48 hours, the great fire had consumed three million acres and took a total of 85 lives, 78 of which were firefighters. Another 125 were reported missing. The area burned was about the size of the state of Connecticut, 130 miles long by 20 to 35 miles wide. The seven to eight billion board feet of merchantable timber destroyed could have been enough lumber to build 50,000 to 55,000 modern houses. It amounted to a loss of approximately $13,470,906 (1910 value). The government's cost of fighting the fire amounted to $795,281. In addition to the human loss of life, the' amount of destruction to animals in the forests was substantial. Those animals that survived showed up in camps, dazed. Small animals could be picked up without harm, and larger animals such as deer could be fed by hand.

Damage from the burn hurt the area's economy for years to follow. The heavy dead timber was a fire hazard and the incidence of reburn has been about 30 to 40 percent. Serious erosion also took place, making revegetation difficult.

Worst of all the after-fire effects was a bark-beetle epidemic. The scorched trees were immediately infested. By 1914, the beetles were invading green timber. Before they were contained, the beetles contaminated millions of board feet of white pine and other valuable trees. Some of the scorched wood was salvaged. Retimbering on the St. Joe, Coeur d' Alene and Lolo forests began in 1912, after the areas had been somewhat cleared. The Forest Service reseeded many of the areas with white and yellow pines.

Scars from the blaze still remain in many places. It will be more than another half century before the areas are completely recovered.

THIS ARTICLE, CIRCA 1970, AN ORIGINALLY TITLED "ALL HELL BROKE LOOSE", IS REPRINTED FROM THE MONTANA HISTORIAN. IT WAS WRITTEN BY TINA SOLBERG AND BILL ELMORE, WITH RESEARCH ASSISTANCE FROM NUMEROUS OTHER MEMBERS OF HAL STEARNS' MONTANA SEMINAR CLASS AT THE UNIVERSITY OF MONTANA. THE PUBLICATION IS NO LONGER IN PRINT.

MONTANA POLITICS

MONTANA'S PHYSICAL GEOGRAPHY REFLECTS THE STATE'S POLITICAL LANDSCAPE: diverse, occasionally eccentric and always unpredictable. The broad high plains of eastern Montana have demanded cautious lifestyles and conservative politics. The towering mountains of our west invited daring and encouraged more liberal politics.

Prior to statehood in 1889, the state was torn between the Civil War hatreds of migrated southern sympathizers and those who had arrived from the north and supported the Union's cause. The incredible riches discovered in the mining camp of Butte gave birth to the politics of both corporate domination and the urban populism of organized labor. Montana, whose birth into statehood was achieved under such conditions, has remained politically factionalized for one hundred and fourteen years.

Montanans have divided our political preferences geographically, east to west, with liberals predominating in the mountainous west and conservatives usually holding sway in the state's eastern high plains. Our political schizophrenia doesn't end there; it is also revealed in our differing ballot choices between state and federal officials. We have generally elected our liberals to the US Congress and kept conservatives at home in our state offices.

The political pulse of Montana can be taken in differing ways. There are polls that purport to measure opinion and mood. There are other barometers of this state's political persuasions — the throb of daily activities, the talk over morning coffee, letters to the editor, the radio talk shows. The surest way, however, to identify a people's political preferences, and particularly their wishes concerning our relationship with the federal government, is to simply go to that second Tuesday every other November and tally their vote choices for national office.

Beginning with our statehood election to the US House of Thomas Carter in 1889, we have elected 15 Democrats, 16 Republicans and 1 Independent to the House. Since statehood, Democrats have served Montana in the House for a total of 104 years. Republicans have served for 82 years. (For many of the years since statehood, we have had two congressional districts.)

Until 1913 members of the US Senate were appointed by the various state legislatures, not directly elected by popular vote. The XVII Amendment to the US Constitution gave direct election authority to the people. Montanans, once granted direct election, have only chosen two Republicans to represent us in the US Senate while electing nine Democratic candidates. Prior to direct elections, our legislatures appointed six Republicans but only three Democrats to the US Senate — perhaps due to the domination of early-day cattle barons and corporations.

Despite our historic electoral preference for Democratic senators, we have reversed ourselves in our choices for president, having voted for 16 Republican candidates for president and giving our majority to only four Democrats: Franklin Roosevelt, Harry Truman, Lyndon Johnson and Bill Clinton.

Our past half century of national election results are particularly revealing about our selection of candidates who favor activist federal government. In 1948 Montanans elected the Democrat Mike Mansfield in the western congressional district and Wesley Dewart, a Republican, in the eastern district. We chose a Democrat, Jim Murray, for the United States Senate. As they had throughout the Depression and war, Montanans in 1948 signaled their support for an activist government by casting 57 percent of their total votes for those candidates for congress and president who had campaigned in favor of an aggressive federal partner. Montanans, like a majority of Americans, held that the federal government embodied a great idea, which is that government can be the instrument of the common purpose of a free people. That half century ago Montanans and Americans knew they were participants with their federal government; together they brought us through a national economic collapse, beat the Nazis and the Japanese in World War II, preserving America against domestic calamity and foreign domination.

Since then and during the past half century our ballot results are equally illuminating. The first thing one notices is this: during the past 55 years, Montanans are closely divided between Democrats and Republicans. Since 1948 we've had 26 elections for federal office. During those years the eastern congressional district has elected a Republican to the US House 18 times, and a Democrat eight times. In the west, Montanans have more than reversed that trend, sending a Democrat to Congress 20 times and a Republican six times. During those same years, we have had 13 US Senate elections. We chose a Democrat 11 times, and a Republican twice. The census results of 1990 reduced our representation in the US House from two to one member and since the ensuing election we have elected a Democrat twice and a Republican four times.

Notably, however, Montanans have, according to their election-day decisions, voted very much the way they did back in 1948: that is, for those federal candidates who, regardless of their campaign rhetoric, have been supportive of an active federal government. Montanans clearly expect that even our most conservative senators and representatives practice the activist habit of bringing home the federal bacon through appropriation. There have been major differences between our members of Congress on what is commonly referred to as social policy: Social Security, Medicare and Medicaid. Our contemporary Democratic and Republican members have often widely differed on welfare, Head Start, the arts, and always they have disagreed about environmental policy. They also have usually disagreed on tax policy and, to some degree, even on defense and foreign policy. However, on those issues concerning federal appropriations which have defined the Western-federal partnership, there has been remarkable agreement regardless of party. Whether conservative or liberal, the members of the Montana congressional delegation have each been eager to, in the notable phrase of former Senator Lee Metcalf, "back up the federal money truck." No one can remember our Senators, Democrat or Republican, ever differing on interstate highway funding for Montana, airline service, airport construction, or federal dollars for superfund clean up. On energy, too, they are clones, all supporting energy research such as MHD in Butte and Billings, and all historically in favor of building hydro-electric dams. (I feel compelled to note here that as Montana's western district congressman, I broke with that tradition to kill the proposed Libby Re-regulating Dam; the first Montana congressman in the state's history to reject a publicly-funded dam intended for his own district.)

On farm payments or ag research there is virtually no difference. One cannot find a single time in half a century when any member of the Montana congressional delegation voted against impact aid dollars for our schools. The list goes on, demonstrating that among the members of the Montana delegation, regardless of whether it was the liberal Arnold Olson in the 1960s or the conservative Conrad Burns in the '90s, there has been a quiet, almost camouflaged but nonetheless remarkable unanimity in support of significant federal spending for this state; in other words — activist federal government.

For 50 years and more, the Iwo Jima generation and the several since, have purposely on each election day, chosen a partnership between their governments: local (including school boards), county, state, and national. Montanans have been wise enough to recognize that the federal partner is necessary to help balance our economy, assist with access and equity in our locally run schools, assure the cleanliness of our air and water, and restrain corporate greed, particularly here in this state.

Only a few years ago I was visiting with a Republican member of the US House from the west who announced that he would be leaving Congress. I recalled that he had first been elected on a platform of opposing "the big spenders in the Congress." I asked him if he had discovered who those "big spenders" are. He smiled and answered, "Yes, conservative senators from the West."

However, as in the words of the song "The times they are a changing." There is no doubt that the federal-state relationship has historically been a very tense fellowship in this state and throughout the West. Although our support for federal spending seems to continue, Montanans recognize a vitality inherent in today's reconsideration of the appropriate federal role. However, as we consider a new relationship between our state and the federal government, we must seek any new order not out of artificially conjured political anger or indignity, but rather with a determination toward what is the best way to accommodate the continuing needs of Montana.

—PAT WILLIAMS

MONTANA'S LEGISLATURE

A BIT OF HISTORY: UPON ATTAINING STATEHOOD, MONTANA'S FIRST LEGISLATIVE session convened in 1889–90 and consisted of 50 members in the House of Representatives (25 Democrats, 25 Republicans) and 16 senators (8 Democrats, 8 Republicans). The Legislature has met at least every other year in Helena since then.

Since it was ratified in 1972, the Montana Constitution has defined the state's legislatures accordingly: "The legislature shall meet each odd-numbered year in regular session of not more than 90 legislative days." However, it does allow for any legislature to increase the limit on the length of any subsequent sessions and also gives the governor or the majority of the members the right to convene in special sessions.

The Constitution sets in stone the legislative numbers, calling for the Senate to be made up of no more than 50 or fewer than 40 members serving four-year terms. The House of Representatives is to include no more than 100 or fewer than 80 members serving two-year terms. Senators and representatives are prohibited from serving more than eight years in any 16-year period. During the early teens, '20s and '30s, the numbers in both houses fluctuated. The Senate first grew to a maximum of 56 members in 1927, and in the House of Representatives to a high of 107 in 1921.

Capitol building, Helena. RICK AND SUSIE GRAETZ

Capitol Rock in the Long Pines, named for its resemblance to the state capitol building. RICK AND SUSIE GRAETZ

The actual number of legislative members is to be determined after each federal census by a commission of five citizens, none of whom may be public officials, that prepares a plan for redistricting and reapportioning the state. Each established House district elects one representative and each senate district is made up of two adjoining house districts.

Montana's 58th Legislative Session in 2003 was made up of 53 Republicans and 47 Democrats in the House of Representatives and 29 Republicans and 21 Democrats in the Senate.

—GRANT SASEK

MONTANA NEWSPAPERS

MONTANA'S FIRST NEWSPAPERS WERE MUCH LIKE THE STATE'S FIRST communities: many disappeared soon after their founding. But just like the gold camps and growing towns they served, a few survived, flourished and went on to define early journalism under Montana's big sky.

Newspapers arrived in Montana with the prospectors. In the early 1860s, small "camp papers" cropped up at gold camps, but none managed to last more than an edition or two. Often, they were just one small page and circulation reached no farther than the site they served. Historians point to the Aug. 27, 1864, premier edition of the Virginia City Montana Post as the beginning of journalism in the state.

The same year that Montana would become a territory, two Virginia City businessmen, John Buchanan and M.M. Manner, ordered a press and other printing equipment to be shipped upriver from St. Louis to Fort Benton, then hauled overland by wagon to Virginia City to start the Post. The men managed to publish the first edition and with one issue under their belt, sold the newspaper to other entrepreneurs. English emigrant and schoolteacher Joseph Dimsdale was hired as editor and while he had no journalistic experience, he leaped into his new profession with much enthusiasm. Although Dimsdale was to die at the young age of 35, before doing so, he secured his place in Montana history as the state's first journalist.

Under Dimsdale's guidance, the Post quickly became a voice in the wilderness — and its target was, as Dimsdale described it, Montana's "wicked side." This weekly newspaper earned a reputation as a champion of the oppressed and an ardent supporter of the Vigilantes — locals who were taking justice into their own hands. News in the Post was slanted to support Vigilante action and Dimsdale even took to running regular columns romanticizing their stories. The Post later published those articles in book form and "The Vigilantes of Montana" became the first book published in Montana. Dimsdale also took advantage of the Post's classified ads to advertise tutoring for $1.50 a week — the first education offered in Montana.

The other cause Dimsdale took on — the very reason Virginia City and the Post existed — was mining. A great deal of space was dedicated to technical mining information that only prospectors would care about. During the Post's life, hundreds of pieces were devoted to the gulches surrounding Virginia City and details of what were found there.

In 1865, a year after the Post first published, Montana saw the arrival of its second newspaper — also located in Virginia City — when Maj. John Bruce began printing The Virginia City Montana Democrat. The first edition of the Democrat marked the beginning of an organized Democratic Party in Montana and the newspaper was not shy about being an advocate for the party's positions.

Neither the Post nor the Democrat lasted more than a few years. The Virginia City Montana Post printed its last issue March 28, 1868. The Democrat had only published a year, until 1866, when it closed so that its press could be used to begin The Rocky Mountain Gazette at a booming gold strike around Last Chance Gulch. By the time the Gazette began publishing in what would become Helena, another newspaper the Helena Radiator was already printing on the gulch. Soon, several Helena businessmen purchased the Radiator's printing press to start up the Helena Herald. The town and the Herald grew quickly and in 1867 the Helena Herald became Montana's first daily newspaper.

For the times, the Herald didn't come cheaply. Subscription rates to Montana's first daily newspaper were $8 a month in gold dust or $10 a month in cash.

Journalism's time had arrived in Montana. Within the next 10 years, a dozen newspapers would begin publishing in Montana's burgeoning communities — and the one thing they all seemed to have in common was an agenda. The Democrat had launched that party's activity in the state and the Bozeman Pick and Plow started printing from Diamond City in 1875 with the promise that it would "Boldly and fiercely champion the cause of the sons of toil."

By the turn of the 20th Century, most Montana cities had several newspapers, each with their distinct purpose and readership. In the year 1900, Helena had the Daily Independent, two German-language newspapers, one Scandinavian-language publication and a weekly targeting Afro-American readers.

Just south of Helena in Butte, 12 newspapers, including three dailies, were printing to announce the arrival of the 20th Century. No other city in Montana has seen the number of journalistic endeavors as Butte. One historian claims that something more than 85 newspapers have been published in Butte since the Butte Miner went to print in 1876.

And while gold mining, politics and agriculture had set the agendas for many of Montana's early newspapers, another type of mining, and another type of newspaper appeared in Butte and Anaconda in the 1880s. Those newspapers would leave a powerful legacy that still lingers with Montana journalism.

During this time, W. A. Clark, one of two "copper kings" making a fortune around Butte and Anaconda, used the pages of his Butte Miner to attack his rival, competing copper king Marcus Daly. Stung by the constant bad press, Daly fired back in 1889 by hiring a long-time professional journalist named John Durston to start the Anaconda Standard. Although the Standard was published in Anaconda, most of its circulation was in nearby Butte. With Clark controlling the Miner and Daly owning the Standard, the fight was on — a battle that grew to near epic proportions when the question was raised of where the state capital should be permanently located.

Daly, who lived near Anaconda, wanted to see it as the capital city and lobbied hard for Anaconda in the Standard. Clark argued in the Miner for locating the capital in Helena. The conflict prompted bold headlines and hosts of accusations from both of the newspapers. Other newspapers jumped into the scrap, including The Colored Citizen, a Helena newspaper targeting black readers. It later was credited with helping sway the decision in Helena's favor.

The clash between the Standard and the Miner continued well past the decision to locate the Capitol in Helena and even beyond the death of Marcus Daly in 1901. Finally, in 1917, a growing labor movement in Butte prompted the two newspapers to join forces to editorialize against the effort. In 1928, the Miner and Standard merged into the Montana Standard in Butte under the ownership of The Anaconda Company, the company founded by Daly.

The Anaconda Company hung on to its founder's philosophy that it made good business sense for a copper company to own newspapers, and the corporation went on to purchase three other major daily newspapers and several other smaller publications across the state. For most of the first half of the 20th Century, the Anaconda Company owned the Montana Standard, The Missoulian, the Helena Independent Record and the Billings Gazette. Of the five largest cities in the state, only Great Falls had a newspaper that wasn't owned by "The Company." This period of Montana journalism referred to as "the copper collar," was a time when the Anaconda Company defined much of Montana's news — and perhaps more importantly, it was a time when the company determined what was not news. Critics charge that the lack of reporting on issues surrounding the company itself was the largest abuse seen during this period.

The copper collar was broken in 1960 when the Anaconda Company sold its Montana papers for $5.7 million to Lee Enterprises, a Midwest-based chain of newspapers. Immediately, concerns were raised across Montana that the papers were just passing from one corporation to another. Lee officials were quick to promise each of them would be independently run to reflect the communities they served. But by then, the Great Falls Tribune, which also had been purchased along the way by an out-of-state corporation, had firmly cemented its reputation throughout Montana as the source for unbiased, complete news coverage. The concerns over distant ownership lessened.

In 1946, 31-year-old Navy veteran Mel Ruder set up shop in a log building in Columbia Falls and began publishing The Hungry Horse News. Situated just outside the gateway to Glacier National Park, Ruder promised readers positive news and plenty of "The three Bs of pictures: babies, beauties and beasts."

In 1964, flood waters ravaged the Flathead region and Ruder responded by working around the clock, using an airplane and boats (some allege rafts) to get his pictures, putting out extra papers and adding two extra editions to the once-a-week press run. The next year, Ruder would become the first Montana journalist to win a Pulitzer Prize. Today, nearly 40 years later, The Hungry Horse News remains the largest paid circulation weekly newspaper in the state.

Ruder would remain Montana's only Pulitzer Prize-winning journalist until 2000, when Great Falls Tribune reporter Eric Newhouse received a Pulitzer for a report on alcoholism. By then, Gannett, one of the largest newspaper chains in the country, owned the Tribune and Lee Enterprises continued to own all of the daily newspapers it had purchased from the Anaconda Company nearly 50 years earlier.

In 2003, 73 weekly newspapers were publishing in Montana — including several that have proven it's hard in Montana to be too small of a town to support a newspaper. The Wibaux Pioneer-Gazette, Terry Tribune, Fairfield Sun Times, Jordan Tribune and Valier Valierian all are long-time weeklies that have survived with circulations below 1,000 readers.

For Montanans who ranch, farm and live in the state's smaller communities, weekly newspapers still provide what daily newspapers from distant cities cannot — news of the events in their communities and in the lives of their neighbors.

By the turn of the 21st Century, another, independently owned form of print journalism was carving out a place for itself in the cities. Several alternative, free weekly newspapers are being published in Montana's larger communities already served by strong daily papers. Just a hint of what Montana journalism was like 100 years ago.

—GRANT SASEK

THE PUBLISHERS THANK MIKE MCINALLY, EDITOR OF THE *MISSOULIAN* AND DAVE SHORS, EDITOR OF THE *INDEPENDENT RECORD* FOR PROVIDING BACKGROUND FOR THIS ESSAY.

WILDERNESS AREAS

THEY RANGE THROUGHOUT MONTANA'S NORTHERN ROCKY MOUNTAINS AND TWO of them grace the prairie in our northeastern corner ... 16 jewels that are part of the National Wilderness System and some of the Big Sky Country's most cherished assets. In short, wilderness is a place where man is only a visitor. These magnificent landscapes are undisturbed and unchanged since the forces of nature created them. And the Wilderness Act of 1964 assures that they will not be altered.

They provide superb outdoor and spiritual experiences for all. In a society besieged by chaos and rampant growth, a sojourn to these special places allows one to become grounded in a simpler world. Roaded buffer zones surround most of them and enable those not so inclined or physically able to walk or ride horses into the backcountry, an opportunity to garner some of the same experiences and see sights similar to those found beyond the trailhead.

The revered Bob Marshall Wilderness, is the most famous of all of Montana's wilderness lands. In August 1940, it was set-aside to honor renowned conservationist and champion of wilderness preservation, Bob Marshall. The original Bob Marshall Wilderness consisted of 950,000 acres. Today, it encompasses more than 1.5 million acres and includes three contiguous wilderness areas ... the Bob Marshall, Scapegoat and Great Bear. With the magnificent Chinese Wall straddling the Continental Divide as its heart, "the Bob" has it all ... high remote peaks, glaciers, big rivers, meadows and dense forests. To visitors from all over the world, this is the epitome of wilderness.

The Scapegoat segment is remarkable in that it was the first "people's Wilderness," so designated through the desire and efforts of Montana folks, rather than achieving the status via a government directive.

The 920,000-acre Absaroka-Beartooth Wilderness, the second best known of Montana's protected areas, continues to be one of the most visited wilderness parcels in the nation. This lake and snowfield dotted country is home to the state's tallest summits earning it the reputation the "roof of Montana." The tundra-like terrain of its high plateau makes exploring relatively easy. Billings residents consider "The A-B" to be their backyard and are not shy about delving into it.

Each of our wilderness areas has it's own special attributes and are well placed throughout the state. Some are small pockets such as the Gates of the Mountains Wilderness near Helena and the Rattlesnake and Welcome Creek Wilderness areas close to Missoula. Local folks take pride in, and feel ownership of these enclaves.

Lonesome Peak, Absaroka-Beartooth Wilderness. RICK AND SUSIE GRAETZ

Three areas are within national wildlife refuges. The UL Bend Wilderness along the big Missouri River is steeped in history from the steamboat era and Lewis and Clark. It is in the center of one of the finest wildlife refuges in the country, the Charles M. Russell National Wildlife Refuge. To the south of Plentywood, the Medicine Lake Wilderness is part of the Medicine Lake National Wildlife Refuge and presents a peaceful wildlife filled haven amidst some of Montana's richest wheat fields. And in the remote Centennial Valley east of Monida Pass, Red Rock Lakes Wilderness is part of the Red Rock Lakes National Wildlife Refuge.

The adjoining Mission Mountain Wilderness (Federal)/Mission Mountains Wilderness (Tribal-Salish Kootenai) protects beautiful sculptured peaks, high lake country and grizzly bear habitat above the Mission Valley south of Flathead Lake. The Cabinet Mountains Wilderness is a 94,000-acre sanctuary of trees, water and rugged peaks, amidst heavily logged terrain near Libby.

Southwest Montana's Anaconda Pintler Wilderness and surrounding wild country has been a destination for generations of hikers, hunters and fishermen from the Anaconda/Butte area. The Continental Divide is its backbone. The more than 250,000-acre Lee Metcalf Wilderness, named for one of Montana's greatest United States Senators, is a treasured place for the folks of Bozeman and the Gallatin Valley. Public interest groups fought long and hard to preserve this area of 10,000 to 11,000-foot peaks, cirque lakes and flower meadows for years. The Lee Metcalf, which includes the Madison

417

Range and Spanish Peaks, is vitally important for protecting the wildlife values of the Yellowstone Park Ecosystem.

Rising from the Bitterroot Valley's west side between Darby and Missoula, some of the most prominent peaks and spectacular relief of the Selway-Bitterroot are found in Montana's almost 250,000-acre share of this 1,340,460-acre wilderness. Idaho claims the rest.

In spite of their enormous importance to Montana, both in economic and quality of life terms, these federally protected mountain and prairie wildlands occupy only minute 3.5 percent of the state's total landmass.

Montana still has more than 9.6 million acres of unprotected public lands not yet scarred by roads and development. They are wilderness in fact, but not by law. We are in a position now to make important decisions concerning them before the chance is lost forever. The paramount question is "how much of this very fragile and untrammeled terrain are we willing to lose?" Development, roads and motorized activities now dominate many of the other mountain state's terrain. Montanan's have indicated we don't intend to go that route and want to keep the wilderness characteristics that allow us to live a rugged way of life that has disappeared elsewhere. Therefore, we must come up with a solution that allows the important timber industry and agriculture to remain strong while still preserving those areas deserving lasting protection. We can't take these priceless resources for granted ... they aren't being produced anymore.

—RICK AND SUSIE GRAETZ

Rock Creek borders the east side of the Welcome Creek Wilderness. RICK AND SUSIE GRAETZ

RESOURCES

HISTORICAL SOCIETY ... A MONTANA TREASURE

Forts, place names, trails and towns no longer in existence are all featured on the first map of the Montana Territory. Walter de Lacy, Surveyor General of the Territory, drew the pen and ink map on linen in 1865 during the state's infancy. The Montana Historical Society not only has this original masterpiece on hand, but also boasts of 8,000 other irreplaceable, historic Montana maps in its collection.

Included are the Sanborn Fire Insurance maps. Started in 1884, they are drawn to scale and show all the streets in over 300 communities, with specific buildings named on some blocks. Up until 1961, they were updated every few years. By viewing them it is possible to document the town's growth and changes.

Then there are the newspapers; 95 percent of all the papers ever published in Montana, dating back to the initial effort, the 1864 Montana Post out of Virginia City, are in the Society's archives and on microfilm. All of the good and bad news is available to those who wish to research the past.

More than 400,000 black and white photographs, going back to the 1800s, depict the evolution of Montana from a Territory to a State.

These are just minute examples of the phenomenal collections stored and taken care of for all of our heirs and us by the Montana Historical Society.

The Society, located in Helena, belongs to all Montanans, not just history buffs and scholars. What is housed in its museum is nothing short of a mirror and record of our heritage. School children, researchers, college students and folks just interested in whom and what went before them, can find all the resources they want.

Early in 1865, a group of some of Montana's most noted citizens, including Granville Stuart, Wilbur Fisk Sanders and mapmaker de Lacy, came together in Stuart's Virginia City store and set the formation of the Society in motion. On February 2, 1865, when the First Territorial Legislature met in Virginia City, they incorporated the Historical Society of Montana. At this point, the second oldest institution of its kind west of the Mississippi River began its reach towards distinction.

The Society's earliest records and collections were stored in the Territorial Auditor's office in Virginia City. The mining camp however was losing population as the gold played out and as a result, Virginia City was soon to lose its status as Territorial Capital to Helena and the collected works were moved there to Wilbur Fisk Sanders' law office. Then on January 9, 1874, these possessions were burned in a fire. The board put out a call to replace much of what was lost, meeting with great success.

In 1887, space was rented in the Lewis and Clark County courthouse. As the public gained access, a paid professional librarian, Laura Howey, was hired in 1898 to oversee the works. Under her competent direction and ability to approach and convince state politicians of the Society's importance, huge strides in professional cataloging and new acquisitions were made. Later in 1902, a move was made to the new State Capitol. In 1907, a description of the Society's assets was published, bringing further attention to the value of the organization. This growth though came to an end. The state's constitution required all public officials to be qualified voters; then, women still lacked that right in Montana. As a result, Howey was not rehired and the Society and its library experienced 25 years of stagnation. Eventually, politics changed and a new librarian, Anne McDonnell, was hired. Highly regarded, she brought the Historical Society back into the light and a renewed period of development ensued.

In 1941, serious efforts were underway to build a home for the ever-expanding library, displays, art and other artifacts. Bonds were approved by the legislature and the Sons and Daughters of Montana Pioneers became partners with the Society in the effort. It was the Pioneer group, which purchased the land for the present-day structure. In 1952, the edifice was finished and the Montana Historical Society had its own quarters.

The late K. Ross Toole, now a legend in the annals of Montana history, was hired as the first professional director in 1951. Toole, a fourth-generation Montanan, helped raise the Historical Society and all it stands for, to the lofty stature it now enjoys. Under his leadership, the Society's acclaimed publication, Montana: the Magazine of Western History, was started, and a new direction was followed. Toole felt the museum had to "tell a coherent story" and collection policies needed to be changed. He stated "... You see, we simply had to make up our minds whether we wanted a meaningless hodgepodge of relics that did not tell a cohesive, chronological story, or whether we wanted a real museum. We chose the latter."

Evidence of his work can clearly be seen today. Aside from the wonderful collection of maps, photographs and newspapers, the Museum features more than 55,000 artifacts relating to the culture of Montana, including approximately 5,000 Native American pieces representing all of Montana's Indian tribes. Other exhibits include displays of the history of Montana's traditional economic activities such as mining, ranching, farming and logging.

And the list of this wealth depicting Montana's story goes on ... the Society holds hundreds of books about the Battle of the Little Big Horn, a large collection of local and county histories, documents of all state agencies, the original Journals of Patrick Gass of the Lewis and Clark Expedition issued in 1807, a microfilm record of livestock brands for Montana from 1873 to the present, diaries of pioneers, journals of the first explorers in Yellowstone National Park, 227 of Charlie Russell's best works, historic photography by Haynes, Huffman and Cameron, displays of old clothing ranging from high society to the miners and the Chinese who lived in the mining camps, and much, much more.

With such a rich and lively history, Montanans are fortunate to have an organization like the Montana Historical Society. They're preserving our memories, enabling us to know where we've come from. An understanding of the past can be essential to enjoying all Montana offers today.
—RICK AND SUSIE GRAETZ

THE LEWIS AND CLARK INTERPRETIVE CENTER

Discovering the "great falls" of the Missouri was one of the highlights of the Corps of Discovery's Montana journey ... portaging the five of them was probably the most difficult task. The Lewis & Clark National Historic Trail Interpretive Center, a "living, breathing history book," as the Great Falls Tribune describes it, is located on the banks of the Missouri in the area of the falls on the northern edge of the city of Great Falls.

To spend a day here is to step back into the Expedition. The place can be likened to a "nerve center" of the Corps of Discovery's time in the state. Not only can you can trace the route of the explorers up the Missouri from St. Louis to its headwaters in Montana, then across the Northern Rocky

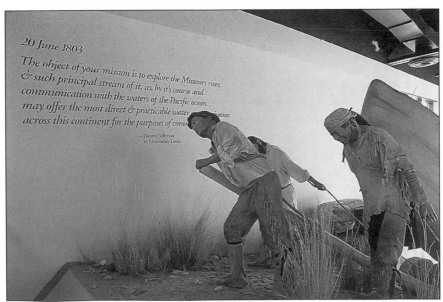

Lewis & Clark Interpretive Center, Great Falls. RICK AND SUSIE GRAETZ

Mountains to the Pacific Ocean and return, but you can also get a great appreciation for the difficulty and diversity of the journey.

Operated by the US Forest Service, the central theme of this 25,000-square-foot treasure house is Lewis and Clark's life amongst the Plains Indians. While you learn the intricacies of the Expedition, you'll also leave with some understanding of the different Indian Nations they encountered and relied heavily on for assistance. In keeping with this theme, the Interpretive Center features a 28-minute, PBS documentary film produced by award winning director Ken Burns.

How the Expedition packed their "baggage," and why they made the caches, what plants and animals they saw, how did the Indians live and what was their reaction to these intruders, and what was the iron boat like? These are just a few of the many questions answered through the panels and interactive displays in the exhibit hall.

Of special interest is a large map compiled from the original drawings of William Clark showing the area they covered. Was there a life for Expedition members when their historical journey ended? The Center has the answer for the explorers as well as the fate of the Indian tribes.

Opportunities for hands-on demonstrations, short programs, presentations and events are numerous; one day may not be enough for a visit. The research library itself demands time. The national archives of the Lewis & Clark Trail Heritage Foundation is located in the Center. This public library has more than 1,000 books and documents on hand, many of them rare or one-of-a-kind. As a result, the center attracts many well known Lewis and Clark scholars.

—RICK AND SUSIE GRAETZ

FORT PECK INTERPRETIVE CENTER AND MUSEUM

In late spring 2004, Missouri River Country will be able to boast of the new 17,500 square foot Fort Peck Interpretive Center and Museum located near the Fort Peck Dam site and the town of Fort Peck. In essence, the facility will be a showcase for the Upper Missouri River in northeast Montana.

The US Army Corps of Engineers will manage the facility and the US Fish and Wildlife Service will feature interpretive displays and programs on the wildlife of the adjacent 1.1 million-acre Charles M. Russell National Wildlife Refuge.

The main theme linking each entity involved will be the Missouri River ... dinosaur and wildlife exhibits, fossils and history. A fresh water aquarium containing the different species of fish living in the river and Fort Peck Lake will be a highlight. This is a region with a colorful past. While only a few hundred folks reside here today, at one time over 50,000 people called this place home. In 1933 during the Great Depression, President Franklin Delano

Roosevelt approved the construction of Fort Peck Dam to control flooding and more importantly to create jobs; 10,500 people found work on the project. An interpretive display will highlight the story of the construction.

Another feature of the museum will be "Peck's Rex," a Tyrannosaurus Rex skeleton, similar to those uncovered just south of Fort Peck and across the lake in the Hell Creek formation. The landscape bordering the lake's southern shores is considered one of the richest fossil beds in the world.

Milk River Observation Point and Lewis and Clark Overlook — Fort Peck area

During their 1804/1805-winter camp in today's North Dakota, the Hidatsa Indians advised Meriwether Lewis and William Clark of several landmarks they would meet on the way to the three forks of the Missouri. On May 8, 1805, the Corps Discovery arrived at "the river that scoalds at all others," and seeing as "...this river posseses a peculiar whiteness, being about the colour of a cup of tea with the admixture of a tabelspoonful of milk. from the colour of the water we called it Milk river."

Clark ascended to the top of the hills just south of the confluence of the Milk and the Missouri to view the landscape and work on his map. Today visitors can climb the same 700-foot rises from an access to the Milk River Observation Point near Fort Peck Dam, off of Hwy 24, and find the same spectacular view, as well as exhibits that interpret the Milk River, the importance of cottonwoods to the Expedition, and profile the Assiniboine Indians that populated this region.

From another vantage position, the Lewis & Clark Overlook, on the south side of Hwy 24, and closer to the lake, the view shed extends out over Fort Peck Lake and the terrain the Corps moved through heading west.

—RICK AND SUSIE GRAETZ

MUSEUM OF THE ROCKIES

They stomp their feet, roar and throw their weight around. Sounding more like assertive two-year-olds than the millions-plus-year-olds they really are, the robotic Triceratops and her babies are the stars of the Museum of the Rockies in Bozeman. Endearing themselves to all who enter, they are just a hint of the phenomenal exhibits both in and out side of the museums walls.

With a mission of understanding, preserving, and interpreting the natural and cultural history of the northern Rocky Mountain region, the Museum of the Rockies has not only taken on the enormous duty of depicting history, but also archaeology, paleontology, ethnology, geology, astronomy, art history, and photography — a task it performs well. Using the extensive permanent collection, which includes approximately 280,000 items — primarily in archaeology, photo-archives, history, vertebrate paleontology, ethnology, geology and fine arts, and the theme of "One Place Through All of Time," the museum allows visitors to travel from prehistoric Montana 4 billion years ago all the way to the next millennium.

One of the most popular stops on the timeline is the Berger Dinosaur Hall where full-sized recreations of the Maiasaura peeblesorum, or "good mother lizard" illustrate their behaviors. World-renowned paleontologist Jack Horner, whose work has forced researchers to reconsider former beliefs about how 80 million years ago dinosaurs lived and reared their young, made the discovery on Egg Mountain near Choteau.

At the Bowman fossil bank, visitors are able to converse with and watch specially trained volunteers prepare dinosaur fossils for further study.

Going back a mere 11 thousand years, experience through dioramas, historic photographs, Native American artifacts and hands-on activities the rich history of the region's earliest Natives' lives, and their progress to their present-day descendants on the seven Indian Reservations in Montana.

A little farther along the timeline and closer to the present, it is possible to experience the daily life on a turn-of-the-century homestead at the Living History Farm. Costumed interpreters will take you back in time as you watch them cooking on a wood burning stove, baking bread, forging iron in the blacksmith shop, doing farm chores, and working in the heirloom garden.

Now, when your feet tell you they've had enough time on the ground, head to the world-class Taylor Planetarium where you can sit back, relax and through the magic of technology that blends the art of astronomy with the art of theatre, magically end your visit.

Extremely well done and highly respected among its fellow museums (or those who run them), the Museum of the Rockies is one of Montana's treasures. This is a place of wonder. Ageless in its appeal, it draws you in and makes you a part of the experience.

—RICK AND SUSIE GRAETZ

ABOUT THE AUTHORS...

Rick and Susie Beaulaurier Graetz
Many of the essays in this book are from their popular syndicated newspaper column *This Is Montana*. Rick is the founder of *Montana Magazine* and *American Geographic Publishing* and teaches a course in Montana Geography at The University of Montana. He and Susie are the publishers of Northern Rockies Publishing and the *Montana Geographic Journal*. The couple has authored numerous Montana books as well as several foreign titles. Their programs and lectures on Montana are much in demand. They live in Helena and Big Sky.

ABOUT THE CONTRIBUTORS...

Dave Alt
Dave Alt picked up a Ph.D. from the University of Texas. After a short tenure in London, he taught geology courses for the next 40 years at the University of Montana. Although now retired, he still teaches. Alt is well know for his Roadside Geology series, including a *Roadside Geology of Montana*, of which he is a co-author. He has also produced a geology text and a recent book, *Glacial Lake Missoula*.

Harry Fritz
Harry Fritz is a professor of history and Chairman of the Department of History at The University of Montana. A 1965 Missoula County High School graduate, Fritz earned a Ph.D. from Washington University in St. Louis. Professor Fritz teaches courses in early American history, American military history, and Montana history. He has twice been UM Teacher of the Year (1972 and 1999) and a Distinguished Service Award winner (1985).

Jeff Gritzner

Professor and Chairman — Department of Geography and Chairman of the Asian Studies Program at the University of Montana — Gritzner earned his Ph.D. from The University of Chicago. Prior to coming to Missoula, he served as a senior associate at the World Resources Institute and a senior program officer at the National Academy of Sciences/National Research Council. His academic research is chiefly in the areas of cultural, historical, and environmental geography.

A.B. Guthrie, Jr.

Considered by many to be Montana's best known and most accomplished writer, Guthrie was "a product of the Rocky Mountain Front" as he often said. His most acclaimed books are *The Way West* and *Big Sky*. *The Way West* earned him the coveted Pulitzer Prize. He also wrote the scripts for two movies … The Kentuckian and Shane.

Joseph Kinsey Howard

Newspaper editor, social and political critic, historian and promoter of regional culture, Howard came to Great Falls at a young age and went on to fame with his newspaper work and writing. His book, *Montana: High, Wide and Handsome*, first published in 1943, was and still is a classic work in Montana history and social criticism.

Richard Hugo

Hugo signed on to teach, and direct the writing program at the University of Montana in 1964 after earning a graduate degree from the University of Washington. His wife, Ripley said he came to Montana because the fishing was better here than in Washington — less brambles. Hugo went on to become an acclaimed poet with several books to his credit.

Wally McRae

Wally has been "a rancher forever," running a multi-generational outfit in the Rosebud Creek area of south central Montana, and a cowboy poet for 40 years with four books to his credit. McRae has received the Governor's Award for the Arts, and a National Heritage Fellowship from the National Endowment for the Arts, the first Montanan to be so honored.

Ken Mielke

Ken came to Montana in 1995 as the Montana National Weather Service Area Manager and meteorologist-in-charge of the Great Falls Weather Forecast Office. Mielke retired from the NWS in 2002 and is now a professor at the University of Great Falls. He has participated in writing numerous weather essays with Rick and Susie Graetz for their newspaper column.

Tom Palmer
Tom Palmer is a Helena writer, editor and award-winning Montana journalist, and has made his home in Montana for more than 20 years. Since 1986, he's tracked conservation issues for Montana Fish, Wildlife & Parks, and remains active in the town of Helena's efforts to preserve open space and provide parks for youth recreation.

John Pulaski
John Pulasky is the staff weathercaster for the Northern Ag Network, broadcasting five daily weathercasts. He also teaches aviation meteorology and aviation history at Rocky Mountain College in Billings, Montana. Most recently, John was one of 35 individuals selected from around the world to receive the National Oceanic and Atmospheric Administration's 2003 "Environmental Hero" award.

Lee Rostad
Lee and her husband Phil ranch on the headwaters of the Musselshell River. Lee is the author of several books including *Meagher County Sketchbook* and *Fourteen Cents and Seven Green Apples*, and numerous magazine articles. A graduate of the University of Montana, she did graduate studies as a Fulbright Scholar at the University of London and has an honorary doctorate degree from Rocky Mountain College. She is a recipient of the Governor's Award in Humanities for 2001.

Grant Sasek
Sasek is a Montana native born and raised in East Helena and a graduate of the University of Montana in Missoula. He is a former long-time reporter with the Independent Record in Helena and works as a freelance writer.

Nicholas Vrooman
Nicholas directs Northern Plains Folklife Resources and is also the Program Manager for Talent Search in the Montana University System office. He has written extensively on the Metis and produced Metis music. He has also served as State Folklorist for Montana and North Dakota. To prepare for all this Vrooman earned three Master's degrees in Education, American Folk Culture and Museum Studies

Pat Williams
Pat served Montana for nine terms in the US House of Representatives from 1979 until 1997. He is now Senior Fellow at the University of Montana's Center for the Rocky Mountain West. Williams teaches at the University, writes a regular syndicated newspaper column and hosts a monthly half-hour program on statewide public radio.

INDEX